D1327094

SIR THOMAS MALORY
AND THE
MORTE DARTHUR

A SURVEY OF
SCHOLARSHIP AND
ANNOTATED BIBLIOGRAPHY

SIR THOMAS MALORY
AND THE
MORTE DARTHUR

A SURVEY OF
SCHOLARSHIP AND
ANNOTATED BIBLIOGRAPHY

Page West Life

Published for the Bibliographical Society
of the University of Virginia by the
UNIVERSITY PRESS OF VIRGINIA
Charlottesville

THE UNIVERSITY PRESS OF VIRGINIA
Copyright © 1980 by the Rector and Visitors
of the University of Virginia

First published 1980

Library of Congress Cataloging in Publication Data
Life, Page West.
Sir Thomas Malory and the Morte Darthur.

Includes index.
1. Malory, Thomas, Sir, 15th cent. Morte d'Arthur—
Bibliography. 2. Malory, Thomas, Sir, 15th cent. —
Criticism and interpretation — History. 3. Arthurian
romances — Bibliography. I. Virginia. University.
Bibliographical Society. II. Title.
Z8545.5.L53 [PR2045] 016.823'2 80-16180
ISBN 0-8139-0868-X

TO MY PARENTS

E. M. and Geraldine West

PREFACE

This work presents a survey of scholarship and an annotated bibliography of Sir Thomas Malory and the MORTE DARTHUR. The bibliography is designed to be as comprehensive as possible through 1977 and
includes items after that date which were available for annotation.
It comprises books and articles especially devoted to Malory and the
MORTE DARTHUR, those containing significant references to these
topics, and reviews of scholarship and criticism. A few bibliographies of Malory studies have appeared:

George Watson, ed. THE NEW CAMBRIDGE BIBLIOGRAPHY OF ENGLISH
    LITERATURE. Cambridge: Cambridge University Press, 1974.
    Vol. 1, 600-1600, columns 674-78.

Eugène Vinaver, ed. THE WORKS OF SIR THOMAS MALORY. 2nd ed.
    Oxford: Clarendon Press, 1967. Vol. 1, pp. cxxxii-cxlii.

Robert H. Wilson. "Malory and Caxton." Chapter 9 in A MANUAL
    OF THE WRITINGS IN MIDDLE ENGLISH, 1050-1500. Ed. Albert
    E. Hartung. New Haven, Conn.: Connecticut Academy of Arts
    and Sciences, 1972. Vol. 3, pp. 909-24.

Thomas C. Rumble. "A Survey of the Editions and Criticism of
    Sir Thomas Malory's MORTE D'ARTHUR." Master's Thesis.
    Tulane University, 1950.

Elizabeth T. Pochoda. "An Annotated Bibliography of All Signif-
    icant Malory Scholarship." ARTHURIAN PROPAGANDA: 'LE
    MORTE D'ARTHUR' AS AN HISTORICAL IDEAL OF LIFE. Chapel
    Hill: University of North Carolina Press, 1971, pp. 141-
    77.

The first three bibliographies are unannotated. Of these, the first
two are selective: the Cambridge bibliography consists of 140 items,
and Vinaver lists approximately 170 "critical works." On the other
hand, the Wilson bibliography is "complete for all serious studies
down through 1955 and . . . include[s] selected important studies to
the date of going to press (February 22, 1971)" [J. Burke Severs, A
MANUAL OF THE WRITINGS IN MIDDLE ENGLISH, 1050-1500, Vol. 1]. Many
unpublished dissertations are excluded, but it is still the most
comprehensive and useful bibliographical list of Malory scholarship
and reviews to date, although the lack of annotation renders it less
useful than one might wish. This bibliography is greatly indebted
to Wilson's work.

    The only models for this bibliography are the annotated biblio-
graphies of Rumble and Pochoda. Rumble's thesis assessing Malory

criticism to 1950 is now of limited value since so much scholarship
has appeared following the publication of Vinaver's edition of the
Winchester Manuscript in 1947. On the other hand, Pochoda's bibliography of 212 items, which she claims comprises "all significant"
Malory scholarship, annotates Malory studies through 1968. Her bibliography has been called "very useful" [Lucy Mitchell, MEDIUM AEVUM,
42 (1973), 286-89] and praised as giving "lucid summary" [P. J. C.
Field, RES, N.S. 23 (1972), 466-68]. But Edward D. Kennedy demonstrates in a review [SPECULUM, 48 (1973), 397-402] that the selection
of items is sometimes arbitrary (including several negligible items
and omitting a number of important studies); moreover, the bibliography lists no scholarly reviews and includes few dissertations and few
studies written abroad.

DESIGN AND SCOPE OF THE BIBLIOGRAPHY

The items within each division of this bibliography are in
chronological order. Authors or reviewers writing in the same year
are listed alphabetically. Each item, whenever possible, is listed
according to the date of its first publication. The indexes generally preclude the need for an extensive system of cross-references;
however, cross-references are given if they provide necessary or useful information. "Book" and "Chapter" refer to Caxton's editorial
divisions of the MORTE DARTHUR; "Tale" refers to Vinaver's editorial
divisions in his edition of the Winchester Manuscript of the MORTE
DARTHUR. Reviews are not listed for items of a bibliographical
nature or for editions of Malory's sources; reviews are listed only
for editions and studies of the MORTE DARTHUR. The list of reviews
for any item may not be complete, though an attempt has been made to
include all reviews located through the use of BOOK REVIEW DIGEST,
INDEX TO BOOK REVIEWS IN THE HUMANITIES, the MODERN HUMANITIES RESEARCH
ASSOCIATION BULLETIN, MODERN LANGUAGE QUARTERLY, Parry and Schlauch
bibliographies [nos. 238, 240], the NATIONAL LIBRARY SERVICE CUMULA-
TIVE BOOK INDEX, and through some use of BOOK REVIEW INDEX, the NEW
YORK TIMES BOOK REVIEW, CURRENT BOOK REVIEW CITATIONS, the READER'S
GUIDE, and the INTERNATIONALE BIBLIOGRAPHIE DER ZEITSCHRIFTEN LITER-
ATUR, c. REZENSIONEN. Reviews in the YEAR'S WORK IN ENGLISH STUDIES
are not included.

I. SURVEY OF SCHOLARSHIP. This introductory survey attempts
to assess past and present scholarship on Malory and the MORTE DAR-
THUR and to update and develop more fully earlier surveys of scholarship:

Eugène Vinaver. "Sir Thomas Malory." ARTHURIAN LITERATURE IN
     THE MIDDLE AGES, ed. Roger Sherman Loomis. Oxford: Clar-
     endon Press, 1959, pp. 541-52.

Elizabeth T. Pochoda. "A Review of Earlier Malory Scholarship

with Some Suggestions for Further Studies." ARTHURIAN PRO-
PAGANDA. Chapter 1, pp. 3-22.

Larry D. Benson. "Sir Thomas Malory's LE MORTE DARTHUR." CRIT-
ICAL APPROACHES TO SIX MAJOR ENGLISH WORKS, ed. R. M. Lumi-
ansky and Herschel Baker. Philadelphia: University of
Pennsylvania Press, 1968, pp. 81-131.

Derek S. Brewer. "The Present State of Malory." FORUM FOR
MODERN LANGUAGE STUDIES, 6 (1970), 83-97; rpt. ARTHURIAN
ROMANCE: SEVEN ESSAYS. Ed. D. D. R. Owen. New York:
Barnes and Noble, 1971.

Robert H. Wilson. "Malory and Caxton." In A MANUAL OF THE WRIT-
INGS IN MIDDLE ENGLISH, 1050-1500. Vol. 3, pp. 757-71.

II. BIBLIOGRAPHY. This has three parts: Editions, Studies, and
Indexes. A. Editions. This consists of (1) a bibliography of materials specifically related to editions of the MORTE DARTHUR (descriptive bibliographies); (2) major editions, reprints, and translations
of sources and analogues of the MORTE DARTHUR; and (3) editions of the
MORTE DARTHUR. This third part is divided into the following categories: Winchester Manuscript, complete editions before 1634, complete
editions after 1634, abridgements, prose adaptations, art editions,
translations, and recordings. "Abridgements" are usually scholarly
editions of parts of the MORTE DARTHUR. "Prose adaptations" are usually popular abridged editions which have modernized spelling, punctuation, and diction, and which are often rewritten by their authors
for a particular audience. Works which contain only brief passages or
selections from the MORTE DARTHUR are not included. "Art editions"
are limited to illustrated "editions de luxe" printed in limited number on fine quality paper. In compiling and annotating the "Editions"
section, I am especially indebted to Eugène Vinaver [MALORY (Oxford:
Clarendon Press, 1929; rpt. 1970), pp. 189-98; THE WORKS OF SIR THOMAS
MALORY, 2nd ed. (Oxford: Clarendon Press, 1967), vol. 3].

B. STUDIES OF THE MORTE DARTHUR. This consists of (1) general
bibliographies of the Arthurian legend and the MORTE DARTHUR (the
PMLA, MHRA, and other annual bibliographies of English literature are
not included); and (2) an annotated list of studies. This, the larg-
est part of the bibliography, consists of books and articles which
contain critical commentary on and references to Malory and the MORTE
DARTHUR. No attempt is made to include material which treats the
topic of Malory as a "source," particularly that which concerns nineteenth-century poetic adaptations of the MORTE DARTHUR. Such studies
are included only if they contain critical commentary on the MORTE
DARTHUR. Similarly, no attempt is made to include all references to
or excerpts from the MORTE DARTHUR (for example, reprintings of Caxton's
preface) contained in literary histories and anthologies or in linguistic surveys and studies. A few literary histories and anthologies,
generally from the late nineteenth and early twentieth centuries, are

included for their antiquarian interest, but the number of such works
in this century makes it impossible to include them all. Materials
unavailable for annotation are indicated by asterisks. In some cases,
when the BIBLIOGRAPHICAL BULLETIN OF THE INTERNATIONAL ARTHURIAN SO-
CIETY provides the only source of information for an item, that annotation is paraphrased and the BBIAS citation is given.

     C. INDEXES. This section contains (1) an index of names (au-
thors, editors, compilers, translators, and illustrators); (2) a title
index; and (3) a subject index.

     In completing this bibliography, I owe special thanks to Profes-
sor Edward D. Kennedy and to Professor George Kane, who offered valu-
able suggestions and criticism at every stage of the project. I should
also like to thank the Interlibrary Loan staff of the University of
North Carolina at Chapel Hill and the North Library staff of the British Library for their patient and efficient assistance. Finally, I
am especially grateful to my husband, Professor Allan R. Life, for
his understanding and encouragement.

LIST OF ABBREVIATIONS

ALMA ARTHURIAN LITERATURE IN THE MIDDLE AGES. Ed. Roger Sherman
   Loomis. Oxford: Clarendon Press, 1959.

ARCHIV ARCHIV FÜR DAS STUDIUM DER NEUEREN SPRACHEN UND LITERATUREN

AUMLA JOURNAL OF THE AUSTRALASIAN UNIVERSITIES LANGUAGE AND LITER-
   ATURE ASSOCIATION

BBIAS BIBLIOGRAPHICAL BULLETIN OF THE INTERNATIONAL ARTHURIAN SO-
   CIETY

BJRL BULLETIN OF THE JOHN RYLANDS LIBRARY

CCM CAHIERS DE CIVILISATION MÉDIÉVALE

CE COLLEGE ENGLISH

CFMA CLASSIQUES FRANÇAIS DU MOYEN ÂGE

CL COMPARATIVE LITERATURE

CLS COMPARATIVE LITERATURE STUDIES

DA[I] DISSERTATION ABSTRACTS [INTERNATIONAL]

EA ÉTUDES ANGLAISES

E.E.T.S. EARLY ENGLISH TEXT SOCIETY
   O.S. Original Series
   E.S. Extra Series

EHR ENGLISH HISTORICAL REVIEW

ELN ENGLISH LANGUAGE NOTES

JEGP JOURNAL OF ENGLISH AND GERMANIC PHILOLOGY

LGRP LITERATURBLATT FÜR GERMANISCHE UND ROMANISCHE PHILOLOGIE

LJ LIBRARY JOURNAL

MHRA MODERN HUMANITIES RESEARCH ASSOCIATION

MLN MODERN LANGUAGE NOTES

MLQ MODERN LANGUAGE QUARTERLY

MLR MODERN LANGUAGE REVIEW

MP   MODERN PHILOLOGY

MS   MEDIAEVAL STUDIES

N & Q   NOTES AND QUERIES

NM   NEUPHILOLOGISCHE MITTEILUNGEN

PBSA   PUBLICATIONS OF THE BIBLIOGRAPHICAL SOCIETY OF AMERICA

PMLA   PUBLICATIONS OF THE MODERN LANGUAGE ASSOCIATION OF AMERICA

PQ   PHILOLOGICAL QUARTERLY

RBPH   REVUE BELGE DE PHILOLOGIE ET D'HISTOIRE

RCHL   REVUE CRITIQUE D'HISTOIRE ET DE LITTÉRATURE

RES   REVIEW OF ENGLISH STUDIES

RLC   REVUE DE LITTÉRATURE COMPARÉE

RP   ROMANCE PHILOLOGY

RR   ROMANIC REVIEW

SATF   SOCIÉTÉ DES ANCIENS TEXTES FRANÇAIS

SEL   STUDIES IN ENGLISH LITERATURE [English Literary Society of
            Japan]

SN   STUDIA NEOPHILOLOGICA

SP   STUDIES IN PHILOLOGY

TLS   [London] TIMES LITERARY SUPPLEMENT

TSE   TEXAS STUDIES IN ENGLISH

TSL   TENNESSEE STUDIES IN LITERATURE

TSLL   TEXAS STUDIES IN LITERATURE AND LANGUAGE

UTQ   UNIVERSITY OF TORONTO QUARTERLY

VQR   VIRGINIA QUARTERLY REVIEW

WSTM   THE WORKS OF SIR THOMAS MALORY.   Ed. Eugène Vinaver.   2nd
            ed. 3 vols. Oxford: Clarendon Press, 1967.

YES   YEARBOOK OF ENGLISH STUDIES

YWES   YEAR'S WORK IN ENGLISH STUDIES

ZFSL   ZEITSCHRIFT FÜR FRANZÖSISCHE SPRACHE UND LITERATUR

ZRP   ZEITSCHRIFT FÜR ROMANISCHE PHILOLOGIE

ZAA   ZEITSCHRIFT FÜR ANGLISTIK UND AMERIKANISTIK

ZAAK   ZEITSCHRIFT FÜR ASTHETIK UND ALLGEMEINE KUNSTWISSENSCHAFT

CONTENTS

SIR THOMAS MALORY
AND THE
MORTE DARTHUR

A SURVEY OF
SCHOLARSHIP AND
ANNOTATED BIBLIOGRAPHY

I. SURVEY OF SCHOLARSHIP

This survey consists of a brief introduction, a section about the identity of Sir Thomas Malory, and five sections about topics which have been prominent in critical discussion of the MORTE DARTHUR. These topics are texts and editions, sources, structure, style, and theme.

INTRODUCTION

Two dates have been particularly important in the history of Malory scholarship in this century: the discovery in 1934 by W. F. Oakeshott of the Winchester Manuscript (now British Library Additional MS. 59678) of the MORTE DARTHUR,[1] and the subsequent publication in 1947 of a three-volume edition of the manuscript by Eugène Vinaver. The importance of these dates can hardly be overestimated. First, the Winchester Manuscript provided a version of the MORTE DARTHUR which differed markedly, and in some respects radically, from what was long believed to be the only extant version of Malory's text, the edition printed in 1485 by William Caxton. Second, the publication of the manuscript provoked discussion and provided a new impetus to Malory scholarship. The most dramatic example of the intense debate caused by the 1947 edition was the controversy sparked by Vinaver's assertion, implicit in the title of his edition (THE WORKS OF SIR THOMAS MALORY), that the MORTE DARTHUR was not a unified work but eight separate romances.

Although recent surveys of scholarship have taken 1947 as a point of departure for discussing criticism of Malory and the MORTE DARTHUR,[2] this survey will discuss trends in critical opinion in both the nineteenth and twentieth centuries. While the interest of modern scholarship in the Winchester Manuscript has provided a stimulus to the study of the MORTE DARTHUR, it has, to some extent, obscured the contributions of critics in the nineteenth and early twentieth centuries to an understanding and appreciation of Malory's work. Many of the critical problems and issues related to Malory and the MORTE DARTHUR which have concerned contemporary critics -- biography, textual issues, source study, structure, style, and theme -- also concerned critics in the nineteenth and early twentieth centuries. This essay will examine how these issues were raised and discussed in the nineteenth century and then developed and given greater focus in the twentieth century. Such an examination shows that in the last hundred years most of these issues have been characterized by controversy.

BIOGRAPHY

The identity of the "Syr Thomas Maleoré, Knyght" who asked his readers to pray for his soul when he completed his work in the "ninth yere of the reygne of Kyng Edward the Fourth"[3] has intrigued and puzzled readers over the centuries. This interest was inevitable given the brevity of Caxton's only reference to Malory in the preface to the 1485 edition of the MORTE DARTHUR. Caxton said that he based his text upon a "copye unto me delyverd, whyche copye syr Thomas Malorye dyd take oute of certeyn bookes of Frensshe and reduced it into En-

glysshe."[4] From this, most scholars have assumed that Caxton knew

little of Malory.[5] For centuries it was believed that Malory was a

Welshman on the grounds that John Bale had stated in 1557 that Malory

was "genere ac patria Brytannus."[6] The strongest proponent of this

view, which was especially popular in the nineteenth century, was the

Celticist John Rhŷs, who argued that the surname "Malory" was a cor-

ruption of "Maelor," a Welsh placename; but this opinion was vigorous-

ly attacked by Kittredge and Vetterman.[7]

In the 1890's, scholars such as T. W. Williams, A. T. Martin,

and Kittredge, working independently, attempted to establish Malory's

identity. The researches of Williams[8] and Martin[9] were overshadowed

by the 1896 publication of Kittredge's influential article "Who Was

Sir Thomas Malory?"[10] In this paper Kittredge methodically argued

the case that Sir Thomas Malory of Warwickshire was the only candidate

who could seriously be considered the author of the MORTE DARTHUR on

the grounds that he fulfilled four necessary conditions:

> (1) He must have been a knight; (2) he must have
> been alive in the ninth year of Edward IV, which
> extended from March 4, 1469, to March 3, 1470
> (both included); (3) he must have been old enough
> in 9 Ed. IV to make it possible that he should
> have written this work. Further, Caxton does not
> say that he received the 'copy' directly from the
> author, and his language may be held to indicate
> that Malory was dead when the book was printed.
> In this case he must have died before the last
> day of July (or June), 1485, and we have a fourth
> condition to be complied with.[11]

Kittredge further elaborated the case for the Warwickshire Malory in

1925, and subsequently new facts about Malory's career were discovered

by Edward Hicks, A. C. Baugh, and E. K. Chambers.[12] Furthermore, the

newly-discovered Winchester Manuscript contained a colophon which appeared to support the supposition that Malory wrote the MORTE DARTHUR
while in prison: "For this was drawyn by a knyght presoner, Sir Thomas Malleorré, that God sende hym good recover."[13]   This seemed to
confirm Kittredge's argument.

Kittredge's case, repeated and elaborated by later writers, assumed the character first of probability and then of fact.   It is not
difficult to see why this happened.   First, Kittredge supposed in
1896 that only one man by the name of Sir Thomas Malory would be living during the last years of Edward IV's reign.[14]   He was able to
document the existence of a Sir Thomas Malory of Warwickshire and
hence it seemed likely to Kittredge, and to readers who accepted his
argument, that this Malory wrote the MORTE DARTHUR.   Second, for many
years no strong argument was advanced in opposition to the Warwickshire candidate.

Recently, however, the Warwickshire Malory has received more
scrutiny.   Gweneth Whitteridge attempted to prove that there were
two Warwickshire Thomas Malorys, one of Newbold Revel and one of Fenny
Newbold,[15] but her argument was disproved by P. J. C. Field, who put
forward evidence to show that Newbold Revel and Fenny Newbold were
names used interchangeably for the same place.[16]   Only one strong
rebuttal of Kittredge has appeared in print: William Matthews argued
in his book THE ILL-FRAMED KNIGHT: A SKEPTICAL INQUIRY INTO THE IDEN-
TITY OF SIR THOMAS MALORY, that the authorship might more suitably be
attributed to a hitherto unknown Thomas Malory of Studley and Hutton
in Yorkshire.[17]   After criticizing the arguments for the Warwickshire

Malory, Matthews argued in support of his own Yorkshire candidate on

the basis of northernisms in the Winchester Manuscript, Malory's use

of northern romances and geographic locations, and his "fondness for

alliterative phrases." Although Vinaver did note in the second edi-

tion of the WORKS that Matthews had proposed an alternative to the

Warwickshire knight, he nevertheless found Matthews' argument weakened

by the fact that there was no evidence that the Yorkshire Malory had

been either a knight or a prisoner.[18]

The controversy over Malory's identity has been related to the

question of whether the MORTE DARTHUR is a "moral" or "immoral" book.

The critic's view of Malory the author has often been conditioned or

complicated by his attitude toward this "morality" issue. In his

preface, Caxton emphasized the moral and didactic qualities of the

work, and most critics have accepted the validity of his statements.

They have also assumed that the moral nature of the work and the moral

character of its author should not be contradictory. Well into the

twentieth century, many of those who believed that Malory was a Welsh-

man also believed that he was a priest; this belief seems to have been

based on the assumption that the MORTE DARTHUR was a moral work and

its corollary that a "moral" book is written by a "moral" man.[19]

This assumption also influenced discussion of the Warwickshire candi-

date, who, as research has revealed, was at various times accused of

theft and rape. C. S. Lewis tried to dismiss the charges against

Malory by pointing out that Malory's actions should not be judged ac-

cording to modern-day standards of criminal behavior.[20] But the moral

paradox between the character of the Warwickshire knight and the

nature of his supposed work has troubled many critics, including Vinaver,[21] who nevertheless accepted the Warwickshire Malory in default of
a better claimant, and William Matthews, whose dissatisfaction with
the Warwickshire Malory's character appears to have been a main reason
for his seeking a better claimant for authorship. Matthews claimed
that this reaction was felt by "mature, sophisticated critics, in no
need of instruction that human behavior is less than consistent and
that literary men often say what literary men fail to do. But whereas
with Leonardo or Dickens they would not be perturbed, with Malory they
are so justly bothered that they cannot leave well or ill alone, but
are impelled to explain one or the other away."[22] It might be pointed
out that Whitteridge's argument for the existence of two Thomas Malorys of Warwickshire, one of Newbold Revel and the other of Fenny Newbold, was based on the supposition that the parliamentary and "criminal'
careers of Malory presented an unacceptable paradox.[23]

The identity of the author of the MORTE DARTHUR has not yet been
determined, and it is likely that his identity will never be established beyond reasonable doubt. Internal evidence for Malory's identity is provided by Malory's statements in the Caxton edition and the
Winchester Manuscript and by Caxton's preface. From these sources, it
is clear that any candidate for authorship must meet these criteria:
he must have been a knight, he must have been a prisoner, and he must
have been living during the ninth year of the reign of Edward IV.
Apart from Caxton's single reference to Sir Thomas Malory in the preface, there are no known contemporary references to Malory as author
of the MORTE DARTHUR. The next references appeared in the following

century. The first was a sentence written in an early sixteenth-
century hand on folio 199^r of the Cambridge SUITE DU MERLIN: "Ci
commence le livre que Sir Thomas Malori chevalier reduce in Engloys
et fuist emprente par William Caxton."[24] The second was a brief biography of Sir Thomas Malory as author which appeared in John Bale's
SCRIPTORUM ILLUSTRIUM MAIORIS BRYTANNIAE. . . CATALOGUS. It is unlikely that external evidence of the sort necessary to prove Malory's
identity, such as letters of Caxton or Malory, specific contemporary
references to Malory as author, or Malory's holograph manuscript,
will ever be found.

Four candidates have been proposed for the authorship of the
MORTE DARTHUR. The Welshman supported by Rhŷs is no longer taken
seriously and probably never existed; the Thomas Malory of Papworth
proposed by Martin has received little support and, like the Yorkshire
claimant of Matthews, cannot be proven to have been a knight. Of all
the contenders, the Warwickshire knight of Kittredge is still the most
widely accepted, but there is no evidence, apart from the fact that he
fulfills the qualifications of being both a knight and a prisoner at
the time the MORTE DARTHUR was written, to connect him with the actual
writing of the work. Only Matthews has undertaken the task of seeking
a plausible alternative to the Warwickshire Malory, and his efforts
demonstrate that until there is evidence to prove a connection between
the Warwickshire knight and the writing of the MORTE DARTHUR, his authorship must be regarded as a possibility and not a certainty.[25]

TEXTS AND EDITIONS

MORTE DARTHUR was first published by William Caxton at Westminster on July 31, 1485.[26] Its early popularity was attested by the appearance of six editions between 1485 and 1634: those of Wynkyn de Worde, 1498, 1529; William Copland, 1557; Thomas East, who printed two editions in 1585; and William Stansby, 1634.[27] After Stansby's edition, the MORTE DARTHUR was not printed until the early nineteenth century when two independent editions appeared in 1816, and the better-known edition by Robert Southey appeared a year later.[28] In the second half of the century, a number of editions, most of them derived from Stansby's edition, were printed.[29]

Nineteenth-century editors were concerned to establish an accurate text of the MORTE DARTHUR, and this goal was best achieved in two editions based on Caxton: Edward Strachey's popular Globe Edition of 1868, and the more scholarly three-volume edition by H. O. Sommer of 1889-91. After Caxton's edition, each black-letter edition had been based on the edition which immediately preceded it: the 1498 Wynkyn de Worde edition was based on Caxton's edition; de Worde's edition of 1529 was based on his own 1498 edition; Copland's 1557 edition was based on de Worde's 1529 edition; East's two editions of 1585, one in folio and one in quarto, were based on Copland's edition; and Stansby's 1634 edition was based on East's folio edition.[30] Edward Strachey estimated that the Stansby text contained approximately 20,000 departures from Caxton's text.[31] Since the 1816 editions and the 1858 Wright edition were derived from Stansby's text, their accuracy was correspondingly poor. Strachey and Sommer aimed to restore Caxton's original text.[32]

An accurate text was prerequisite to sound studies of Malory's
sources, style, and language. Indeed, there was little scholarly criticism of the MORTE DARTHUR until Strachey's Globe Edition of 1868, and
the interest in Malory's work was given an even greater impetus in the
last decade of the nineteenth century by the publication of Sommer's
edition. Must of this interest was initially focused on source study
but later dealt with the related issues of structure, theme, and style.
Some questions were typical: Was Malory a "translator" and "compiler,"
or was he an "original" writer? Was the MORTE DARTHUR, as Caxton
argued, a "moral" and didactic work, or was it, as Ascham claimed,
an "immoral" work full of "bold bawdry and open manslaughter"? How
was Malory's style to be described and analyzed?

In the early 1930's, Vinaver was preparing to edit the MORTE DAR-
THUR from Caxton's text when, in 1934, W. F. Oakeshott's discovery of
the manuscript of Malory's work in the Moberly Library at Winchester
College forced him to abandon the Caxton project in order to edit the
manuscript. The text of the newly discovered manuscript had eight
major divisions instead of Caxton's twenty-one, and it differed con-
siderably from the text of the Caxton edition, particularly in the
division concerning Arthur's Roman campaign. C. S. Lewis described
Oakeshott's find as the "most startling literary discovery of the century" and said that it "reduced Malory scholarship to a state of
suspense for the next fourteen years."[33] When Vinaver's three-volume
edition appeared as THE WORKS OF SIR THOMAS MALORY, its title clearly
expressed Vinaver's judgment that Malory had written eight separate

romances; those who believed that he had intended to write a single

work, the MORTE DARTHUR,[34] objected to the title of Vinaver's edition.

For the next twenty years, Malory scholarship was chiefly concerned

with this structural issue. The relationship of Caxton's edition to

the Winchester Manuscript received little discussion, for most critics

accepted Vinaver's view that the two texts derived from a common

source but that Caxton did not use the manuscript in preparing his

edition.[35] The recent quincentenary of Caxton's founding of the first

English press, however, encouraged discussion of Caxton's role as a

printer and editor. A number of articles and books on this topic

have appeared,[36] and in one of these, Lotte Hellenga and Hilton Kelli-

her jointly challenged the view that the Winchester Manuscript had no

connection with Caxton's printing shop at Westminster. Pointing out

that the manuscript contained traces of printer's ink and offsets of

letters belonging to Caxton's types two and four, they argued that

Caxton may well have used the manuscript in preparing his edition.[37]

SOURCE STUDY

That Malory drew on French and English sources in writing the

MORTE DARTHUR had long been recognized, but there was no attempt to

identify the specific sources until the eighteenth century, when, in

the 1770's, Thomas Warton claimed that Malory used the French Prose

LANCELOT.[38] Some years later, Walter Scott noted Malory's use of the

French Prose TRISTAN,[39] and Henry Weber expressed the opinion that

Malory had used the English "fair unknown" romances LIBEAUS DESCONUS

and IPOMEDON for his story of GARETH.[40] Most critics sought to identify Malory's French sources, but by the end of the nineteenth

century, they were also studying his English sources.[41] In his edi-

tion of Caxton, Sommer accurately identified most of the sources that

Malory used.[42]

Malory's use of various sources may have been the reason why

nineteenth-century critics frequently referred to Malory as a "trans-

lator," "compiler," and occasionally "chronicler."[43] The connotations

of these nouns were sometimes neutral but often negative. To Moritz

Trautmann, Malory was only a "Zusammenstoppler,"[44] and to Alfred Nutt

he was a "most unintelligent compiler."[45] To Henry Ellis and to many

others, Malory's book was a "mere compilation."[46] This negative and

condescending attitude persisted. The MORTE DARTHUR was regarded as

a "typical collective romance. . . made. . . by aggregation," an "ill-

digested collection of fragments."[47] And in 1929, Vinaver referred

to Malory's work as a "slightly modified and condensed translation of

the French Arthurian novels."[48]

In the nineteenth century, many were content to call the MORTE

DARTHUR a "translation" or "compilation." On the other hand, there

were some who perceived that Malory showed some degree of originality

in writing the work. In 1862, George Marsh wrote:

> The Morte d'Arthur is not, indeed, a work of Eng-
> lish invention, nor, on the other hand, is it just
> to style it simply a translation. No continuous
> French original for it is known; but it is a com-
> pilation from various French romances, harmonized
> and connected so far as Malorye was able to make a
> consistent whole of them, by supplying here and
> there links of his own forging.[49]

Later in the century others expressed this opinion, and some claimed

that Malory was much more than a "mere literary carpenter."[50] Edward

Strachey applied the term "maker" to Malory,[51] and Walter Raleigh
called him an "artist conscious of his art."[52] The opinion that Sommer's research on Malory's sources "much reduced the old knight's
claim to originality"[53] was not in fact true. Few strong cases for
Malory's "originality" were made before 1890, and although some critics for years after that date still called Malory a "compiler" and
"translator," Sommer's identification of Malory's sources finally allowed scholars to make detailed comparisons of the text and its
sources and to achieve a greater appreciation of Malory's accomplishment
Sommer believed that Malory was no "mere translator" and thought that
the term "adapter" more appropriately described him. He said that
Malory "evidently endeavoured--and with no little measure of success--
to weld into an harmonious whole the immense mass of French romance.
After a comparison with his sources, his work gives the impression
that he did not servilely copy his originals, but that he had read
various versions, and that he impressed upon the whole the stamp of
his originality."[54] Vinaver, the next major editor of the MORTE DAR-
THUR, also came to hold this opinion, though he was at first skeptical
of Malory's claim to originality.[55] The most vociferous advocate of
Malory's originality and of his claim to artistic achievement was
George Saintsbury, who called the MORTE DARTHUR a "great and original
book"[56] and defended Malory against the charge that he was only a
compiler.[57] Saintsbury wrote that "in what he omits, as well as in
his treatment of what he inserts, he shows nothing short of genius.
Those who call him a mere, or even a bad compiler, either have not
duly considered the matter or speak unhappily."[58] Saintsbury's

influence on Malory scholarship was apparent in Vida D. Scudder's LE

MORTE DARTHUR OF SIR THOMAS MALORY AND ITS SOURCES. In this important

book, the first full-length study of Malory's work, Scudder echoed

Saintsbury by stating that Malory showed "great original genius in

creating the MORTE DARTHUR from a number of sources."[59]

The assumption that Malory's work was to be understood in refer-

ence to its sources was implicit in the use of such terms as "trans-

lator," "compiler," and "original" writer. Those words reflected the

belief that Malory's artistic achievement could be measured by com-

parison of his work with its sources. It was necessary, however, to

establish as accurately as possible, given the probability that some

of the particular manuscripts which Malory used were no longer extant,

what sources he actually used before it could be determined how he

used them. Since the publication of Sommer's edition, knowledge of

the sources and Malory's handling of them has been expanded, especial-

ly by Eugène Vinaver[60] and Robert H. Wilson.[61] In addition, new texts

of some of Malory's sources, such as the Cambridge SUITE DU MERLIN and

the Leningrad Manuscript of the Prose TRISTAN, have been discovered.[62]

And more recently, there has been some interest in Spanish analogues

of the MORTE DARTHUR for the light that they shed on Malory's sources.[63]

In his criticism of the MORTE DARTHUR, Vinaver has in his own

words tended to project Malory against his French rather than his Eng-

lish background.[64] Vinaver's knowledge of Malory's French sources is

apparent in his criticism and Malory scholars are indebted to his work;

nevertheless, because of Vinaver's emphasis on Malory's French sources,

study of his English sources and background was a secondary

consideration for many years. The Winchester Manuscript provided evi-

dence that Malory followed the Alliterative MORTE ARTHURE more close-

ly than had been believed,[65] and Robert H. Wilson and E. Talbot

Donaldson showed that Malory used the Stanzaic MORTE ARTHUR in Caxton's

Book 18.[66] These two romances were the English sources which most in-

fluenced the MORTE DARTHUR, but Malory also used the fifteenth-century

metrical chronicle of John Hardyng.[67] Furthermore, Robert H. Wilson,

William Matthews, and Larry D. Benson suggested that Malory might

have had considerable knowledge of the English romance tradition.[68]

The recognition and discussion of Malory's English sources have en-

couraged critics to determine his place in the English romance tradi-

tion and to study his work in a context other than that provided by

his French sources.

Source study has been an important catalyst in Malory scholarship.

It has been useful for discussion of the structure of the MORTE DARTHUR

and for analysis of its style and thematic content, but even in the

later nineteenth century, some scholars argued that source study was

receiving too much emphasis. Saintsbury was among the first to criti-

cize what he called the "direction which modern study so often takes,

of putting inquiry into origins above everything, and neglecting the

consideration of the work as work"[69] and to label source study as "la-

borious and respectable, but rather superfluous."[70] Such an opinion,

however, could only be expressed after Malory's sources had been iden-

tified and source study was exerting influence on criticism of the

MORTE DARTHUR.

STRUCTURE

Defining the structure of the MORTE DARTHUR has been the problem
almost exclusively of twentieth-century critics. In the nineteenth
century, identification of Malory's sources took precedence over
structural analysis of the work. Those who regarded the MORTE DARTHUR
as a "translation" or "compilation" gave little attention to examination of its structure. Those terms were alone sufficient to describe
it. William Minto skeptically wrote that "it is vain to look for any
profound and consistent unity in such a compilation of the unconcerted
labours of different authors."[71] If critics addressed structural issues at all, they generally used vague language in their discussions.
Bernard ten Brink acknowledged that the MORTE DARTHUR had a "kind of
unity"[72] and Alfred Nutt thought that it was "some sort of whole."[73]
F. J. Furnivall coined a phrase popular with later writers when he
called it a "most pleasant jumble and summary of the Arthur Legends."[74]
But nineteenth-century critics who called Malory's work "original"
were forced to discuss and label its structure in terms other than
"translation" or "compilation." The words "epic" and "romance" were
frequently applied; moreover, the importance of the novel in the nineteenth century encouraged comparison between the MORTE DARTHUR and the
novel, in which Malory's work was found wanting. When critics said,
for example, that the unity of the MORTE DARTHUR was disturbed by
multiplicity and similarity of incident,[75] they were judging the work
according to Aristotelian principles of structural unity. In the
twentieth century the premise that Malory should be judged according
to these principles has been challenged, particularly by Vinaver.[76]

The intense study of French medieval literature in the late nineteenth

century was instrumental in developing both an understanding of the

artistic principles which governed the medieval romance genre and a

critical vocabulary with which to discuss it. In his ÉTUDE SUR LE

LANCELOT EN PROSE (1918), Ferdinand Lot coined the term "entrelace-

ment," the "device of interweaving a number of separate themes,"[77]

but it was Vinaver who popularized the use of this word in discussing

his theory that Malory unravelled the interlace structure of his

sources.

Shortly after the discovery of the Winchester Manuscript in 1934,

Oakeshott and Vinaver stated in a number of articles[78] that the manu-

script was of the utmost importance for illuminating critical problems

connected with the MORTE DARTHUR, which until that time was known only

through texts derived from Caxton's 1485 edition, and also for recon-

structing Malory's original text. Vinaver concluded that the "tradi-

tional unity" of the MORTE DARTHUR should be attributed to Caxton ra-

ther than to Malory.[79] In his 1947 edition, Vinaver asserted that

Malory wrote not one but eight separate romances; he based this asser-

tion on evidence provided by Caxton's preface and the explicits and

inconsistencies within the manuscript.[80] When the Winchester Manu-

script was published, it was to be expected that Vinaver's radical

view of the MORTE DARTHUR as eight romances would cause dissent. Such

a revolutionary theory forced reconsideration of the earlier assump-

tions concerning the structure of Malory's work and medieval author-

ship in general. The debate which ensued between Vinaver and his

critics dominated Malory scholarship for the next twenty years.[81]

Among those most critical of Vinaver's judgment were R. M. Lumiansky
and Charles Moorman, whose views were published in a number of books
and articles.[82] The proponents of the "unity" school argued against
Vinaver's statement that the explicits offered conclusive proof that
the work was eight romances[83] and stated that "chronological inconsistencies" were proof of a "planned chronology which makes use of
cross reference and retrospective narrative in order to establish its
sequence of events."[84] The controversy over the "unity" of the MORTE
DARTHUR led to examination and discussion of the word "unity" as a
critical term. Lumiansky postulated two types of unity: "historical
unity" (did Malory intend to write a single book?) and "critical
unity" (does the MORTE DARTHUR exist as a single work, regardless of
Malory's authorial intentions?) and claimed that the work contained
both types of unity.[85] The proponents of "unity" argued against the
views of Vinaver, who rarely replied to his opponents in print,[86] but
Arthur K. Moore denied the arguments of the "unity" proponents on the
grounds that they "demonstrate the sheer fatuousness of affirming or
denying unity without reference to the conditions of its achievement";
moreover, he claimed, they showed "confusion of matters of opinion and
of fact, critical intentionalism, and abuse of rules of evidence."[87]

Between the extreme opinions about the structure of the MORTE
DARTHUR, a number of critics attempted to find a "middle" view. These
were critics who, while unable to accept Vinaver's conclusions, were
also unable to accept the opinion of Lumiansky and Moorman that the
MORTE DARTHUR provided evidence of artistic unity and sometimes found
that their arguments were "overzealous" and "overly ingenious."[88]

R. S. Loomis believed that the MORTE DARTHUR had a general design but
not "unity" in the modern sense[89]; Robert H. Wilson believed that the
work had a "partial unity" and that Malory might have conceived of a
general plan for his work only as he was writing it[90]; Stephen Knight
proposed that the MORTE DARTHUR had two types of structure, the first
five tales being "episodic" and the last three forming a "coherent
narrative"[91]; and D. S. Brewer preferred to use the term "cohesion"
(suggested to him by Vinaver) to describe the structure.[92] The two
most influential spokesmen for the "middle-of-the-road" view were
Brewer and C. S. Lewis, who held "clear-headed reservation and cautious disagreement with Vinaver."[93] To Brewer, the structure of the
MORTE DARTHUR could be compared with the "walls of a city, enclosing
a variety of dwellings, as the walls of Chester and York enclose
buildings of every date from Rome to the present day, yet still make
one medieval city."[94] And Lewis pointed out that Malory would not
have understood modern discussions of "unity" in his work: "It would
be no use asking him how many books he thought he had written; he
would think we meant the material volumes of 'quairs.' If we asked
him, 'How many tales?' he might enumerate more than eight. . . . If
we talked to him about 'artistic unity,' he would not understand."[95]

Several years after the publication in 1890 of Sommer's research
on Malory's sources, Saintsbury asserted that some critics were placing too much emphasis on source study; similarly, some years after
the publication of the Winchester Manuscript in 1947, critics such as
Brewer and Lewis began to question the importance and relevance of the
"unity" debate to Malory scholarship and encouraged study not of the

structure of the MORTE DARTHUR but of neglected aspects of the work such as its style and historical context.[96] But the "unity" debate which occupied Malory scholarship for two decades did serve two useful purposes. First, it led to a closer examination of the Caxton edition and cast light on Caxton's editorial procedures. Second, it encouraged scholars to study each of the eight tales separately to understand more fully Malory's development as a writer.[97]

The most controversial issue concerning study of the individual tales was the problem of establishing their order of composition. Since the order in the Winchester Manuscript and Caxton's edition was the same, it would appear that the tales were transmitted in that order, but Vinaver argued that this was not the actual order of composition. He believed in fact that Malory wrote Tale 2 (Caxton's Book 5) before Tale 1 and that Tale 2 represented Malory's first attempt to write an Arthurian romance. This view, though accepted by many, has received some criticism.[98]

STYLE

Since Thomas Warton first discussed the MORTE DARTHUR in his OBSERVATIONS ON THE FAERIE QUEENE in 1762, critics have argued over the nature and artistic value of Malory's work, but there was one point on which they generally agreed, and one element of his work which they have almost universally praised: his style. Virtually all the general discussions of the MORTE DARTHUR written in the nineteenth century attempted to define its appeal for the reader. To Sir Walter Scott, Malory's style had a "simplicity bordering upon the sublime."[99]

This opinion was echoed by later writers who said that it was a style

of "wonderful simplicity and of wonderful effectiveness"; "dignified,

simple, and generally direct. . . charmingly quaint"; "vigorous and

fresh"; "genial, unobtrusive, dignified, rich in feeling and clear in

expression."[100] Two adjectives frequently used to describe it were

"simple" and "dignified." To the critics of the late nineteenth and

early twentieth centuries who attempted to analyze its style, the

MORTE DARTHUR had a "subtle, magnetic charm which is irresistible."[101]

Very often, however, the critical response more accurately described

the reader's response to the style rather than the style itself.[102]

For example, one critic said that Malory's language was "exactly what

it ought to be" and another said that Malory "conceals the means by

which he obtains his complete result."[103] Such responses were affec-

tive, not analytical. They nevertheless showed that many critics re-

garded Malory's style as unique and original even though they were

content to use only a small number of adjectives to discuss it. There

were few objective data for analyzing Malory's style, and only a few

books attempted to discuss Malory's syntax and vocabulary.[104] It is

fair to say that the critic regarded himself as having the function of

conveying to a general audience the response of an intelligent reader

and not that of a linguistic specialist. Vinaver offered the most

concrete and objective analysis of Malory's style published before the

discovery of the Winchester Manuscript.[105]

Some analyses of Malory's style addressed the problem of defining

Malory's place in the English prose tradition and of analyzing both

influences on his style and the influence which his style exerted on later generations. For many years the most influential discussion of

this topic was R. W. Chambers' "On the Continuity of English Prose

from Alfred to the School of More," in which Chambers asserted that

although Malory was an important English writer, his work was not

very significant in the development of the English secular prose tra-

dition. He was, Chambers said, a "tributary to the main stream of

continuous English prose."[106] In the last two decades, Chambers'

view has been challenged. A. A. Prins claimed that "for all the gal-

licisms in vocabulary, [Malory's] kind of prose is far less gallicized

in phraseonomy or latinized in syntax" than that of More,[107] and R. M.

Wilson and Norman Davis held the opinion that Chambers underestimated

Malory's importance in the development of the English prose tradi-

tion.[108] Their opinion was not without precedent, however; Saintsbury

had written in 1912 that Malory's influence on Elizabethan prose was

greater than had at that time been realized.[109]

Vinaver's edition of the Winchester Manuscript made possible a

number of linguistic studies of Malory's syntax, grammar, and vocabu-

lary; two of the earliest important studies to appear were comparisons

of word-order in the Winchester Manuscript and Caxton's edition.[110]

Although this edition did provide a stimulus for linguistic study of

the MORTE DARTHUR, Brewer stressed, over twenty years after publica-

tion of the manuscript, that a "full and satisfactory treatment of

style depends on a firmer basis of linguistic knowledge and comparison

than we yet possess."[111] In the last fifteen years, Japanese scholars

have analyzed Malory's grammar and syntax.[112] The recent stylistic

analyses of the MORTE DARTHUR by P. J. C. Field and Mark Lambert have not been dependent on linguistic studies of Malory's grammar, vocabu-

lary, and syntax. These two critics have stated that Malory's style

should be discussed in the context of the prose traditions of his own

time. Field, in the first major book-length study of Malory's style,

emphasized Malory's affinities with the direct and colloquial style

of the chronicle tradition.[113] Lambert, whose work was indebted to

Field, stressed the importance of determining what prose style charac-

teristics Malory held in common with his sources and contemporaries.

He stated that the stylistic characteristics of fifteenth-century

prose could not be "subtracted" from Malory's work to determine what

was original or distinctive in Malory's style; this could best be seen

in sections where differences between the style of the MORTE DARTHUR

and that of Malory's sources could be analyzed.[114] These two discus-

sions of his style and its relation to other aspects of the MORTE

DARTHUR owed more to the interest generated by Vinaver's edition of

the Winchester Manuscript and to surveys of scholarship which have

stressed the need for stylistic analysis than they owed to linguistic

studies.

THEME

The first editors of the MORTE DARTHUR were its first critics.

In his preface to the 1485 edition, Caxton stressed the moral and

didactic elements of the work. He printed it

> to the entente that noble men may see and lerne
> the noble actes of chyvalrye, the jentyl and
> vertuous dedes that somme knyghtes used in tho
> days, by whyche they came to honour, and how
> they that were vycious were punysshed and ofte

> put to shame and rebuke. . . . Doo after the
> good and leve the evyl, and it shal brynge
> you to good fame and renommee. . . . But all
> is wryton for our doctryne, and for to beware
> that we falle not to vyce nor synne . . . .[115]

Although it might be claimed that Caxton emphasized the morality of

the work in hopes of increasing his sales, it is more likely that

Caxton's statements were sincere. And Wynkyn de Worde interpolated

in Book 21, Chapter 12, of the 1498 edition, a passage in which he

pointed out the moral utility of the MORTE DARTHUR. This passage was

also printed in the subsequent black-letter editions.

> Therfor me thynketh this present boke callid
> La mort dathur [sic] is ryght necessary often
> to be radde. For in it shal ye fynde the
> gracious knyghtly and vertuous werre of moost
> noble knyghtes of the worlde, wherby they gate
> praysyng contynuell. Also me semyth by the
> oft redyng therof. ye shal gretly desyre tacus-
> tome yourself in folowynge those gracyous
> knyghtly dedes. That is to seye, to drede god,
> and love ryghtwisnes, faythfully & courageously
> to serve your soverayne prynce. And the more
> that god hath geven you the tryumfall honour,
> the meeker ye oughte to be, ever feryng the
> unstablynesse of this dysceyvable worlde.[116]

There seems to be little reason why de Worde should have interpolated

this passage so close to the end of the work unless it expressed his

convictions.

A vehement detractor of the morality of the MORTE DARTHUR was

Roger Ascham, who in THE SCHOLEMASTER (1570) charged that the romance

was "bold bawdry and open manslaughter."[117] That this charge was tak-

en seriously by later generations is suggested in William Stansby's

"advertissement" to the 1634 edition.

> Thus, reader, I leave thee at thy pleasure to
> reade but not to judge, except thou judge

> with understanding. The asse is no competent
> judge betwixt the owle and the nightingale
> for the sweetnes of their voices; . . . Neither
> is it beseeming for a man to censure that which
> his ignorance cannot perceive, or his pride and
> malice will prejudicate or cavill at.

The issue whether the romance was "moral" or "immoral" interested

nineteenth-century critics. The judgment of some was impaired by the

assumption that the artistic aims of Tennyson and other poets who

utilized Arthurian materials should also have been the artistic aims

of Malory.[118] Not all or indeed most nineteenth and early twentieth-

century readers applied these ethical and literary standards to the

MORTE DARTHUR. The poetry of Tennyson, Morris, and Swinburne certain-

ly increased the popularity of the MORTE DARTHUR in the nineteenth

century, which is evident from the number of popular editions which

were printed. The defense of the morality of the MORTE DARTHUR was

prompted by an awareness, among the better critics, that a proper

consideration of Malory's work required both abstraction from the

work of the Victorian poets, whose themes were not always those of

Malory, and a sense of historical perspective.[119] Many of those who

did not find the MORTE DARTHUR "immoral" dismissed the relevance of

the "moral" question and discussed thematic content instead. One of

these, Edward Strachey, isolated what he believed to the theme of

the work:

> It is what Carlyle would have called the peren-
> nial battle between God and the devil,--the
> context between man's free will and his circum-
> stances; the nemesis which attends his way
> during that contest, and his triumph by help of
> a higher power than his own.[120]

Saintsbury, who first stated clearly that the MORTE DARTHUR was concerned with love, religion, and war,[121] ascribed Malory's impor-

tance to his recognition that "in the combination of the Quest of the

Grail with the loves of Lancelot and Guinevere lay the kernel at once

and conclusion of the whole matter."[122] The theme of conflicting

loyalties was stressed by Scudder, Chambers, and Vinaver. Scudder

identified a conflict of loyalty in duties to lord, lady, and God

(reflecting the tripart subject matter of love, religion, and war);

Chambers wrote that the "ultimate debate. . . is not between the

ideals of Camelot and the ideals of Corbenic, but a purely human one,

the familiar conflict between human love and human loyalty"; and Vina-

ver found that the conflict of loyalties was "inherent in the tradi-

tional doctrine and practice of chivalry."[123]

Most critics have assumed that the MORTE DARTHUR reflected the

times in which Malory lived and wrote, the last years of the Wars of

the Roses, and many have believed that the turmoil of the mid-fifteenth

century led Malory to idealize the past. To these critics Malory's

attitude was "nostalgic" and "escapist." In CHIVALRY IN ENGLISH LIT-

ERATURE, William Henry Schofield called the MORTE DARTHUR a "work of

retrospect, tinged with sadness for the passing of the good old days;

a work of idealism, troubled with knowledge of miserable facts daily

indulged; a work of patriotism, written when the land was being wasted

by civil strife; a work of encouragement to the right-minded, and of

warning to the evil-minded, among men of that class in which the

author lived and moved."[124] It is a fair presumption that Malory's

work contains references, direct or indirect, to political and social

problems which existed at the time he wrote. It is difficult to

imagine that Malory's depiction of the decline of Arthurian society
and the reasons for this do not, in some measure, reflect those of his
time. But Malory's personal sympathies and attitudes may be impossible
to determine with certainty and internal evidence of the MORTE DARTHUR
to support them must be used with care. Assumptions about Malory's
attitude to his historical background, for example, have led many critics to search for parallels between events and historical individuals
of the fifteenth century and events and characters of the MORTE DARTHUR.
Nellie Slayton Aurner, who believed that Malory wrote an "allegorical
presentation of the rise and downfall of a united English chivalry
under the Lancastrian dynasty,"[125] saw specific parallels between Arthur in various sections of the work and Henry IV, Henry V, and Henry
VI.[126] She presented parallels between historical events in the Warwickshire Malory's life and fictional events in the MORTE DARTHUR as
evidence for his authorship. Most critics have accepted that Malory
was a Lancastrian,[127] and some have been more judicious than Aurner in
assessing the possible influence of fifteenth-century political strife
on Malory's work. George R. Stewart, who argued from geographical
references in the MORTE DARTHUR that Malory was a Lancastrian, thought
that Malory's association of the traitors with the southwest of England, a Yorkist stronghold, betrayed his Lancastrian sympathies.[128]
And Edward D. Kennedy, who accepted the premise that Malory was a Lancastrian involved in the politics of his day, suggested that Malory's
depiction of Arthur's attitude toward his queen may have been influenced by Edward IV's unpopular marriage to Elizabeth Wydville in 1464;
nevertheless, he stressed that the MORTE DARTHUR was not a "political

allegory."[129]

Some critics stated that Malory was trying to reestablish the
lost age of chivalry and its ideals in an England torn by civil strife
for a didactic and exemplary purpose, not to evoke or chronicle a lost
and longed-for past but to revitalize and instruct a degenerate present. Arthur B. Ferguson argued that Malory was concerned with the
"ethical value of chivalry in his own day" and wanted the MORTE DAR-
THUR to serve as an exemplum for the present.[130] On the other hand,
Elizabeth T. Pochoda claimed that Malory was not presenting Arthurian
society as a political model for the late fifteenth century but was
exposing its inadequacy as such as model.[131] In recent years, study
has been focused on Malory's concept of chivalry in relation to the
historical, political, and cultural milieu of the fifteenth century
and on defining as precisely as possible his concepts of chivalry,
honor, truth, and knighthood. In MALORY'S 'MORTE DARTHUR,' Larry D.
Benson argued that Malory's attitude was not nostalgic or escapist but
"realistic" and that his work dealt with the practical concerns of his
aristocratic class.[132]

CONCLUSION

The aim of this survey has been to show that the major critical
issues connected with the work which have occupied twentieth-century
critics -- Malory's identity, texts and editions of the MORTE DARTHUR,
source study, structure, style, and theme -- developed from discussion
of those topics in the last half of the nineteenth century and were
stimulated by Vinaver's edition of the Winchester Manuscript. Critics

have come to accept the premise that the MORTE DARTHUR should not be
judged by contemporary literary standards, and they have generally
dismissed the importance of classifying the work as "epic," "romance,"
"chronicle," or early "novel." The plea for establishing sound prem-
ises on which the MORTE DARTHUR could be judged was stated by Saintsbury:

> It is what the artist does with his materials,
> not where he gets them, that is the question.
> And Malory has done, with his materials, a very
> great thing indeed. . . . Sometimes he may not
> take the best available version of a story;
> but we must ask ourselves whether he knew it.
> Sometimes he may put in what we do not want:
> but we must ask ourselves whether there was
> not a reason for doing so, to him if not to us.
> What is certain is that he, and he only in any
> language, makes of this vast assemblage of
> stories one story, and one book.[133]

Malory scholarship has generally been dominated by an "either. . .
or" fallacy: either one accepted the authorship of the Warwickshire
Malory, or he was faced with the fact that the Sir Thomas Malory who
wrote the MORTE DARTHUR was only a name; either one accepted that
study of the MORTE DARTHUR was dependent on source study, or he depre-
ciated the value of source study altogether; Malory was either a "Zusammenstoppler" or he was an "artist conscious of his art"[134]; the
MORTE DARTHUR was either eight separate romances or a "unified" single
work.[135] Admittedly, such assertions on both sides often encouraged
specious argumentation and rigidity of opinion. The "either. . . or"
debates have nevertheless forced reconsideration of important issues
and generated new ideas and a synthetic approach to Malory scholarship. Matthews has offered a strong case against uncritical acceptance

of the authorship of the Warwickshire Malory who has long been thought

to be the writer of the MORTE DARTHUR. There is general acceptance of

the opinion that source study is very useful for assessing Malory's

work but should not take precedence over study of the MORTE DARTHUR

itself. The debate over whether Malory was a "compiler" or a "maker"

has given way to the view that critics should study his development as

a writer. And the "unity" debate has encouraged critics to interpret

the structure of the MORTE DARTHUR according to the aesthetic princi-

ples of the medieval romance, not the modern novel, and to suggest

critical terms other than "unity" for discussing it.

ENDNOTES

[1] For an account of the discovery, see W. F. Oakeshott, "The Find-
ing of the Manuscript," ESSAYS ON MALORY, ed. J. A. W. Bennett (Oxford:
Clarendon Press, 1963), pp. 1-6. See also his articles in the London
TIMES, June 26, 1934, p. 17; Aug. 25, 1934, pp. 11, 12; and TLS, Sept.
27, 1934, p. 650. The manuscript has been reproduced in THE WINCHESTER
MALORY; A FACSIMILE, with an introduction by N. R. Ker. E.E.T.S. Sup-
plemental Series, No. 4. London and New York: Oxford University
Press, 1976.

[2] These include Eugène Vinaver, "Sir Thomas Malory," ALMA, ed. R.
S. Loomis (Oxford: Clarendon Press, 1959), pp. 541-52; Larry D. Ben-
son, "Sir Thomas Malory's LE MORTE DARTHUR," CRITICAL APPROACHES TO
SIX MAJOR ENGLISH WORKS, ed. R. M. Lumiansky and Herschel Baker (Phil-
adelphia: University of Pennsylvania Press, 1968), pp. 81-131; D. S.
Brewer, "The Present State of Malory," FORUM FOR MODERN LANGUAGE STUD-
IES, 6 (1970), 83-97; rpt. in ARTHURIAN ROMANCE: SEVEN ESSAYS, ed.
D. D. R. Owen (New York: Barnes and Noble, 1971); Elizabeth T. Pocho-
da, ARTHURIAN PROPAGANDA: 'LE MORTE DARTHUR' AS AN HISTORICAL IDEAL
OF LIFE (Chapel Hill: University of North Carolina Press, 1971), pp.
3-22; R. H. Wilson, "Malory and Caxton," A MANUAL OF THE WRITINGS IN
MIDDLE ENGLISH, 1050-1500, ed. Albert E. Hartung (New Haven: Connect-
icut Academy of Arts and Sciences, 1972), vol. 3, pp. 757-71.

[3] Eugène Vinaver, ed., THE WORKS OF SIR THOMAS MALORY, 2nd ed.
(Oxford: Clarendon Press, 1967), vol. 3, p. 1260. This work is here-
after abbreviated as WSTM, and unless otherwise indicated, all subsequent references will be to this edition.

[4]Ibid., vol. 1, p. cxlv.

[5]N. F. Blake recently suggested that Caxton concealed his knowledge of Malory because he was afraid that Malory's reputation might
harm the sale of the book. See "Caxton Prepares His Edition of the
MORTE DARTHUR," JOURNAL OF LIBRARIANSHIP, 8 (Oct. 1976), 280.

[6]SCRIPTORUM ILLUSTRIUM MAIORIS BRYTANNIAE. . . CATALOGUS, 2nd ed.
(Basel, 1557-59), vol. 1, p. 628.

[7]G. L. Kittredge, "Who Was Sir Thomas Malory?" HARVARD STUDIES
AND NOTES IN PHILOLOGY AND LITERATURE, 5 (1896), 97-106; E. Vetterman,
DIE BALEN-DICHTUNGEN UND IHRE QUELLEN, ZRP Beiheft 60 (1918), 53-60.

[8]"Sir Thomas Malory," ATHENAEUM, 1896, pt. 2, pp. 64-65; 98.
Williams found that a "Thomas Malorie, miles" was excluded from a
general pardon issued 8 Edward IV, but Kittredge identified him with
his own Warwickshire candidate ["Who Was Sir Thomas Malory?" pp. 88-
90].

[9]"Sir Thomas Malory," ATHENAEUM, 1897, pt. 2, pp. 353-54; "The
Identity of the Author of the 'Morte d'Arthur,' with Notes on the Will
of Thomas Malory and the Genealogy of the Malory Family," ARCHAEOLOGIA,
56 (1898), 165-82. Martin documented the existence of a Thomas Malory
of Papworth, Huntingdonshire (died 1469), and argued that he was the
author.

[10]"Who Was Sir Thomas Malory?" pp. 85-106. Kittredge's identification of the author of the MORTE DARTHUR with Sir Thomas Malory of
Warwickshire was first announced in a paper at Columbia University,
March 15, 1894, and was first printed in JOHNSON'S UNIVERSAL CYCLO-
PAEDIA, 5 (1894), 498. H. O. Sommer had mentioned this Thomas Malory
in his edition of LE MORTE DARTHUR [(London: David Nutt, 1890), vol.
2, p. 1, footnote 3], but Sommer did not claim that this Malory wrote
the work.

[11]"Who Was Sir Thomas Malory?" pp. 86-87.

[12]G. L. Kittredge, SIR THOMAS MALORY (Barnstable: Privately
printed, 1925; rpt. Folcroft Library Editions, 1974); Edward Hicks,
SIR THOMAS MALORY: HIS TURBULENT CAREER (Cambridge: Harvard University Press, 1928; rpt. Octagon Books, 1970); A. C. Baugh, "Documenting
Sir Thomas Malory," SPECULUM, 8 (1933), 3-29; E. K. Chambers, SIR
THOMAS MALORY (London: English Association, 1922; rpt. 1976), p. 16;
rpt. in SIR THOMAS WYATT AND SOME COLLECTED STUDIES (London: Sidgwick
and Jackson, 1933), pp. 44-45. For a history of the research concerning the Warwickshire Malory, see Richard D. Altick, THE SCHOLAR ADVEN-
TURERS (New York: Macmillan, 1950), pp. 65-85.

[13]WSTM, vol. 1, p. 180.

[14]As subsequent research proved, this supposition was false.

[15]"The Identity of Sir Thomas Malory, Knight-Prisoner," RES, N.S. 24 (1973), 257-65.

[16]"Sir Thomas Malory, M.P.," BULLETIN OF THE INSTITUTE OF HISTOR-ICAL RESEARCH, 47 (1974), 24-35.

[17]Berkeley: University of California Press, 1966. Matthews sum-marized and analyzed the cases for the Welsh Malory (pp. 5, 35-37), the Papworth Malory (pp. 5-7, 37-38), and the Warwickshire Malory (pp. 7-34, 39-74).

[18]WSTM, vol. 1, p. xxi. For more extensive remarks, see Vinaver's edition of KING ARTHUR AND HIS KNIGHTS (London and New York: Oxford University Press, 1968; rpt. 1975), p. 228. In an otherwise favorable review, D. S. Brewer also noted this weakness ["The Present Study of Malory," pp. 85-88]. Matthews did argue in his book that the term "knight-prisoner" might indicate that Malory was a prisoner of war and not a criminal.

[19]For example, J. R. Clarke [KING ARTHUR: HIS RELATION TO HISTORY AND FICTION (Gloucester: John Bellow, [1880]), p. 19] said that "wheth-er Sir Thomas Malory was a knight or not, he constantly throughout his narrative reveals his character as an ecclesiastic, while describing the vices and the errors of the character he depicts."

[20]"The MORTE DARTHUR," TLS, June 7, 1947, p. 273; rpt. STUDIES IN MEDIEVAL AND RENAISSANCE LITERATURE (Cambridge: Cambridge University Press, 1966), pp. 104-05. Hicks and Altick also tried to extenuate the charges against Malory's character.

[21]WSTM, vol. 1, pp. xxvi-xxix. Vinaver claimed that the reader's belief in Malory's "morality" came from Caxton's preface where Caxton said that the book should be read for moral improvement. Vinaver therefore denied that there was a "moral cleavage between the book and the man to whom it has been attributed" (p. xxvii).

[22]"His paradox is too absolute: a book that delightfully and ap-parently convincedly exhorts and exemplifies to an ideal behavior, con-trasting with a career that seems to have been substantially devoted to what the ideal specifically condemns." [THE ILL-FRAMED KNIGHT, p. 50.]

[23]"The Identity of Sir Thomas Malory, Knight-Prisoner," pp. 257-65.

[24]WSTM, vol. 3, p. 1280. Vinaver stated that this is the "only reference to Malory yet found in an Old French manuscript."

[25]Larry D. Benson praised Matthews' "skeptical" and cautious view [MALORY'S 'MORTE DARTHUR' (Cambridge: Harvard University Press, 1976), p. ix].

[26]Two copies of Caxton's edition are extant: a perfect copy in
the Pierpont Morgan Library, New York, and an imperfect copy in the
John Rylands Library, Manchester.   In the nineteenth century, these
copies were called the Osterley Park and Althorp copies, respectively.
The Pierpont Morgan copy has been reproduced in facsimile by the Scolar Press in association with the library (1976). For a history of
these two copies, see Seymour de Ricci, A CENSUS OF CAXTONS (Oxford:
Bibliographical Society, 1909), p. 81, n. 76.

[27]For discussion of how the early (black-letter) editions and
important nineteenth-century editions are related, see H. O. Sommer,
ACADEMY, 34 (1888), 273, and his edition of LE MORTE DARTHUR (London:
David Nutt, 1890; rpt. New York: AMS Press, 1973), vol. 2, pp. 15-17.
For bibliographical information, see Sommer's edition, vol. 2, pp. 1-
14; Eugène Vinaver, MALORY (Oxford: Clarendon Press, 1929; rpt. 1970),
pp. 189-95.

[28]Barry Gaines discussed these editions in "The Editions of Malory in the Early Nineteenth Century," PUBLICATIONS OF THE BIBLIOGRA-
PHICAL SOCIETY OF AMERICA, 68 (1974), 1-17.

[29]Among these are Thomas Wright, 1858; Edward Strachey [Globe
Edition], 1868; F. J. Simmons and John Rhŷs, 1893-94; Ernest Rhys,
[1892?]; Israel Gollancz [Temple Classics], 1897; A. W. Pollard [Li-
brary of English Classics], 1900; Dent [Everyman edition], 1906. Some
popular abridgements were edited by J. T. Knowles, 1862; Edward Conybeare, 1868; B. Montgomerie Ranking, [1871]; Sidney Lanier, 1880;
Ernest Rhys, 1886; Charles Morris, 1892; A. T. Martin, 1896; W. E.
Mead, 1897.

[30]H. O. Sommer, "The Relationships of the Several Editions of Malory's 'Morte Darthur,'" ACADEMY, 34 (1888), 273.

[31]"Caxton's 'Morte Darthur,'" ACADEMY, 29 (1886), 220.

[32]Strachey stated that after collating the Althorp and Osterley
Park copies of the Caxton edition, he was satisfied that his edition
was a "more accurate reproduction of Caxton's text than any other
except that of Southey" [MORTE DARTHUR (London and Philadelphia: Macmillan, 1868), p. xviii]. It should be noted that William Upcott,
not Southey, was the textual editor for the 1817 edition, which was
based on Caxton's edition, and that the text was not as accurate as
Strachey believed [Sommer, ACADEMY, 34 (1888), 273]. Sommer's statement of his aim may be found in LE MORTE DARTHUR, vol. 2, p. 17.
Vinaver was critical of Sommer's work. In collating the edition with
the Rylands copy of Caxton's edition, Vinaver claimed to have found
over a hundred mistakes (WSTM, vol. 1, p. cxxxi).

[33]"The 'Morte Darthur,'" TLS, June 7, 1947, p. 273; rpt. STUDIES
IN MEDIEVAL AND RENAISSANCE LITERATURE (Cambridge: Cambridge University Press, 1966), p. 103.

[34]It should be noted that the first edition to use this title
after Caxton was the 1816 reprint of Stansby's edition which is sometimes attributed to Haslewood (WSTM, vol. 1, p. xl).

[35]WSTM, vol. 1, p. cii–ciii.

[36]N. F. Blake, CAXTON: ENGLAND'S FIRST PUBLISHER (New York:
Barnes and Noble, 1975); N. F. Blake, "Caxton Prepares His Edition of
the MORTE DARTHUR," JOURNAL OF LIBRARIANSHIP, 8 (1976), 272–85; Richard Deacon, A BIOGRAPHY OF WILLIAM CAXTON (London: Frederick Muller,
1976); George D. Painter, WILLIAM CAXTON: A QUINCENTENARY BIOGRAPHY
OF ENGLAND'S FIRST PRINTER (London: Chatto and Windus, 1976).

[37]"The Malory Manuscript," THE BRITISH LIBRARY JOURNAL, 3 (Autumn
1977), 91–113.

[38]THE HISTORY OF ENGLISH POETRY FROM THE CLOSE OF THE ELEVENTH
TO THE COMMENCEMENT OF THE EIGHTEENTH CENTURY (London: J. Dodsley,
1774–81), vol. 2, p. 235 note.

[39]Introduction to SIR TRISTRAM (Edinburgh: Constable, 1804),
p. lxxx.

[40]METRICAL ROMANCES OF THE THIRTEENTH, FOURTEENTH, AND FIFTEENTH
CENTURIES (Edinburgh: Constable, 1810), vol. 3, pp. 363–64.   Benson
revived this theory in MALORY'S 'MORTE DARTHUR.'

[41]Trautmann first discussed Malory's use of the Alliterative MORTE
ARTHURE in "Der Dichter Huchown und seine Werke," ANGLIA, 1 (1878),
145–46.   The relationship between the MORTE DARTHUR and the Stanzaic
MORTE ARTHUR was argued in a series of articles by H. O. Sommer and
J. D. Bruce.   See Sommer's edition, vol. 3; Bruce, ANGLIA, 23 (1900),
67–100; Bruce, Introduction to LE MORTE ARTHUR (E.E.T.S., London:
Trübner, 1903), pp. vii–xxx; Sommer, ANGLIA, 29 (1906), 529–38; Bruce,
"A Reply to Dr. Sommer," ANGLIA, 30 (1907), 209–16.

[42]Sommer discussed Malory's use of each source in LE MORTE DAR-
THUR, vol. 3.   Some of this information had already appeared as "The
Sources of Malory's 'Le Morte Darthur,'" ACADEMY, 37 (1890), 11–12.

[43]The term "chronicler" was found less often than the other two.
Cf. W. E. Gladstone, GLEANINGS OF PAST YEARS, 1844–78 (London: John
Murray, 1879), vol. 2, p. 152; George W. Cox, AN INTRODUCTION TO THE
SCIENCE OF COMPARATIVE MYTHOLOGY AND FOLKLORE (London: Kegan Paul,
1881), p. 313.   Recently, Malory's relationship and indebtedness to
the chronicle tradition has received considerable attention.   P. J. C.
Field [ROMANCE AND CHRONICLE: A STUDY OF MALORY'S PROSE STYLE (Bloom-
ington: Indiana University Press, 1971), p. 37] stated that Malory
put "romance material into chronicle form."   See also Mark Lambert's
MALORY: STYLE AND VISION IN 'LE MORTE DARTHUR' (New Haven, Conn.:
Yale University Press, 1975).   Lambert discussed characteristics of

prose style which Malory held in common with contemporary writers and with his sources in Chapter 1.

[44]"Der Dichter Huchown und seine Werke," ANGLIA, 1 (1878), 145.

[45]STUDIES ON THE LEGEND OF THE HOLY GRAIL (London: David Nutt, 1888), p. 236.

[46]SPECIMENS OF EARLY ENGLISH METRICAL ROMANCES (London: Longmans, 1805), vol. 1, p. 308. Cf. S. Humphreys Gurteen, THE ARTHURIAN EPIC (New York and London: G. P. Putnam, 1895; rpt. New York: Haskell House, 1965), p. 84.

[47]Charles Sears Baldwin, AN INTRODUCTION TO ENGLISH MEDIEVAL LITERATURE (New York and London: Longmans, 1914), p. 165; William Morris, Letter to the PALL MALL GAZETTE, rpt. in THE COLLECTED WORKS OF WILLIAM MORRIS (London: Longmans, 1914), vol. 22, p. xv.

[48]MALORY (Oxford: Clarendon Press, 1929; rpt. 1970), p. 29.

[49]THE ORIGIN AND HISTORY OF THE ENGLISH LANGUAGE AND OF THE EARLY ENGLISH LITERATURE IT EMBODIES (London: Sampson Low, 1862), p. 487.

[50]Frederick Dixon, "The Round Table," TEMPLE BAR, 109 (Sept.-Dec. 1896), 210. Ernest Rhys [LIBRARY OF THE WORLD'S BEST LITERATURE, ed. C. D. Warner (New York: Peale, 1897), vol. 17, p. 9645], said that Malory was "much more" than a "mere compiler and book-maker." Sidney Lanier [THE BOY'S KING ARTHUR (New York: Scribner, 1880), p. xx] likewise claimed that the MORTE DARTHUR was no "mere compilation."

[51]MORTE DARTHUR (London and Philadelphia: Macmillan, 1868), p. viii.

[52]THE ENGLISH NOVEL (New York: Scribner, 1894), p. 14.

[53]Harold Littledale, ESSAYS ON LORD TENNYSON'S IDYLLS OF THE KING (New York: Macmillan, 1893), p. 24.

[54]"The Sources of Malory's 'Le Morte Darthur,'" ACADEMY, 37 (1890), 11.

[55]See especially the "Preface to the 1970 Impression" in MALORY (Oxford: Clarendon Press, 1929; rpt. 1970). In 1929, Vinaver believed that Malory had written a single work.

[56]A SHORT HISTORY OF ENGLISH LITERATURE (New York: Macmillan, 1898; rpt. 1960), p. 196. See also A HISTORY OF ENGLISH PROSE RHYTHM (Bloomington: Indiana University Press, 1912; rpt. 1965), pp. 82-92.

[57]THE ENGLISH NOVEL (New York: E. P. Dutton, 1913), pp. 24-27. See also A HISTORY OF ENGLISH PROSE RHYTHM, pp. 82-83.

[58] THE FLOURISHING OF ROMANCE (New York: Scribner, 1897), p. 105.

[59] New York: E. P. Dutton, 1917; rpt. 1921, p. 366.

[60] See LE ROMAN DE TRISTAN ET D'ISEUT DANS L'OEUVRE DE THOMAS MA-
LORY (Paris: Champion, 1925); MALORY (Oxford: Clarendon Press, 1929;
rpt. 1970); and the Commentaries in WSTM, vol. 3.

[61] CHARACTERIZATION IN MALORY: A COMPARISON WITH HIS SOURCES
(Chicago, 1934; rpt. Norwood, Pa.:   Norwood Editions, 1975); "Malory
and the PERLESVAUS," MP, 30 (1932), 13-22; "The 'Fair Unknown' in Malory," PMLA, 58 (1943), 1-21; "Malory's Naming of Minor Characters,"
JEGP, 42 (1943), 364-85; "Malory's French Book Again," CL, 2 (1950),
172-81; "The Prose LANCELOT in Malory," TEXAS STUDIES IN ENGLISH, 32
(1953), 1-13; "Addenda on Malory's Minor Characters," JEGP, 55 (1956),
563-87; "The Rebellion of the Kings in Malory and in the Cambridge SUITE
DU MERLIN," TEXAS STUDIES IN ENGLISH, 31 (1952), 13-26.   References to
other articles by Wilson appear in footnotes below.

[62] For an account of the discovery of the Cambridge SUITE DU MER-
LIN, see Eugène Vinaver, "La genèse de la SUITE DU MERLIN," MÉLANGES
DE PHILOLOGIE. . . ERNEST HOEPFFNER (Paris: Les Belles Lettres, 1949),
pp. 295-300; also WSTM, vol. 3, pp. 1279-82.   For information about
the Leningrad Manuscript, see WSTM, vol. 3, p. 1449.

[63] See WSTM, vol. 3, p. 1267; Thomas C. Rumble, "The Tale of Tris-
tram: Development by Analogy," MALORY'S ORIGINALITY, ed. R. M. Lumi-
ansky (Baltimore: Johns Hopkins Press, 1964), pp. 130-39; Edward D.
Kennedy, "Arthur's Rescue in Malory and the Spanish TRISTAN," N & Q,
N.S. 17 (1970), 6-10; Edward D. Kennedy, "Malory and the Spanish
TRISTAN: Further Parallels," N & Q, N.S. 19 (1972), 7-10.

[64] WSTM, "Preface to the First Edition," vol. 1, p. x.

[65] Eugène Vinaver and E. V. Gordon, "New Light on the Text of the
Alliterative MORTE ARTHURE," MEDIUM AEVUM, 6 (1937), 81-98.   See also
R. H. Wilson, "Some Minor Characters in the MORTE ARTHURE," MLN, 71
(1956), 475-80.

[66] These two critics argued against Vinaver's statement ["Notes
on Malory's Sources," ARTHURIANA, 1 (1928-29), 64-66] that Malory made
extensive use of the MORT ARTU in Caxton's Book 18; they claimed that
Malory's source was the Stanzaic MORTE ARTHUR.   See Wilson, "Malory,
the Stanzaic MORTE ARTHUR, and the MORT ARTU," MP, 37 (1939), 125-38;
Donaldson, "Malory and the Stanzaic LE MORTE ARTHUR," SP, 47 (1950),
460-72; and Wilson, "Notes on Malory's Sources," MLN, 66 (1951), 22-
26.   Wilson and Donaldson ended the debate over Malory's use of the
Stanzaic MORTE ARTHUR which Sommer and Bruce had initiated (see footnote 41).

[67] See WSTM, vol. 3, p. 1405; William Matthews, THE TRAGEDY OF

ARTHUR (Berkeley: University of California Press, 1960), p. 172; Edward D. Kennedy, "Malory's Use of Hardyng's Chronicle," N & Q, N.S. 16 (1969), 167-70; R. H. Wilson, "More Borrowings from Hardyng's Chronicle," N & Q, N.S. 17 (1970), 208-10.

[68] See R. H. Wilson, "Malory's Early Knowledge of Arthurian Romance," TSE, 29 (1950), 33-50; William Matthews, THE ILL-FRAMED KNIGHT, Chapter 3 ("The Locale of the MORTE DARTHUR"); Larry D. Benson, MALORY'S 'MORTE DARTHUR,' Chapter 2 ("Malory and English Romance").

[69] THE ENGLISH NOVEL, p. 24. W. Lewis Jones [KING ARTHUR IN HISTORY AND LEGEND (Cambridge: Cambridge University Press; New York: G. P. Putnam, 1912)] shared this opinion, and Vida D. Scudder [LE MORTE DARTHUR OF SIR THOMAS MALORY AND ITS SOURCES, Part 3] stressed that source study must be used with caution.

[70] A SHORT HISTORY OF ENGLISH LITERATURE, p. 196. Cf. Edmund Reiss, SIR THOMAS MALORY (New York: Twayne, 1966), Chapter 1.

[71] CHARACTERISTICS OF ENGLISH POETS FROM CHAUCER TO SHIRLEY (London: Blackwood, 1874), p. 107.

[72] HISTORY OF ENGLISH LITERATURE, ed. Alois Brandl, trans. L. Dora Schmidz (London: Bell, 1896), vol. 3, p. 46.

[73] ACADEMY, 29 (1886), 196.

[74] LA QUESTE DEL SAINT GRAAL (London: Roxburghe Club, 1864), p. iii.

[75] See, for example, Howard Maynadier, THE ARTHUR OF THE ENGLISH POETS (New York: Houghton Mifflin, 1907), p. 229; F[rederick] Ryland, "The Morte D'Arthur," THE ENGLISH ILLUSTRATED MAGAZINE, 6 (1888-89), 57-58.

[76] For discussion of these theories, see MALORY (Oxford: Clarendon Press, 1929; rpt. 1970), preface; WSTM, vol. 1, pp. xlvi-xlvii, lxiv-lxxiii; "Form and Meaning in Medieval Romance," The Presidential Address of the Modern Humanities Research Association, Leeds, 1966; À LA RECHERCHE D'UNE POÉTIQUE MÉDIÉVALE (Paris: Nizet, 1970); and THE RISE OF ROMANCE (Oxford: Clarendon Press, 1970), especially Chapters 5-7.

[77] THE RISE OF ROMANCE, p. 71. One critic of Vinaver's interpretation of Malory's narrative technique was Benson, who called the MORTE DARTHUR a "one-volume prose history" [MALORY'S 'MORTE DARTHUR'].

[78] See footnote 1. W. F. Oakeshott, "Caxton and Malory's MORTE DARTHUR," GUTENBERG-JAHRBUCH, 10 (1935), 112-16; and "The Manuscript of the MORTE DARTHUR," DISCOVERY, 16 (1935), 45-46. See also Eugène Vinaver, "Malory's MORTE DARTHUR in the Light of a Recent Discovery,"

BJRL, 19 (1935), 438-57; "New Light on Malory's MORTE DARTHUR," YORK-
SHIRE SOCIETY FOR CELTIC STUDIES, 1935-36, pp. 18-20.

[79]"New Light on Malory's MORTE DARTHUR," p. 20.

[80]See WSTM, vol. 1, pp. xxxv-xxxviii. Vinaver made three claims
in support of the theory. First, he claimed that Caxton's preface
("Wherfore, such as have late ben drawn oute bryefly into Englysshe
. . .") refers to a number of volumes, so that the "conclusion naturally suggests itself that what he published was a collection of works,
not a single composition." Second, the Winchester Manuscript contained
distinct explicits at the end of each of the eight major divisions of
the manuscript, and the first explicit showed clearly that Malory had
no intention to continue his work. Third, the text contained numerous
inconsistencies. "An author who regards each of his works as a separate 'tale' or 'book' would hardly think it necessary to make them
consistent in every detail with one another."

[81]For useful bibliographies of the controversy, see Stephen
Knight, THE STRUCTURE OF SIR THOMAS MALORY'S ARTHURIAD (Sydney: Syd-
ney University Press, 1969), Chapters 1 and 2; Robert W. Ackerman,
"'The Tale of Gareth' and the Unity of LE MORTE DARTHUR," PHILOLOGICAL
ESSAYS. . . HERBERT DEAN MERITT, ed. James L. Rosier (Hague: Mouton,
1970), pp. 196-203; James D. Merriman, THE FLOWER OF KINGS (Lawrence:
University of Kansas Press, 1973), pp. 186-88.

[82]These are too numerous to mention. The essential arguments may
be found in a collection of essays edited by Lumiansky, MALORY'S ORIG-
INALITY: A CRITICAL STUDY OF 'LE MORTE DARTHUR' (Baltimore: Johns
Hopkins, 1964). The opinions of Moorman may be found in THE BOOK OF
KYNG ARTHUR: THE UNITY OF MALORY'S MORTE DARTHUR (Lexington: Univer-
sity of Kentucky Press, 1965), which incorporates earlier articles.

[83]See Thomas C. Rumble, "The First Explicit in Malory's MORTE
DARTHUR," MLN, 71 (1956), 564-66. R. H. Wilson, though not associated
with the "unity" school, wrote a judicious critique of Vinaver's views
on the explicits and inconsistencies in "How Many Books Did Malory
Write?" TSE, 30 (1951), 1-23.

[84]Charles Moorman, "Internal Chronology in Malory's MORTE DAR-
THUR," JEGP, 60 (1961), 243. See similar opinions in R. M. Lumiansky,
"The Question of Unity in Malory's MORTE DARTHUR," TULANE STUDIES IN
ENGLISH, 5 (1955), 33-39. See Stephen Knight, THE STRUCTURE OF SIR
THOMAS MALORY'S ARTHURIAD, pp. 13-19; Ellyn Olefsky, "Chronology,
Factual Consistency, and the Problem of Unity in Malory," JEGP, 68
(1969), 57-73; Robert H. Wilson, "Chronology in Malory," STUDIES IN
LANGUAGE, LITERATURE AND CULTURE OF THE MIDDLE AGES AND AFTER, ed.
E. Bagby Atwood and Archibald A. Hill (Austin: University of Texas
Press, 1969), pp. 324-34.

[85]"The Question of Unity in Malory's MORTE DARTHUR," pp. 32 ff.

[86] WSTM, vol. 1, pp. xli-li.

[87] "Medieval English Literature and the Question of Unity," MP, 65 (1968), 297.

[88] James D. Merriman, THE FLOWER OF KINGS, p. 17. Also see William Matthews' review of MALORY'S ORIGINALITY, SPECULUM, 41 (1966), 155-59.

[89] THE DEVELOPMENT OF ARTHURIAN ROMANCE (New York: Harper and Row, 1964), pp. 171-73.

[90] "How Many Books Did Malory Write?" TSE, 30 (1951), 21-23.

[91] THE STRUCTURE OF SIR THOMAS MALORY'S ARTHURIAD, p. 76.

[92] "'the hoole book,'" ESSAYS ON MALORY, ed. J. A. W. Bennett (Oxford: Clarendon Press, 1963), p. 42.

[93] Knight, p. 11.

[94] THE MORTE DARTHUR: PARTS SEVEN AND EIGHT (London: Edward Arnold, 1968), p. 22.

[95] "The English Prose MORTE," ESSAYS ON MALORY, pp. 21-22.

[96] Mark Lambert [MALORY: STYLE AND VISION IN 'LE MORTE DARTHUR,' p. x] shared this attitude. "There is the question of unity in Malory's tales: in this tourney I do not ride." He added that "after twenty years of investigating unity it is time for us to take the fruit, leave the chaff, and rotate our crops."

[97] Vinaver [WSTM, vol. 1, "Preface to the First Edition"] and Wilson ["How Many Books Did Malory Write?" p. 23] have urged study of the individual tales. For examples of such studies, see the following: P. E. Tucker ["Chivalry in the MORTE," ESSAYS ON MALORY, pp. 64-103] discussed the development of Malory's concept of chivalry; Michael Stroud ["Malory and the Chivalric Ethos," MS, 36 (1974), 331-53] studied Malory's concept of chivalry in Tale 2; and Edward D. Kennedy ["Malory's King Mark and King Arthur," MS, 37 (1975), 190-234] argued that Tale 5 influenced Malory's depiction of Arthur in later tales.

[98] Vinaver's opinion [WSTM, vol. 1, pp. li-lvi] was supported by Ján Šimko [WORD-ORDER IN THE WINCHESTER MANUSCRIPT AND IN WILLIAM CAXTON'S EDITION OF THOMAS MALORY'S MORTE DARTHUR (Halle: Niemeyer, 1957)]. Others challenged Vinaver's view. See reviews by J. A. W. Bennett [RES, 25 (1949), 163-64] and Larry D. Benson ["Sir Thomas Malory's LE MORTE DARTHUR," CRITICAL APPROACHES TO SIX MAJOR ENGLISH WORKS, p. 95]. For more detailed criticism, see Edward D. Kennedy, "The Arthur-Guenevere Relationship in Malory's MORTE DARTHUR," STUDIES IN THE LITERARY IMAGINATION, 4 (1971), 29-40; and Toshiyuki Takamiya,

"'Wade,' 'dryvande,' and 'Gotelake'--Three Notes on the Order of Composition in the MORTE DARTHUR," STUDIES IN ENGLISH LITERATURE, English No., 1974, pp. 131-48; and William Matthews, "Where Was Siesia-Sessoyne?" SPECULUM, 49 (1974), 680-86. Terence McCarthy [Caxton and the Text of Malory's Book 2," MP, 71 (1973), 144-52] attempted to establish the order of composition by analyzing stylistic differences.

[99]MARMION (Edinburgh: Constable, 1808), p. iii.

[100]John W. Hales, ENGLISH PROSE SELECTIONS, ed. Henry Craik (New York: Macmillan, 1893), vol. 1, p. 61; Howard Maynadier, THE ARTHUR OF THE ENGLISH POETS (New York: Houghton Mifflin, 1907), p. 244; A. T. Martin, SELECTIONS FROM MALORY'S LE MORTE D'ARTHUR (New York: Macmillan, 1896), p. xxxvi; F. J. Snell, THE AGE OF TRANSITION, 1400-1580 (London: George Bell, 1905), vol. 2, pp. 87-88.

[101]S. Humphreys Gurteen, THE ARTHURIAN EPIC (New York: Putnam, 1895), p. 85.

[102]P. J. C. Field, ROMANCE AND CHRONICLE: A STUDY OF MALORY'S PROSE STYLE (Bloomington: Indiana University Press, 1971), "Preliminaries."

[103]Alfred Nutt, STUDIES ON THE LEGEND OF THE HOLY GRAIL (London: David Nutt, 1888), p. 236; G. Gregory Smith, THE TRANSITION PERIOD (New York: Scribner, 1900), p. 331.

[104]Among these are Hermann Römstedt, DIE ENGLISCHE SCHRIFTSPRACHE BEI CAXTON (Göttingen, 1891); Charles Sears Baldwin, THE INFLECTIONS AND SYNTAX OF THE MORTE D'ARTHUR (Boston: Ginn, 1894); George Hempl, "The Verb in the 'Morte D'Arthur,'" MLN, 9 (1894), 240-41; Charlotte Fromm, ÜBER DEN VERBALEN WORTSCHATZ IN SIR THOMAS MALORYS 'LE MORTE DARTHUR' (Marburg, 1914); Arie Dekker, SOME FACTS CONCERNING THE SYNTAX OF MALORY'S 'MORTE DARTHUR' (Amsterdam: Portielje, 1932); Gera Winkler, DAS RELATIVUM BEI CAXTON UND SEINE ENTWICKLUNG VON CHAUCER BIS SPENSER (Saalfield, 1933); Arie Dekker, "On the Syntax of the English Verb from Caxton to Dryden," NEOPHILOLOGUS, 20 (1935), 113-20.

[105]See Chapter 8 ("Translation and Style") in MALORY, pp. 100-08.

[106]Introduction to Nicholas Harpsfield's THE LIFE AND DEATH OF SIR THOMAS MOORE [sic], ed. Elsie V. Hitchcock, E.E.T.S. (London: Trübner, 1932; rpt. 1950), p. cxli. Chambers' pronouncement was repeated, sometimes verbatim. Chambers "rightly saw that the main stream could not flow through the prose of. . . Malory. Important as [he is] in the full story of our prose, [he does] not help us to understand which way it was moving [H. S. Bennett, "Fifteenth Century Secular Prose," RES, 21 (1945), 257]. "Malory remains as a beautiful inland lake, cut off from the outer world" [H. S. Bennett, CHAUCER AND THE FIFTEENTH CENTURY (Oxford: Clarendon Press, 1947; rpt. 1965), pp. 202-03].

[107]FRENCH INFLUENCE IN ENGLISH PHRASING (Leiden: Leiden University Press, 1952), p. 18.

[108]R. M. Wilson, "On the Continuity of English Prose," MÉLANGES . . . FERNAND MOSSÉ (Paris: Didier, 1959), p. 493. Norman Davis, "Styles in English Prose of the Late Middle and Early Modern Period," ACTES DU VIIIe CONGRÈS DE LA FÉDÉRATION INTERNATIONALE DES LANGUES ET LITTÉRATURES MODERNES (Liège, 1961), pp. 165-81. Davis believed that fifteenth-century prose style was more dependent on epistolary and stylistic conventions than had been previously thought. See "Style and Stereotype in Early English Letters," LEEDS STUDIES IN ENGLISH, 1 (1967), 7-17.

[109]A HISTORY OF ENGLISH PROSE RHYTHM, p. 92.

[110]Ján Šimko, WORD-ORDER IN THE WINCHESTER MANUSCRIPT AND IN WILLIAM CAXTON'S EDITION OF THOMAS MALORY'S MORTE DARTHUR (1485)--A COMPARISON (Halle: Niemeyer, 1957); and Arthur Sandved, STUDIES IN THE LANGUAGE OF CAXTON'S MALORY AND THAT OF THE WINCHESTER MANUSCRIPT (Oslo: Norwegian University Press, 1968).

[111]"The Present Study of Malory," p. 88.

[112]See especially articles by Kunio Nakashima published in the BULLETIN OF THE ENGLISH LITERARY SOCIETY OF NIHON UNIVERSITY and IN SPITE OF THE THIRTEEN SUPERSTITION; and by Shunichi Noguchi in HIROSHIMA STUDIES IN ENGLISH LANGUAGE AND LITERATURE and STUDIES IN ENGLISH LITERATURE [English Literary Society of Japan].

[113]ROMANCE AND CHRONICLE: A STUDY OF MALORY'S PROSE STYLE (Bloomington: Indiana University Press, 1971). See also Shunichi Noguchi, "The Paradox of the Character of Malory's Language," HIROSHIMA STUDIES IN ENGLISH LANGUAGE AND LITERATURE, 13 (1967), 115 ff.

[114]MALORY: STYLE AND VISION IN 'LE MORTE DARTHUR' (New Haven, Conn.: Yale University Press, 1975).

[115]WSTM, vol. 1, pp. cxlv-cxlvi. It should be noted that Caxton acknowledged that there was some "evyl" and "synne" in the work.

[116]THE NOBLE AND JOYOUS BOKE ENTYTLED LE MORTE DARTHUR, ed. A. S. Mott (Oxford: Printed for the Shakespeare Head Press. . . by Basil Blackwell, 1933), vol. 2, pp. 370-71.

[117]For a defense of the attacks made on the romances by Ascham and other humanists, see Robert P. Adams, "'Bold Bawdry and Open Manslaughter': The English New Humanist Attack on Medieval Romance," HUNTINGTON LIBRARY QUARTERLY, 23 (1959), 33-48.

[118]See, for example, Canon Dawson, "The Morals of the Round Table," LIVING AGE, 267 (Dec. 3, 1910), 606-10. F. J. Snell [THE AGE OF

TRANSITION, 1400-1580 (London: George Bell, 1905), vol. 2, p. 89]
claimed that the great defect of the moral character of Malory's romance was its disrespect for the sanctity of marriage.

[119] See Edward R. Russell, THE BOOK OF KING ARTHUR. A PAPER READ
BEFORE THE LITERARY AND PHILOSOPHICAL SOCIETY OF LIVERPOOL (Liverpool:
Marples, 1889); and George Newcomen, "The Lovers of Launcelot," NEW
IRELAND REVIEW, 11 (1899), 44-50.

[120] "Talk at a Country House: 'Down to Tower'd Camelot,'" ATLAN-
TIC MONTHLY, 73 (1894), 52. This opinion is repeated by A. T. Martin
[Introduction, SELECTIONS FROM MALORY'S LE MORTE D'ARTHUR (New York:
Macmillan, 1896), p. xxii]: "From the internal evidence of the book
it seems clear that to Malory the whole story presented itself as the
definite working out of a great tragedy, the punishment of an unconscious sin." The theme of fate was also emphasized by K. M. Loudon
[TWO MYSTIC POETS AND OTHER ESSAYS (Oxford: Blackwell, 1922), pp. 31-
82].

[121] "The Round Table stories, merely as such, illustrate Valour;
the Graal stories, Religion; the passion of Lancelot and Guinevere
with the minor instances, Love." [THE ENGLISH NOVEL (New York: Dutton, 1913), p. 27.]

[122] A SHORT HISTORY OF ENGLISH LITERATURE (New York: Macmillan,
1898; rpt. 1960), p. 197.

[123] See Vida D. Scudder, LE MORTE DARTHUR OF SIR THOMAS MALORY AND
ITS SOURCES; E. K. Chambers, SIR THOMAS MALORY (London: English Association, 1922; rpt. 1976), p. 9; rpt. in SIR THOMAS WYATT AND SOME
COLLECTED STUDIES (London: Sidgwick and Jackson, 1933), p. 33; Eugène Vinaver, THE RISE OF ROMANCE (Oxford: Clarendon Press, 1970),
p. 131; see also WSTM, vol. 3, p. xcvi.

[124] Cambridge: Harvard University Press, 1912, p. 87. Cf. "Faced
with the horrors of internecine strife and the uncertainty of the future, Malory naturally enough fell back on remembrances of the past
and tried to find in them a picture of glory and prosperity, as well
as the cause which had led to the decay of the great kingdom of Arthur" [Eugène Vinaver, MALORY, p. 110]. The MORTE DARTHUR has been
described as the "funeral oration," the "swan-song," and the "Indian
summer" of Arthurian chivalry [A. L. Morton, "The Matter of Britain,"
ZAA, 8 (1960), 24; Vida D. Scudder, LE MORTE DARTHUR OF SIR THOMAS
MALORY AND ITS SOURCES, p. 362; and William W. Lawrence, MEDIEVAL
STORY (New York: Columbia University Press, 1911), pp. 137-38].

[125] "Sir Thomas Malory--Historian," PMLA, 48 (1933), 389.

[126] Ibid., pp. 367-77. Vinaver believed that in Tale 2 Malory
attempted to glorify Henry V [WSTM, vol. 3, pp. 1367-68]. For refu-
tation, see William Matthews, "Where Was Siesia-Sessoyne?" SPECULUM,
49 (1974), 680-86.

[127] In the only article to argue against Malory's Lancastrian partisanship ["The Political Bias of Malory's MORTE DARTHUR," VIATOR, 5 (1974), 364-86], Richard R. Griffith asserted that Edward IV was a more likely parallel to Arthur than Henry VI, but Griffith was unable to explain why, if Malory were a Yorkist, he should have been in prison in the 1460's.

[128] "English Geography in Malory's MORTE D'ARTHUR," MLR, 30 (1935), 204-09.

[129] "Malory and the Marriage of Edward IV," TSLL, 12 (1970-71), 155-62.

[130] THE INDIAN SUMMER OF ENGLISH CHIVALRY (Durham: Duke University Press, 1960), p. 58.

[131] ARTHURIAN PROPAGANDA: 'LE MORTE DARTHUR' AS AN HISTORICAL IDEAL OF LIFE (Chapel Hill: University of North Carolina Press, 1971). For criticism of this view, see Edward D. Kennedy, "Malory's King Mark and King Arthur," MEDIAEVAL STUDIES, 37 (1975), 190 ff.

[132] Cambridge: Harvard University Press, 1976.

[133] THE ENGLISH NOVEL (New York: Dutton, 1913), p. 25.

[134] "On the nature of Malory's work two widely differing views have been expressed. Sir Edward Strachey regards him as having consciously planned and produced a great prose epic, while others look on him as a 'Zusammenstoppler,' a more or less clumsy manufacturer of a literary patchwork quilt" [A. T. Martin, ed., SELECTIONS FROM MALORY'S LE MORTE D'ARTHUR (New York: Macmillan, 1896), pp. xxi-xxii].

[135] Mark Lambert stated that the question of unity has been presented as an "absolute choice" [MALORY: STYLE AND VISION IN 'LE MORTE DARTHUR,' p. x].

II. BIBLIOGRAPHY

A. EDITIONS

1. Descriptive Bibliographies

1. Ames, Joseph. TYPOGRAPHICAL ANTIQUITIES: BEING AN HISTORICAL
    ACCOUNT OF PRINTING IN ENGLAND. London: Printed by W. Faden,
    1749. [See nos. 2, 4.]

    Caxton edition, pp. 43-46; de Worde edition, p. 86.

2. Herbert, William. TYPOGRAPHICAL ANTIQUITIES, OR AN HISTORICAL
    ACCOUNT OF THE ORIGIN AND PROGRESS OF PRINTING IN GREAT BRITAIN
    AND IRELAND. Begun by the late Joseph Ames. . . Augmented by
    William Herbert. 3 vols. London, 1785-90. [See nos. 1, 4.]

    See vol. 1, pp. 57-61. Herbert believes that Ames saw a Caxton
    edition and thinks it curious that Ames failed to note who
    owned it.

3. Panzer, Georg Wolfgang Franz. ANNALES TYPOGRAPHICI AB ARTIS INVENTAE
    ORIGINE AD ANNUM MD. Norimbergae: Impensis Joannis Eberhardi
    Zeh, Bibliopolae, 1795.

    Caxton edition, vol. 3, p. 555, no. 21; de Worde edition, p. 558,
    no. 42.

4. Dibdin, Thomas Frognall. TYPOGRAPHICAL ANTIQUITIES. . . [by Joseph
    Ames, augmented by William Herbert]. Enlarged by Thomas Frognall
    Dibdin. 4 vols. London, 1810-19. [See nos. 1, 2.]

    Caxton edition, vol. 1, pp. cviii, 241-55; de Worde edition,
    vol. 2, pp. 81-82; Copland edition, vol. 3, p. 143.

5. _____. BIBLIOTHECA SPENCERIANA; OR A DESCRIPTIVE
    CATALOGUE OF THE BOOKS PRINTED IN THE FIFTEENTH CENTURY . . . IN
    THE LIBRARY OF GEORGE JOHN EARL SPENCER. London: Longman, Hurst
    and Co., 1814. [Supplemented by no. 6.]

    de Worde edition (1498) in vol. 4, pp. 403-09, no. 907.

6. _____. SUPPLEMENT TO THE BIBLIOTHECA SPENCERIANA
    [no. 5]. London: Shakespeare Press, 1822.

Caxton edition, vol. 6, p. 213, no. 1194. This includes a note
on the eleven leaves reproduced in facsimile by Whittaker from
the perfect Osterley Park copy of the Caxton edition for the
imperfect Althorp copy.

7. Hain, Ludovici. REPERTORIUM BIBLIOGRAPHICUM. 2 vols. Stuttgar-
    tiae, 1826–38. [Supplemented by no. 14.]

    Caxton edition, vol. 1, p. 230, no. 1864; de Worde edition
    (1498), no. 1865.

8. Collier, J[ohn] Payne. A CATALOGUE, BIBLIOGRAPHICAL AND CRITICAL,
    OF EARLY ENGLISH LITERATURE. London, 1837. Published as A BIB-
    LIOGRAPHICAL AND CRITICAL ACCOUNT OF THE RAREST BOOKS IN THE
    ENGLISH LANGUAGE. 2 vols. London: Joseph Lilly, 1865.

    East folio edition, pp. 11–13 [1837 ed.]; vol. 1, pp. 31–32
    [1865 ed.]; Stansby edition, pp. 13–14 [1837 ed.]; vol. 1,
    pp. 32–33 [1865 ed.].

9. Lowndes, William Thomas. THE BIBLIOGRAPHER'S MANUAL OF ENGLISH
    LITERATURE. 1857; new rev. ed. by Henry G. Bohn. 4 vols. Lon-
    don: Henry G. Bohn, 1864.

    See vol. 1, pp. 74–75.

10. Blades, William. THE LIFE AND TYPOGRAPHY OF WILLIAM CAXTON, ENG-
    LAND'S FIRST PRINTER. 2 vols. London: Joseph Lilly, 1861–63.
    Rpt. New York: Burt Franklin, 1971. [Burt Franklin Bibliogra-
    phical and Reference Series.]

    Typographical description, vol. 2, pp. 176–78.

    Note: This book was issued in 1877 in a condensed version with
    the title THE BIOGRAPHY AND TYPOGRAPHY OF WILLIAM CAXTON, ENG-
    LAND'S FIRST PRINTER. See rev. ed. of the 1877 issue, London:
    Kegan Paul, Trench, Trübner and Co., 1897, pp. 304–06.

11. Hazlitt, W. Carew. HAND-BOOK TO THE POPULAR, POETICAL AND DRAMA-
    TIC LITERATURE OF GREAT BRITAIN. London: John Russell Smith,
    1867.

    List of black-letter editions, pp. 13–14.

12. Strachey, Edward. MORTE DARTHUR; SIR THOMAS MALORY'S BOOK OF
    KING ARTHUR AND OF HIS NOBLE KNIGHTS OF THE ROUND TABLE. [Globe
    edition.] London and Philadelphia: Macmillan, 1868, pp. xxxi–
    xxxvii.

13. Sommer, H.Oskar, ed. LE MORTE DARTHUR BY SYR THOMAS MALORY. Lon-
    don: David Nutt, 1889–91. Rpt. New York: AMS Press, 1973.
    Vol. 2, pp. 2–25.

14. Copinger, W[alter] A[rthur]. SUPPLEMENT TO HAIN'S REPERTORIUM
    BIBLIOGRAPHICUM [no. 7]. 2 vols. London: Henry Sotheran and
    Co., 1895-1902.

    Caxton edition, vol. 1, p. 53, no. 1864.

15. Mead, William E. SELECTIONS FROM SIR THOMAS MALORY'S MORTE DAR-
    THUR. Boston: Ginn and Co., 1897; rev. 1901, pp. xxiii-xxv.

16. Hoe, Robert. CATALOGUE OF BOOKS BY ENGLISH AUTHORS WHO LIVED
    BEFORE THE YEAR 1700. 5 vols. New York: n. p., 1903.

    Stansby edition, vol. 1, pp. 13-14 (reproduces the frontis-
    piece); Caxton edition, vol. 3, p. 104; Southey 1817 edition,
    vol. 3, p. 105; Wright 1858 edition, vol. 3, p. 106.

17. Ricci, Seymour de. A CENSUS OF CAXTONS. Illustrated Monographs
    issued for the Bibliographical Society, No. 15. Oxford:
    Printed for the Bibliographical Society, 1909, p. 81, no. 76.

18. Esdaile, Arundell. A LIST OF ENGLISH TALES AND PROSE ROMANCES
    PRINTED BEFORE 1740. London: Printed for the Bibliographical
    Society, 1912, pp. 96-97.

19. Duff, E[dward] Gordon. FIFTEENTH CENTURY ENGLISH BOOKS: A BIB-
    LIOGRAPHY OF BOOKS AND DOCUMENTS PRINTED IN ENGLAND AND OF
    BOOKS FOR THE ENGLISH MARKET PRINTED ABROAD. Illustrated Mono-
    graphs issued for the Bibliographical Society, No. 18. Oxford:
    Printed for the Bibliographical Society, 1917, p. 80, nos. 283,
    284.

20. Aurner, Nellie Slayton. CAXTON, MIRROUR OF FIFTEENTH-CENTURY
    LETTERS; A STUDY OF THE LITERATURE OF THE FIRST ENGLISH PRESS.
    New York and Boston, 1926; rpt. Russell and Russell, 1965,
    p. 222.

21. Pollard, A[lfred] W[illiam], and G. R. Redgrave. A SHORT-TITLE
    CATALOGUE OF BOOKS PRINTED IN ENGLAND,SCOTLAND, AND IRELAND
    AND OF ENGLISH BOOKS PRINTED ABROAD, 1475-1640. London: The
    Bibliographical Society, 1926; 2nd ed. rev. and enlarged begun
    by W. A. Jackson and F. S. Ferguson, completed by Katharine F.
    Pantzer. Vol. 2 (I-Z). London: Published for the Bibliogra-
    phical Society by Oxford University Press, 1976.

    See nos. 801-806 in 1926 ed. under "Arthur."

22. Vinaver, Eugène. MALORY. Oxford: Clarendon Press, 1929; rpt.
    with a new preface, 1970, pp. 189-98.

    List with annotations of all important editions through the
    nineteenth century.

23. Hodnett, Edward. ENGLISH WOODCUTS, 1480-1535. London: Printed for the Bibliographical Society by Oxford University Press, 1935; rpt. with "additions and corrections," 1973.

   Commentary on the woodcuts in the de Worde editions on pp. 309-13.

24. Walker, R[ainforth] A[rmitage]. LE MORTE DARTHUR WITH BEARDSLEY ILLUSTRATIONS, A BIBLIOGRAPHICAL ESSAY. Bedford, [England]: Published by the Author, 1945.

25. Farrar, Clarissa P., and Austin P. Evans. BIBLIOGRAPHY OF ENGLISH TRANSLATIONS FROM MEDIEVAL SOURCES. [Records of Civilization, Sources and Studies, No. 39.] New York: Columbia University Press, 1946, nos. 2623-30 on pp. 310-11. [Supplemented by no. 28.]

26. Rumble, Thomas C. "A Survey of the Editions and Criticism of Sir Thomas Malory's MORTE D'ARTHUR." Master's Thesis. Tulane University, 1950.

27. O'Dell, Sterg. A CHRONOLOGICAL LIST OF PROSE FICTION IN ENGLISH PRINTED IN ENGLAND AND OTHER COUNTRIES, 1475-1640. Cambridge, Mass.: Technology Press of M. I. T., 1954.

   Black-letter editions, pp. 24, 25, 30, 35, 50, 107.

28. Ferguson, Mary Anne Heyward. BIBLIOGRAPHY OF ENGLISH TRANSLATIONS FROM MEDIEVAL SOURCES [Records of Civilization, Sources and Studies, No. 88.] New York and London: Columbia University Press, 1974. [Supplements no. 25.]

   Vinaver editions, p. 153, no. 1339.

2. Major Editions, Reprints, Translations

of Sources of the MORTE DARTHUR

A. French Sources

SUITE DU MERLIN

29. Paris, Gaston, and Jacob Ulrich, eds. MERLIN, ROMAN EN PROSE DU
XIIIe SIÈCLE, PUBLIÉ AVEC LA MISE EN PROSE DU POËME DE MERLIN
DE ROBERT DE BORON, D'APRÈS LE MANUSCRIT APPARTENANT À M. ALFRED
H. HUTH. SATF. 2 vols. Paris: Firmin Didot, 1886.

The introduction discusses Malory's use of the SUITE DU MERLIN
as found in the Huth Manuscript (British Museum Additional MS.
38117). [Until the discovery of the Cambridge Manuscript by
Eugène Vinaver in 1945 (see nos. 131 and 542), the Huth Manuscript was the only known version of Malory's source.]

30. Sommer, H. Oskar, ed. DIE ABENTEUER GAWAINS, YWAINS UND LE MOR-
HOLTS MIT DEN DREI JUNGFRAUEN AUS DER TRILOGIE (DEMANDA) DES
PSEUDO-ROBERT DE BORON, DIE FORTSETZUNG DES HUTH-MERLIN. NACH
DER ALLEIN BEKANNTEN HS. NR. 112 DER PARISER NATIONAL-BIBLIOTHEK.
ZRP Beiheft 47. Halle: Niemeyer, 1913.

Comparing Malory's Book 4, Chapters 20-24, with the Huth MERLIN,
Sommer finds Malory's version is much shorter and concludes that
Malory either misunderstood or altered his source. [Sommer re-
tracts statements made in no. 40.]

31. Legge, Mary Dominica, ed. LE ROMAN DE BALAIN; A PROSE ROMANCE OF
THE THIRTEENTH CENTURY. Introduction by Eugène Vinaver. Manchester: Manchester University Press, 1942.

The introduction (pp. ix-xxxii) contains a few remarks on Malory's version of the Balin story.

32. Micha, Al[exandre]. "Fragment de la Suite-Huth du MERLIN." RO-
MANIA, 78 (1957), 37-45.

An edition of the Siena fragment.

33. Bogdanow, Fanni. "The SUITE DU MERLIN and the Post-Vulgate ROMAN
DU GRAAL." ALMA, pp. 325-35.

34. _____. LA FOLIE LANCELOT; A HITHERTO UNIDENTIFIED POR-
    TION OF THE 'SUITE DU MERLIN' CONTAINED IN MSS. B. N. FR. 112
    and 12599. Beihefte zur ZRP, Heft 109 (1965).

35. _____. THE ROMANCE OF THE GRAIL. New York: Barnes
    and Noble; Manchester: Manchester University Press, 1966.
    [Also listed as no. 686.]

    See the Introduction and Chapter 1 ("The Known Texts of the
    'Suite du Merlin'"). Description of the manuscripts is in the
    "Bibliography," pp. 271-73. See Appendix II, pp. 228-41 (Siena
    fragment), and pp. 241-49 (Cambridge Additional MS. 7071).

36. Campbell, David E., trans. THE TALE OF BALAIN, FROM THE ROMANCE
    OF THE GRAIL, A 13TH CENTURY FRENCH PROSE ROMANCE. Evanston,
    [Ill.]: Northwestern University Press, 1972.

    A translation of Cambridge Additional MS. 7071 [described in
    WSTM, 1947 ed., vol. 3, pp. 1277-80; 1967 ed., vol. 3, pp. 1279-
    82].

37. Briel, Henri de, trans. LE ROMAN DE MERLIN L'ENCHANTEUR. Paris:
    C. Klincksieck, 1971.

PROSE TRISTAN

38. Löseth, E[ilert]. LE ROMAN EN PROSE DE TRISTAN, LE ROMAN DE PA-
    LAMÈDE ET LA COMPILATION DE RUSTICIEN DE PISE, ANALYSE CRITIQUE
    D'APRÈS LES MANUSCRITS DE PARIS. [Bibliothèque de l'École des
    Hautes Études, 82e fasc.] Paris: Bouillon, 1891; rpt. New
    York: Burt Franklin, 1970.

    Contains a brief comparison of this version and Malory's treat-
    ment of Tristan (pp. xxii-xxiii). See also Löseth's subsequent
    studies of Tristan manuscripts in the British Museum (1905) and
    in Rome and Florence (1924).

39. Bédier, Joseph. LE ROMAN DE TRISTAN PAR THOMAS, POÈME DU XIIIe
    SIÈCLE. SATF. 2 vols. Paris: Firmin Didot, 1902-05; rpt.
    1961.

    See Appendice I in vol. 2, pp. 321-95. "Les parties anciennes
    du roman en prose française" [MSS. B. N. fr. 103 and 727].
    These sections are translated in no. 43.

40. Sommer, H. Oskar, ed. "Galahad and Perceval. From the 'Tristan'
    MS. Add. 5474, FF. 142c-164b, British Museum." MP, 5 (Jan.
    1908), 55-84, 181-200, 291-341.

Some commentary on Malory's characterization of Perceval and Malory's use of sources. [Opinions retracted in no. 30, pp. xx, xxiii.]

41. Vinaver, Eugène. ÉTUDES SUR LE 'TRISTAN' EN PROSE: LES SOURCES, LES MANUSCRITS. BIBLIOGRAPHIE CRITIQUE. Paris: Honoré Champion, 1925.

42. Murrel, E. S. "The Death of Tristan from Douce MS. 189." PMLA, 43 (1928), 343-83.

43. Champion, Pierre, trans. LE ROMAN DE TRISTAN ET ISEULT, TRADUCTION DU ROMAN EN PROSE DU QUINZIÈME SIÈCLE. [Bibliothèque de Cluny, vol. 20.] Paris: Éditions de Cluny, 1938.

    A translation from MS. fr. 103 as represented in the Bédier edition [no. 39], vol. 2, pp. 321-95.

44. Johnson, F. C., ed. LA GRANT YSTOIRE DU MONSIGNOR TRISTAN, 'LI BRET.' THE FIRST PART OF THE PROSE ROMANCE OF TRISTAN FROM ADV. MS. 19.1.3. IN THE NATIONAL LIBRARY OF SCOTLAND. Edinburgh and London: Oliver and Boyd, 1942.

45. Pickford, Cedric E., ed. ALIXANDRE L'ORPHELIN; A PROSE TALE OF THE FIFTEENTH CENTURY. [French Classics, Extra Series.] Manchester: Manchester University Press, 1951.

    The text is that of Pierpont Morgan MS. 41. This corresponds to the MORTE DARTHUR, Book 10, Chapters 32-40, and to Winchester Manuscript ff. 260^v-268^r. Pickford notes that in adapting this story from the French, Malory added an ending in which King Mark is slain (pp. xviii-xix).

46. Vinaver, Eugène. "The Prose TRISTAN." ALMA, pp. 339-47.

47. Curtis, Renée L., ed. LE ROMAN DE TRISTAN. Vol. 1. Munich: Max Hueber, 1963. Vol. 2. Leiden: E. J. Brill, 1976.

48. Spector, Norman B. THE ROMANCE OF TRISTAN AND ISOLT. Foreward by Eugene Vinaver. Evanston, Ill.: Northwestern University Press, 1973.

    Text is based on Bibliothèque Nationale MS. 103 of the Prose TRISTAN and on an episode in B. N. MS. 757.

49. Baumgartner, Emmanuele. LE 'TRISTAN EN PROSE.' Genève: Droz, 1975.

50. TRISTAN, 1489. Introductory note by C. E. Pickford. London: Scolar Press, 1976.

A facsimile of the 1489 edition published by Jehan Le Bourgoys
of a version of the TRISTAN closely related to Bibliothèque Na-
tionale MS. 103. The facsimile reproduces a copy of the edition in the Bodleian Library.

VULGATE PROSE LANCELOT

51. Paris, Paulin. LES ROMANS DE LA TABLE RONDE. Paris: Léon Tech-
    ener, 1867-77. Tomes 3-5: LANCELOT DU LAC.

52. Sommer, H. Oskar, ed. LE LIVRE DE LANCELOT DEL LAC. THE VULGATE
    VERSION OF THE ARTHURIAN ROMANCES, EDITED FROM MANUSCRIPTS IN
    THE BRITISH MUSEUM. Vols. 3-5. Washington: Carnegie Insti-
    tute, 1910-12.

    Text is that of British Museum Additional MS. 10293.

53. Bräuner, Gerhard, et al., eds. DER ALTFRANZÖSISCHE PROSAROMAN
    VON LANCELOT DEL LAC. . . VERSUCH EINER KRITISCHEN AUSGABE NACH
    ALLEN BEKANNTEN HANDSCHRIFTEN, by pupils of Professor Eduard
    Wechssler, in the MARBURGER BEITRÄGE ZUR ROMANISCHEN PHILOLOGIE.
    Hefte 2, 6, 8, 19. Marburg: Ebel, 1911-16.

54. Lot, Ferdinand. ÉTUDE SUR LE LANCELOT EN PROSE. [Bibliothèque
    de l'École des Hautes Études, 226e fasc.] Paris, 1918.

55. Boulenger, Jacques. LES ROMANS DE LA TABLE RONDE NOUVELLEMENT
    RÉDIGÉS. 4 vols. Paris, 1922-23. (1) L'HISTOIRE DE MERLIN
    L'ENCHANTEUR; LES ENFANCES DE LANCELOT. (2) LES AMOURS DE
    LANCELOT DU LAC; GALEHAUT, SIRE DES ILES LOINTAINES. (3) LE
    CHEVALIER A LA CHARRETTE; LA CHATEAU AVENTUREUX. (4) LE SAINT
    GRAAL; LA MORT D'ARTUS.

56. Lot-Borodine, Myrrha, and Gertrude Schoepperle. LANCELOT DU LAC
    MIS EN NOUVEAU LANGAGE. New York and Oxford, 1926.

57. Paton, Lucy Allen, trans. SIR LANCELOT OF THE LAKE. A FRENCH
    PROSE ROMANCE OF THE THIRTEENTH CENTURY. Trans. from MS. in
    the Bibliothèque Nationale (Fonds français, 344) with an Intro-
    duction and Notes. [Broadway Medieval Library.] New York:
    Harcourt, Brace, and Co.; London: G. Routledge and Sons, 1929.
    [Abridgement.]

58. Hutchings, Gweneth, ed. LE ROMAN EN PROSE DE LANCELOT DU LAC.
    LE CONTE DE LA CHARRETTE. Paris: Droz, 1938.

59. Frappier, Jean. "The Vulgate Cycle." ALMA, pp. 295-318.

60. LANCELOT DU LAC, 1488. A Scolar Press Facsimile. 2 vols. London:
    Scolar Press, 1973; rpt. 1975.

Vol. 1 was originally published by Jehan and Gaillard Le Bourgeois; Vol. 2 by Jehan du Pré. The facsimile is reproduced
from a copy of the edition in the National Library of Wales.

VULGATE QUESTE DEL SAINT GRAAL

61. Furnivall, Frederick J., ed. LA QUESTE DEL SAINT GRAAL IN THE
    FRENCH PROSE OF (AS IS SUPPOSED) MAISTRES GAUTIERS MAP, OR
    WALTER MAP. Printed for the Roxburghe Club. London: J. B.
    Nichols and Sons, 1864.

    Text is that of British Museum MS. Royal 14.E.iii. [This edi-
    tion is also listed as no. 286.]

62. Sommer, H. O., ed. "The Queste of the Holy Grail; forming the
    third part of the Trilogy indicated in the SUITE DU MERLIN
    Huth MS." ROMANIA, 36 (1907), 369-402, 543-90.

63. _____, ed. LES AVENTURES OU LA QUESTE DEL SAINT GRAAL.
    THE VULGATE VERSION OF THE ARTHURIAN ROMANCES, EDITED FROM
    MANUSCRIPTS IN THE BRITISH MUSEUM. Vol. 6. Washington: Car-
    negie Institute, 1913.

    Text is that of British Museum Additional MS. 10294 with vari-
    ants from other British Museum manuscripts.

64. Pauphilet, Albert. ÉTUDES SUR LA QUESTE DEL SAINT GRAAL ATTRI-
    BUÉE À GAUTIER MAP. Paris: Honoré Champion, 1921.

65. _____, trans. LA QUESTE DU SAINT GRAAL. Paris, 1923.
    [A modern French translation of no. 66.]

66. _____, ed. LA QUESTE DEL SAINT GRAAL, ROMAN DU XIIIe
    SIÈCLE. CFMA, no. 33. Paris: Honoré Champion, 1923; rpt.
    1949. [Translated in no. 65.]

    Text is based on MS. 77 of the Palais des Arts Library in Lyon.

67. Comfort, William Wistar, trans. THE QUEST OF THE HOLY GRAIL.
    London and Toronto: J. M. Dent, 1926.

68. Vinaver, Eugène. MALORY. Oxford: Clarendon Press, 1929; rpt.
    1970.

    In Appendix III (pp. 155-58), Vinaver compares Malory's Book 15
    with portions of Bibliothèque Nationale MS. 120.

69. Matarasso, P. M., trans. THE QUEST OF THE HOLY GRAIL. Harmonds-
    worth, Middlesex; and Baltimore: Pengiun, 1969; often re-
    printed.

In the introduction (pp. 27-29), Matarasso repeats many of Vinaver's theories about Malory's use of the French QUESTE.

VULGATE MORT ARTU

70. Bruce, J[ames] Douglas, ed. MORT ARTU: AN OLD FRENCH PROSE RO-
    MANCE OF THE XIIIth CENTURY.   EDITED FROM MS. 342. . . OF THE
    BIBLIOTHÈQUE NATIONALE. Halle: Niemeyer, 1910.

    The introduction (p. viii) contains a note on the relationships
    of the MORTE DARTHUR, the Stanzaic MORTE ARTHUR, and the MORT
    ARTU.

71. Sommer, H. Oskar, ed. LA MORT LE ROI ARTUS. THE VULGATE VERSION
    OF THE ARTHURIAN ROMANCES, EDITED FROM MANUSCRIPTS IN THE BRIT-
    ISH MUSEUM. Vol. 6. Washington: Carnegie Institute, 1913.

    Text is based on British Museum Additional MS. 10294.

72. Frappier, Jean, ed. LA MORT LE ROI ARTU, ROMAN DU XIIIe SIÈCLE.
    [Collection des Textes Littéraires Français.] Paris: Droz,
    1936; 2nd ed., Genève: Droz, and Lille: Giard, 1954; 2nd rev.
    ed., Genève: Droz, and Paris: Minard, 1956. [For a transla-
    tion of the second edition, see no. 75.]

    Frappier's introduction is essentially the same as his article
    "The Vulgate Cycle," ALMA, pp. 294-302 [no. 59], with modifica-
    tions and the addition of more textual and manuscript informa-
    tion.

73. _____. ÉTUDE SUR LA MORT LE ROI ARTU, ROMAN DU XIIIe
    SIÈCLE. DERNIÈRE PARTIE DU LANCELOT EN PROSE. Seconde édition
    revue et augmentée. [Publications Romanes et Françaises, 70.]
    Genève: Droz; Paris: Minard, 1961.

74. Cable, James, trans. THE DEATH OF KING ARTHUR. Trans. with an
    Introduction by James Cable. Harmondsworth, Middlesex; and
    Baltimore: Penguin, 1971; rpt. 1975.

    The Introduction (pp. 9-21) contains analyses of Arthur, Guine-
    vere, Lancelot, and Gawain.

75. Carman, J. Neale, trans. FROM CAMELOT TO JOYOUS GARD: THE OLD
    FRENCH LA MORT LE ROI ARTU. Edited with an Introduction by
    Norris J. Lacy. Lawrence, Manhattan, Wichita: University
    Press of Kansas, 1974.

    Text is based on the Frappier second edition [no. 72].

PERLESVAUS

76. Potvin, Ch[arles]. PERCEVAL LE GALLOIS OU LE CONTE DU GRAAL PUB-
    LIÉ D'APRES LES MANUSCRITS ORIGINAUX. [Société des Bibliophiles
    Belges. Publications, No. 21.] 6 vols. Mons: Société des Bib-
    liophiles, 1866-71.

    See vol. 1 (1866). Text is based on MS. 11145 in the Biblio-
    thèque Royale of Brussels. [For a translation, see no. 77.]

77. Evans, Sebastian, trans. THE HIGH HISTORY OF THE HOLY GRAIL.
    2 vols. London: J. M. Dent, 1898; 2nd ed., 1899, and often
    reprinted; 1st ed. rpt. Cambridge: James Clarke, 1969.

    A translation of the Potvin edition [no. 76].

78. Nitze, William A., and T. Atkinson Jenkins, eds. LE HAUT LIVRE DU
    GRAAL; PERLESVAUS. 2 vols. Chicago: University of Chicago
    Press, 1932-37; rpt. New York: Phaeton Press, 1972.

    Text is based on MS. Hatton 82 of the Bodleian Library. Vol. 1:
    Text, Variants, Glossary. Vol. 2: Commentary.

79. Nitze, William A. "Perlesvaus." ALMA, pp, 263-73.

                    b. Spanish Analogues

80. EL BALADRO DEL SABIO MERLIN CON SUS PROFECIAS. Burgos: Juan de
    Burgos, 1498.

    The only extant copy is in the Oviedo University Library.
    [See also no. 87.]

81. LA DEMANDA DEL SANCTO GRIAL. Primera Parte: EL BALADRO DEL SABIO
    MERLIN CON SUS PROFECIAS. Segunda Parte: LA DEMANDA DEL SANCTO
    GRIAL CON LOS MARAVILLOSOS FECHOS. Sevilla, 1535.

    The three complete copies are in the National Library of Madrid,
    the Advocates Library of Edinburgh, and the Bibliothèque Na-
    tionale. [For a reprint, see no. 82.]

82. Bonilla y san Martin, Adolfo, ed. EL BALADRO DEL SABIO MERLIN.
    PRIMERA PARTE DE LA DEMANDA DEL SANCTO GRIAL. LIBROS DE CABAL-
    LERIAS. Primera Parte: Ciclo Artúrico. [Nueva Biblioteca de
    Autores Españoles, vol. 6.] Madrid: Bailly Ballière é hijos,
    editores, 1907, pp. 3-162. [A reprint of the 1535 edition,
    no. 81.]

83. _____, ed. LIBRO DEL ESFORÇADO CAVALLERO DON TRISTÁN DE
LEONIS Y DE SUS GRANDES FECHOS EN ARMAS. [Valladolid, 1501.]
Sociedad de Bibliófilos Madrileños, 6. Madrid, 1912. Also contained in LIBROS DE CABALLERIAS, primera parte, pp. 339-457 [no.
82].

84. Bohigas Balaguer, P[edro]. LES TEXTOS ESPAÑOLES Y GALLEGO-PORTU-
GUESES DE LA DEMANDA DEL SANCTO GRIAL. REVISTA DE FILOLOGÍA
ESPAÑOLA, anejo 7. Madrid, 1925.

85. Entwistle, William J. ARTHURIAN LEGEND IN THE LITERATURES OF THE
SPANISH PENINSULA. London, 1925.

86. Northup, George Tyler, ed. EL CUENTO DE TRISTAN DE LEONIS, EDITED
FROM THE UNIQUE MANUSCRIPT VATICAN 6428. Chicago: University
of Chicago Press, 1928.

87. Bohigas Balaguer, Pedro, ed. EL BALADRO DEL SABIO MERLIN SEGÚN
EL TEXTO DE LA EDICIÓN DE BURGOS DE 1498. [Selecciones Biblió-
filas, segunda serie.] 3 vols. Barcelona, 1957-62.

88. Malkiel, María Rosa Lida de. "Arthurian Literature in Spain and
Portugal." ALMA, pp. 406-18.

89. Bodganow, Fanni. THE ROMANCE OF THE GRAIL. New York: Barnes
and Noble; Manchester: Manchester University Press, 1966, pp.
287-89.

c. English Sources

HARDYNG'S CHRONICLE

90. THE CHRONICLE OF JHON [sic] HARDYNG, FROM THE FIRST BEGYNNYNG OF
ENGLANDE, UNTO THE REIGNE OF KYNG EDWARD THE FOURTH WHER HE
MADE AN END OF HIS CHRONICLE. Londini: Richardi Graftoni, 1543.

Grafton printed two editions in 1543.

91. THE CHRONICLE OF IOHN HARDYNG. . .[with] A BIOGRAPHICAL AND LITER-
ARY PREFACE, AND AN INDEX, BY HENRY ELLIS. London: Printed for
F. C. and J. Rivington, 1812.

ALLITERATIVE MORTE ARTHURE

92. Halliwell, James Orchard, ed. MORTE ARTHURE. THE ALLITERATIVE
ROMANCE OF THE DEATH OF KING ARTHUR. Now first printed from a
manuscript in Lincoln Cathedral. For private circulation:
Brixton Hall, 1847.

93. Perry, George G., ed. MORTE ARTHURE. EDITED FROM ROBERT THORN-
    TON'S MANUSCRIPT (AB. 1440 A.D.) IN THE LIBRARY OF LINCOLN
    CATHEDRAL. E.E.T.S., O.S., No. 8. London: Trübner and Co.,
    1865. [Revised in no. 94.]

94. Brock, Edmond, ed. MORTE ARTHURE, OR THE DEATH OF ARTHUR. EDITED
    FROM ROBERT THORNTON'S MS. IN THE LIBRARY OF LINCOLN CATHEDRAL.
    A new edition. E.E.T.S., O.S., No. 8. London: Trübner and Co.,
    1871; often reprinted. [A revision of no. 93.]

95. Banks, Mary Macleod, ed. MORTE ARTHURE. AN ALLITERATIVE POEM OF
    THE 14TH CENTURY. New York and London: Longmans, Green and Co.,
    1900.

    In the introduction (p. 127), Banks states that the MORTE DAR-
    THUR, Book 5, is "based on a version which apparently differed
    slightly from this." [For a modern prose translation, see no.
    96.]

96. Boyle, Andrew, trans. MORTE ARTHUR: TWO EARLY ENGLISH ROMANCES.
    With an Introduction by Lucy Allen Paton. [Everyman edition.]
    London: J. M. Dent; New York: E. P. Dutton, [1912], pp. 1-93.

    A modern prose translation of the Alliterative MORTE ARTHURE
    based on the Banks edition [no. 95]. In the Introduction, Paton
    refers to Malory's use of the two poems as sources (see pp.
    xiii-xv).

97. Björkman, Erik, ed. MORTE ARTHURE, MIT EINLEITUNG, ANMERKUNGEN
    UND GLOSSAR. [Alt-und Mittelenglische Texte, 9.] Heidelberg:
    Carl Winters; New York: G. E. Strechert and Co., 1915.

98. Finlayson, John, ed. MORTE ARTHURE. [York Medieval Texts.]
    Evanston, Ill.: Northwestern University Press; London: Edward
    Arnold, 1967.

    A textbook edition for undergraduates with select bibliography,
    appendices, and glossary.

99. Benson, Larry D., ed. KING ARTHUR'S DEATH; THE MIDDLE ENGLISH
    STANZAIC MORTE ARTHUR AND ALLITERATIVE MORTE ARTHURE. [The Li-
    brary of Literature, 20.] Indianapolis: Bobbs-Merrill, 1974.

    A textbook edition for undergraduates.

100. Krishna, Valerie S., ed. THE ALLITERATIVE MORTE ARTHURE: A CRIT-
     ICAL EDITION. New York: Burt Franklin, 1976.

STANZAIC MORTE ARTHUR

101. Ponton, Thomas, ed. LE MORTE ARTHUR. THE ADVENTURES OF SIR
      LAUNCELOT DU LAKE. Roxburghe Club. London: Printed by Wil-
      liam Bulmer and Co., Shakespeare Printing-Office, 1819.

102. Furnivall, F[rederick] J., ed. LE MORTE ARTHUR, EDITED FROM THE
      HARLEIAN MS. 2252 IN THE BRITISH MUSEUM. With a prefatory
      essay on Arthur by the late Herbert Coleridge. London and Cam-
      bridge, Mass.: Macmillan, 1864.

      Furnivall discusses whether Malory and the author of the Stan-
      zaic MORTE ARTHUR used a source related to the MORT ARTU, or
      whether Malory had seen LE MORTE ARTHUR. Coleridge (pp.
      xxviii-lvi) compares the Arthurian works of Malory and Geof-
      frey of Monmouth.

103. Bruce, J[ames] Douglas, ed. LE MORTE ARTHUR, A ROMANCE IN STAN-
      ZAS OF EIGHT LINES, RE-EDITED FROM MS. HARLEY 2252 IN THE
      BRITISH MUSEUM. E.E.T.S., No. 88. London: Trübner and Co.,
      1903; reissued 1930, 1959.

104. MORTE ARTHUR: TWO EARLY ENGLISH ROMANCES. With an Introduction
      by Lucy Allen Paton. [Everyman edition.] London: J. M. Dent;
      New York: E. P. Dutton, [1912], pp. 95-201.

      It is not clear whether Lucy Allen Paton or Andrew Boyle
      edited the text.

105. Hemingway, Samuel B., ed. LE MORTE ARTHUR; A MIDDLE ENGLISH
      METRICAL ROMANCE. [Riverside Literature Series.] New York
      and Boston: Houghton Mifflin; London: George G. Harrap, 1912.

      A textbook edition based on the Bruce edition [no. 103].

106. Benson, Larry D. KING ARTHUR'S DEATH; THE MIDDLE ENGLISH STAN-
      ZAIC MORTE ARTHUR AND ALLITERATIVE MORTE ARTHURE. Indianapolis:
      Bobbs-Merrill, 1974.

      A textbook edition based on the Bruce edition [no. 103].

107. Hissiger, P. F., ed. LE MORTE ARTHUR: A CRITICAL EDITION.
      [Studies in English Literature, No. 96.] Paris: Mouton, 1975.

      This contains a summary of critical opinion on Malory's use of
      the poem in Tales 7 and 8.

3. Manuscript and Editions of the MORTE DARTHUR

a. Manuscript

108. British Library Additional Manuscript 59678. Formerly called the "Winchester Manuscript," Manuscript 13, Warden and Fellows' Library, Winchester College, folios 9^a–484^b preserved (late fifteenth century). Reproduced in facsimile in no. 109.

109. THE WINCHESTER MALORY; A FACSIMILE, with an Introduction by N. R. Ker. E.E.T.S. Supplemental Series, No. 4. London and New York: Oxford University Press, 1976.

Chapters in the Introduction are 1. Number of leaves and their condition and foliation. 2. Watermarks. 3. Quiring and leaf marks. 4. Dimensions and ruling. 5. The two scribes and their script. 6. Decoration and paragraph marks. 7. Binding. 8. History.

b. Complete Editions Before 1634

110. William Caxton's edition of the MORTE DARTHUR (THE NOBLE AND JOYOUS BOOKE ENTYTLED LE MORTE DARTHUR) published at Westminster, July 31, 1485.

The colophon reads: The Noble and Joyous book entytled le morte Darthur/Notwythstondyng it treateth of the byrth/lyf/ and actes of the sayd kyng Arthur/of his noble knyghtes of the rounde table/theyr meruayllous enquestes and aduentures/ thachyeuyng of the sangreal/& in thende the dolorous deth & departyng out of thys world of them al/whiche book was reduced in to englysshe by syr Thomas Malory knyght as afore is sayd/ and by me deuyded in to XXI bookes chaptyred and enprynted/ and fynnysshed in thabbey westmestre he last day of Juyl the yere of our lord/M/CCCC/LXXXV/Caxton me fieri fecit.

Reproduced in facsimile in no. 111. For bibliographical information, see de Ricci [no. 17]. Two copies survive: a perfect copy in the Pierpont Morgan Library, New York; and an imperfect copy (missing leaves supplied in facsimile from the Pierpont Morgan copy) in the John Rylands Library, Manchester.

111. SIR THOMAS MALORY: LE MORTE DARTHUR. PRINTED BY WILLIAM CAXTON 1485. Reproduced in facsimile from the copy in the Pierpont

Morgan Library, New York, with an Introduction by Paul Needham. London: Scolar Press in association with the Pierpont Morgan Library, 1976.

The five-page introduction contains bibliographical information about the editions and about the history of the Pierpont Morgan and Rylands copies of Caxton's edition.

112. Wynkyn de Worde, Westminster, 1498. THE BOOKE OF THE NOBLE KYNG. KYNG ARTHUR SOMETYME KYNGE OF ENGLONDE OF HIS NOBLE ACTES AND FEATES OF ARMES AND CHYVALRYE, HIS NOBLE KNYGHTES AND TABLE ROUNDE AND IS DEVYDED IN TO. XXI. BOOKES.

This edition is reprinted in no. 113. The extant copy of this edition is in the John Rylands Library, Manchester.

113. THE NOBLE AND JOYOUS BOKE ENTYTLED LE MORTE DARTHUR. Ed. A. S. Mott. 2 vols. Oxford: Printed at the Shakespeare Head Press . . . and published for the Press by Basil Blackwell, 1933.

A reprint of the unique copy of the edition printed by Wynkyn de Worde in 1498, and now in the John Rylands Library, Manchester [no. 112]. Modernized spelling and punctuation.
   a. T. S. Eliot [no. 474].
   b. A. Machen, OBSERVER, Dec. 17, 1933.
   c. TLS, Nov. 23, 1933, p. 811.

114. Wynkyn de Worde, 1529. A reprint of the 1498 edition, with successive variations. THE BOOKE OF THE MOOST NOBLE AND WORTHY PRINCE KYNG. KYNG ARTHUR SOMETYME KYNGE OF GRETE BRYTAYNE NOW CALLED ENGLONDE WHICHE TREATETH OF HIS NOBLE ACTES AND FEATES OF ARMS AND OF CHYVALRYE. OF HIS NOBLE KNYGHTES OF THE TABLE ROUNDE AND THIS VOLUME IS DEVYDED IN TO XXI. BOOKES.

The extant copy is in the British Library.

115. Wyllyam Copland, 1557. THE STORY OF THE MOST NOBLE AND WORTHY KYNGE ARTHUR, THE WHICHE WAS ONE OF THE WORTHYES CHRYSTEN, AND ALSO OF HIS NOBLE AND VALIAUNTE KNYGHTES OF THE ROUNDE TABLE. Newly imprynted and corrected. Imprynted at London by Wyllyam Copland.

Three copies, only one of which is perfect, are in the British Library.

116. Thomas East, c1585. Two editions, one in folio and one in quarto. THE STORYE OF THE MOST NOBLE AND WORTHY KYNGE ARTHUR, THE WHICH WAS THE FYRST OF THE WORTHYES CHRYSTEN, AND ALSO OF HYS NOBLE AND VALYAUNT KNYGHTES OF THE ROUNDE TABLE. Newly imprynted and corrected, between Paules Wharfe and Baynardes Castell by Thomas East.

A complete copy of the folio edition is in the British Library.

117. William Stansby, 1634. THE MOST ANCIENT AND FAMOUS HISTORY OF
     THE RENOWNED PRINCE ARTHUR, KING OF BRITAINE WHEREIN IS DE-
     CLARED HIS LIFE AND DEATH, WITH ALL HIS GLORIOUS BATTAILES
     AGAINST THE SAXONS, SARACENS, AND PAGANS, WHICH (FOR THE HONOUR
     OF HIS COUNTRY) HE MOST WORTHILY ATCHIEUED. AS ALSO, ALL THE
     NOBLE ACTS, AND HEROICKE DEEDS OF HIS VALIANT KNIGHTS OF THE
     ROUND TABLE. Newly refined and published for the delight, and
     profit of the Reader. London: Printed by William Stansby for
     Iacob Bloome.

     Two copies, one of which is perfect, are in the British Library.
     This edition includes a "Preface, or Advertissement to the
     Reader, for the better illustration and understanding of this
     famous Historie."

c. Complete Editions After 1634

118. LA MORT D'ARTHUR. THE MOST ANCIENT AND FAMOUS HISTORY OF THE RE-
     NOWNED PRINCE ARTHUR AND THE KNIGHTS OF THE ROUND TABLE. 3
     vols. London: R. Wilks, 1816. [Modernized. Based on the
     Stansby edition.]

119. THE HISTORY OF THE RENOWNED PRINCE ARTHUR, KING OF BRITAIN; WITH
     HIS LIFE AND DEATH, AND ALL HIS GLORIOUS BATTLES. LIKEWISE,
     THE NOBLE ACTS AND HEROIC DEEDS OF HIS VALIANT KNIGHTS OF THE
     ROUND TABLE. 2 vols. London: Published by J. Walker and Co.,
     1816. [Modernized. Based on the Stansby edition.]

120. THE BYRTH, LYF, AND ACTES OF KYNG ARTHUR; OF HIS NOBLE KNYGHTES
     OF THE ROUNDE TABLE, THEYR MERVEYLLOUS ENQUESTES AND ADVENTURES,
     THACHYEUYNG OF THE SANC GREAL; AND IN THE END LE MORTE DARTHUR,
     WITH THE DOLOROUS DETH AND DEPARTYNG OUT OF THYS WORLDE OF
     THEM AL. With an Introduction and Notes, by Robert Southey,
     Esq. 2 vols. London: Printed from Caxton's Edition, 1485,
     for Longman, Hurst, Rees, Orme, and Brown . . . by Thomas
     Davison, 1817.

     The Preface contains discussion of Arthurian romance. Southey
     calls Malory a "compiler" (pp. xxvi–xxviii). He claims that
     this edition is a "reprint with scrupulous exactness from the
     first edition by Caxton, in Earl Spencer's library." Actually,
     Southey is responsible only for the Introduction and Notes,
     William Upcott for the text. This edition is reprinted in
     no. 207.

121. LA MORT D'ARTHURE. THE HISTORY OF KING ARTHUR AND OF HIS KNIGHTS
     OF THE ROUND TABLE COMPILED BY SIR THOMAS MALORY, KNT. edited
     from the text of the edition of 1634, with introduction and

notes by Thomas Wright, Esq. 3 vols. London: John R. Smith,
1858; 2nd ed., 1865, 1866; 3rd ed., London: Reeves and Turner,
1889.   Published in "Sir John Lubbock's Hundred Books, No. 49,"
London: Routledge, 1893.

The introduction contains discussion of the 1816 and 1817 editions (vol. 1, pp. v-xvii).   Wright wishes to print an edition
widely accessible to the public.   He reprints the title page
and preface of the Stansby edition.

122.   Strachey, Edward, ed.   MORTE DARTHUR; SIR THOMAS MALORY'S BOOK
OF KING ARTHUR AND OF HIS NOBLE KNIGHTS OF THE ROUND TABLE.
The Original Edition of Caxton revised for Modern Use with an
Introduction.   [Globe edition.]   London and Philadelphia:
Macmillan, 1868; 2nd ed., 1868; index added, 1869; introduction
revised, 1891; often reprinted.   [Partially modernized; expur-
gated.]

Strachey claims that Malory is no "mere compiler and translator" but a "maker" whose work has an "epic unity and harmony"
(p. viii).   He defends Malory's characterization of Gawaine and
the "morality" of the work.   In his discussion of previous
editions, Strachey attacks Upcott's editing of the 1817 edition [no. 120].
   a.   ATHENAEUM, 1868, pt. 1, p. 694.
   b.   W. Minto, ACADEMY, vol. 38, p. 273.
   c.   T. S. Eliot, SPECTATOR, vol. 152, p. 278.

123.   Sommer, H. Oskar, ed.   LE MORTE DARTHUR BY SYR THOMAS MALORY, THE
ORIGINAL EDITION OF WILLIAM CAXTON NOW REPRINTED AND EDITED
WITH AN INTRODUCTION AND GLOSSARY. . . WITH AN ESSAY ON MALORY'S
PROSE STYLE BY ANDREW LANG.   3 vols.   London: David Nutt, 1889-
91; rpt. New York: AMS Press, 1973.

Vol. 1: Text.   Vol. 2:   The Introduction contains the following: Sir Thomas Malory and the various editions of LE MORTE
DARTHUR; relation of the different editions of LE MORTE DARTHUR
to one another; the present edition; list of errors, omissions,
and orthographical irregularities in Caxton's impression; result of the collation of Whittaker's facsimiles with the original pages; notes on the language of LE MORTE DARTHUR; list of
the various readings between Caxton's and Wynkyn de Worde's
editions; list of names and places; and glossary.   Vol. 3:
"Introductory Essay by Andrew Lang" and "Studies on the Sources
of LE MORTE DARTHUR."   Lang compares the MORTE DARTHUR and
Homeric epic.   Sommer discusses Malory's use of each of his
sources.
   a.   Lionel Johnson, ACADEMY, 38 (1890), 237-39.
   b.   NATION, 50 (Jan. 2, 1890), 15-16.
   c.   NATION, 51 (Sept. 4, 1890), 196-97.
   d.   ATHENAEUM, 1891, pt. 2, pp. 612-13.

e. N. Kellner, ENGLISCHE STUDIEN, 15 (1891), 424-25.
f. E. Kölbing, ENGLISCHE STUDIEN, 15 (1891), 425-27; 16 (1892), 403-05.
g. SPECTATOR, 67 (Sept. 19, 1891), 385-87.
h. Edward Strachey [no. 320].
i. K. D. Bülbring, LGRP, 13 (1892), 296.
j. NATION, 54 (Jan. 21, 1892), 58.
k. W. W. Greg, FOLK-LORE, 12 (1901), 491.
l. E. Vinaver [no. 441], pp. 128 ff.

124. Simmons, F. J., ed. THE BIRTH, LIFE AND ACTS OF KING ARTHUR, OF HIS NOBLE KNIGHTS OF THE ROUND TABLE, THEIR MARVELLOUS ENQUESTS AND ADVENTURES, THE ACHIEVING OF THE SAN GREAL, AND IN THE END LE MORTE D'ARTHUR, WITH THE DOLOROUS DEATH AND DEPARTING OUT OF THIS WORLD OF THEM ALL.--The text as written by Sir Thomas Malory and imprinted by William Caxton at Westminster the year 1485 and now spelled in modern style, with an introduction by Professor [John] Rhŷs, and embellished with many original designs by Aubrey Beardsley. London: J. M. Dent, 1893-94; rpt. 2nd ed., 1909; 3rd ed., 1927, including note on Aubrey Beardsley by Aymer Vallance and bibliographical note on Beardsley's illustrations by R. A. Walker [see no. 24]. This edition is also listed as no. 205.

The text is "modernized in spelling and punctuation" and is based on the 1817 Southey edition with some variants from the Sommer edition. In the Preface (pp. xi-xxxvi), Rhŷs argues that Malory was Welsh and discusses the origin of the Arthurian cycles and the historicity of Arthur.
    a. NATION, 58 (Apr. 5, 1894), 255-56.
    b. CRITIC, N.S. 21 (May 26, 1894), 354.
    c. ATLANTIC MONTHLY, 74 (Sept. 1894), 413-14.
    d. ATHENAEUM, Dec. 22, 1894, pp. 866-67.
    e. CRITIC, N.S. 23 (June 29, 1895), 473.
    f. ATHENAEUM, 1909, pt. 2, p. 703.

125. Rhys, Ernest, ed. THE NOBLE AND JOYOUS HISTORY OF KING ARTHUR. 2 vols. [The Scott Library.] London: Walter Scott, [1892?]. [Modernized. Based on the Stansby edition.]

126. Gollancz, Israel, ed. LE MORTE DARTHUR BY SIR THOMAS MALORY. 4 vols. [The Temple Classics.] London: J. M. Dent, 1897; often reissued.

127. Pollard, A. W., ed. LE MORTE DARTHUR. SIR THOMAS MALORY'S BOOK OF KING ARTHUR AND OF HIS NOBLE KNIGHTS OF THE ROUND TABLE. [Library of English Classics.] 2 vols. London and New York: Macmillan, 1900. Often reprinted. Subsequent editions illustrated by W. Russell Flint and Robert Gibbings [nos. 206, 208.]

Text is modernized in spelling but based on the Sommer edition. In a "bibliographical note" (pp. v-viii), Pollard calls Caxton's

preface "a brief criticism, which, on the points on which it
touches, is still the soundest and most sympathetic that has
been written." In using his sources, Malory showed "skill,
approaching to original genius."
    a. ATHENAEUM, 1910, pt. 2, p. 496.

128. LE MORTE D'ARTHUR BY SIR THOMAS MALORY. [Everyman edition.]
    2 vols. London: J. M. Dent; New York: E. P. Dutton, 1906.
    Often reprinted. Issued as one volume in the "Dent's Double
    Volumes" Series, 1933.

    This is a reprint of the 1893 Dent edition edited by F. J.
    Simmons. For the general contents of the introduction by John
    Rhỹs, see no. 124.

129. Vinaver, Eugène, ed. THE WORKS OF SIR THOMAS MALORY. 3 vols.
    Oxford: Clarendon Press, 1947. Reprinted with corrections,
    1948.

    See the second edition [no. 131] for annotation. This edition
    was also issued as one volume [no. 130].
    a. John E. Housman, ERASMUS, 1 (1947), 921-25.
    b. F. G. Kenyon, TLS, June 7, 1947, p. 281.
    c. [C. S. Lewis, no. 535.]
    d. E. M. W. Tillyard, "Malory Re-edited," CAMBRIDGE REVIEW,
        69 (Oct. 25, 1947), pp. 54 f.
    e. TLS, May 24, 1947, p. 258.
    f. M[ario] R[oques], ROMANIA, 70 (1948-49), 555-56.
    g. M. Schlauch, N.Y. TIMES BOOK REVIEW, Sept. 12, 1948,
        p. 28.
    h. R. H. Wilson, MP, 46 (1948), 136-38.
    i. E. C. Batho, MLR, 44 (1949), 260.
    j. J. A. W. Bennett, RES, 25 (1949), 161-67.
    k. W. A. Nitze [no. 576].
    1. J. Šimko [no. 577].

130. _____, ed. THE WORKS OF SIR THOMAS MALORY. [Oxford
    Standard Authors.] London: Oxford University Press, 1954;
    2nd ed., 1971. Issued in paperback, 1977.

    A one-volume edition of nos. 129, 131, excluding most of the
    introduction, critical apparatus, commentary, index, and bib-
    liography.
    Reviews of the first edition:
    a. Donald C. Baker, BOOKS ABROAD, 29 (1955), 350.
    b. T. A. Birrell, ENGLISH STUDIES, 36 (1955), 332.
    c. Madeleine Blaess, MLR, 50 (1955), 524-25.
    d. Denis Donoghue, STUDIES, 44 (1955), 382-83.
    e. F. Mossé, EA, 8 (1955), 337-38.
    f. D. C. Muecke, "Some Notes on Vinaver's Malory," MLN, 70
        (1955), 325-28.

g. F. Wölcken, ARCHIV, 191 (1955), 361.
h. Paul A. Brown, MLN, 71 (1956), 514-15.
i. Helaine Newstead, SPECULUM, 31 (1956), 420-21.

Reviews of the second edition:
a. J. M. Cowen, N & Q, 217 (1972), 30-31.
b. P. J. C. Field, SN, 41 (1972), 180-84.
c. M. Dubois, EA, 26 (1973), 225-26.
d. K. H. Göller, ANGLIA, 91 (1973), 124.

131. _____, ed. THE WORKS OF SIR THOMAS MALORY. 2nd ed.
     3 vols. Oxford: Clarendon Press, 1967.

In the "Preface to the First Edition" reprinted in this second
edition, Vinaver discusses the discovery of the Winchester
Manuscript and admits his tendency to interpret Malory in terms
of his French background. The "Preface to the Second Edition"
announces revisions which appear in the new edition: revised
critical apparatus, enlarged commentary, modification of editorial principles, and a discussion of the "unity" issue.
There is a new collation of the text with the Winchester Manuscript and Caxton's edition, and a new interpretation of THE
TALE OF KING ARTHUR based on a new version of the French source
of the tale.

The "Introduction" contains four chapters. Chapter 1 ("The
Knight-Prisoner") discusses Malory's biography. Vinaver up-
holds the candidacy of Thomas Malory of Newbold Revel, Warwickshire, though he has some reservations about the identification.
In Chapter 2 ("The Story of the Book"), Vinaver restates his
belief that the MORTE DARTHUR is eight separate romances and
replies to his critics. The explicits, he claims, most clearly demonstrate that each tale is a separate entity. Vinaver
concedes that the work may contain unity of characterization,
but he believes that the separate romances show that no structural unity was intended. Chapter 3 ("The Writer's Progress")
concerns style, structure, and interpretation. Vinaver
praises Malory's style, which has "simplicity and power."
Malory's French sources contained a wealth of episodic material
and characters; Malory reduced these materials and altered
their arrangement from "interweaving" to "progressive" exposi-
tion. In the last two tales, Malory succeeded in imposing his
own sens on the matiere of the Arthurian romances. The central
theme of the MORTE DARTHUR is the "tragic conflict of two
loyalties. . . , the heroic loyalty of man to man. . . [and]
the blind devotion of the knight-lover to his lady." Chapter
4 ("The Method of Editing") provides information on the texts,
principles of reconstructing the original, and the present
edition.

An annotated bibliography of important Malory studies follows

the Introduction. Vol. 3 contains a commentary, an index of
proper names, a glossary by G. L. Brook, and corrigenda. The
commentary contains critical notes, a discussion of each tale
and its sources, and a bibliography of materials relevant to
each tale.
    a. J. Lawlor, CRITICAL QUARTERLY, 10 (1968), 397.
    b. F. Lecoy, ROMANIA, 89 (1968), 286.
    c. J. M. Cowen, MLR, 64 (1969), 629-30.
    d. W. Goldhurst, NEW LEADER, Jan. 20, 1969, p. 20.
    e. J. A. W. Bennett, RES, N.S. 21 (1970), 192-93.
    f. D. S. Brewer, MEDIUM AEVUM, 39 (1970), 35-39.
    g. Robert Guiette, RBPH, 49 (1971), 244-45.
    h. Peter H. Salus, ENGLISH STUDIES, 52 (1971), 455.
    i. J. M. Cowen, N & Q, N.S. 19 (1972), 30.
    j. P. J. C. Field, SN, 41 (1972), 180-84.
    k. K. H. Güller, ANGLIA, 91 (1973), 121-24.

132. Cowen, Janet, ed. SIR THOMAS MALORY: LE MORTE D'ARTHUR. Intro-
     duction by John Lawlor. 2 vols. Harmondsworth, Middlesex;
     and Baltimore: Penguin English Library, 1969.

     The text is based on Caxton's edition. In the Introduction
     (pp. vii-xxxi), Lawlor discusses the controversies about Malo-
     ry's identity and the unity of the MORTE DARTHUR. Lawlor says
     that Malory unravels his sources, placing structural emphasis
     on the downfall of the kingdom, and achieves a more realistic
     tone than was present in his sources.
         a. S. S. Hussey, N & Q, N.S. 17 (1970), 319-20.
         b. W. O. Evans, LANGUAGE AND STYLE, vol. 5, pp. 67-73.

                  d. Abridgements

133. K[nowles], J[ames] T. THE STORY OF KING ARTHUR AND HIS KNIGHTS
     OF THE ROUND TABLE. Compiled and arranged by J. T. K. with
     illustrations by G. H. Thomas. London: Griffith and Farran,
     1862. Numerous editions.

134. Conybeare, Edward. LA MORTE D'ARTHUR: THE HISTORY OF KING
     ARTHUR. COMPILED BY SIR THOMAS MALORY. London: Edward Moxon,
     1868.

     Conybeare tries to "put into a more popular form one of the
     least appreciated works in the English language" (p. iii).

135. LIFE AND EXPLOITS OF KING ARTHUR AND HIS KNIGHTS OF THE ROUND
     TABLE, A LEGENDARY ROMANCE. London: Milner and Co., [1878].
     Also published [c1890].

136. Lanier, Sidney. THE BOY'S KING ARTHUR; BEING SIR THOMAS MALORY'S

HISTORY OF KING ARTHUR AND HIS KNIGHTS OF THE ROUND TABLE.
Edited for boys, with an introduction. Illustrated by Alfred
Kappes. New York: Charles Scribner's Sons; London: Sampson
Low, 1880. Often reprinted, with illustrations by other art-
ists, including N. C. Wyeth.

In the Introduction, Lanier calls the MORTE DARTHUR not a
"mere compilation" but a "work in which so much of [Malory]
is mingled that it is largely. . . his own" (p. xx).

137. Rhys, Ernest, ed. MALORY'S HISTORY OF KING ARTHUR AND THE QUEST
OF THE HOLY GRAIL. [FROM THE MORTE D'ARTHUR.] Edited, with
general introduction to the "Camelot Classics," by Ernest
Rhys. London: Walter Scott; New York: W. J. Gage, 1886.

In the Introduction (pp. v-xxxv), Rhys discusses the English
prose tradition and Malory's place and importance in it.

138. Morris, Charles. KING ARTHUR AND THE KNIGHTS OF THE ROUND TA-
BLE. A MODERNIZED VERSION OF THE MORTE DARTHUR. London:
W. W. Gibbings, 1892.

Morris claims that "Malory was not solely an editor. He was
in a large sense a creator. It was coarse and crude material
with which he had to deal, but in his hand its rude prose
gained a degree of poetic fervor" (p. 9).

139. Martin, A[lfred] T., ed. SELECTIONS FROM MALORY'S LE MORTE
D'ARTHUR. Edited with introduction, notes, and glossary.
London and New York: Macmillan, 1896; rpt. London, 1924.

The text is based on Strachey's edition [no. 122]. Martin
believes that Malory conceived his work as a "great tragedy,
the punishment of an unconscious sin" (p. xxii). In the Introduction (pp. vii-xxxvi), Martin discusses Malory's sources,
prose style, and characterizations.
    a. C. S. Baldwin, JGP [JEGP], vol. 2 [n.d.], pp. 103-05.

140. Mead, William Edward, ed. SELECTIONS FROM SIR THOMAS MALORY'S
MORTE DARTHUR. [Athenaeum Press Series.] London and Boston:
Ginn and Co., 1897; revised, 1901.

The text is based on the Sommer edition [no. 123] and includes
Books 1, 2, 13, 17, 18, and 21. The edition has an introduction, notes, glossary, and indexes. The Introduction discusses
Malory's identity (with a biographical chapter by G. L. Kittredge), editions of the MORTE DARTHUR, Malory's sources, the
popularity and influence of the work, and aspects of its language, syntax, diction, and style. Mead says that Malory was
"more than a mere translator" (p. liii) but that his originality is difficult to assess since his exact manuscript sources

are not known.
    a. C. S. Baldwin, JGP [JEGP], vol. 2 [n.d.], pp. 103-05.

141. THE STORY OF ELAINE: THE FAIR MAID OF ASTOLAT BY SIR THOMAS
      MALORY. [Astolat Oakleaf Series.] Guildford: Astolat Press,
      1903. Also published in different format, London: Siegle,
      Hill, and Co., [1910].

142. THE BOOK OF SIR GALAHAD AND THE ACHIEVEMENT OF THE ADVENTURE OF
      THE SANCGREAL BY SIR THOMAS MALORY. [Oakleaf Series.] Lon-
      don: Astolat Press, 1904. Also published in different for-
      mat, London: Siegle, Hill, and Co., [1911].

143. Child, Clarence Griffin, ed. THE BOOK OF MERLIN [and] THE BOOK
      OF SIR BALIN, FROM MALORY'S KING ARTHUR, WITH CAXTON'S PREFACE.
      Edited with an introductory sketch and glossary. [Riverside
      Literature Series.] Boston and New York: Houghton Mifflin;
      London: George G. Harrap, 1904.

      Based on the Sommer edition [no. 123]. Modernized spelling.
      The "introductory sketch" (pp. iii-xvii) discusses theme,
      structure, and style.

144. Swiggett, Douglas W., ed. SELECTIONS FROM SIR THOMAS MALORY'S
      LE MORTE DARTHUR. Edited with introduction, notes, and glos-
      sary. New York: Macmillan, c1909 [1918].

      Based on the Pollard edition [no. 127].

145. Wragg, H., ed. SELECTIONS FROM MALORY. Oxford: Clarendon
      Press, 1912. [Abridged. Also see no. 430.]

146. Pollard, Alfred W., ed. THE ROMANCE OF KING ARTHUR AND HIS
      KNIGHTS OF THE ROUND TABLE. Abridged from Malory's MORTE
      D'ARTHUR. Illustrated by Arthur Rackham. London and New
      York: Macmillan, 1917; reissued New York: Weathervane Books,
      n.d.

147. THE NOBLE TABLE OF THE SANGREAL. DRAWN OUT OF THE FRENCH TONGUE
      BY SIR THOMAS MALORY, KT., AND FIRST PUBLISHED BY MASTER WIL-
      LIAM CAXTON. Edited by a Graduate of Cambridge. [The Pil-
      grim's Books, No. 4.] London: Philip Allan, 1920; 2nd ed.,
      1923; 3rd ed., 1924.

148. THE DEATH OF KING ARTHUR, BEING THE TWENTY-FIRST BOOK OF SIR
      THOMAS MALORY'S BOOK OF KING ARTHUR AND OF HIS NOBLE KNIGHTS
      OF THE ROUND TABLE. With illustrations designed and engraved
      on wood by Catherine Donaldson. London: Macmillan, 1928.

149. Babington, P. L., ed. SELECTIONS FROM LE MORTE D'ARTHUR. Lon-
      don: Sidgwick and Jackson, 1929.

Based on the Pollard edition [no. 127]. Contains an introduction and a bibliographical note.

150. Crump, Geoffrey H. A SHORTER MALORY. Edited with an introduction. London and New York: Thomas Nelson, 1930. [Extracts. Modernized spelling.]

151. Aurner, Nellie Slayton, ed. MALORY: AN INTRODUCTION TO THE MORTE D'ARTHUR. New York: Thomas Nelson, 1938.

Aurner discusses the Warwickshire Malory's biography. She believes that the MORTE DARTHUR has originality and a tripartite structure emphasizing loyalty to lord, lady, and God. Unlike Scudder [no. 402], however, who believes that the work reflects the age of chivalry, Aurner thinks that Malory wrote about his time, not a "lost age."

152. Sanders, Charles R., and Charles E. Ward, eds. THE MORTE DARTHUR BY SIR THOMAS MALORY: AN ABRIDGEMENT. New York: F. S. Crofts and Co., 1940.

153. LANCELOT AND GUINEVERE. New edition, with drawings by Lettice Sandford; text established by Professor Vinaver, with spelling and punctuation newly modernized. London: Folio Society, 1953.

Based on the 1947 Vinaver edition [no. 129].

154. Vinaver, Eugène, ed. THE TALE OF THE DEATH OF KING ARTHUR. Oxford: Clarendon Press; New York: Oxford University Press, 1955.

The text is a "revised form [of] all the relevant sections" of the 1947 edition [no. 129]. This edition contains an introduction (pp. vii-xxvi), commentary, bibliography, glossary, and index. Vinaver traces the theme of the fall of Arthur's kingdom from Geoffrey of Monmouth and the Vulgate cycle to Layamon, the Alliterative MORTE ARTHURE, and the Stanzaic MORTE ARTHUR. The major theme of the MORTE DARTHUR is "divided allegiances" -- man to man, and man to lady.
    a. M. Blaess, MLR, 50 (1955), 524-25.
    b. N & Q, N.S. 2 (1955), 365-66.
    c. TLS, Jan. 28, 1955, p. 60; April 29, 1955, p. 255.
    d. D. S. Brewer [no. 606].
    e. R. T. Davies, RES, N.S. 7 (1956), 330-31.
    f. H. Newstead, SPECULUM, 31 (1956)., 420-21.
    g. D. Bethurum, JEGP, 56 (1957), 125-26.

155. _____, ed. KING ARTHUR AND HIS KNIGHTS, SELECTIONS FROM THE WORKS OF SIR THOMAS MALORY. [Riverside Editions.] Boston: Houghton Mifflin, 1956. Revised and enlarged edition, 1968. [See no. 158.]

In the Introduction, Vinaver discusses <u>entrelacement</u> in early
romance and Malory's attempt to condense and unravel his
sources. Selections are Merlin, Balin, Pelleas and Ettard,
the Knight of the Cart, Lancelot and Elaine, the Holy Grail,
the Poisoned Apple, and the Fair Maid of Astolat. Bibliographical notes.
   a. N. C. Starr, CE, 19 (1957-58), 86.

156. Davies, R[eginald] T[horne], ed. SIR THOMAS MALORY: KING ARTHUR
      AND HIS KNIGHTS; A SELECTION FROM WHAT HAS BEEN KNOWN AS LE
      MORTE DARTHUR. New York: Barnes and Noble; London: Faber and
      Faber, 1967. Also issued by Faber in paperback, 1968.

      The text, based on the Winchester Manuscript with the conclu-
      sion added from Sommer's edition, is for the non-specialist.
      In the Introduction (pp. 13-26), Vinaver discusses Malory's re-
      duction of his sources, his interlace technique, and the his-
      tory of the Winchester Manuscript and the Caxton edition.
      Davies acknowledges that the MORTE DARTHUR has serious struc-
      tural flaws but sees "unity" in the whole.
      a. J. A. Christie, HIBBERT JOURNAL, Autumn, 1967, p. 36.
      b. TLS, Nov. 30, 1967, p. 1126.
      c. M.-M. Dubois, EA, 21 (1968), 407.
      d. P. E. Tucker, N & Q, N.S. 15 (1968), 152-53.

157. Brewer, D[erek] S., ed. THE MORTE DARTHUR: PARTS SEVEN AND
      EIGHT BY SIR THOMAS MALORY. Edited with an introduction,
      notes, and glossary. [York Medieval Texts.] London: Edward
      Arnold, 1968. Evanston, Ill.: Northwestern University Press,
      1972.

      The text is based on the one-volume 1954 Vinaver edition [no.
      130] with some variants from the Winchester Manuscript and the
      Caxton edition. Spelling is modernized. In the Introduction
      (pp. 1-37), Brewer discusses theme, structure, style, and char-
      acterization. He believes that the work has a "combination
      of romantic remoteness" and "contemporary relevance" that ap-
      pealed to Malory's generation and also appeals to the present
      age. The MORTE DARTHUR expresses the "need to reconcile the
      individual's demands with those of society, to recognize and
      cherish personal integrity, and true love, and to create a
      good society" (p. 1). Malory emphasized honour ("worship")
      rather than love, and its loyalties to king, fellowship, and
      lady. Though the final tragedy had multiple causes, the diver-
      gence between honour and virtue is central. Honour consists
      of maintaining public reputation and is therefore only the ap-
      pearance of virtue; but for Arthur and for Malory, "true"
      honour and virtue are necessary but unattainable. Malory
      effectively portrays character through action and speech, and
      his prose style combines "colloquial liveliness" and "ceremoni-
      ous dignity." According to Brewer, modern concepts of "organic

unity" should be abandoned in discussion of the structure of the MORTE DARTHUR.

158. Vinaver, Eugène, ed. KING ARTHUR AND HIS KNIGHTS: SELECTED TALES BY SIR THOMAS MALORY. Edited with an introduction. Originally published under a slightly different title, New York: Houghton Mifflin, 1956 [see no. 155]; rev. ed., New York and London: Oxford University Press, 1968; rpt. 1975.

This edition differs from that of 1956 in that it includes the TALE OF THE DEATH OF ARTHUR and a bibliographical notice containing an updated list of critical studies (pp. 227-31) which apply to the tales in this edition.
   a. J. M. Cowen, N & Q, 221 (1976), 515.

159. Field, P. J. C., ed. SIR THOMAS MALORY: LE MORTE DARTHUR. THE SEVENTH AND EIGHTH TALES. [London Medieval and Renaissance Series.] London: Hodder and Soughton; New York: Holmes and Meier, 1978.

The text is based on the Winchester Manuscript. Introduction (pp. 1-67) and commentary.

e. Adaptations

160. Frith, Henry. KING ARTHUR AND HIS KNIGHTS OF THE ROUND TABLE. With original illustrations by F. A. Fraser. London: Routledge, 1884.

161. Edwardson, E. THE COURTEOUS KNIGHT AND OTHER TALES BORROWED FROM SPENSER AND MALORY. Illustrated by Robert Hope. Edinburgh and London: Thomas Nelson, 1899.

162. Macleod, Mary. THE BOOK OF KING ARTHUR AND HIS NOBLE KNIGHTS. STORIES FROM SIR THOMAS MALORY'S MORTE DARTHUR. Introduction by John W. Hales. Illustrated from drawings by A. G. Walker. London: Wells Gardner, Darton, and Co., 1900. Often published, sometimes with different title.

163. Clay, Beatrice. STORIES FROM LE MORTE DARTHUR AND THE MABINOGION. Illustrated by C. E. Hughes. [Temple Classics for Young Children.] London: J. M. Dent, 1901. Often published, sometimes with different title.

164. Pyle, Howard. THE STORY OF KING ARTHUR AND HIS KNIGHTS. New York: Charles Scribner's Sons; London: George Newnes, 1903; rpt. 1933.

165. Allen, J. C. TALES OF KING ARTHUR AND THE ROUND TABLE. Adapted

from the Book of Romance by Andrew Lang. Illustrations by
H. J. Ford. London: Longmans, Green and Co., 1905.

166. Cutler, U. Waldo. STORIES OF KING ARTHUR AND HIS KNIGHTS. Retold from Malory's 'Morte Darthur.' London: George G. Harrap, 1905. Published under different titles, 1911, 1933.

167. MacGregor, Mary. STORIES OF KING ARTHUR'S KNIGHTS. TOLD TO
THE CHILDREN. With pictures by Katharine Cameron. London:
T. C. and E. C. Jack, [1905].

168. Pyle, Howard. THE STORY OF THE CHAMPIONS OF THE ROUND TABLE.
New York: Charles Scribner's Sons; London: George Newnes,
1905; rpt. 1933; rpt. New York: Dover, 1968.

169. _____. THE STORY OF SIR LAUNCELOT AND HIS CHAMPIONS.
New York: Charles Scribner's Sons; London: Chapman and Hall,
1907; rpt. 1933.

170. Sterling, Mary Blackwell. THE STORY OF GALAHAD. RETOLD FROM
LE MORTE D'ARTHUR OF SIR THOMAS MALORY AND THE ORIGINAL
STORIES. Illustrated by William Ernest Chapman. London:
Grant Richards; New York: E. P. Dutton, 1908.

171. THE CHILDREN'S KING ARTHUR. STORIES FROM TENNYSON AND MALORY.
London: Henry Frowde, and Hodder and Soughton, [1909].

172. Baldwin, James. STORIES OF THE KING. New York: American Book
Co., 1910.

173. Haydon, A. L. STORIES OF KING ARTHUR. Illustrations by Arthur
Rackham. London and New York: Cassell, 1910.

174. KING ARTHUR AND HIS KNIGHTS. [Stories Old and New.] London:
Blackie and Son, [1910].

175. Pyle, Howard. THE STORY OF THE GRAIL AND THE PASSING OF ARTHUR.
New York: Charles Scribner's Sons, 1910; rpt. 1933.

176. Senior, Dorothy. THE KING WHO NEVER DIED. TALES OF KING ARTHUR.
London: Adam and Charles Black, 1910.

177. Gilbert, Henry. KING ARTHUR'S KNIGHTS: THE TALES RETOLD FOR
BOYS AND GIRLS. Illustrated by Walter Crane. Edinburgh and
London: T. C. and E. C. Jack, 1911; also published, 1933,
[1934].

178. Lea, John. TALES OF KING ARTHUR AND THE ROUND TABLE. [Told for
the Bairns.] London: S. W. Partridge, [1920].

179. Ashley, Doris. KING ARTHUR AND THE KNIGHTS OF THE ROUND TABLE.

Illustrated by Arthur A. Dixon and edited by Capt. E. Vreden-
burg. London: Raphael Tuck, [1922].

180. Allen, Philip Schuyler, ed. KING ARTHUR AND HIS KNIGHTS: A
NOBLE AND JOYOUS HISTORY. Illustrated by Mead Schaeffer and
John R. Neill. [Windemere Series.] Chicago and New York:
Rand McNally, 1924.

181. Creswick, Paul. KING ARTHUR. THE STORY OF THE ROUND TABLE. Illustrated by B. Westmaroff and L. D'Emo. New York: American
Book Co., 1925.

182. Winder, Blanche. STORIES OF KING ARTHUR. With Forty-eight
Colour Plates by Harry G. Theaker. London: Ward, Lock, and
Co., [1925].

183. Alexander, Ann D. WOMEN OF THE MORTE DARTHUR. TWELVE OF THE
MOST ROMANTIC OF THE WORLDS [sic] LOVE STORIES. Selected from
Malory's MORTE DARTHUR and illustrated by Ann D. Alexander.
London: Methuen, 1927.

184. Merchant, Elizabeth Lodor. KING ARTHUR AND HIS KNIGHTS. Illustrated by Frank Godwin. Philadelphia: John C. Winston, 1927.

185. STORIES OF KING ARTHUR AND HIS KNIGHTS. Illustrated by R. B.
Ogle. [Epworth Children's Classics.] London: Epworth Press,
[1927].

186. KING ARTHUR AND HIS KNIGHTS. STORIES OF THE ROUND TABLE BASED
ON LE MORTE D'ARTHUR. By Sir Thomas Malory. [Brodie Books,
No. 45.] London: James Brodie, [1928].

187. Rutley, C[ecily] M. STORIES OF KING ARTHUR'S KNIGHTS. Illustrations by Alfred Pearse. London: R. T. S. Office, [1929].

188. Hampden, John. KNIGHTS OF THE ROUND TABLE. TAKEN FROM 'LE
MORTE D'ARTHUR' BY SIR THOMAS MALORY. London and Edinburgh:
Thomas Nelson, [1930].

189. STORIES OF KING ARTHUR'S KNIGHTS TOLD TO THE CHILDREN. [Nelson's
Bumper Books.] London: Thomas Nelson, [1930].

190. Price, Eleanor C. THE ADVENTURES OF KING ARTHUR. ARRANGED FROM
THE 'MORTE DARTHUR' OF SIR THOMAS MALORY. Illustrated by
Rowland Wheelwright. Cover and border design by G. P. Mickle-
wright. London: J. Coker, 1931; also published 1933, [1948].

191. Campbell, Stuart. KING ARTHUR AND HIS KNIGHTS. London and Glas-
gow: Collins' Clear-Type Press, [1933]; also published under
the title STORIES OF KING ARTHUR, 1935, 1938, and under other
titles, two editions, [1941]; and 1964.

192. Lee, F. H. THE CHILDREN'S KING ARTHUR. Illustrated by Honor C.
     Appleton. With a frontispiece by Rowland Wheelwright. London:
     George G. Harrap, 1935.

193. Martin, Constance M. KING ARTHUR AND HIS KNIGHTS. FROM THE
     STORY BY SIR THOMAS MALORY. Illustrated by Gerald Ososki.
     [Riverside Readers.] London: Philip and Tacey, [1935]; also
     published [1948].

194. STORIES FROM KING ARTHUR. [Great Writers for Young Readers.]
     London: Oxford University Press, 1935.

195. Harrison, G. B. NEW TALES FROM MALORY. Illustrated by C. Walter
     Hodges. London: Thomas Nelson, 1939.

196. Cooke, Brian Kennedy. KING ARTHUR OF BRITAIN. FROM SIR THOMAS
     MALORY'S MORTE D'ARTHUR. Illuminated in the style of early
     English miniatures by Anthony Rado. Leicester: Edmund Ward,
     1946; rpt. 1951, 1954; 2nd ed. illustrated by Gay Galsworthy,
     1961.

197. _____. SIR LANCELOT. FROM SIR THOMAS MALORY'S MORTE
     D'ARTHUR AND OTHER SOURCES. Illustrated after Walter-Colours
     by W. Russell Flint. Leicester: Edmund Ward, 1951.

198. _____. THE HOLY GRAIL. FROM SIR THOMAS MALORY'S
     MORTE D'ARTHUR AND OTHER SOURCES. Illustrated from the "Codice
     Palatino" in the Florence Museum. Leicester: Edmund Ward, 1953.

199. Green, Roger Lancelyn. KING ARTHUR AND HIS KNIGHTS OF THE ROUND
     TABLE. NEWLY RE-TOLD OUT OF THE OLD ROMANCES. Illustrated by
     Lotte Reiniger. [Puffin Story Books, No. 73.] London: Pen-
     guin, 1953; rpt. London: Faber and Faber, 1957.

200. Hadfield, Alice M. KING ARTHUR AND THE ROUND TABLE. Illustrated
     by Donald Seton Cammell. London: J. M. Dent; New York: E. P.
     Dutton, 1953.

201. Fraser, Antonia. KING ARTHUR AND THE KNIGHTS OF THE ROUND TABLE.
     Illustrated by Rebecca Fraser. [First published, Heirloom Li-
     brary, 1954.] London: Sidgwick and Jackson, 1970.

202. Cooke, Brian Kennedy. THE QUEST OF THE BEAST. FROM SIR THOMAS
     MALORY'S 'MORTE D'ARTHUR' AND OTHER SOURCES. Illustrations in
     the text from "Tavola Rotonda" (Cod. Pal. 556) by Courtesy of
     the National Library, Florence. London: Edmund Ward, 1957.

203. Baines, Keith. SIR THOMAS MALORY'S LE MORTE D'ARTHUR: KING AR-
     THUR AND THE LEGENDS OF THE ROUND TABLE. A Rendition in modern
     idiom by Keith Baines, with an introduction by Robert Graves.
     Decorative illustrations by Enrico Arno. London: George G.
     Harrap; New York: Bramwell House; New York: New American

Library [Mentor Classics], 1962.

The text is based on the 1947 and 1954 Vinaver editions [nos. 129, 130]. Abridged and modernized.
  a. TLS, Apr. 2, 1964, p. 274.

204. Steinbeck, John. THE ACTS OF KING ARTHUR AND HIS NOBLE KNIGHTS, FROM THE WINCHESTER MANUSCRIPTS OF THOMAS MALORY AND OTHER SOURCES. Ed. Chase Horton. New York: Farrar, Straus, and Giroux; London: Heinemann, 1976.

A retelling of Tales 1 and 3 of the MORTE DARTHUR. The Appendix contains the correspondence of Steinbeck concerning the project.
  a. P. L. Adams, ATLANTIC MONTHLY, 238 (Nov. 1976), 118.
  b. BOOKLIST, 73 (Oct. 15, 1976), 294, 316.
  c. Edmund Fuller, WALL STREET JOURNAL, Nov. 19, 1976, p. 1.
  d. J. Gardner, N.Y. TIMES BOOK REVIEW, Oct. 24, 1976, p. 31.
  e. G. A. Masterton, LJ, 101 (Oct. 15, 1976), no. 2178.
  f. CHOICE, 14 (Mar. 1977), 64.
  g. M. S. Cosgrave, HORN BOOK, 53 (Oct. 1977), 561.
  h. Cynthia Johnson, SCHOOL LIBRARY JOURNAL, 23 (Apr. 1977), 84.
  i. Derek Mahon, NEW STATESMAN, 93 (Feb. 11, 1977), 195.
  j. Diana Rowan, CHRISTIAN SCIENCE MONITOR, Jan. 12, 1977, p. 23.
  k. T. A. Shippey, TLS, Apr. 29, 1977, p. 536.
  l. M. C. Williams, NEW REPUBLIC, 176 (Feb. 5, 1977), 34-35.
  m. John Ditsky, AMERICAN LITERATURE, 49 (Jan. 1978), 633-35.

f. Art Editions

205. Simmons, F. J., ed. THE BIRTH, LIFE AND ACTS OF KING ARTHUR. Illustrated by Aubrey Beardsley. London: J. M. Dent, 1893-94; 2nd ed., 1909; 3rd ed., 1927. [For full citation, see no. 124.]

Beardsley's illustrations are reproduced in facsimile from this edition in ILLUSTRATIONS FOR LE MORTE DARTHUR. Arranged by Edmund V. Gillon, Jr. New York: Dover, 1972. For bibliographical information about the illustrations, see no. 24.

206. THE BOOK OF KING ARTHUR AND OF HIS NOBLE KNIGHTS OF THE ROUND TABLE. BY SIR THOMAS MALORY, KNIGHT. Illustrated by W. Russell Flint. 4 vols. [Riccardi Press Books.] London: Philip Lee Warner, Publisher to the Medici Society, 1910-11; rpt. 1920, 1923, 1927 (in one volume), 1929.

The text is based on the 1900 Pollard edition [no. 127]. This edition contains forty-eight color plates reproduced after original watercolor drawings.

207. THE NOBLE AND JOYOUS BOOK ENTYTLED LE MORTE DARTHUR NOTWYTHSTOND-
     YNG IT TREATETH OF THE BYRTH, LYF, AND ACTES OF THE SAYD KING
     ARTHUR, OF HIS NOBLE KNYGHTES OF THE ROUNDE TABLE, THEYR MER-
     VAYLLOUS ENQUESTES AND ADVENTURES, THACHYEVYNG OF THE SANGREAL
     & IN THENDE THE DOLOROUS DETH AND DEPARTYNG OUT OF THYS WORLDE
     OF THEM AL, WHICHE BOOK WAS REDUCED IN TO ENGLYSSHE BY SYR
     THOMAS MALORY, KNYGHT. Illustrated by Charles M. Gere and
     Margaret Gere. Chelsea: The Ashendene Press, 1913.

     The text is based on the 1817 Southey edition [no. 120].

208. LE MORTE DARTHUR; THE STORY OF KING ARTHUR AND OF HIS NOBLE
     KNIGHTS OF THE ROUND TABLE WRITTEN BY SIR THOMAS MALORY, FIRST
     PRINTED BY WILLIAM CAXTON, NOW MODERNISED, AS TO SPELLING AND
     PUNCTUATION. 3 vols. Illustrated with wood engravings by
     Robert Gibbings & Printed at the Golden Cockerel Press, Lon-
     don, for the Limited Editions Club, New York, 1936.

     The text is based on the 1900 Pollard edition [no. 127].

209. THE BOOK OF THE HOLY GRAIL FROM THE MORTE D'ARTHUR BY SIR THOMAS
     MALORY TOGETHER WITH WILLIAM CAXTON'S PROLOGUE. Birmingham
     School of Printing, Central School of Arts and Crafts, 1934.

     Contains seven full-page wood engravings.

210. LANCELOT AND ELAINE, BEING THE EIGHTH TO THE TWENTIETH CHAPTERS
     OF THE EIGHTEENTH BOOK OF SIR THOMAS MALORY'S LE MORTE DARTHUR
     WITH ENGRAVINGS BY JOAN HASSALL. Printed and published by
     Hague and Gill, 1948.

     Contains two engravings. The text is that of the Sommer edi-
     tion [no. 123] with no corrections of Caxton's misprints.

                    g. Translations

211. Rüttgers, Severin. HERR LANZELOT UND DAS FRAÜLEIN VON ASTOLAT.
     Dusseldorf: Ohle, 1912.

212. Undset, Sigrid. FORTAELLINGER OM KONG ARTUR OG RIDDERNE AV DET
     RUNDE BORD. Fortalt paa norsk. Oslo: Aschehoug and Co.,
     1915; rpt. 1953.

     This was translated into Polish as LEGENDY O KRÓLU ARTURZE I
     RYĆERZACH OKRAGLEGO STOŁU. Warszawa: Pax, 1957.

213. Lachmann, Hedwig. DIES EDLE UND FREUDENREICHE BUCH HEISSET DER
     TOD ARTHURS OBZWAR ES HANDELT VON GEBURT, LEBEN UND TATEN DES
     GENANNTEN KÖNIGS ARTHUR VON SEINEN EDELN RITTERN VOM RUNDEN
     TISCHE UND IHREN WUNDERBAREN FAHRTEN UND ABENTEUERN VON DER

VOLLENDUNG DES HEILIGEN GRALS UND SCHIESSLICH VON IHRER ALLER SCHMERZLICHEM TODE UND ABSCHEIDEN VON DIESER WELT. 3 Bd. Einleitung von Severin Rüttgers (pp. v-xix). Leipzig: Infel Verlag, [1923].

214. Vallvé, Manuel. LOS CABALLEROS DE LA TABLE REDONDA; LEYENDAS RELATADAS A NIÑOS POR MANUEL VALLVÉ, CON ILLUSTRACIONES DE JOSÉ SEGRELLES. 4. ed. Barcelona: Araluce, [1932?].

215. Eilian, John. BRENIN ARTHUR Y PLANT. Wedi ei hail-adrodd yn Gymraeg gan John Eilian. O Stori Saesneg F. H. Lee. A'i darlunio gan Honor C. Appleton. [Silff Lyfrau'r Plant.] London: George G. Harrap, 1953.

216. Dubois, Marguerite-Marie. SIR THOMAS MALORY; LE ROMAN D'ARTHUR ET DES CHEVALIERS DE LA TABLE RONDE. Extraits choisis d'après l'édition originale du MORTE DARTHUR de Caxton avec les principes variantes du manuscrit de Winchester. [Collection Bilingue des Classiques Étrangers.] Paris: Aubier, 1948.

Introduction (pp. 9-53). English text with French translation on facing page. Dubois says that Malory intended neither to celebrate a chivalric past nor to edify the present. Critics should not search for modern structural "unity" in his work.

217. Urgan, Mina. ARTHUR' ÜN ÖLÜMÜ. Dünya edebiyatİndan tercümeler. Indiliz Klâsikleri, No. 55. 4 vols. in 3. Istanbul: Millİ Egitim Basİmevi, 1948.

218. Naudé, Adèle. KONING ARTHUR EN SY RIDDERS. Vertel deur Adèle Naudé. [Ons eie boekrak.] Kaapstad, 1950.

219. Hopp, Zinken. KONG ARTHUR OG RIDDERNE AV DET RUNDE BORD. Tegninger av Odd Brockmann. Bergen: J. W. Elde, c1951.

220. O BASILIAS ARTHOUROS KAI OI IPPOTES TĒS STRŌNGYLĒS TRAPEZĒS. Metaphrasē Phōkiōnos Kōnsta. Athēnai: Atlantis, c1956.

Published under a slightly different title, Athēnai: M. Pechlibanidēs, [1970?].

221. Baldini, Gabriele. LA PIU BELLE PAGINE DELLA LETTERATURA INGLESE. Vol. 1: The Fair Maid of Astolat. Milano, 1958.

222. Cahn, Jan. ARTUŠOVA SMRT. Přeložil Jan Caha. [Živá díla minulosti, sv. 25.] Praha, Státni Naklad. Krásné Literatury, Hudby a Uměni, 1960.

223. Denis, Alberto. OS CAVALEIROS DO REI ARTUR. [Grandes Obras da Literatura Universal.] São Paulo: Edições e Publicações Brasil, 1963.

224. Tormos, Pilar Grimaldo. LOS CABALLEROS DE LA TABLA REDONDA. Illustraciones [de] Mario Logli y Gabriele Santini. [Biblio-
teca Zagal 3. Serie Literatura.] Barcelona: Editorial Teide,
1963.

225. Omer, Devorah. ABIRE HA-SHULḤAN HE-'AGOL. n. p., 1966.

226. Shimuzu, Aya. ĀSA Ō DENSETSU KENKYŪ. n. p., 1966.

227. Egunova, N. A. SMERT' ARTURA. n. p., 1968.

228. Tellér, Gyula. ARTHUR KIRÁLYNAK ES VITÉZEINEK, A KEREK ASZTAL
LOVAGJAINAK HISTÓRIÁJA. Budapest: Magyar Helikou, 1970.

229. Brink, André P. KONING ARTHUR EN SY RIDDERS VAN DIE RONDE TAFEL
In Afrikaans oorvertel deur André P. Brink. Gabaseer op die
oorspronklike teks van Sir Thomas Mallory. Kaapstad en Pre-
toria, 1968.

230. Volpi, Domenico. ARTU E I CAVALIERI DELLA TAVOLA ROTONDA. Firen-
ze: Giunti Bemporad Marzocco, 1972.

231. Leão, Pepita de. O REI ARTUR E SENS CAVALEIROS DE SIR THOMAS MA-
LORY. n. p., 1973.

232. Bernshtein, I. M. THOMAS MALORY: LE MORTE DARTHUR. Moscow:
Nauka, 1974.

    A complete translation based on Caxton's edition with Beardsley
    illustrations at the beginning of each chapter. Critical es-
    says are at the end of the work (pp. 765-833).

233. Findeisen, Helmut. DIE GESCHICHTEN VON KÖNIG ARTUS UND DEN RIT-
TERN SEINER TAFELRUNDE. 2 vols. n. p., 1975. Published in
3 vols., illustrated by Beardsley, n. p., 1976.

h. Recordings

234. LE MORTE D'ARTHUR, adapted from Sir Thomas Malory and produced
by John Barton. Three records. Argo Record Co., 1963. RG
227-29.

    A condensed version of the last book. The text is based on
    Caxton's edition with some use of Vinaver's edition of the
    Winchester Manuscript.

235. LE MORTE D'ARTHUR; LAUNCELOT AND GUENEVER. Read by Siobhan McKen-
na. Caedmon TC 1374. 1972.

Notes on the slipcase by Helaine Newstead.

236. THE CAMBRIDGE TREASURY OF ENGLISH PROSE. Vol. 1: MALORY TO DONNE. Caedmon TC 1054.

B. STUDIES OF THE MORTE DARTHUR

1. General Bibliographies of the Arthurian Legend

and the MORTE DARTHUR

237. Wells, John Edwin. A MANUAL OF THE WRITINGS IN MIDDLE ENGLISH, 1050-1400. New Haven, Conn.: Yale University Press, 1916-52.

238. Bruce, James Douglas. THE EVOLUTION OF ARTHURIAN ROMANCE FROM THE BEGINNINGS DOWN TO THE YEAR 1300. 2 vols. Baltimore: Johns Hopkins, 1923; 2nd ed. with a bibliographical supplement by Alfons Hilka. 2 vols. in 1. Genève: Slatkine Reprints, 1974.

239. Tucker, Lena Lucille, and Allen R. Benham. A BIBLIOGRAPHY OF FIFTEENTH-CENTURY LITERATURE. [University of Washington Publications in Language and Literature.] Seattle: University of Washington Press, 1928, pp. 125-28.

240. Parry, John J., ed. A BIBLIOGRAPHY OF CRITICAL ARTHURIAN LITERATURE FOR THE YEARS 1922-29. New York: MLA, 1931.

241. Harding, Jane D. THE ARTHURIAN LEGEND: A CHECKLIST OF BOOKS IN THE NEWBERRY LIBRARY. Chicago: Newberry Library, 1933.

242. Parry, John J., and Margaret Schlauch. A BIBLIOGRAPHY OF CRITICAL ARTHURIAN LITERATURE FOR THE YEARS 1930-35. New York: MLA, 1936.

243. THE CAMBRIDGE BIBLIOGRAPHY OF ENGLISH LITERATURE. Ed. F. W. Bateson. Cambridge: Cambridge University Press, 1940. Vol. 1.

244. Parry, John J., and Paul Brown. "A Bibliography of Critical Arthurian Literature for the Year. . . ." MLQ. Vols. 1 (1940)-24 (1963).

245. Northup, Clark S., and John J. Parry. "The Arthurian Legends: Modern Retellings of the Old Stories: An Annotated Bibliography." JEGP, 43 (1944), 173-221.

246. Chambers, E[dmund] K. "Bibliography." ENGLISH LITERATURE AT
      THE CLOSE OF THE MIDDLE AGES. [Oxford History of English
      Literature, Vol. 2, Pt. 2.] Oxford: Clarendon Press, 1946,
      pp. 206-07, 229-31.

247. Holmes, Urban T. THE MEDIEVAL PERIOD. [A Critical Bibliography
      of French Literature, Vol. 1.] Syracuse, N.Y.: Syracuse Uni-
      versity Press, 1947; enlarged ed., 1952.

      See Chapter 10 ("Matière de Bretagne") by John J. Parry,
      Helaine Newstead, and William Roach.

248. Vinaver, Eugène, ed. THE WORKS OF SIR THOMAS MALORY. Oxford:
      Clarendon Press, 1947. Vol. 3, pp. 1652-58.

249. International Arthurian Society. BIBLIOGRAPHICAL BULLETIN.
      Vol. 1 (1949) -

250. Brown, Paul A. "The Arthurian Legends: Supplement to Northup
      and Parry's Annotated Bibliography with Further Supplement by
      John J. Parry." JEGP, 49 (1950), 208-16.

251. Bossuat, Robert. MANUEL BIBLIOGRAPHIQUE DE LA LITTÉRATURE FRAN-
      ÇAISE AU MOYEN AGE. Melun: d'Argences, 1951. Supplements,
      Paris: d'Argences, 1955, 1961.

252. Woledge, Brian. BIBLIOGRAPHIE DES ROMANS ET NOUVELLES EN PROSE
      FRANÇAISE ANTÉRIEURS À 1500. [Société de Publications Romanes
      et Françaises, No. 42.] Genève: Droz; Lille: Giard, 1954.
      Supplement for 1954-73. Genève: Droz, 1975.

253. Loomis, Roger Sherman, ed. ARTHURIAN LITERATURE IN THE MIDDLE
      AGES: A COLLABORATIVE HISTORY. Oxford: Clarendon Press, 1959.

254. Davies, R. T. "Bibliographical Note." ESSAYS ON MALORY. Ed.
      J. A. W. Bennett. Oxford: Clarendon Press, 1963, pp. 146-47.

255. Fisher, John H., ed. THE MEDIEVAL LITERATURE OF WESTERN EUROPE:
      A REVIEW OF RESEARCH, MAINLY 1930-1960. New York: MLA, 1966,
      pp. 100-01.

256. Vinaver, Eugène, ed. THE WORKS OF SIR THOMAS MALORY. 2nd ed.
      Oxford: Clarendon Press, 1967. Vol. 1, pp. cxxxii-cxlii.

257. Matthews, William. OLD AND MIDDLE ENGLISH LITERATURE. [Golden-
      tree Bibliographies.] New York: Appleton-Century-Crofts,
      1968.

258. THE NEW CAMBRIDGE BIBLIOGRAPHY OF ENGLISH LITERATURE. Ed. George
      Watson. Cambridge: Cambridge University Press, 1971. Vol. 1.

259. Pochoda, Elizabeth T. ARTHURIAN PROPAGANDA: 'LE MORTE DARTHUR'
      AS AN HISTORICAL IDEAL OF LIFE. Chapel Hill: University of
      North Carolina Press; London: Oxford University Press, 1971,
      pp. 141-77.

260. Wilson, Robert H. "Malory and Caxton." A MANUAL OF THE WRITINGS
      IN MIDDLE ENGLISH, 1050-1500. Ed. Albert E. Hartung. New Ha-
      ven, Conn.: Connecticut Academy of Arts and Sciences, 1972.
      Vol. 3, pp. 909-24.

                2. Studies of Malory and the MORTE DARTHUR

261. Caxton, William. Preface to the 1485 edition of the MORTE DAR-
      THUR.

262. Worde, Wynkyn de. Interpolation in Book 21, Chapter 12, of the
      1498 edition of the MORTE DARTHUR. Quoted from the 1933 Mott
      edition [no. 113], vol. 2, pp. 370-71.

      "O ye myghty and pompous lordes shynynge in the glory transy-
      tory of thys unstable lyf, as in regnynge over reames. greate
      & myghte countres. fortified wyth stronge castles & tournes,
      edified with many a ryche cite. Ye also ye fyers & myghty
      chyvalers so valyaunte in aventurous dedes of armes: Behold
      beholde: se how this myghty conquerour Arthur, whom in his
      humayne lyf, all the world doubted: ye also this noble quene
      Guenever, that sometyme sate in her chare adourned wyth golde,
      perle and precious stones: now lye full lowe in obscure fosse
      or pytte coveryd wyth cloddes of erth & clay
      "Beholde also this myghty champyon Launcelot, pyerles of
      knyghthode: se now how he lyeth grovelynge on the colde molde.
      now beynge so feble and faynt, that somtyme was so terrible:
      how & in what manere oughte ye to be so desyrous of the mon-
      dayne honour so daungerous. Therfor me thynketh this present
      boke called La mort dathur [sic] is ryght necessary to be
      radde. For in it shal ye fynde the gracious knyghtly and ver-
      tuous werre of moost noble knyghtes of the worlde, wherby they
      gate praysyng contynuell. Also me semyth by the oft redyng
      therof. ye shal gretly desyre tacustome yourself in folowynge
      those gracyous knyghtly dedes. That is to saye, to drede god,
      and love ryghtwisnes, faythfully & courageously to serve your
      soverayne prynce. And that more than god hath geven you the
      tryumfall honour, the meker ye oughte to be, ever feryng the
      unstablynesse of this dyseeyvable worlde."

      Note: Copland, East, and Stansby reprinted this interpolation
      in their editions.

263. Leland, John. ASSERTIO INCLYTISSIMI ARTURII REGIS BRITANNIAE.
      London, 1544; published under the title A LEARNED AND TRUE AS-
      SERTION OF THE ORIGINAL, [sic] LIFE, ACTES, AND DEATH OF THE
      MOST NOBLE, VALIANT, AND RENOUMED [sic] PRINCE ARTHURE. KING
      OF GREAT BRITTAINE. Newly translated into English by Richard
      Robinson. London: John Wolfe, 1582.

      Leland includes "Thomas Melorius" among the "Brittaine writ-
      ers" on whose testimonies his book is based. He remarks
      (p. 13, left): "And because I have againe entred into the
      Misteries of sacred Antiquitie and am descended a curious
      searcher into the bowels thereof, it liketh me to bring forth
      to light an other matter, namely Arthures Seale, a monument
      most cunningly engraven, auncient, and reverent. Concerning
      which, Caxodunus maketh mention, yet breefly and sclenderly
      in his preface to the history of Arthure: which the common
      people readeth printed in the English tongue."

264. Bale, John. ILLUSTRIUM MAIORIS BRITANNIAE SCRIPTORUM, HOC EST,
      ANGLIAE, CAMBRIAE, AC SCOTIAE SUMMARIUM. Ipswich, 1548; 2nd
      ed., Basel, 1557-59, under the title SCRIPTORUM ILLUSTRIUM
      MAIORIS BRYTANNIAE QUAM NUNC ANGLIAM & SCOTIAM VOCANT: CATA-
      LOGUS.

      [The following is taken from the 2nd ed., vol. 1, pp. 628-29.]

                    Thomas Mailorius. LII.

      Thomas Mailorius, genere ac patria Brytannus, heroici animi
      ac generosi studii homo, inter eius temporis alumnos, variis
      variarum virtutum & fortunarum dotibus emicuit. Est Mailoria,
      ut in antiquarum dictionum syllabo Lelandus habet, in finibus
      Cambriae regio quaedam, Devae flumini vicina, quam & alibi
      quoque a fertilitate & armorum fabrefactura commendat. Inter
      diversas reipublicae curas non remisit ille literarum studia,
      sed succisivis horis historias legere dulcissimum decebat,
      & quasdam in ipsis jucundae vetustatis, reliquias quasi prae
      oculis videre. Unde in earum lectione diutissime versatus, ex
      multis authoribus, & libris Latine ac Gallice scriptis, magno
      labore collegit, atque in linguam nostram vertit.
                    Acta regis Arthuri, Lib. 1.
                    De mensa rotunda eiusdem Lib. 1.
      Praeter haec nihil eum edidisse novi, nec in bibliopolarum
      officinis amplius quicquam vidi. Ab huius libris, aniles fa-
      bulas, quibus abundat, necessario resecandas esse putarim, ut
      veritas in historia servetur. Clarvisse his diebus fertur.

      Note: Bale's association of Malory with Wales is based on the
      following statements by John Leland. (1) "Mailoria, regio
      in finibus Cambriae Devae flu. vicina. Et hęc quidem dividitur
      in Cambrianan, quę nunc Bromefeld, & Saxonicam." ["Syllabus

et interpretatio antiquarum dictionum." GENETHLIACON ILLUS-
TRISSIMI EĀDUERDI. London, 1543 [1544], p. 44; also, THE
ITINERARY OF JOHN LELAND THE ANTIQUARY, ed. Thomas Hearne.
Oxford, 1769, vol. 9, p. xxxvii.] (2) An account of "Eng-
lisch Maylor" and "Walch Maylor" on the south and north sides
of the River Dee, respectively. [ITINERARY, ed. Hearne, 1769,
vol. 5, pp. 31-33; THE ITINERARY OF JOHN LELAND, ed. Lucy T.
Smith. London, 1964 [1907], vol. 3, pp. 69-71.]

265. Ascham, Roger. THE SCHOLEMASTER. London: Printed by John Daye,
     1570, pp. 27-28.

     A famous denunciation of the MORTE DARTHUR. "In our forefa-
     thers tyme, whan Papistrie, as a standyng poole, covered and
     overflowed all England, fewe bookes were read in our tong,
     savyng certaine bookes of Chevalrie, as they sayd, for pas-
     time and pleasure, which, as some say, were made in Monaster-
     ies, by idle Monkes, or wanton Chanons: as one for example,
     MORTE ARTHURE: the whole pleasure of which booke standeth
     in two speciall poyntes, in open mans slaughter [sic], and bold
     bawdrye: In which booke those be counted the noblest Knightes,
     that do kill most men without any quarell, and commit fowlest
     aduoulteres by sutlest shiftes: as Sir Launcelote, with the
     wife of King Arthure his master: Syr Tristram with the wife
     of King Marke his uncle: Syr Lamerocke with the wife of King
     Lote, that was his own aunte. This is good stuffe, for wise
     men to laughe at, or honest men to take pleasure at. Yet I
     know, when Gods Bible was banished the Court, and MORTE ARTHURE
     received into the Princes chamber. What toyes, the dayly
     readyng of such a booke, may worke in the will of a yong ientle-
     man, or a yong mayde, that liveth welthelie and idlelie, wise
     men can judge, and honest men do pitie. And yet ten MORTE
     ARTHURES do not the tenth part so much harme, as one of these
     bookes, made in Italie, and translated in England.

     Note: In TOXOPHILUS [London: Edward Whytchurch, 1545], Ascham
     alludes to the MORTE DARTHUR in the Preface: "In our fathers
     tyme nothing was red, but bookes of fayned chevalrie, wherin
     a man by redinge, shuld be led to none other ende, but onely
     to manslaughter and baudrye. Yf any man suppose they were good
     ynough to passe the time with al, he is deceyved. For surelye
     vayne woordes doo woorke no smal thinge in vayne, ignoraunt,
     and younge mindes, specially yf they be gyven any thynge ther-
     unto of theyr owne nature."

266. Laneham, Robert. Letter describing the visit of Elizabeth I to
     Kenilworth, 1575. [See no. 289.]

267. [Gascoigne, George.] THE PRINCELYE PLEASURES AT THE COURTE OF
     KENELWOORTH: THAT IS TO SAYE, THE COPIES OF ALL SUCH VERSES,
     PROSES, OR POETICALL INVENTIONS, AND OTHER DEVICES OF PLEASURE,
     AS WERE THERE DEVISED, AND PRESENTED, BY SUNDRY GENTLEMEN,

BEFORE THE QUENE'S MAIESTIE, IN THE YEARE 1575. Imprinted at
London, by Rychard Ihones, 1576. Rpt. London: F. Marshall,
1821. Or see THE COMPLETE WORKS OF GEORGE GASCOIGNE. Ed.
John W. Cunliffe. Cambridge: Cambridge University Press,
1907-10; rpt. Grosse Point, Michigan: Scholarly Press, 1969,
vol. 2, pp. 91-131.

The "Ladie of the Lake" and Merlin are characters in the entertainment and attest to the popularity of the MORTE DARTHUR during Elizabeth's reign.

268. Camden, William. REMAINES OF A GREATER WORKE, CONCERNING BRIT-
      AINE, THE INHABITANTS THEREOF, THEIR LANGUAGES, NAMES, SUR-
      NAMES, EMPRESES, WISE SPEECHES, POËSIES, AND EPITAPHES.
      London: Simon Waterson, 1605.

      Camden's attribution of the origins of the names Lancelot and
      Tristram to the MORTE DARTHUR ("king Arthurs historie") attests
      to its popularity. See pp. 61, 71.

269. Stansby, William. Preface to the 1634 edition of the MORTE DAR-
      THUR [no. 117]. Reprinted in the Wright edition [no. 121].

270. Dugdale, William. ANTIQUITIES OF WARWICKSHIRE ILLUSTRATED;
      FROM RECORDS, LEIGER-BOOKS, MANUSCRIPTS, CHARTERS, EVIDENCES,
      TOMBES, AND ARMES. London: Thomas Warren, 1656; 2nd ed., rev.
      and augmented by William Thomas. 2 vols. Osborn and Longman,
      1730. Numerous later editions.

      Genealogical and biographical materials relating to the War-
      wickshire Malorys and to Richard Beauchamp, Earl of Warwick.
      See 1656 ed., pp. 55-56; 2nd ed., 1730, vol. 1, pp. 81-83.
      [John Malory] "left issue Thomas; who, in K. H. 5. time, was
      of the retinue to Ric. Beauchamp E. Warr. at the siege of
      Caleys, and served there with one lance and two Archers; re-
      ceiving for his lance and I. Archer xx.li. per an. and their
      dyet; and for the other Archer, X. marks and no dyet.
      "This Thomas, being a Kt. in 23. H. 6. served for this shire
      in the Parliam. then held at Westm. and dying 14 Martii
      10. E. 4. lyeth buryed under a marble in the Chappell of Sir
      Francis at Gray Friers, near Newgate in the Suburbs of London"
      (p. 56, col. b).

271. Nicolson, William. THE ENGLISH HISTORICAL LIBRARY: OR, A SHORT
      VIEW AND CHARACTER OF MOST OF THE WRITERS NOW EXTANT, EITHER
      IN PRINT OR MANUSCRIPT; WHICH MAY BE SERVICEABLE TO THE UNDER-
      TAKERS OF A GENERAL HISTORY OF THIS KINGDOM. London, 1696.

      This reference attests to the popularity of the MORTE DARTHUR.
      "Tho. Malory (a Welsh Gentleman) wrote King Arthur's Story in
      English; a Book that is, in our Days, often sold by the Ballad-

singers with the like Authentick Records of Guy of Warwick and
Bevis of Southampton" (vol. 1, p. 98).

272.   Warton, Thomas. OBSERVATIONS ON THE FAERIE QUEENE OF SPENSER.
       London: R. and J. Dodsley, 1754; 2nd ed., corrected and en-
       larged, 2 vols., London: R. and J. Dodsley, 1762; rpt. New
       York: Greenwood Press, 1968.

       The first critical discussion of Malory in the eighteenth cen-
       tury. See 1st ed., pp. 15-28; 2nd ed., pp. 19-37. Warton
       analyzes Spenser's use of the MORTE DARTHUR in the FAERIE
       QUEENE and claims that "there is great reason to conclude. . .
       that [MORTE DARTHUR] was a favorite and reigning romance about
       the age of queen Elizabeth; or at least one very well known
       and much read at that time" (p. 21). As proof, he cites a
       passage from Robert Laneham's letter [see no. 289] which de-
       scribes the entertainment for Elizabeth at Kenilworth in 1575.
       He also claims that the MORTE DARTHUR "seems to have extended
       its reputation beyond the reign of queen Elizabeth" (p. 26).
       [See nos. 557 and 446.]

273.   Johnson, Samuel, ed. THE PLAYS OF WILLIAM SHAKESPEARE. London:
       Printed for J. and R. Tonson, 1765.

       See Vol. 8, Appendix ("Notes to the Fourth Vol."). In a note
       about p. 300, Johnson comments on the line "I remember at
       mile-end Green, when I lay at Clement's Inn, I was Sir Dagonet
       in Arthur's Shew." Johnson: "Arthur's Shew seems to have been
       a theatrical representation made out of the old romance of
       MORTE ARTHUR, the most popular one of our author's age."

274.   Warton, Thomas. THE HISTORY OF ENGLISH POETRY FROM THE CLOSE
       OF THE ELEVENTH TO THE COMMENCEMENT OF THE EIGHTEENTH CENTURY.
       London: J. Dodsley, 1774-81; 2nd ed., 1775-81; revised by
       W. Carew Hazlitt, London, 1871.

       Warton believes that Stephen Hawes was probably familiar with
       Caxton's edition of the MORTE DARTHUR (see footnote, vol. 2,
       p. 235) and that "much, if not most" of the MORTE DARTHUR was
       based on the French romance of LANCELOT. Warton comments on
       Shallow's line ("I was then Sir Dagonet in ARTHUR'S SHOW") in
       HENRY IV, PART 2: "ARTHUR'S SHOW, here supposed to have been
       presented at Clement's-inn, was probably an interlude or masque,
       which actually existed, and was very popular, in Shakespeare's
       age: and seems to have been compiled from Mallory's MORTE
       ARTHUR, or the history of King Arthur, then recently published,
       and the favorite and most fashionable romance" (vol. 2, p. 405).

275.   Scott, Walter, ed. Introduction. SIR TRISTREM; A METRICAL RO-
       MANCE OF THE THIRTEENTH CENTURY BY THOMAS OF ERCILDOUNE, CALLED
       THE RHYMER. Edited from the Auchinleck MS. Edinburgh:

Archibald Constable, 1804; 2nd ed., 1806; 3rd ed., 1811; 4th
ed., 1819.

"The HISTORY OF TRISTREM was not, so far as I know, translated
into English as a separate work; but his adventures make a
part of the collection, called the MORTE ARTHUR, containing
great part of the history of the Round Table, extracted at
Hazard, and without much art or combination, from the various
French prose folios on that favourite topic. This work was
compiled by Sir Thomas Malory, or Maleore, in the ninth year
of the reign of Edward IV. and printed by Caxton. It has since
undergone several editions, and is in the hands of most antiquaries and collectors. Those, unaccustomed to the study of
romance, should beware of trusting to this work, which mis-
represents the adventures, and traduces the character of Sir
Gawain, and other renowned Knights of the Round Table" (1st
ed., p. lxxx).

Note: In the 3rd ed., 1811, the following sentence was added
at the end of this paragraph: "It is, however, a work of
great interest, and curiously written in excellent old English,
and breathing a high tone of chivalry."

276. Ellis, George. SPECIMENS OF EARLY ENGLISH METRICAL ROMANCES.
      3 vols. London: Longman, Hurst, Rees and Orme, 1805.

      Ellis calls the MORTE DARTHUR a "mere compilation." He does
      not believe that the author of the Stanzaic MORTE ARTHUR used
      Malory's work as a source. See vol. 1, pp. 308, 368.

277. Burnett, George. SPECIMENS OF ENGLISH PROSE-WRITERS, FROM THE
      EARLIEST TIMES TO THE CLOSE OF THE SEVENTEENTH CENTURY. 3
      vols. London: Longman, Hurst, Rees and Orme, 1807.

      See vol. 1, pp. 247-59. Burnett quotes Caxton's prologue and
      selected passages. He thinks that Malory was a Welsh priest.

278. Scott, Walter. MARMION; A TALE OF FLODDEN FIELD. Edinburgh:
      Archibald Constable, 1808.

      See Note 1 in "Notes to Canto First," pp. iii-v. "The Romance
      of the Morte Arthur [sic] contains a sort of abridgment
      of the most celebrated adventures of the Round Table; and,
      being written in comparatively modern language, gives the
      general reader an excellent idea of what romances of chivalry
      actually were. It has also the merit of being written in pure
      old English; and many of the wild adventures which it contains,
      are told with a simplicity bordering upon the sublime."

279. Weber, Henry, ed. METRICAL ROMANCES OF THE THIRTEENTH, FOUR-
      TEENTH, AND FIFTEENTH CENTURIES. Edinburgh: Archibald Con-
      stable, 1810. Vol. 3, pp. 363-64.

Weber notes the resemblance of Ipomydon to Libeaus Desconus
and Malory's Beaumains. He says that Malory "undoubtedly
borrowed" his story from either IPOMYDON or LIBEAUS DESCONUS.
[Benson revived Weber' theory. See no. 884.]

280. Scott, Walter. "Romance." SUPPLEMENT TO THE FOURTH, FIFTH,
AND SIXTH EDITIONS OF THE ENCYCLOPAEDIA BRITANNICA. Edinburgh:
Archibald Constable, 1824. Vol. 6, pp. 435-56. Reprinted in
THE MISCELLANEOUS PROSE WORKS OF SIR WALTER SCOTT, 1834, vol.
6, pp. 127-216; and in ESSAYS ON CHIVALRY, ROMANCE, AND THE
DRAMA [Chandos Classics], London: Frederick Warne, [1888].

"Sir Thomas Malory, indeed, compiled from various French au-
thorities, his celebrated MORTE D'ARTHUR, indisputably the
best Prose Romance the language can boast" (p. 455). Scott
says that Gawain is "usually represented as courteous; Kay
as rude and boastful; Mordred as treacherous; and Sir Launcelot as a true, though sinful lover, and in all other respects
a model of chivalry" (p. 440).

281. Watt, Robert. BIBLIOTHECA BRITANNICA; OR A GENERAL-INDEX TO
BRITISH AND FOREIGN LITERATURE. Edinburgh: Archibald Constable, 1824. Vol. 2, p. 638.

"This Romance seems to have been drawn from many French and
Welsh writers. It is composed in a very legendary style, and
shows the compiler to have been a Welsh priest, as some have
already supposed."

282. Hallam, Henry. INTRODUCTION TO THE LITERATURE OF EUROPE IN THE
FIFTEENTH, SIXTEENTH, AND SEVENTEENTH CENTURIES. 4th ed.
London: John Murray, 1854. Vol. 2, p. 218.

Hallam calls the MORTE DARTHUR a "translation from several
French romances" written in a "very spirited language."

283. "Literature of the Legends of King Arthur." CHRISTIAN EXAMINER,
67 (Nov. 1859), 391-408.

The author discusses the 1858 Wright edition [no. 121] and
the theme of conflict of good and evil in the MORTE DARTHUR.
See pp. 394-95.

284. "La Mort D'Arthur." DUBLIN UNIVERSITY MAGAZINE, 55 (April 1860),
497-512.

Plot summary of the MORTE DARTHUR with commentary.

285. Marsh, George P. THE ORIGIN AND HISTORY OF THE ENGLISH LANGUAGE
AND OF THE EARLY ENGLISH LITERATURE IT EMBODIES. London:
Sampson Low, 1862; revised ed., New York: Charles Scribner's
Sons, 1885.

Marsh criticizes Southey's remarks on Malory's language [no.
120] as "very superficial criticism" and claims that "The Morte
d'Arthur [sic] is not . . . a work of English invention, nor,
on the other hand, is it just to style it simply a translation.
No continuous French original of it is known; but it is a
compilation from various French romances, harmonized and connected so far as Malorye was able to make a consistent whole
of them, by supplying here and there links of his own forg-
ing" (p. 487).

286. Furnivall, Frederick J., ed. LA QUESTE DEL SAINT GRAAL IN THE
      FRENCH PROSE OF (AS IS SUPPOSED) MAISTRES GAUTIERS MAP, OR
      WALTER MAP. Printed for the Roxburghe Club. London: J. B.
      Nichols and Sons, 1864. [Also listed as no. 61.]

      "I cannot find that any separate English translation of LA
      QUESTE exists. But this is less to be regretted, inasmuch as
      Syr Thomas Maleore, in his most pleasant jumble and summary of
      the Arthur Legends, has, with a true instinct, abstracted the
      Quest at much greater length than the other portions of the
      story, rightly recognising its greater beauty and deeper spir-
      itual meaning" (p. iii).

287. Strachey, Edward. "Interpolations in Southey's 'Morte D'Arthur.'"
      ATHENAEUM, 1867, pt. 2, p. 306.

      Strachey believes that eighteen pages of interpolations in the
      1817 Southey edition were taken by Upcott, the textual editor
      of the edition, from the 1634 Stansby edition and not from the
      Spencer copy of the Caxton edition on which the Southey edi-
      tion was based. [See also ATHENAEUM, 1867, pt. 2, p. 807;
      and no. 288.]

288. _____. "[Interpolations in] Southey's 'Morte Arthur'"
      [sic].   ATHENAEUM, 1868, pt. 1, pp. 323-24.

      Strachey concludes that Upcott used the Wynkyn de Worde edition
      of 1498 to supply the eighteen interpolated pages in the 1817
      Southey edition [see no. 287].

289. Furnivall, Frederick J., ed. CAPTAIN COX, HIS BALLADS AND BOOKS;
      OR ROBERT LANEHAM'S LETTER. London: Taylor and Co., 1871.
      Reprinted as ROBERT LANEHAM'S LETTER. London: For the New
      Shakspere [sic] Society by Kegan Paul, Trench, Trübner and Co.,
      1890, 1907.

      Furnivall reprints Robert Laneham's letter, in which Laneham
      describes Elizabeth's visit to Kenilworth in 1575, a certain
      Captain Cox, and ballads and books that Cox knew (see pp. 28
      f). Among these is "King Arthurz book" which Furnivall iden-
      tifies with the MORTE DARTHUR (see pp. xv-xvi). In his

commentary, Furnivall credits the downfall of Arthur's kingdom to Arthur's begetting of Mordred.

Note: One ballad sung by a minstrel to Elizabeth ["a sollem song, warranted for story out of King Arthurz acts, the first booke and 26. chapter" (see pp. 41-42)] is also called "King Ryence's Challenge" and is printed in Francis James Child, ENGLISH AND SCOTTISH BALLADS, 1858, vol. 1, pp. 121-23; and in Thomas Percy, RELIQUES OF ANCIENT ENGLISH POETRY, 1765, vol. 3, pp. 25-27.

290. Odgers, W. Blake. KING ARTHUR AND THE ARTHURIAN ROMANCES; A PAPER READ BEFORE THE BATH LITERARY AND PHILOSOPHICAL ASSOCIA-TION. Dec. 22nd, 1871. London: Longmans, Green; Bath: William Lewis, [1872].

Odgers compares Malory and Tennyson to Homer and Virgil (pp. 56-61).

291. Minto, William. CHARACTERISTICS OF ENGLISH POETS FROM CHAUCER TO SHIRLEY. Edinburgh and London: William Blackwood, 1874; 2nd ed., 1885.

See "Sir Thomas Malory," pp. 104-11. Minto discusses the structure and unity of the MORTE DARTHUR. He sees the figure of Arthur as the main unifying force but says that "it is vain to look for any profound and consistent unity in such a compilation of the unconcerted labours of different authors" (p. 107).

292. Preston, Harriet W. "The Arthuriad." ATLANTIC MONTHLY, 38 (Aug. 1876), 129-42.

A general comparison of the Arthurian materials of Geoffrey of Monmouth, French romance, Malory, and Tennyson.

293. Brink, Bernhard ten. GESCHICHTE DER ENGLISCHEN LITERATUR. Ed. Alois Brandl. Strassburg: Trübner, 1893 [1877]. Bd. 2, pp. 396-98. Translated as HISTORY OF ENGLISH LITERATURE. [Bohn's Standard Library.] London: George Bell, 1896. Vol. 3 [trans. L. Dora Schmitz], pp. 43-46.

Ten Brink discusses the structure of the MORTE DARTHUR. He believes that the work is primarily a compilation but does have a "kind of unity" (p. 46).

294. Trautmann,Moritz. "Der Dichter Huchown und seine Werke." ANGLIA, 1 (1878), 109-49.

See pp. 145-46. Trautmann believes that Malory ("der Zusammen-stoppler") made extensive use of the Alliterative MORTE ARTHURE in Book 5.

295. "Geoffrey of Monmouth." ENCYCLOPAEDIA BRITANNICA. 9th ed.
      Edinburgh: Adam and Charles Black, 1879. Vol. 10, p. 173,
      col. 1.

      The author claims that the MORTE DARTHUR is the English ILIAD.

296. Gladstone, W[illiam] E. GLEANINGS OF PAST YEARS, 1844-78. Vol.
      II: PERSONAL AND LITERARY. London: John Murray, 1879.

      See Chapter 3, pp. 150-54. Gladstone compares late redactions
      of the Arthurian romances, including the MORTE DARTHUR, with
      late redactions of the Charlemagne romances.

297. Clarke, J[ohn] R. KING ARTHUR: HIS RELATION TO HISTORY AND FIC-
      TION; A LECTURE DELIVERED TO THE GLOUCESTER LITERARY AND SCIEN-
      TIFIC SOCIETY. Gloucester: John Bellows, Steam Press, [1880].

      A summary and appreciation of the MORTE DARTHUR with comments
      on theme, characterization, and Malory's personality.

298. Cox, George W. AN INTRODUCTION TO THE SCIENCE OF COMPARATIVE
      MYTHOLOGY AND FOLKLORE. London: Kegan Paul, 1881.

      "There can be no question that in the chronicle of Malory we
      have a number of stories, the connexion between some of which
      is very slender, and which have been pieced together with no
      great dexterity and skill" (p. 313).

299. Paris, Gaston. "Études sur les Romans de la Table Ronde. Lance-
      lot du Lac. II. Le Conte de la Charrette." ROMANIA, 12
      (1883), 459-534.

      See pp. 498 f. Paris states that Malory was chiefly a trans-
      lator. He examines Book 19, Chapters 1 - 9, which differ
      from Chrétien de Troyes' version of the cart episode. Malory's
      version is divided into two sections, the first of which is
      based on a French source independent of that which Chrétien
      used; the second part derives ultimately from Chrétien's ver-
      sion.

300. Branscheid, P. "Über die Quellen des Stabreimenden MORTE AR-
      THURE." ANGLIA, 8 (1885), 179-236.

      See pp. 220-21. Malory's use of the Alliterative MORTE AR-
      THURE in Book 5.

301. McNeill, George P., ed. SIR TRISTREM. [Publications of the
      Scottish Text Society.] Edinburgh and London: William Black-
      well, 1886.

      For brief comments on Malory's use of the Tristan story, see
      p. xxiii.

302. Nutt, Alfred. [Review article.] Ernest Rhys, ed., MALORY'S
      HISTORY OF KING ARTHUR AND THE QUEST OF THE HOLY GRAIL. ACAD-
      EMY, 29 (1886), 195-96.

      Nutt denies both that the MORTE DARTHUR is an "epic" and that
      the Grail quest has "'spiritual significance.'" He concludes
      that the MORTE DARTHUR is a "late attempt at fusing into some
      sort of whole a number of independent, often discordant, sto-
      ries." [See no. 303.]

303. Strachey, Edward. "Caxton's 'Morte Darthur.'" ACADEMY, 29
      (1886), 220.

      A response to Nutt's statement [no. 302] that Rhys's edition
      (a reprint of Wright's reprint of the 1634 Stansby edition)
      is a faithful reproduction of Caxton's text. Strachey claims
      that the Stansby edition has about 20,000 variants from Cax-
      ton's edition and that his own Globe Edition is the only one
      to reproduce Caxton's original text.

304. Märtens, Paul. "Zur Lanzelotsage: Eine literarhistorische Un-
      tersuchung." ROMANISCHE STUDIEN. Ed. Eduard Boehmer. Bonn:
      Eduard Weber, 1888. Bd. 5, Heft 18, pp. 557-706.

      See p. 562. Malory's use of the French Prose LANCELOT and
      some bibliographical information about the Wright and Strachey
      editions.

305. Nutt, Alfred. STUDIES ON THE LEGEND OF THE HOLY GRAIL. London:
      David Nutt, 1888.

      "Malory is a wonderful example of the power of style. He is
      a most unintelligent compiler. He frequently chooses out of
      the many versions of the legend, the longest, most wearisome,
      and least beautiful; his own contributions to the story are
      beneath contempt as a rule. But his language is exactly what
      it ought to be, and his has remained in consequence the classic
      English version of the Arthur story" (p. 236).

306. Sommer, H. Oskar. "The Relationship of the Several Editions of
      Malory's 'Morte Darthur.'" ACADEMY, 34 (1888), 273.

      Sommer describes the black-letter editions and their textual
      relationships.

307. Russell, Edward R. THE BOOK OF KING ARTHUR. A Paper read before
      the Literary and Philosophical Society of Liverpool on the 16th
      of December, 1889. Liverpool: D. Marples, 1889.

      General discussion of style, characterization, and structural
      weaknesses of the MORTE DARTHUR. Russell claims that the

morality of the work must not be censured by comparison with
contemporary moral standards. He finds the MORTE DARTHUR in-
ferior to works of the Renaissance. "The charm of it must be
admitted; the value of it is but moderate" (p. 37).

308. Ryland, F[rederick]. "The Morte D'Arthur." THE ENGLISH ILLUS-
      TRATED MAGAZINE, 6 (1888-89), 55-64, 86-92.

      This article is illustrated with wood-engraved drawings by
      Henry Ryland. F[rederick] Ryland discusses the narrative
      structure of the MORTE DARTHUR. He believes that Malory was
      more than a translator: "His share in the work must not be
      overlooked. . . . He deserves at any rate the honour which is
      due to patient editing" (pp. 55-56). He compares the work to
      medieval art and architecture, emphasizing that, in both,
      form is subordinated to subject matter. Both have "rich multi-
      plicity of detail," "wealth of ornament," and are "essentially
      excursive and episodical" (p. 57). The chief unifying element
      in the MORTE DARTHUR is the "element of prophecy" which raises
      the reader's suspense.

309. Tennyson, Alfred. "To the Queen." THE WORKS OF ALFRED LORD
      TENNYSON. London and New York: Macmillan, 1888. Vol. 3,
      lines 34-45 of the poem.

                                    --But thou, my Queen,
      Not for itself, but thro' thy living love
      For one to whom I made it o'er his grave
      Sacred, accept this old imperfect tale,
      New-old, and shadowing Sense at war with Soul
      Rather than that gray king, whose name, a ghost,
      Streams like a cloud-man-shaped, from mountain peak,
      And cleaves to cairn and cromlech still; or him
      Of Geoffrey's book, or him of Malleor's, one
      Touch'd by the adulterous finger of a time
      That hover'd between war and wantonness,
      And crownings and dethronements.

310. Sommer, H. O. "The Facsimile Pages in Lord Spencer's Copy of
      Malory's 'Morte Darthur.'" ACADEMY, 35 (1889), 95, 288.

      Sommer discusses the twenty-one pages lacking in Lord Spencer's
      copy of the MORTE DARTHUR (on which the 1817 Southey edition
      is based) and which were later added to Lord Spencer's copy
      from the Osterley Park copy of Caxton's edition by Whittaker.
      Sommer collates the original with the facsimile pages and
      finds very few variants.

311. "An Arthurian Journey." ATLANTIC MONTHLY, 65 (June 1890), 811-29.

      Summaries of and commentary on the Arthurian works of Malory
      and Tennyson. "The prose Morte d'Arthur [sic] is a patchy bit

of work; the edges of the scraps seldom meet exactly. It is
easy to recognize different versions of one story in several
adventures which are narrated as happening at distinct times
and places. Even by its own system of chronology and geography there are discrepancies and contradictions; it is full of
clumsy translations. . . . But the same spirit animates the
whole book, and that was infused by Sir Thomas Malory" (p. 821).

312. Brown, Anna Robertson. "Wynkyn de Worde's 'Morte Darthur.'"
      ACADEMY, 38 (1890), 91; reply by H. O. Sommer, p. 112.

      Brown states tht two of the ten leaves missing from the 1498
      Wynkyn de Worde edition may be found in Douce Fragments 10,
      Bodleian Library. Sommer replies that he knew of the fragments
      but that they are not related to the 1498 edition.

313. Kellner, Leon, ed. Introduction. CAXTON'S BLANCHARDYN AND EG-
      LANTINE. E.E.T.S., E.S., No. 58. London: Trübner and Co.,
      1890; rpt. 1906.

      Kellner discusses Caxton's syntax and uses some examples from
      the MORTE DARTHUR.

314. Minto, W[illiam]. "English Scholars and the 'Morte Darthur.'"
      ACADEMY, 38 (1890), 273-74.

      A reply to L. Johnson's review of Sommer's edition [ACADEMY,
      38 (1890), 237-39]. Minto claims that English scholars deserve
      more credit for their work on the MORTE DARTHUR than Johnson
      allows. He cites Strachey's Globe Edition as an example.

315. Sommer, H. Oskar. "The Sources of Malory's 'Le Morte Darthur.'"
      ACADEMY, 37 (1890), 11-12.

      Source and manuscript information for each of the twenty-one
      books of the MORTE DARTHUR. Sommer claims that Malory is no
      "mere translator" but an adapter of English and foreign mate-
      rials. "He evidently endeavoured--and with no little measure
      of success--to weld into an harmonious whole the immense mass
      of French romance. After a comparison with his sources, his
      work gives the impression that he did not servilely copy his
      originals, but that he had read various versions, and that he
      impressed upon the whole the stamp of his own originality"
      (p. 11).

316. "Dunheved." "Sir Thomas Malory's 'Castle Terabil.'" N & Q,
      Ser. 7, vol. 12 (1891), 412; Ser. 8, vol. 4 (1893), 232-33.

      The author identifies Malory's "Castle Terabil" with "Dunheved
      Castle, Launceston," sometimes called "Castle Terrible."
      [See no. 318.]

317. Rhŷs, John. STUDIES IN THE ARTHURIAN LEGEND. Oxford: Clarendon
      Press, 1891.

      Rhŷs discovers the origins of some of the characters, places,
      and stories of the MORTE DARTHUR in Welsh myth.

318. Robbins, Alfred F. "Sir Thomas Malory's 'Castle Terabil.'"
      N & Q, Ser. 7, vol. 12 (1891), 41.

      Robbins suggests that "Castle Terabil" is the castle of Launces-
      ton, sometimes called "Castle Terrible." [See no. 316.]

319. Römstedt, Hermann. DIE ENGLISCHE SCHRIFTSPRACHE BEI CAXTON.
      Göttingen, 1891.

      A 54-page dissertation on Caxton's phonology. Baldwin [no. 326]
      calls this work useful.

320. Strachey, Edward. "Le Morte Darthur." LITERARY OPINION: AN
      ILLUSTRATED REVIEW OF ENGLISH AND FOREIGN LITERATURE, 7 (July
      1891), 108-09.

      A review of Sommer's edition [no. 123] with bibiliographical
      information about editions of the MORTE DARTHUR and the history
      of the sales of the two copies of the Caxton edition.

*321. Norton, Samuel Wilber. "The Verb in Malory's MORTE D'ARTHUR."
       Dissertation. University of Michigan, 1892.

322. Hales, John W. "Malory." ENGLISH PROSE SELECTIONS. Ed. Henry
      Craik. London and New York: Macmillan, 1893. Vol. 1, pp.
      60-76.

      Hales uses only Caxton's preface to supply biographical infor-
      mation about Malory. He says that the MORTE DARTHUR is "ar-
      ranged with remarkable skill and judgment. . . written in a
      style of wonderful simplicity and of wonderful effectiveness"
      (pp. 60-61).

323. L[ee], S[idney]. "Sir Thomas Malory." DICTIONARY OF NATIONAL
     BIOGRAPHY. Ed. Leslie Stephen and Sidney Lee. London: Smith,
     Elder, and Co., 1893. Vol. 35, pp. 439-40.

     Lee surveys the candidates for the authorship of the MORTE
     DARTHUR, lists Malory's sources, discusses his use of them,
     and praises his style.

324. Littledale, Harold. ESSAYS ON LORD TENNYSON'S IDYLLS OF THE KING.
     London and New York: Macmillan, 1893.

     Littledale states that "it is not impossible that Malory's
     standpoint was that of the quasi-historian at least as much

as of the romance-writer. These legends had a concrete reality for him that they have not for us, and whenever he feels
that he is too unreal, he shelters himself by saying that so
it is written in the French Book" (p. 24).

325. Murray, James A. H. "'Daw' in Malory's 'Morte Darthur.'" ACAD-
EMY, 44 (1893), 464.

In his edition [no. 123], book 11, chapter 10, Sommer defines
"daw" as "to moisten, sprinkle with cold water." Murray defines it as "to awake from a swoon."

326. Baldwin, Charles Sears. THE INFLECTIONS AND SYNTAX OF THE MORTE
D'ARTHUR OF SIR THOMAS MALORY: A STUDY IN FIFTEENTH-CENTURY
ENGLISH. Boston: Ginn and Co., 1894.

In the preface, Baldwin claims that the "linguistic value of
the MORTE D'ARTHUR is equal to its literary value." His book
is a linguistic study of the work as representative of the
period between Chaucer and Spenser.
    a. ATHENAEUM, 1894, pt. 2, p. 386.
    b. K. Bülbring, BEIBLATT ZUR ANGLIA, 5 (1895), 323.
    c. CRITIC, N.S. 23 (1895), 473.
    d. N. Kellner, ENGLISCHE STUDIEN, 22 (1899), 79.

327. Capper, E. "The Kamalot of Romance." GOOD WORDS, 35 (1894),
37-42.

Capper suggests possible geographical locations for Camelot
and other places in the MORTE DARTHUR.

328. Hempl, George. "The Verb in the 'Morte D'Arthur.'" MLN, 9
(1894), 240-41.

A study of the inflected verbs in the MORTE DARTHUR. Hempl
corrects Baldwin's study [no. 326] with the help of an unpublished thesis [no. 321]. See reply by Baldwin [no. 333].

329. Kittredge, G[eorge] L[yman]. "Sir Thomas Malory, or Maleore."
JOHNSON'S UNIVERSAL CYCLOPAEDIA, 5 (1894), 498.

Kittredge first proposes in print the identification of Sir
Thomas Malory of Warwickshire as the author of the MORTE DAR-
THUR.

330. McNary, Sarah J. "Beowulf and Arthur as English Ideals." POET-
LORE, 6 (1894), 529-36.

McNary praises Malory as a writer who told the "composite" Arthurian legend in "strong prose."

331. Raleigh, Walter. THE ENGLISH NOVEL, BEING A SHORT SKETCH OF ITS
      HISTORY. New York: Charles Scribner's; London: John Murray,
      1894; rpt. 1925.

      See pp. 13-17. Raleigh denies that the MORTE DARTHUR has a
      "finely ordered artistic structure" but sees within it excel-
      lent narrative qualities and style. Malory is an "artist con-
      scious of his art" (p. 14).

332. Strachey, Edward. "Talk at a Country House: 'Down to Tower'd
      Camelot.'" ATLANTIC MONTHLY, 73 (1894), 46-55.

      A defense of Malory and the MORTE DARTHUR and an advertisement
      for Strachey's Globe Edition. He presents his views in the
      narrative framework of a question-and-answer dialogue between
      a certain "Foster" and a Squire (Strachey).

333. Baldwin, Charles Sears. "The Verb in the 'Morte d'Arthur.'"
      MLN, 10 (1895), 46-47.

      Baldwin acknowledges Hempl's corrections [no. 328].

334. Gurteen, S[tephen] Humphreys. THE ARTHURIAN EPIC. New York and
      London: G. P. Putnam's Sons, 1895; rpt. New York: Haskell
      House, 1965.

      See pp. 6 ff. and 82 ff. Gurteen claims that the MORTE DARTHUR
      is not an "original work but simply a compilation. . . . It con-
      tains no well-conceived plot, or rather no plot at all. . . .
      Still, the MORT DARTHUR, with all its imperfections, has a subtle
      magnetic charm which is irresistible" (pp. 84-85).

335. Wechssler, Eduard. ÜBER DIE VERSCHIEDENEN REDAKTIONEN DES ROBERT
      VON BORRON ZUGESCHRIEBENEN GRAAL-LANCELOT-CYKLUS. Halle:
      Niemeyer, 1895.

      Discussion of the MORTE DARTHUR and its sources (pp. 22-37).

336. Wuelker, Richard Paul. DIE ARTHURSAGE IN DER ENGLISCHEN LITERA-
      TUR. Leipzig: Edelmann, 1895.

      Wuelker quotes long passages from Caxton's preface and from
      the MORTE DARTHUR. General remarks on Malory's historical con-
      text, Caxton's role as editor, and characterization.

337. Blake, C. J. "The Creators of English Romance. I. Sir Thomas
      Malory and the 'Morte D'Arthur.'" GREAT THOUGHTS FROM MASTER
      MINDS, 26 (Oct. 1896), 35-36.

      Summary of Caxton's preface and the MORTE DARTHUR. Blake
      calls Malory's style "simple" and "lucid."

338. Dixon, Frederick. "The Round Table." TEMPLE BAR, 109 (Sept.-
      Dec. 1896), 201-13.

See pp. 209-12. Dixon believes that Malory is no "mere literary carpenter" but used his materials with an "individuality entirely his own" (p. 210). He defends the morality of the work.

339. Kittredge, George Lyman. "Who Was Sir Thomas Malory?" HARVARD STUDIES AND NOTES IN PHILOLOGY AND LITERATURE, 5 (1896), 85-106; rpt. Boston, 1897.

See no. 329. Kittredge argues that Sir Thomas Malory of New-bold Revel, Warwickshire, mentioned in Dugdale's ANTIQUITIES OF WARWICKSHIRE [no. 270], wrote the MORTE DARTHUR because his life parallels the biographical information provided by Caxton's preface, the conclusion of the final book, and the colophon. "From these passages it appears that any Sir Thomas Malory advanced as the author. . . must fulfill the following conditions: (1) He must have been a knight; (2) he must have been alive in the ninth year of Edward IV, which extended from March 4, 1469, to March 3, 1470 (both included); (3) he must have been old enough in 9 Ed. IV to make it possible that he should have written this work. Further, Caxton does not say that he received the 'copy' directly from the author, and his language may be held to indicate that Malory was dead when the book was printed. In this case he must have died before the last day of July (or June), 1485, and we have a fourth condition to be complied with" (pp. 86-87). Kittredge attacks John Rhŷs's proposal that Malory was Welsh. He believes that the Warwickshire Malory is the same Malory mentioned by Williams [no. 340] as being excluded from a general pardon issued 8 Ed. IV. Kittredge summarizes this argument in no. 342. [For studies which advance Kittredge's argument, see nos. 376, 406, 418, 434, 463; for opposition to his argument, see no. 697.]
a. Gaston Paris, ROMANIA, 27 (1898), 321.

340. Williams, T. W. "Sir Thomas Malory." ATHENAEUM, 1896, pt. 2, pp. 64-65.

Williams notes the exclusion of a "Thomas Malorie, miles" from a pardon issued 8 Edward IV (in a Wells Cathedral manuscript). He believes that Malory may have fled to the continent and that the inclusion of his name among a number of Welsh names may indicate that he was a Welshman.

341. _____. "Sir Thomas Malory." ATHENAEUM, 1896, pt. 2, p. 98.

Williams believes that a pardon cited in Warkworth's CHRONICLE is identical to the one mentioned in no. 340. [For objection to this view, see no. 339, p. 89, footnote 1.]

342. Kittredge, George L[yman]. "Sir Thomas Malory and His Family."

SELECTIONS FROM SIR THOMAS MALORY'S MORTE DARTHUR. Ed. William
Edward Mead. [Athenaeum Press Series.] Boston and London:
Ginn and Co., 1897.

A summary of Kittredge's argument that Sir Thomas Malory of
Warwickshire wrote the MORTE DARTHUR [see nos. 329, 339].
Information on the family and career of Richard Beauchamp, Earl
of Warwick, Malory's military commander.

343. Martin, A. T. "Sir Thomas Malory." ATHENAEUM, 1897, pt. 2, pp.
      353–54.

      Martin announces the discovery and summarizes the contents of
      the will of Thomas Malory of Papworth, Huntingdonshire, dated
      September 16, 1469, and proved October 27, 1469. Martin be-
      lieves that this Malory may be identical to the "Thomas Malorie
      miles" exempted from a general pardon granted 8 Edward IV [see
      no. 340].

344. P[aris], G[aston]. "Fragment du 'Vallet à la cote Mal taill iee.'"
      ROMANIA, 26 (1897), 276–80.

      See p. 280. Paris believes that Gareth's nickname should be
      "Beau Mauvais" instead of "Beaumayns" and that Malory misinter-
      preted it.

345. Rhys, Ernest. "Sir Thomas Malory and the Morte d'Arthur." LI-
      BRARY OF THE WORLD'S BEST LITERATURE, ANCIENT AND MODERN. Ed.
      Charles Dudley Warner. New York: R. S. Peale and J. A. Hill,
      1897. Vol. 17, pp. 9645–54.

      Rhys thinks it "highly probable" that Malory was a Welsh cleric.
      Malory is "much more than the mere compiler and book-maker that
      some critics have been content to call him."

346. Saintsbury, George. THE FLOURISHING OF ROMANCE AND THE RISE OF
      ALLEGORY. New York: Charles Scribner's Sons; London: William
      Blackwood, 1897; rpt. London, 1907.

      Saintsbury thinks the MORTE DARTHUR is a very moral work. Ma-
      lory's task in adapting the Vulgate Cycle was to "adjust and
      bring out the full epic completeness of the legend" (p. 127).

347. [Tennyson, Hallam.] ALFRED LORD TENNYSON: A MEMOIR. BY HIS
      SON. London: Macmillan and Co., 1897.

      See vol. 1, p. 194. Hallam Tennyson quotes a letter from Ed-
      ward Fitzgerald in which Fitzgerald reported a conversation
      between himself and Alfred Lord Tennyson. "Of the Chivalry Ro-
      mances he said to me, 'I could not read "Palmerin of England"
      nor "Amadis," nor any other of those Romances through. The

"Morte d'Arthur" is much the best: there are very fine things
in it, but all strung together without Art.'"

348. Weston, Jessie L. THE LEGEND OF SIR GAWAIN. [Grimm Library, No.
      7.] London: David Nutt, 1897.

      Weston finds Malory's treatment of Gawain "remarkably inconsis-
      tent." Lancelot supplants Gawain in importance. See pp. 103 ff.

349. Martin, A. T. "The Identity of the Author of the 'Morte d'Ar-
      thur,' with Notes on the Will of Thomas Malory and the Genea-
      logy of the Malory Family." ARCHAEOLOGIA, 56 (1898), 165-82.

      Martin discusses two Thomas Malorys: Thomas Malory of Papworth,
      Huntingdonshire (died 1469), and Thomas Malory "miles" (died
      1471 according to the Northampton Inquisition of that year).
      Martin believes that the latter is probably the Sir Thomas Ma-
      lory excluded from a general pardon issued 8 Edward IV and that
      the title "miles" is the only information which connects him
      with the MORTE DARTHUR. He believes that the Papworth Malory
      wrote the work and uses a statement by John Bale [no. 264] to
      make the identification.

350. _____. "'Mailoria' and Sir Thomas Malory." ATHENAEUM,
      1898, pt. 2, p. 98.

      Martin connects Thomas Malory of Papworth with the area called
      "Mailoria" in Shropshire, which John Bale associated with the
      writer of the MORTE DARTHUR [no. 264].

351. _____. "Society of Antiquaries--June 16." ATHENAEUM,
      1898, pt. 1, p. 827, col. 1.

      Martin believes that Thomas Malory of Papworth wrote the MORTE
      DARTHUR. The fact that the birthplace of this Malory is close
      to the area "Mailoria" which John Bale identified with Malory
      [see no. 264] favors his argument. Martin concedes that his
      argument is weakened by the fact that the Papworth Malory was
      never called a "knight." [See note in ATHENAEUM, 1898, pt. 2,
      p. 98, col. 3, for discussion of possible locations for "Mail-
      oria."]

352. Saintsbury, George. A SHORT HISTORY OF ENGLISH LITERATURE. Lon-
      don: Macmillan, 1898; rpt. New York: St. Martin's Press, 1960.

      See pp. 195-97. Saintsbury calls the MORTE DARTHUR a "great
      and original book" (p. 196). Malory "grasped, and this is his
      great and saving merit as an author, the one central fact of
      the story--that in the combination of the Quest of the Graal
      with the loves of Lancelot and Guinevere lay the kernel at
      once and the conclusion of the whole matter. And last (his

great and saving merit as a writer) he told his tale in a manner which is very nearly impeccable" (p. 197).

353. Walther, Marie. MALORY'S EINFLUSS AUF SPENSER'S FAERIE QUEENE.
Dissertation. Heidelberg. Rpt. Eisleben: August Klüppel,
[1898].

General remarks about the MORTE DARTHUR in the opening pages.
Walther claims that parallels of characterization, narrative
plan, and detail show that the work exerted considerable influence on Spenser's FAERIE QUEENE.

354. Chrétien de Troyes. LANCELOT (DER KARRENRITTER). Ed. Wendelin
Foerster. [Christian von Troyes sämtliche erhaltene Werke.]
Halle: Niemeyer, 1899.

See vol. 4, pp. xxx ff.for a comparison of the knight of the
cart story in the works of Chrétien de Troyes and Malory.

355. Newcomen, George. "The Lovers of Launcelot (A Critical Study of
Sir Thomas Malory's Epic.)" NEW IRELAND REVIEW, 11 (1899),
44-50.

Newcomen stresses that the MORTE DARTHUR should not be read
with preconceived notions derived from nineteenth-century adaptations of the work. MORTE DARTHUR is not an "immoral"
work, but "like a true artist, Malory puts before us [a] picture of human frailty and of inevitable fate" (p. 45).

356. Ranken, J. "Tintagel." ART JOURNAL, N.S. 15 (1899), 19-24.

A description of Tintagel, Cornwall, and its Arthurian associations, with drawings by F. W. Sturge.

357. Weston, Jessie L. KING ARTHUR AND HIS KNIGHTS: A SURVEY OF AR-
THURIAN ROMANCE. [Popular Studies in Mythology, Romance, and
Folklore, No. 4.] London: David Nutt, 1899.

Weston emphasizes that Malory's work does not follow early
Arthurian legends.

358. Bruce, J[ames] Douglas. "The Middle English Metrical Romance
'Le Morte Arthur,' [Harleian MS. 2252]: Its Sources and Its
Relation to Sir Thomas Malory's 'Morte Darthur.'" ANGLIA, 23
(1900), 67-100.

This article begins the controversy between Bruce and Sommer
over the relationship of the Stanzaic MORTE ARTHUR and Malory's
later books, a relationship which Sommer initially discussed
in volume 3 of his edition of the MORTE DARTHUR [no. 123].
Sommer, according to Bruce, believes that Malory did adapt the

Stanzaic MORTE ARTHUR. In Bruce's opinion, Malory did not adapt the work; both versions derive from a common source, a modified version of the Mort Arthur section of the Old French Prose LANCELOT. Bruce summarizes his argument in no. 365.

359. Hughes, Thomas. THE MISFORTUNES OF ARTHUR. Ed. Harvey Carson Grumbine. [Li terarhistorische Forschungen, Heft 14.] Berlin: Emil Felber, 1900.

In the Introduction, Grumbine discusses the influence of the MORTE DARTHUR on Hughes' play, which Grumbine believes is less than generally thought.

360. Schüler, Meier. SIR THOMAS MALORYS 'LE MORTE D'ARTHUR' UND DIE ENGLISCHE ARTHURDICHTUNG DES XIX JAHRHUNDERTS. Strassburg: Singer, 1900.

Though Schüler's study concentrates on nineteenth-century English adaptations of the MORTE DARTHUR, it contains bibliographical information about nineteenth-century editions of the work, lists abridgements and modernizations, and contains some comments by nineteenth-century writers, critics, and editors about the importance of the work.

361. Smith, G[eorge] Gregory. THE TRANSITION PERIOD. Vol. 4 of PERIODS OF EUROPEAN LITERATURE. Ed. [George] Saintsbury. London and Edinburgh: William Blackwood; New York: Charles Scribner's Sons, 1900.

See pp. 330-33. An impressionistic description of Malory's style. "It is not that Malory is ingenuously simple, or takes no pains in the selection of vocabulary, or arranges the matters of Arthur at haphazard, but rather that he conceals the means by which he obtains his complete result" (p. 331).

362. Weston, Jessie L. THE LEGEND OF SIR LANCELOT DU LAC. [Grimm Library, No. 12.] London: David Nutt, 1901.

See pp. 45 f. Use of the Lancelot story in the MORTE DARTHUR. Weston claims that Malory's source for this material was not Chrétien de Troyes.

363. "Humour in Malory." ACADEMY, 62 (1902), 17-18.

The author uses Book 5, Chapter 5, as an example of the "unconscious humour" in the MORTE DARTHUR, which usually derives from "quaint" and "archaic" words whose meanings have changed since Malory's time.

364. Brown, Arthur C. L. "Iwain: A Study in the Origins of Arthurian Romance." HARVARD STUDIES AND NOTES IN PHILOLOGY AND LITERATURE, 8 (1903), 1-147.

See pp. 142–44. Brown notes similarities between the GARETH section and Chrétien de Troyes' IVAIN. Malory's version, a "late and extremely confused form" of the story, derives from an old Celtic tale that was reworked by some transcriber who knew the IVAIN.
a. W. A. Nitze, MLN, 19 (1904), 82.

365. Bruce, J[ames] Douglas, ed. Introduction. LE MORTE ARTHUR, A ROMANCE IN STANZAS OF EIGHT LINES. E.E.T.S., E.S., No. 88. London: Kegan Paul, Trench, Trübner, and Co., 1903, pp. vii-xxx.

Bruce believes that Sommer's study of Malory's sources [no. 123, vol. 3, pp. 249 ff.] is derivative. He summarizes the argument that he made against Sommer's work in no. 358.

366. Garnett, Richard, and Edmund Gosse. ENGLISH LITERATURE: AN ILLUSTRATED RECORD. London: William Heinemann; New York: Macmillan, 1903. Vol. 1, pp. 258-64.

General survey article. The authors stress Malory's powers of narration.

367. Gilson, J. P. "Sir Thomas Malory." ATHENAEUM, 1903, pt. 1, p. 275.

Gilson thinks that a Thomas Malory who was a member of the Malory family of Kirkby Malory, Leicestershire, may have written the MORTE DARTHUR.

368. Paton, Lucy Allen. STUDIES IN THE FAIRY MYTHOLOGY OF ARTHURIAN ROMANCE. [Radcliffe College Monograph, No. 13.] Boston, 1903; 2nd ed., enlarged with a Survey of Scholarship on the Fairy Mythology Since 1903 and a Bibliography by Roger Sherman Loomis. [Burt Franklin Bibliographical Series, No. 18.] New York: Burt Franklin, 1960.

Paton discusses the Celtic fairy queen motifs in Arthurian romance, including the MORTE DARTHUR.

369. Duff, Edward Gordon. WILLIAM CAXTON. Chicago: Caxton Club, 1905.

See pp. 63-65. Duff calls the MORTE DARTHUR "perhaps the most interesting volume Caxton ever printed" and describes the history of the ownership of the two copies of the Caxton edition.

370. Ker, W. P. ESSAYS ON MEDIEVAL LITERATURE. New York and London: Macmillan, 1905.

See pp. 22-27. Ker believes that Malory created an artistic work and a prose style of his own.

371. Snell, F[rederick] J[ohn]. THE AGE OF TRANSITION, 1400-1580. In
     HANDBOOKS OF ENGLISH LITERATURE. Ed. John W. Hales. London:
     George Bell and Sons, 1905. Vol. 2, pp. 83-90.

     Snell presents a fuller critical discussion than is found in
     most literary histories of this time. He condemns the theory
     that Malory was Welsh and prefers the Warwickshire candidate
     proposed by Kittredge. Malory is a "creative artist" (p. 87)
     and "essentially a poet" (p. 88); his style is "genial, unob-
     trusive, dignified, rich in feeling, and clear in expression"
     (pp. 87-88). In general, Snell opposes the view that the
     MORTE DARTHUR is immoral, but he does say that the "great blot
     of the book is undoubtedly its want of respect for the sanctity
     of marriage" (p. 89).

372. Sommer, H. Oskar. "On Dr. Douglas Bruce's Article: 'The Middle-
     English "Le Morte Arthur."'" ANGLIA, 29 (1906), 529-38.

     Sommer replies to Bruce's criticism of his interpretation of
     the relationship between the MORTE DARTHUR and the Stanzaic
     MORTE ARTHUR [see nos. 358, 365]. Sommer claims that his opin-
     ions are not derivative and that Bruce either misread or misin-
     terpreted his opinions. "What I thought and still think is,
     that while writing this portion of his work, Malory had besides
     a French source, a copy of 'Morte Arthur' as represented by the
     Harl. MS. before him, and to this fact the peculiar coincidences
     and similarities etc. are due." [See Bruce's reply, no. 374.]

373. Weston, Jessie L. THE LEGEND OF SIR PERCEVAL. [Grimm Library,
     Nos. 17, 19.] 2 vols. London: David Nutt, 1906-09.

     See vol. 2, p. 287. Weston refers to "Malory's noble and dig-
     nified prose."

374. Bruce, J[ames] Douglas. "A Reply to Dr. Sommer." ANGLIA, 30
     (1907), 209-16.

     Bruce, adamant in his opinions on the relationship between the
     MORTE DARTHUR and the Stanzaic MORTE ARTHUR, writes a heated
     reply to Sommer [no. 372].

375. Golther, Wolfgang. TRISTAN UND ISOLDE IN DEN DICHTUNGEN DES MIT-
     TELALTERS UND DER NEUEN ZEIT. Leipzig: Hirzel, 1907.

     See pp. 365 f. and 384 f. Golther stresses the importance of
     Malory's version of the Tristan legend for nineteenth-century
     poets.

376. Maynadier, [Gustavus] Howard. THE ARTHUR OF THE ENGLISH POETS.
     London: Constable and Co.; New York: Houghton Mifflin, 1907;
     rpt. Boston: Houghton Mifflin, 1935.

See Chapter 13 (pp. 218-46). Maynadier quotes passages from
Kittredge's article on the Warwickshire Thomas Malory [no. 339].
That Malory had some originality is seen in his conception of
a plan for the MORTE DARTHUR, his emphasis on Arthur as a central figure, and his selection of story, incident, and detail.
On the other hand, Maynadier believes that Malory's characterizations are weak and that the unity of the MORTE DARTHUR is
disturbed by multiplicity of incident. The best feature of
the work is Malory's style, which has "beautiful rhythm" and
is "dignified, simple, and generally direct."

Note: On p. 246, Maynadier quotes a letter of Kittredge. In
it Kittredge corrects the date of the Warwickshire Malory's
death from March 14, 1470, to 1471. [Also see no. 418.]
   a. ACADEMY, 73 (Nov. 31, 1907), 182-84.
   b. CONTEMPORARY REVIEW, 112 (Dec. 1907), Literary Supp. 3,
      pp. 11-13.
   c. NATION, 84 (June 27, 1907), 594-95; 85 (Aug. 8, 1907),
      117-18.
   d. Arthur Machen, "The Matter of Romance" in THE GLORIOUS
      MYSTERY (Chicago: Covici-McGee, 1924), pp. 49-56.

377. S.-B., R. "Sir Thomas Malory." N & Q, Ser. 10, vol. 7 (1907),
     88.

The author suggests that a "Thomas Malarie [sic] miles," excluded from a general pardon granted by Edward IV in 1469, may
have written the MORTE DARTHUR.

378. Proby, William (Earl of Carysfort), ed. THE PAGEANTS OF RICHARD
     BEAUCHAMP, EARL OF WARWICK, REPRODUCED IN FACSIMILE FROM THE
     COTTONIAN MS. JULIUS E. IV. [Roxburghe Club, No. 151.] Oxford:
     Privately Printed, 1908.

These "pageants" (53 pencil drawings which depict episodes
from the life of Richard Beauchamp, Earl of Warwick) and the
accompanying commentaries are sometimes said to be the work of
John Rous, the Warwickshire antiquarian. Proby doubts this.

Note: The pageants and commentary are printed also in Joseph
Strutt, HORDA ANGEL-CYNNAN (London, 1775-76), vol. 2, pp. 121 ff.

379. Brown, A[rthur] C. L. "Balin and the Dolorous Stroke." MP, 7
     (1909), 203-06.

Brown calls attention to the publication of the DEMANDA DEL
SANCTO GRIAL, the Spanish version of Malory's source for Book
2. Before its publication only the Huth manuscript, which
lacks two leaves in the section where the dolorous stroke is
described, was known. Brown finds a Celtic analogue to Malory's
story of the dolorous stroke in "The Blinding of Cormac."

380. Carter, Charles Henry. "Ipomedon, an Illustration of Romance
     Origin." HAVERFORD ESSAYS: STUDIES IN MODERN LITERATURE. . .
     F. B. GUMMERE. Haverford, Penn., 1909, pp. 235-70.

     Carter notes that the Book of GARETH is similar to both IPOME-
     DON and LE BEL INCONNU but does not attempt to analyze the
     source relationships specifically.

381. Griffith, Reginald Harvey. "Malory, Morte Arthure, and Fiera-
     bras." ANGLIA, 32 (1909), 389-98. Also in Collected Mono-
     graphs, n. d., vol. 312.

     Griffith believes that Book 5 of the MORTE DARTHUR derives
     from the MORTE ARTHURE, which derives in turn from FIERABRAS.
     He notes Christian-Pagan parallels between the characters Ga-
     wain and Priamus in the MORTE DARTHUR, and Oliver and Fierabras
     in FIERABRAS. [See no. 838.]

*382. Williams, T. W. SIR THOMAS MALORY AND THE MORTE DARTHUR. Bris-
     tol, n. p., 1909.

383. Dawson, Canon. "The Morals of the Round Table: Malory's 'Morte
     d'Arthur' Compared with the 'Idylls of the King.'" LIVING
     AGE, 267 (Dec. 3, 1910), 606-10.

     Dawson judges Malory and the MORTE DARTHUR by late nineteenth-
     century standards and assumes that Malory's aim in writing
     his work should have been that of Tennyson and other Victorian
     poets. Dawson stresses the ideal of chivalry in Malory's
     work but considers Malory and his age barbaric.

384. W[eston], J[essie] L. "Sir Thomas Malory." ENCYCLOPAEDIA BRI-
     TANNICA. 11th ed. New York: Encyclopaedia Britannica, Inc.,
     1910. Vol. 17, p. 496.

     Weston accepts Kittredge's Warwickshire Malory as the author
     of the MORTE DARTHUR. In this work (an "imperishable monument
     of English language and literature"), Malory's best feature is
     his prose style. She claims that Malory does not attempt to
     reconcile contradictions in his sources (for example, the
     characterization of Gawain).

385. Brown, Arthur C. L. "Chrétien's 'Yvain.'" MP, 9 (1911), 109-28.

     See p. 118. Brown draws parallels between an old version of
     the YVAIN and an incident in the MORTE DARTHUR, Book 7. "It
     does not seem to me absurd to hold that the late and confused
     story in Malory may retain primitive incidents lost in the
     YVAIN, e.g. the Isle of 'Avylyon,' and Lynet's conjuring up a
     knight to fight Gareth."

386. Jones, W[illiam] Lewis. KING ARTHUR IN HISTORY AND LEGEND.
      Cambridge: Cambridge University Press, 1911; New York: G. P.
      Putnam, 1912.

      See pp. 1-10, 113-15. Jones discusses Caxton's preface. He
      is critical of the value of source study for study of the MORTE
      DARTHUR and states that Malory is important for his prose style
      and for his story of Arthur and the Round Table.

387. Lawrence, William Witherle. MEDIEVAL STORY. New York: Columbia
      University Press, 1911; 2nd ed., 1926.

      See pp. 137-38. Lawrence emphasizes Malory's role as a trans-
      lator. "His whole rendering of the Arthurian story. . . is
      like the Indian summer of the age of chivalry."

388. Saintsbury. George. A HISTORY OF ENGLISH PROSE RHYTHM. London:
      Macmillan; Bloomington: Indiana University Press, 1912; rpt.
      1965.

      See pp. 82-92. Saintsbury dismisses the question whether Ma-
      lory "compiled" his work. Malory "supplied a mortar of style
      and a design of word-architecture for his brute material of
      borrowed brick or stone, which is not only miraculous, but, in
      the nature even of miraculous things, uncompilable from any
      predecessor" (p. 82). The MORTE DARTHUR is stylistically
      graceful and dignified and shows a "quite new rhythm." Saints-
      bury praises the skilful mixture of narrative and dialogue and
      claims that, though Malory's achievement may have been "half-
      accidental," his influence on the next century was greater
      than has been realized.

389. Schofield, William Henry. "Malory." CHIVALRY IN ENGLISH LITERA-
      TURE: CHAUCER, MALORY, SPENSER AND SHAKESPEARE. [Harvard
      Studies in Comparative Literature, No. 2.] Cambridge: Harvard
      University Press; London: Oxford University Press, 1912, pp.
      75-123.

      Schofield admits that the MORTE DARTHUR has "faults" and "in-
      consistencies," but he upholds the artistic value of Malory's
      work. He calls Ascham [no. 265] a "prejudiced pedant" (p. 79)
      and says that Malory's depiction of chivalry had a didactic
      aim. The MORTE DARTHUR is a "work of retrospect, tinged with
      sadness for the passing of the good old days; a work of ideal-
      ism, troubled with knowledge of miserable facts daily indulged;
      a work of patriotism, written when the land was being wasted
      by civil strife; a work of encouragement to the right-minded,
      and of warning to the evil-minded, among men of that class in
      which the author lived and moved" (p. 87).

390. Bruce, J[ames] Douglas. "The Development of the Mort Arthur

Theme in Mediaeval Romance." ROMANIC REVIEW, 4 (1913), 403-71.

Bruce makes a detailed comparison of how Malory's Books 18, 20, and 21 differ from their source, the MORT ARTU. "Malory's changes. . . in nearly all instances are due to the desire to compress the narrative into a smaller compass. He effects his purpose. . . by omissions and by combining conversations or episodes that are separated in M[ORT] A[RTU]" (p. 424).
   a. E. Brugger, ZFSL, 47 (1925), 98-105.

391. Saintsbury, George. THE ENGLISH NOVEL. [The Channels of English Literature.] London: J. M. Dent; New York: E. P. Dutton, 1913.

Saintsbury calls Malory an "artist," not a "compiler." He believes that Malory had "what no compiler as such can have--because the moment he has it he ceases to be a compiler, and becomes an artist--the sense of grasp, the power to put his finger, and to keep it, on the central pulse and nerve of the story. That he did this deliberately is so unlikely as to be practically impossible: that he did it is certain" (p. 27). Furthermore, he says that Malory successfully connected what he calls the three motifs of chivalry and romance--Valour, Love, and Religion--and that he had considerable success in depicting character.

392. Spence, Lewis. A DICTIONARY OF MEDIEVAL ROMANCE AND ROMANCE WRITERS. London: George Routledge and Sons; New York: E. P. Dutton, 1913.

Book-by-book plot summary of the MORTE DARTHUR.

393. Baldwin, Charles Sears. AN INTRODUCTION TO ENGLISH MEDIEVAL LITERATURE. New York and London: Longmans, Green, and Co., 1914.

See pp. 161-69. Baldwin is critical of Malory and his work. He believes that Malory looked to the past (idealized chivalry) and ignored the present (the War of the Roses), and that his work is a "typical collective romance. . . made. . . by aggregation" (p. 165). The "childish compound sentences" of Malory's prose are "characteristic, not of Malory, but of the half-formed sentence habit of his time" (pp. 166-67).

394. Bausenwein, Josef. "Die poetischen Bearbeitungen der Balin-und Balansage von Tennyson und Swinburne und ihr Verhältnis zu Malory." Dissertation. Heidelberg: Würzburg, 1914.

The chief interest of this study is Tennyson and Swinburne, but Bausenwein does compare the Strachey, Wright, and Sommer editions of the MORTE DARTHUR.

395. Fromm, Charlotte. ÜBER DEN VERBALEN WORTSCHATZ IN SIR THOMAS
      MALORYS ROMAN 'LE MORTE DARTHUR.' Marburg, 1914.

      Part I consists of an etymological index of verbs, with origins
      and probable origins of Old English, Old Norse, German, French,
      and Latin verbs; Part 2 discusses historical and stylistic sig-
      nificance of Malory's usage. Fromm concludes that Malory uti-
      lized vocabulary with great skill.

396. Morris, William. Letter to the PALL MALL GAZETTE; rpt. in THE
      COLLECTED WORKS OF WILLIAM MORRIS. . . WITH INTRODUCTIONS BY
      HIS DAUGHTER MAY MORRIS. London: Longmans, Green and Co.,
      1914. Vol. 22, p. xv.

      Morris includes the MORTE DARTHUR among a list of books which
      "profoundly impressed" him. "I know this is an ill-digested
      collection of fragments, but some of the best of the books it
      is made from (Lancelot is the best of them) are so long and so
      cumbered with unnecessary matter that one is thankful to Mal-
      lory after all."

397. Saintsbury, George. A FIRST BOOK OF ENGLISH LITERATURE. London:
      Macmillan, 1914.

      See pp. 60-61. Saintsbury says that Malory's style is the
      "most perfect of the kind shown in any language." It is "so
      perfect and final" that "it has had no continuation in English:
      it has been imitated, but that is all" (p. 60).

398. D'Evelyn, Charlotte. "Sources of the Arthur Story in Chester's
      LOVES MARTYR." JEGP, 14 (1915), 75-88.

      D'Evelyn notes "close verbal resemblances" between LOVES MARTYR
      and the opening chapters of the MORTE DARTHUR.

*399. Gilchrist, Olive Bacon. "The Moral Code of Chivalry as Reflected
      in Malory's MORTE D'ARTHUR." Dissertation. Boston University,
      1916.

400. Pulver, J. "Music in Malory's 'Arthur.'" MUSICAL NEWS, 51 (1916)
      377; revised in MONTHLY MUSICAL RECORD, 59 (1929), 3-4.

      The references to music in the MORTE DARTHUR provide information
      about secular medieval music in general. For example, Tristram's
      association with the harp shows that music was one of the accom-
      plishments of a gentleman.

401. Quiller-Couch, Arthur. "On the Capital Difficulty of Prose." ON
      THE ART OF WRITING: LECTURES DELIVERED IN THE UNIVERSITY OF
      CAMBRIDGE 1913-1914. Cambridge: Cambridge University Press,
      1916.

See pp. 107-10. Description of Malory's prose style as simple and beautiful.

402. Scudder, Vida D. LE MORTE DARTHUR OF SIR THOMAS MALORY AND ITS SOURCES. New York: E. P. Dutton; London: J. M. Dent, 1917. Rpt. as LE MORTE DARTHUR OF SIR THOMAS MALORY; A STUDY OF THE BOOK AND ITS SOURCES, 1921.

Scudder asserts that the MORTE DARTHUR should be examined as an integrated, artistic work independent of its sources, for "the longer one studies Malory the clearer grows the conviction that his book is a coherent work of art" (p. 182). Malory's romance is a retrospective vision of the glories of the past, written for the degenerate present. While granting that the work does not show classical concepts of unity, Scudder claims that when Malory's work is compared with earlier Arthurian romances, one does feel that Malory conceived the MORTE DARTHUR as a whole. Thematically, he aims to "present the controlling interests of the Middle Ages,--love, religion, war,--in their ideal symmetry and their actual conflict. Malory's way of doing this is to tell the story of the rise and fall of chivalry with its three loyalties, to the overlord, to the lady, and to God, as symbolized in the fate of that fair fellowship, the Round Table" (p. 185). Gawain, Tristram, and Galahad symbolize these three loyalties; Lancelot embodies the clash of all three. The MORTE DARTHUR therefore has a tripartite structure which emphasizes, in turn, each of the loyalties.

Scudder has an opening discussion of Malory's predecessors and concludes the book with a brief discussion of Malory and his sources. Malory showed "great original genius" (p. 366) in creating MORTE DARTHUR from various sources; the essential difference between the work and its sources is the "intensification of purpose" (p. 402) in the former. In Scudder's view, the end of the tragedy is optimistic, showing not the triumph of evil but the sadness that comes when loyalties cannot be reconciled.

    a. George L. Hamilton, RR, 9 (1918), 345-47.
    b. R. S. Loomis, RR, 9 (1918), 441-47.
    c. W. E. Mead, JEGP, 17 (1918), 476-82.
    d. TLS, Jan. 19, 1922, p. 39.

403. Vetterman, E. DIE BALEN-DICHTUNGEN UND IHRE QUELLEN. ZRP Beiheft 60. Also Halle: Niemeyer, 1918.

See Chapter 4 (pp. 52-84). Vetterman claims that a comparison of Malory's Book of BALIN and its source, as represented by the Huth manuscript, shows that he translated from a French source now represented by that manuscript. The Book of BALIN, approximately a fourth the length of its source, is greatly indebted to the French original. After examining the additions, omissions, and alterations which Malory made, Vetterman compares

his work and the Huth manuscript in terms of characterization
and motivation and finds that Malory failed to understand his
source. The opening section of the chapter analyzes and criticizes John Rhŷs's argument that Malory was a Welshman and a
native of "Mailoria" [no. 124].
    a. R. Zenker, ARCHIV, 141 (1921), 150-61.
    b. L. H. Loomis [no. 428].

404. Vechtman-Veth, A. C. E. "Lancelot and Guinevere." ENGLISH STUD-
      IES, 3 (1921), 161-66.

      General remarks on the characterizations of Lancelot and
      Guinevere.

405. Zenker, Rudolf. FORSCHUNGEN ZUR ARTUSEPIK; 1 IVAINSTUDIEN. ZRP
      Beiheft 70. Halle: Niemeyer, 1921.

      See pp. 304 ff. Comparison of Malory's Book of GARETH and Chré-
      tien de Troyes' IVAIN and other "fair unknown" romances. Zenker
      believes that Malory's version is based on a form of the IVAIN
      older than that of Chrétien and provides evidence that such a
      version existed.

406. Chambers, E[dmund] K. SIR THOMAS MALORY. [English Association
      Pamphlet, No. 51.] London, 1922; rpt. 1976. Rpt. in SIR THOM-
      AS WYATT AND SOME COLLECTED STUDIES. London: Sidgwick and
      Jackson, 1933.

      Chambers criticizes the inconsistent characterization and lack
      of unified structure that he finds in the MORTE DARTHUR. He
      characterizes Malory's prose style as having vivid words, men-
      tion of "outdoor sights and sounds," and dialogue which is
      brief, terse, and understated. Malory's grail story, which
      Chambers believes is thematically irrelevant, is unsatisfactory
      because the "ultimate debate, upon which the fortunes of Arthur
      and his fellowship break and are dissolved, is not between the
      ideals of Camelot and the ideal of Corbenic, but a human one,
      the familiar conflict between human love and human loyalty"
      (p. 9). Books 20 and 21 are Aristotelian in structure. Cham-
      bers states that the MORTE DARTHUR does reveal moral interests
      and aristocratic ideals and that Malory wrote "with an eye on
      the fifteenth century" (p. 14).

      Note: On p. 16, Chambers uses evidence unavailable to Kittredge
      to correct some details in Kittredge's biography of the Warwick-
      shire Malory.
      a. E. C. B., MLR, 29 (1934), 493.
      b. C. S. L[ewis], [no. 476].
      c. A. Koszul, REVUE ANGLO-AMÉRICAINE, 12 (1935), 532-33.
      d. F. M. Padelford, MLN, 50 (1935), 207.
      e. Mario Praz, ENGLISH STUDIES, 17 (1935), 184-85.
      f. CHOICE, 3 (1966), 518.

407. Entwistle, William J. "Geoffrey of Monmouth and Spanish Litera-
     ture." MLR, 17 (1922), 381-91.

     Entwistle compares some sections of the NOBILIARIO, an early
     fourteenth-century work, and the death of Arthur and Guinevere
     in Malory's Book 21.

408. Loudon, K[atherine] M. TWO MYSTIC POETS AND OTHER ESSAYS. Ox-
     ford: Basil Blackwell, 1922.

     See "King Arthur: Malory and Tennyson" (pp. 31-82). Loudon
     emphasizes the role of fate in determining the events of the
     MORTE DARTHUR and sees the begetting of Mordred as the cause of
     the downfall of the Round Table. Characters are the instru-
     ments of fate.

409. Anscombe, Alfred. "Hrethel the Great in Arthurian Romance."
     N & Q, Ser. 12, vol. 12 (1923), 327-29.

     Hrethel the Great, king of the Geats and father of Beowulf's
     mother, appears in the MORTE DARTHUR as one of the eleven kings
     ruling Britain in 459 who opposed Arthur's title of dux bel-
     lorum. He is called "Cradelment," king of North Wales (Cumbria).

410. Cross, Tom Peete. "The Passing of Arthur." THE MANLY ANNIVERSARY
     STUDIES IN LANGUAGE AND LITERATURE. Chicago: University of
     Chicago Press, 1923, pp. 284-94.

     Cross asserts that the multiple versions of Arthur's passing
     caused Malory to give a confusing account of the story. The
     original source of the story is Celtic and is best preserved
     in the Irish TÁIN BÓ FRÁICH.

411. Holthausen, F. "Zum alliterierenden Morte Arthure." BEIBLATT
     ZUR ANGLIA, 34 (1923), 91-93; 36 (1925), 188.

     Placename variants in the Alliterative MORTE ARTHURE and the
     MORTE DARTHUR.

412. Loomis, Gertrude Schoepperle. "Arthur in Avalon and the Banshee."
     VASSAR MEDIEVAL STUDIES. Ed. Christabel F. Fiske. New Haven,
     Conn.: Yale University Press, 1923, pp. 3-25.

     After examining the story of Arthur's death, references to
     Avalon, and the role of Morgan in Arthurian romance, Loomis
     discusses Malory's version and his indebtedness to the MORT
     ARTU. She notes that, although Malory says that Arthur goes
     to Avalon to have his wounds healed, Morgan never says that
     she will heal them or take him to Avalon.

413. Baker, Ernest A. THE HISTORY OF THE ENGLISH NOVEL. New York:

Barnes and Noble; London: H. F. and G. Witherby, 1924; rpt.
1957. Vol. 1, chapter 6, pp. 148-207.

Baker states that the MORTE DARTHUR has "unity" because of the
focus on Arthur, the importance of the Lancelot-Guinevere passion and the quest of the Grail throughout the story, and the
theme of duty and honor. The confusing chronology and topo-
graphy deny "unity." Though the work is not a novel, it does
show Malory's interest in character and motivation. The Grail
section is especially important since events are determined
more by actions here than in other parts of the work.

414. Cooksey, Charles F. "The 'Morte D'Arthur.'" NINETEENTH CENTURY,
      95 (1924), 852-59.

      A general appreciation of the MORTE DARTHUR and discussion of
      geographical locations associated with it.

415. Brugger, E. "Der Dichter Bledri-Bleheri-Breri." ZFSL, 47 (1925),
      162-85.

      A note on the MORTE DARTHUR and the name Bleoberys appears in
      a footnote on p. 178.

416. Entwistle, William J. THE ARTHURIAN LEGEND IN THE LITERATURES
      OF THE SPANISH PENINSULA. London: J. M. Dent; New York: E.
      P. Dutton, 1925.

      A few references to the MORTE DARTHUR in connection with Span-
      ish versions of the Arthurian legend, especially the DEMANDA
      DEL SANCTO GRIAL and the BALADRO DEL SABIO MERLIN.

417. Golther, Wolfgang. PARZIVAL UND DER GRAL IN DER DICHTUNG DES
      MITTELALTERS UND DER NEUZEIT. Stuttgart: J. B. Metzler, 1925;
      rpt. New York: AMS Press, 1974.

      Golther praises Malory's originality ("Die Darstellung wirkt
      wie ein ursprüngliches englisches Werk, nicht wie eine bloße
      Übertragung aus dem Französischen") (p. 269). He also praises
      his style.

418. Kittredge, George Lyman. SIR THOMAS MALORY. Barnstable: Pri-
      vately Printed, 1925. Rpt. Folcroft, Penn.: Folcroft Library
      Editions, 1974; also rpt. Somerset Publications, 1976.

      Kittredge advances further evidence that Thomas Malory of War-
      wickshire is the only possible candidate for the authorship of
      the MORTE DARTHUR. In reply to Martin's proposal [no. 349]
      that, of the two Thomas Malorys alive in 1469 (Thomas Malory
      of Papworth, Huntingdonshire, and Thomas Malory of Newbold and
      Winwick, Warwickshire), the Papworth Malory is the most likely

contender, Kittredge claims that this opinion is incorrect
since the Papworth Malory was an "armiger" and not a "knight."
He defends, however, Martin's identification of Sir Thomas Malory of Warwickshire and Sir Thomas Malory of the Northampton
Inquisition as one and the same man. Finally, Kittredge states
that Dugdale [no. 270] was wrong to assign the date of the Warwickshire Malory's death as March 14, 10 Edward IV (1470); he
argues for a 1471 date. [See also no. 376.]

419. Ven-Ten Bensel, Elise F. W. M. THE CHARACTER OF KING ARTHUR IN
     ENGLISH LITERATURE. Amsterdam: H. J. Paris, 1925; rpt. New
     York: Haskell House, 1966.

     See Chapter 6 (pp. 139-54). According to the author, the MORTE
     DARTHUR shows Malory's "fixedness of purpose and uniformity of
     design in his grand, harmonious conception of the whole, in
     spite of his deviations, inconsistencies, and irrelevancies."
     Unity can be seen in Malory's focus on the causes of the down-
     fall and in his development of the character of King Arthur.
     Though the characterization is not consistent, Arthur does be-
     come more virtuous as he grows older and exerts a strong moral
     influence over his knights. Malory skilfully alters and blends
     the Christian and supernatural elements in the character of Ar-
     thur which he inherited from his sources. Arthur is the central
     figure of the work: his ideals give stability and purpose to
     the realm, but his followers, not understanding his goals and
     ideals, fail to maintain them.
         a. M. Gaster, FOLK-LORE, 37 (1926), 404-05.
         b. G. Hübener, BEIBLATT ZUR ANGLIA, 37 (1926), 263-65.
         c. John J. Parry, MLN, 42 (1927), 417-20.

420. Vinaver, Eugène. LE ROMAN DE TRISTAN ET ISEUT DANS L'OEUVRE DE
     THOMAS MALORY. Paris: Honoré Champion, 1925.

     Vinaver determines the sources of Malory's TRISTRAM material
     and compares them with Malory's version. He concludes that the
     TRISTRAM derives from a source now represented by three manu-
     scripts in the Bibliothèque Nationale, MSS. fr. 103, 334, and
     99. Malory's version is about one sixth as long as his source
     and is characterized by fewer knightly adventures. Moreover,
     Malory identifies characters not identified in his source,
     reduces the number of minor characters, and sometimes two
     characters into a single one. The love of Tristram and Iseut
     is one of simple human volition, not one of overwhelming pas-
     sion induced by a love potion; indeed, the love story is
     subordinated to Tristram's feats of chivalry, and Malory sup-
     presses elements in his source which do not support the empha-
     sis on chivalry. Vinaver regards Malory primarily as a
     translator but praises his command of French and his style.
         Appendices to the book are a comparison of the MORTE DARTHUR

and MSS. 103, 334, and 99; an erratum of Caxton; orthography
of proper names; and a summary table of concordances for the
French manuscripts.
a. E. Bourciez, RCHL, 93 (1926), 450-53.
b. F. Desonay, RBPH, 5 (1926), 1023-25.
c. A. Hilka, ZRP, 46 (1926), 511-12.
d. M. Roques, ROMANIA, 52 (1926), 237.
e. E. K. Chambers, MLR, 22 (1927), 97-98.
f. W. Golther, LGRP, 48 (1927), 406-08.
g. E. Brugger, ZFSL, 51 (1928), 131-69.
h. L. E. Winfrey, MP, 26 (1928), 231-33.

421. Aurner, Nellie Slayton. CAXTON, MIRROUR OF FIFTEENTH-CENTURY
LETTERS; A STUDY OF THE LITERATURE OF THE FIRST ENGLISH PRESS.
London: Philip Allan and Co., 1926; rpt. New York: Russell
and Russell, 1965.

See pp. 194-99. After praising Malory for giving later generations a great work and praising Caxton for disseminating Malory's work, Aurner discusses theme, style, and structure in the
MORTE DARTHUR.

422. Legouis, Émile. A HISTORY OF ENGLISH LITERATURE. Trans. Helen
Douglas Irvine. New York: Macmillan; London: J. M. Dent,
1926; often revised and reprinted.

An appreciative criticism of the MORTE DARTHUR as "England's
first book in poetic prose."

423. Ray, B. K. [Vesantakumāra Rāya.] "The Character of Gawain."
DACCA UNIVERSITY BULLETIN, No. 11. Published for the University of Dacca by Oxford University Press, 1926.

Ray opposes Scudder's view [no. 402] that the "inconsistencies"
in Gawain's character reveal his essential human nature, his
mixture of both good and evil. He believes that Malory's
characterization of Gawain is conflicting and that Malory was
evidently unable to reconcile the discrepancies in his sources.

424. Zenker, Rudolf. "Weiteres zur Mabinogionfrage." ZFSL, 48 (1926),
32, 57, 99.

Zenker sees resemblances between sections of the MABINOGION
and Malory's Book of GARETH. Though unknown, the source of the
GARETH section is undoubtedly French.

425. Chambers, E[dmund] K. ARTHUR OF BRITAIN. London: Sidgwick and
Jackson, 1927.

Sources for particular scenes in the MORTE DARTHUR.
a. G. H. Gerould, SPECULUM, 3 (1928), 259-62.

426. Erskine, John. "Further Gossip about King Arthur's Court; MORTE D'ARTHUR." DELINEATOR, 110 (May 1927), 44, 84, 87; revised as "Malory's LE MORTE D'ARTHUR." THE DELIGHT OF GREAT BOOKS. Indianapolis: Bobbs-Merrill, 1928, pp. 53-71.

Stories from the MORTE DARTHUR illustrate Erskine's thesis that Malory's forte is depiction of incident rather than character. He says that Malory should not be discussed from the viewpoint of Victorian interpretations of the Arthurian stories.

427. Hammond, Eleanor Prescott, ed. ENGLISH VERSE BETWEEN CHAUCER AND SURREY. London: Cambridge University Press; Durham, N. C. Duke University Press, 1927; rpt. 1965.

See pp. 33-35. Hammond has a high opinion of Malory's place in literary history and of his abilities as a prose writer. His ability to extricate causality from events and his emphasis on the theme of loyalty--that no man can uphold the three loyalties of knight to lord, lady, and God, equally--constitute his great contribution to the Arthurian legend.

428. Hibbard, Laura A. "Malory's Book of Balin." MEDIAEVAL STUDIES IN MEMORY OF GERTRUDE SCHOEPPERLE LOOMIS. New York: Columbia University Press, 1927, pp. 175-95; rpt. in ADVENTURES IN THE MIDDLE AGES by Laura Hibbard Loomis. New York: Burt Franklin, 1962, pp. 51-65.

Hibbard argues against Vetterman's conclusions about Malory's Book of Balin [no. 403]. Vetterman stated that the changes Malory made in reducing his source, the Huth MERLIN, to a fourth of its length, generally weakened the story and showed that Malory failed to understand both the story and its significance. After comparing the Book of Balin and its source, however, Loomis concludes that "with absolute unity of effect, with a terseness of style that yet keeps cadences of haunting beauty, Malory achieves in the Book of Balin a version that no one has ever bettered" (p. 196).

429. Loomis, Roger Sherman. CELTIC MYTH AND ARTHURIAN ROMANCE. New York: Columbia University Press, 1927.

Loomis refers to the Celtic sources of Malory's materials.

430. Robinson, F[rederic] W. A COMMENTARY AND QUESTIONNAIRE ON 'SELECTIONS FROM MALORY.' (EDITED BY H. WRAGG, CLARENDON PRESS.) London: Sir Isaac Pitman and Sons, 1927.

A study guide keyed for use with no. 145.

431. Byles, A. T. "Medieval Courtesy Books and the Prose Romances of

Chivalry." CHIVALRY. Ed. Edgar Prestage. London and New
York: Alfred A. Knopf, 1928, pp. 183-206.

Byles states that both Malory and Caxton emphasized that noble
birth and character is important to the knight.

432. Fox, Marjorie B. "Sir Thomas Malory and the 'Piteous History of
      the Morte of King Arthur.'" ARTHURIANA, 1 (1928), 30-36.

By considering Books 18, 19, and 21 in relation to their
sources, the Stanzaic MORTE ARTHUR and the MORT ARTU, Fox examines Malory's departures from his sources to ascertain his
artistic purpose. She concludes that he preserved the general
story but tried within individual incidents to furnish reasons
and motives for actions; he gave names to characters and towns
and created a geographical scheme; he adopted characters from
his sources but showed more interest in action than in personality; and he displayed interest in the psychology of his
characters and emphasized their nobility even in defeat.

433. Heinemann, Elfriede. DAS BILD DER DAME IN DER ERZÄHLENDEN DICH-
      TUNG ENGLANDS VON MALORY BIS SPENSER. Quakenbrück, 1928.

In the first chapter, Heinemann identifies the qualities that
characterize the women of the MORTE DARTHUR: noble birth,
beauty, kindness, wisdom, passion, devotion, loyalty, and
affinities for religion.

434. Hicks, Edward. SIR THOMAS MALORY: HIS TURBULENT CAREER. Cam-
      bridge: Harvard University Press, 1928; rpt. Octagon Books,
      1970.

Hicks' biographical study of the Warwickshire Malory is based
on Kittredge's article [no. 339] and subsequent research by
Kittredge and others, including evidence which Hicks himself
discovered in the Public Records Office. Hicks tends to excuse
Malory's criminal offenses, to cast Malory's character in the
best possible light, and to interpret the man in terms of
"biographical evidence" found in the MORTE DARTHUR. The Appendices reprint court records concerning Malory's alleged criminal offenses.
      a. TLS, Dec. 20, 1928, p. 1006.
      b. E. K. Chambers, RES, 5 (1929), 465-67.
      c. F. Delatte, RBPH, 8 (1929), 593.
      d. W. A. Nitze, MP, 26 (1929), 372-73.
      e. ARCHIV, 158 (1930), 147-48.
      f. A. C. Baugh, JEGP, 29 (1930), 452-57.
      g. C. H. Williams, HISTORY, N.S. 15 (1930), 84.
      h. E. Bernbaum, MLN, 46 (1931), 97-98.
      i. CHOICE, 8 (1971), 675.

435. Jaffray, Robert. KING ARTHUR AND THE HOLY GRAIL. New York and
     London: G. P. Putnam's Sons, 1928.

     See Chapter 13, "Malory's MORTE DARTHUR: Concluding Notes"
     (esp. pp. 165-68). Jaffray paraphrases Caxton's preface and
     the contents of each book of the MORTE DARTHUR. "Malory's
     work is easily obtainable for reference in one of the various
     reprints which have been made for modern readers; but the
     wearisome expansion of unimportant incidents makes it rather
     dull reading" (p. 168).

436. Loomis, Roger Sherman. "Gawain, Gwri, and Cuchulinn." PMLA,
     43 (1928), 384-96.

     Brief discussion of Gawain and Gareth in the MORTE DARTHUR
     and their relationships to characters in its sources.

437. Read, Herbert E. "Sir Thomas Malory and the Sentiment of Glory."
     TLS, June 21, 1928, pp. 457-58; rpt. with minor revisions as
     "Malory." THE SENSE OF GLORY: ESSAYS IN CRITICISM. Cambridge:
     Cambridge University Press, 1929, pp. 33-56; and in COLLECTED
     ESSAYS IN LITERARY CRITICISM. London: Faber and Faber, 1938,
     pp. 168-82.

     Read attempts to identify the "universal" in the MORTE DARTHUR
     to help modern readers respond to the work. To Read, the MORTE
     DARTHUR reflects the desire for glory, to be more than oneself,
     to win "worship." Glory is achievement through action, a
     search to be what one can be (potentiality) rather than what
     one is (reality). The story of Gareth particularly exemplifies
     the search for glory.
     a. NEW STATESMAN, Dec. 21, 1929, p. 369.
     b. N & Q, 157 (1929), 305.
     c. TLS, Oct. 10, 1929, p. 786.

438. Vinaver, Eugène. "Notes on Malory's Sources." ARTHURIANA, 1
     (1928), 64-66.

     Vinaver believes that the source of Book 18 is French and gives
     evidence for Malory's possible misreading of a passage in the
     MORT ARTU as proof. He also suggests that the Huth manuscript
     of MERLIN is the source for Malory's story of Merlin.

439. App, August J. LANCELOT IN ENGLISH LITERATURE: HIS ROLE AND
     CHARACTER. Washington: Catholic University of America, 1929;
     rpt. Haskell House, 1969.

     See Chapters 3 and 4 (pp. 53-90). App discusses Malory's de-
     velopment of the character of Lancelot. Lancelot is the hero
     of the Grail quest, and in this adventure he achieves true
     humility; his greatest moment of glory is his healing of Sir

Urry. At the end, however, Lancelot's lie about his involve-
ment with the Queen shows that he is less than perfect, but
even this makes Lancelot seem more human.

440. THE SYMBOLIC MEANING OF THE STORY OF KING ARTHUR. Tintagel:
Published at King Arthur's Hall, [1929].

The author interprets the events of the MORTE DARTHUR symboli-
cally. He retells the story and comments on the symbolic
meaning of each event.

441. Vinaver, Eugène. MALORY. Oxford: Clarendon Press, 1929; rpt.
with a new preface, 1970; rpt. Folcroft, Penn.: Folcroft Library Editions, 1977.

See esp. Chapters 3 ("Narrative Technique"), 4 ("Romance and
Realism") and 6 ("Camelot and Corbenic"). Vinaver believes
that the MORTE DARTHUR is a "slightly modified and condensed
translation of the French Arthurian novels" (p. 29). In reducing his sources and attempting to simplify them, Malory
sometimes made indiscriminate omissions which obscure the
narrative; he "failed to weld the rambling episodes of the
French cycle into a harmonious whole, and retained a mass of
stories unconnected with each other and often irrelevant to
the main theme" (p. 110). The TRISTRAM and GARETH sections
are examples. The MORTE DARTHUR shows tendencies toward a
"realism" that is "fundamentally prosaic and practical" (p. 51).
Fondness for "specifying the economic and legal aspects of
feudal contracts" (pp. 49-50) and descriptive details of dress
and scenery, and for suppressing the magical and supernatural
elements of the romance form characterize this realism. It is
possible that Malory failed to understand the meaning of the
Grail quest in his source because he omitted questions of religious doctrine, but Malory's aim was not to condemn but to
praise chivalry and he therefore emphasized the Grail adventure
as a feat of earthly chivalry. "Faced with two main themes and
forced to subordinate one, Malory made Corbenic a province of
Camelot" (p. 84). The turmoil of the war of the Roses led Malory
to long for the chivalric ideals of the past, and in disentangli
the threads of Arthurian romance, Malory succeeded in writing
a "national epic" (p. 110). According to Vinaver, Malory's
style--"the art of combining pathos and simplicity, romance
and epic straightforwardness"--is among his most impressive
achievements and contributes to the "strange magnetism" (p. 111)
of the MORTE DARTHUR. MALORY has three appendices: "Materials
for Malory's Biography," "The Sources of the MORTE DARTHUR,"
and "Malory's Version of the 'Quest of the Holy Grail.'" It
also has a bibliography of editions (with commentary) and of
critical works (with brief annotations), and an index.
    a. R. Bossuat, RCHL, 97 (1930), 125-27.
    b. O. Burdette, MERCURY, 20 (1930), 467-69.

c. E. K. Chambers, RES, 6 (1930), 336-39.
d. C. F., STUDI MEDIEVALI, 3 (1930), 157.
e. Edmund G. Gardner, MLR, 25 (1930), 219-22.
f. W. Golther, LGRP, 51 (1930), 183-84.
g. M. D. L., OXFORD MAGAZINE, June 19, 1930, p. 906.
h. R. S. Loomis, N.Y. HERALD-TRIBUNE BOOK SECTION, Sept. 14, 1930, p. 10.
i. N & Q, 158 (1930), 70.
j. F. Mossé, LES LANGUES MODERNES, 28 (1930), 345-46.
k. James B. Munn, SPECULUM, 5 (1930), 460-61.
l. M. R., ROMANIA, 56 (1930), 159.
m. TLS, Feb. 13, 1930, p. 115.
n. H. Waddell, NEW STATESMAN, Mar. 15, 1930, p. xii.
o. E. Bernbaum, MLN, 46 (1931), 98.
p. J. H. Falconer, ENGLISH STUDIES, 13 (1931), 15-17.
q. W. A. Nitze, MP, 28 (1931), 364-66.
r. W. Preusler, ANGLIA, 42 (1931), 17-19.
s. A. E. H. Swaen, NEOPHILOLOGUS, 16 (1931), 295-96.
t. CHOICE, 8 (1971), 554.
u. Janet M. Cowen, N & Q, N.S. 18 (1971), 310.

442. Cross, Tom Peete, and William A. Nitze. LANCELOT AND GUENEVERE: A STUDY ON THE ORIGINS OF COURTLY LOVE. Chicago: University of Chicago Press, 1930.

The authors state that the Guenevere abduction scene in the MORTE DARTHUR differs from that found in the work of Chrétien de Troyes but ultimately derives from it.

443. Gardner, Edmund G. THE ARTHURIAN LEGEND IN ITALIAN LITERATURE. New York: E. P. Dutton; London: J. M. Dent, 1930.

See Chapters 4, 7, and 9. In his discussion of Italian Arthurian literature, Gardner compares works such as the TRISTANO RICCARDIANO and the TAVOLA RITONDA with the MORTE DARTHUR.

444. Roberts, W. Wright. "William Caxton, Writer and Critic." BJRL, 14 (1930), 410-22. Also Manchester, 1930.

General comments on the MORTE DARTHUR and Caxton's preface.

445. Schutt, J. H. "A Guide to English Studies." ENGLISH STUDIES, 12 (1930), 98-108.

See pp. 102-04. Schutt calls Malory a "literary artist of considerable genius" and claims that he should be studied "as a story-teller, as a character-draughtsman, and as a prose writer" (p. 103).

446. Dennis, Leah. "The Text of the Percy-Warton Letters." PMLA, 46 (1931), 1166-1201.

This contains 38 letters of Thomas Percy and Thomas Warton, some of which refer to the MORTE DARTHUR. See esp. letter 1 [Percy to Warton, May, 1761] and letter 6 [Warton to Percy, 1761].

447. Frappier, Jean. "Sur un remaniement de la MORT ARTU dans un manuscrit du XIVe siècle: le Palatinus Latinus 1967." RO-MANIA, 57 (1931), 214-22.

This copy of the MORT ARTU contains the final parting scene of Lancelot and Guenevere, which is notably absent from the other manuscript versions of the MORT ARTU. The remanieur of this Vatican manuscript and Malory worked independently; the manuscript is not Malory's source for his version of the parting scene. Frappier judges that the Vatican version of the parting scene is superior to that in the MORTE DARTHUR.

448. Goldman, Marcus Selden. SIR PHILIP SIDNEY AND THE ARCADIA. Dissertation, 1931. Urbana: University of Illinois Press, 1934.

See Chapter 8 ("Malory's MORTE D'ARTHUR in the ARCADIA"). Goldman claims that the MORTE DARTHUR is a source of incidents, characters, setting, mood, and verbal echoes for Sidney's AR-CADIA.
    a. F. Brie, ENGLISCHE STUDIEN, 70 (1935), 287-88.
    b. F.-C. D., REVUE ANGLO-AMÉRICAINE, 12 (1935), 534-35.
    c. J. M. Purcell, PQ, 14 (1935), 379-80.
    d. TLS. April 4. 1935, p. 231.
    e. Allan H. Gilbert, JEGP, 35 (1936), 151-53.

449. Hittmair, Rudolf, ed. WILLIAM CAXTON, ENGLANDS ERSTER DRUCKER UND VERLEGER. Innsbruck: Wagner'sche Universitäts-Buchhand-lung, 1931.

This book contains a few references to Malory and the MORTE DARTHUR, which Hittmair calls the last outstanding work of the Middle Ages.

450. Buchanan, Alice. "The Irish Framework of GAWAIN AND THE GREEN KNIGHT." PMLA, 47 (1932), 315-38.

See pp. 336-37. Buchanan sees a combination of the Temptation and the Beheading Test, two Celtic motifs, in the Book of GARETH.

451. Byrne, Sister Mary. THE TRADITION OF THE NUN IN MEDIEVAL ENG-LAND. Dissertation, 1932. Washington: Catholic University of America, 1932.

Byrne states that Arthurian romances generally present a

realistic nun-abbess figure. In the MORTE DARTHUR, Perceval's
sister may represent a nun-abbess figure. Guinevere, however,
is a romanticized image of the nun.

452. Chambers, R[aymond] W. "The Continuity of English Prose from
      Alfred to More and His School." Introduction to Nicholas
      Harpsfield, THE LIFE AND DEATH OF SIR THOMAS MOORE. Ed. Elsie
      Vaughn Hitchcock. [E.E.T.S., No. 186.] London: Oxford Uni-
      versity Press, 1932, pp. xlv-clxxiv. Also rpt., London, 1950.

      See pp. cxxxviii f. and cxlviii f. Chambers says that Malory,
      though he is an important writer, is not very significant in
      the development of the English secular prose tradition; he is
      a "tributary to the main stream of continuous English prose,
      which runs strongest and deepest through the channel of our
      religious literature" (p. cxli). The prose of Sir Thomas More
      exerted more influence on the Renaissance than that of Malory.
      The humanists regarded the MORTE DARTHUR as "decaying chival-
      ry" (p. cl).

453. Dekker, Arie. SOME FACTS CONCERNING THE SYNTAX OF MALORY'S
      'MORTE DARTHUR.' Amsterdam: Portielje, 1932.

      Dekker calls Malory's language "representative" of the language
      of the late fifteenth century and discusses his grammatical us-
      age, taking examples and formulating from them rules for what
      he considers to be the most important aspects of Malory's syn-
      tax.
          a. Eilert Edwall, ANGLIA, 45 (1934), 139-40.

454. Houghton, R. E. C. "Letter of Matthew Arnold." TLS, May 19,
      1932, p. 368.

      Houghton contrasts the Tristram and Iseult story in the works
      of Arnold and Malory. "Malory, if he has not purposely de-
      graded Tristram, has weakened and obscured the utter devasta-
      tion of the lovers."

455. Lewis, Charles Bertram. CLASSICAL MYTHOLOGY AND ARTHURIAN RO-
      MANCE. London and New York: Oxford University Press, 1932.

      Similarities between Malory's Book 7 and the EREC, LE BEL IN-
      CONNU, YVAIN, FERGUS, LI CHEVALIERS AS DEUS ESPEES, the Prose
      LANCELOT, PERCEVAL continuations, and the JOIE DE LA CORT
      theme.

456. Morgan, Mary Louis. GALAHAD IN ENGLISH LITERATURE. Dissertation.
      Washington: Catholic University of America, 1932.

      See Chapter 5, "Galahad in Malory's MORTE DARTHUR" (pp. 71-89).
      Morgan discusses Malory's version of the Grail quest and

attempts to furnish further proof for Vinaver's argument about
Malory's use of the French QUESTE [see no. 441].

457. Remigereau, François. "Tristan 'Maître de Vénerie' dans la tra-
      dition anglaise et dans le roman de Thomas." ROMANIA, 58
      (1932), 218-37.

      The hunting traditions which legends say that Tristram intro-
      duced into England were ultimately of Norman origin.

458. Vinaver, Eugène. "A Romance of Gaheret." MEDIUM AEVUM, 1 (1932),
      157-67.

      Malory's Book of GARETH is a "fairly faithful adaptation" of a
      lost romance of Gawain's youngest brother Gaheret in the Prose
      TRISTAN cycle. Gareth is the same as the French Gaheret.

459. White, Irma Reed. "Loves Martyr." TLS, July 21, 1932, p. 532.

      White proposes that Chester used the 1557 Copland edition of
      the MORTE DARTHUR "in wholesale fashion" for the Arthurian ma-
      terials in LOVES MARTYR.

460. Wilson, Robert H. CHARACTERIZATION IN MALORY: A COMPARISON WITH
      HIS SOURCES. Dissertation. University of Chicago, 1932. Chi-
      cago: University of Chicago Libraries, 1934; rpt. Norwood,
      Penn.: Norwood Editions, 1975.

      Wilson seeks to determine how character portrayal in the MORTE
      DARTHUR differs from that in Malory's sources and why Malory's
      alterations are significant. He concludes that Malory identi-
      fies anonymous characters and creates more consistent charac-
      terizations than he found in his sources. Wilson believes that
      some of the major characters of the MORTE DARTHUR do achieve
      some degree of originality. Arthur is Malory's most original
      characterization: an ideal king, a just ruler, Arthur never-
      theless helps to bring about the downfall of his kingdom by his
      partiality for Gawain. On the whole, Malory's changes in char-
      acterization are important because they create characters whose
      personalities help to motivate the action.

461. _____. "Malory and the PERLESVAUS." MP, 30 (1932),
      13-22.

      A comparison of the PERLESVAUS and the MORTE DARTHUR, Book 6,
      Chapters 14-15 (the story of the Chapel Perilous). Wilson
      states that the two versions show parallels in narrative detail.
      He believes the Chapel Perilous story in the MORTE DARTHUR de-
      rives ultimately from the PERLESVAUS but that Malory may have
      used a copy of the Agravain material that incorporated this
      story from the PERLESVAUS.

462. Aurner, Nellie Slayton. "Sir Thomas Malory--Historian?" PMLA,
      48 (1933), 362-91.

      Aurner defends Kittredge's argument that Thomas Malory of War-
      wickshire wrote the MORTE DARTHUR. She believes that the MORTE
      DARTHUR "gives an unmistakeable reflection of the impressions
      which would have stamped themselves on the consciousness of a
      man living through the events which this Malory of Warwickshire
      must have experienced" (p. 362). She also thinks that many of
      the characters and events of the work are based on actual peo-
      ple and events of the first half of the fifteenth century. For
      instance, the depiction of Arthur parallels the life and per-
      sonality of Henry IV in the early books, Henry V in the middle
      books, and Henry VI in the last books. Malory transforms the
      historical events of his time into fictional events of romance
      and achieves an "allegorical presentation of the rise and down-
      fall of a united English chivalry under the Lancastrian dynasty"
      (p. 389).

463. Baugh, Albert C. "Documenting Sir Thomas Malory." SPECULUM, 8
      (1933), 3-29.

      Baugh finds more evidence concerning the Warwickshire Malory's
      alleged criminal offenses and his legal convictions, especial-
      ly Malory's part in the Coombe Abbey raid and his imprisonment.
      The evidence shows that Malory was in trouble for a ten-year
      period after his first prison conviction in 1451. Since the
      last evidence shows that Malory was imprisoned in Newgate in
      1460, Baugh thinks he may have died there.

464. Caldwell, James R., ed. EGER AND GRIME. [Harvard Studies in
      Comparative Literature, No. 9.] Cambridge: Cambridge Univer-
      sity Press, 1933.

      Caldwell suggests that a reviser of EGER AND GRIME borrowed
      the detail of Ironside's preparation for battle from the MORTE
      DARTHUR.

465. Greenwood, Alice D. CAMBRIDGE HISTORY OF ENGLISH LITERATURE.
      Ed. A. W. Ward and A. R. Waller. Vol. 2: THE END OF THE MID-
      DLE AGES. New York: Macmillan; Cambridge: Cambridge Univer-
      sity Press, 1933 [1912]. "English Prose in the Fifteenth Century."

      See pp. 335-37. A general appreciation of the MORTE DARTHUR.
      The work is a "scarcely Christianised fairy tale" and its style
      is simple and "childlike." Greenwood emphasizes its atmosphere
      of unreality. "This indescribable conviction of magic places
      Malory's characters outside the sphere of criticism, since,
      given the atmosphere, they are consistent with themselves and
      their circumstances. Nothing is challenged, analysed or em-
      phasised; curiosity as to causation is kept in abeyance;

retribution is worked out, but, apparently, unconsciously"
(p. 337).

Note: Greenwood's discussion appears on pp. 84-86 of THE CON-
CISE CAMBRIDGE HISTORY OF ENGLISH LITERATURE. [Ed.] George
Sampson. 3rd ed. rev. by R. C. Churchill. Cambridge: Cam-
bridge University Press, 1970 [1941].

466. Loomis, Roger Sherman. "The Visit to the Perilous Castle: A
Study of the Arthurian Modifications of an Irish Theme." PMLA,
48 (1933), 1000-35. Rpt. in STUDIES IN MEDIEVAL LITERATURE:
A MEMORIAL COLLECTION OF ESSAYS. New York: Burt Franklin,
1970, pp. 99-134.

See pp. 1021-23. The Book of GARETH derives from a lost
French romance that is related to the BEL INCONNU romances but
also includes details from earlier romances. The Gringamore
episode in Book 7 contains details from the Champion's Bargain
motif and the Visit to Curoi's Fortress.
a. Lewis Thrope, RBPH, 52 (1974), 198-201.

467. Sparnaay, H. HARTMANN VON AUE; STUDIEN ZU EINER BIOGRAPHIE.
Halle: Niemeyer, 1933-38. Vol. 2 (1938), pp. 21-22.

Sparnaay discusses Malory's GARETH in relation to other "fair
unknown" romances. GARETH is representative of a primitive
tale from which the IWEIN derived.

*468. Stephens, G. Arbour. MALLORY'S LAND OF GOIRE OR HOUSE OF MOST
WORSHIP. Aberystwyth, 1933.

469. Vinaver, Eugène. "The Legend of Wade in the MORTE DARTHUR."
MEDIUM AEVUM, 2 (1933), 135-36.

Vinaver believes that Lady Linet's line to Beaumains ('Were
thou a wyȝte as ever was Wade') from Book 7, Chapter 9, echoes
a passage from the Alliterative MORTE ARTHURE, line 964, which
Malory must have remembered from his use of this source in
Book 5.

470. Waite, Arthur Edward. THE HOLY GRAIL. London: Rider and Co.,
1933.

Comparisons of the story of the Grail quest in Arthurian romance, including the MORTE DARTHUR.

471. Whitehead, F[rederic]. "On Certain Episodes in the Fourth Book
of Malory's MORTE DARTHUR." MEDIUM AEVUM, 2 (1933), 199-216.

I. Whitehead conjectures from a comparison of the story of
Pelleas and Ettard in the MORTE DARTHUR and in Fr. MS. B. N.

112 (not Malory's source) that the manuscript contains essentially the same story as Malory's lost source and that differences between the two represent Malory's own changes. (In the French story, Ettard seduces Gawain; in the MORTE DARTHUR, vice-versa). Whitehead attributes the change to what he believes is Malory's lack of understanding of and lack of sympathy with the courtly love tradition. II. Malory's source for Book 4, Chapters 24–28, was similar to B. N. MS. 112. Malory made his own changes, emphasizing physical prowess in arms rather than promiscuous love interest. [See no. 582.]

472. Winkler, Gera. DAS RELATIVUM BEI CAXTON UND SEINE ENTWICKLUNG VON CHAUCER BIS SPENSER. Saalfeld: Günthers Buchdruckerei, 1933.

Winkler examines the use of relatives by both Malory and Caxton and concludes that Caxton seems to have reproduced Malory's usage.

473. "Chrétien de Troyes." TLS, Nov. 15, 1934, pp. 781–82.

Speculation about Malory's identity and his "French book" (see opening paragraph).

474. Eliot, T. S. "Le Morte Darthur." SPECTATOR, 152 (Feb. 23, 1934), 278.

In this review of the 1933 reprint of Wynkyn de Worde's 1498 edition [no. 113], Eliot compares Malory to Sophocles and Homer. "He is a kind of crude northern Homer, a fine prose writer, just lacking the poet's power over the word."

475. Kapp, Rudolf. HEILIGE UND HEILIGENLEGENDEN IN ENGLAND. Halle: Niemeyer, 1934.

See pp. 108–10. Kapp interprets the story of Galahad and the Grail quest as saint's legend.

476. L[ewis], C. S. Review of E. K. Chambers, "Sir Thomas Malory" in SIR THOMAS WYATT AND SOME COLLECTED STUDIES [no. 406]. MEDIUM AEVUM, 3 (1934), 237–40.

Lewis disagrees with the criteria by which Chambers and Vinaver interpret the Grail section of the MORTE DARTHUR. He maintains that the Round Table knights cannot be judged according to scales of "worldly-spiritual" (Vinaver) or "good-bad" (Chambers) but rather on a scale of "bad-good-best." The Grail story is not, as Chambers and Vinaver claim, ill-fitted to the whole but is "an essential part of the tragedy of Lancelot. . . that he should have been given the chance of escaping from this human level on which the tragedy is foredoomed, and should have failed to take it" (p. 240).

477. "Malory's 'Morte D'Arthur.'" BJRL, 18 (1934), 15.

A note on the reprint of the Wynkyn de Worde edition of 1498
[no. 113], the only known copy of which is in the John Rylands
Library, Manchester. "This edition may be said to bridge the
gap between Caxton's original edition of 1485, which was reproduced by Oskar Sommer in 1891, and Wynkyn de Worde's second
edition of 1529, on which most modern editions are based."

478. [Oakeshott, W. F.] "A 'Morte Darthur' Manuscript." [London]
TIMES, June 26, 1934, p. 17.

Oakeshott announces the discovery of the Winchester Manuscript
and notes that it contains numerous variants from the Caxton
edition. [W. W. Greg, in a letter to the editor, Aug. 30, 1934,
p. 13, praises this article and requests that the Winchester
Manuscript be printed in its entirety in Vinaver's forthcoming
edition.]

479. Oakeshott, W[alter] F. "A Malory Manuscript: The Discovery at
Winchester." [London] TIMES, Aug. 25, 1934, pp. 11, 12.

Oakeshott attributes the late discovery of the Winchester Manuscript to missing leaves at the beginning and end. He discusses the probable dating of the manuscript (1470 to 1480),
the importance of the colophons at the end of each tale, and
Caxton's role as editor.

480. _____. "The Text of Malory." TLS, Sept. 27,
1934, p. 650.

A description of the Winchester Manuscript, its scribal tradition, its subdivisions and colophons, and its relation to Caxton's edition and to Malory's holograph.

481. Schirmer, Walter F. "Dichter und Publikum zu Ende des 15 Jahrhunderts in England." ZAAK, 28 (1934), 220.

Schirmer believes that Malory tried to recapture the significance of a lost past for his own time.

482. Dekker, Arie. "Some Observations in Connection with B. Trnka:
On the Syntax of the English Verb from Caxton to Dryden."
NEOPHILOLOGUS, 20 (1935), 113-20.

Dekker adds verbs to Baldwin's list [no. 326] and comments on
Malory's use of verbs.

483. "Malory's Mort d'Arthur." BJRL, 19 (1935), 19-21.

This article, announcing Vinaver's forthcoming edition of the

Winchester Manuscript, contains general remarks on the manuscript and its relation to Caxton's preface and edition.

484. Oakeshott, Walter F. "Caxton and Malory's MORTE DARTHUR." GUTENBERG-JAHRBUCH, 10 (1935), 112-16.

Oakeshott claims that the discovery of the Winchester Manuscript throws light on Caxton's edition and his editorial practices and procedures. By undertaking to revise such a vast work as the MORTE DARTHUR, especially in view of his own responsibilities, Caxton showed great industry. From an examination of the Caxton and Winchester versions of a passage in Book 5 (Tale 2), Oakeshott shows that Caxton tried to eliminate obscure words and archaisms and to simplify; he attributes Caxton's inconsistencies to the necessary haste of his work. Caxton's printer's copy of the MORTE DARTHUR was a scribal manuscript but not Malory's holograph.

485. _____. "The Manuscript of the MORTE DARTHUR." DISCOVERY; A MONTHLY POPULAR JOURNAL OF KNOWLEDGE, 16 (1935), 45-46.

Oakeshott states that the Winchester Manuscript would probably have been discovered earlier if the entry in the catalogue of Winchester manuscripts which described it had not been misleading. The manuscript, written probably between 1469 and 1486, is neither Malory's holograph nor the manuscript which Caxton used. A comparison of Book 5 of the Caxton edition and Tale 2 of the Winchester Manuscript reveals significant differences between the two, especially Caxton's attempt to modernize the language of his original.

486. O'Loughlin, J. L. N. "The Middle English Alliterative 'Morte Arthure.'" MEDIUM AEVUM, 4 (1935), 153-68.

O'Loughlin claims that textual study of the MORTE DARTHUR can possibly throw light on editorial problems in the Alliterative MORTE ARTHURE.

487. Stewart, George R. "English Geography in Malory's 'Morte D'Arthur.'" MLR, 30 (1935), 204-09.

Malory was "translating and reworking the Arthurian story for Englishmen of the fifteenth century, and his geographical references show that he felt himself to be rescuing the story not only from the French language but also from the fog of myth which had enveloped what was, presumably to Malory, the figure of a true English monarch" (p. 205). Malory made geographical references not previously found in Arthurian romance; he identified Camelot with Winchester, Joyous Gard with Northumberland, and Astolat with Guildford. In addition, his geography shows

anti-Yorkist sentiment. The traitors, for example, are associated with the southwest of England, a Yorkist stronghold.

488. Vinaver, Eugène. "Malory's MORTE DARTHUR in the Light of a Recent Discovery." BJRL, 19 (1935), 438-57. Also published as
a monograph, Manchester University Press, 1935.

Vinaver wishes "to give a preliminary survey of some of the
problems arising out of the newly discovered text" (p. 439)
and to establish, from the evidence provided by the text and
its sources, Malory's aims and purposes. He believes that no
"composite" text is possible; the critic must edit the extant
text, though examination of its French sources can be helpful.
He hypothesizes that the Caxton and Winchester versions derive
from a manuscript X which in turn derives from Malory's copy,
and discusses how the two versions and the French sources il-
luminate difficult passages. The Winchester Manuscript attests
to Malory's desire to emphasize the glory of knighthood; Malory
indeed may have regarded the composition of the MORTE DARTHUR
as a pious task.
    a. TLS, Sept. 5, 1935, pp. 554-55.

489. _____. "New Light on Malory's 'Morte Darthur' (What
Caxton Did to the 'Morte Darthur')." YORKSHIRE SOCIETY FOR
CELTIC STUDIES, Session 1935-36, pp. 18-20.

Vinaver claims that a comparison of the Winchester Manuscript
and Caxton's edition reveals that Malory wrote not a unified
book but a number of "self-contained units" (p. 19). Caxton
is responsible for editing the separate sections as a single
work, omitting all but the final explicit and giving the work
its present title. "It was Caxton who made this collection
into a single epic, and in this sense it is to him, not to Malory, that we owe the traditional unity of LE MORTE DARTHUR"
(p. 20).

490. Frappier, Jean. ÉTUDE SUR LA MORT LE ROI ARTU, ROMAN DU XIIIe
SIÈCLE. [Publications Romanes et Françaises, No. 70.] Paris:
Minard, 1936; 2nd ed., 1961.

Frappier describes the MORTE DARTHUR as "une véritable somme
de la légende arthurienne." He claims that Malory preferred
the MORT ARTU to the entire LANCELOT because of its dramatic
qualities.

491. Lewis, C. S. THE ALLEGORY OF LOVE: A STUDY IN MEDIEVAL TRADI-
TION. New York: Oxford University Press, 1936; rpt. 1975.

Lewis denies that the MORTE DARTHUR has any unifying design.
"Malory so often leaves his separate stories unfinished or
else, if he finishes them, fails to interlock them all (so

that they drop away from the rest of the book as independent
organisms) and is. . . generally confused" (p. 300).
a. S. A. Coblentz, NEW YORK TIMES, July 5, 1936, p. 12.
b. William Empson, SPECTATOR, 157 (Sept. 4, 1936), 389.
c. Albert Guerard, Jr., BOOKS, Oct. 18, 1936, p. 14.
d. SATURDAY REVIEW OF LITERATURE, 14 (Aug. 1, 1936), 23.
e. TLS, June 6, 1936, p. 475.
f. T. A. Kirby, MLN, 52 (1937), 515-18.
g. Edgar C. Knowlton, JEGP, 26 (1937), 124-26.
h. F. Krog, ANGLIA, 48 (1937), 333-38.
i. Kathleen Tillotson, RES, 13 (1937), 477-79.
j. Mona Wilson, ENGLISH, 1 (1937), 344-46.
k. O. Elton, MEDIUM AEVUM, 6 (1937), 34-40.
l. George R. Coffman, SP, 35 (1938), 511-15.
m. G. Bonnard, ENGLISH STUDIES, 21 (1939), 78-82.
n. SATURDAY REVIEW OF LITERATURE, Nov. 1, 1958, p. 38.

492. MacNeice, Louis. "Sir Thomas Malory." THE ENGLISH NOVELISTS:
A SURVEY OF THE NOVEL. Ed. Derek Verschoyle. New York: Har-
court, Brace, and Co., 1936, pp. 19-29.

Discussion of the MORTE DARTHUR as a "novel."

493. Newstead, Helaine. "The JOIE DE LA CORT Episode in EREC and the
Horn of Bran." PMLA, 51 (1936), 13-25.

See p. 22. Newstead states that Gareth's battle with the Red
Knight of the Red Launds (Book 7, Chapters 15-18) preserves
little of the original Celtic motif of the horn of Bran.

494. Oakeshott, W[alter] F. "Arthuriana at Winchester." WESSEX: AN
ANNUAL RECORD OF THE MOVEMENT FOR A UNIVERSITY OF WESSEX. Vol.
3, No. 3. Published by the Pilgrim Press Ltd., for University
College, Southampton, 1936, pp. 74-78.

Oakeshott suggests that the Winchester Manuscript was bought
for the monastic library of St. Swithun's when Prince Arthur,
son of Henry VII, was christened at Winchester. It may have
been sent from the cathedral library to the college in 1645
as a gift from Oliver Cromwell.

495. Powys, Llewelyn. "Love at Camelot." NINETEENTH CENTURY AND
AFTER, 120 (Oct. 1936), 490-96.

Impressionistic discussion of the MORTE DARTHUR. "By Malory's
art fragments of the Arthurian legend were woven together as
plain as scenes on a tapestry" (p. 491).

496. Thornton, Sister Mary Madelina. "Malory's LE MORTE D'ARTHUR as
a Christian Epic." M. A. Thesis. University of Illinois-
Urbana, 1936.

Thornton wishes to "examine LE MORTE D'ARTHUR in the light of
epic theory, considering the book as a conscious literary mas-
terpiece, to individualize it as a romantic epic, and to determine its relationship to other Christian epics" (p. 9).
Malory's characters acknowledge that Christianity is important
in their lives though they do fail to achieve its goals.

497. Wedgwood, Josiah C. HISTORY OF PARLIAMENT: . . . 1439-1509.
     2 vols. London, 1936-38. Vol. 2, pp. xix, 63.

     References to the Warwickshire Malory's career in Parliament.

498. Baker, Imogene. THE KING'S HOUSEHOLD IN THE ARTHURIAN COURT FROM
     GEOFFREY OF MONMOUTH TO MALORY. Dissertation. Washington:
     Catholic University of America, 1937.

     Baker states that the MORTE DARTHUR retains early English tra-
     ditions concerning the king's household, a motif generally
     derived from the chronicle tradition. "Malory's composite
     work is representative of the treatment of the household con-
     vention in English romance. He adapts it only so far as he
     finds it useful" (p. 154).
       a. Karl Brunner, LGRP, 61 (1940), 26-27.

499. Fox, Ralph. THE NOVEL AND THE PEOPLE. London: Lawrence and
     Wishart, 1937.

     A Marxist interpretation of the MORTE DARTHUR. Fox says that
     the work has "all the elements of that most pernicious form
     of bourgeois literature, Romanticism." Malory is the "first
     great escapist, a man seeking refuge from a present both fear-
     ful and repellent in an idealized past. He abandoned realism,
     or rather, it never existed for him" (p. 48).

500. Francis, J. H. FROM CAXTON TO CARLYLE; A STUDY OF THE DEVELOP-
     MENT OF THE LANGUAGE, COMPOSITION, AND STYLE IN ENGLISH PROSE.
     Cambridge: Cambridge University Press, 1937.

     See pp. 23-29. Commentary on a passage from the story of Balin.
     Francis takes this passage as an example of Malory's style and
     concludes that Malory was a "master of narrative" (p. 28).

501. Vinaver, E[ugène] and E. V. Gordon. "New Light on the Text of
     the Alliterative MORTE ARTHURE." MEDIUM AEVUM, 6 (1937), 81-98.

     Vinaver and Gordon state that the Winchester Manuscript pro-
     vides evidence that the source of Caxton's Book 5 is the Allit-
     erative MORTE ARTHURE (though not the Thornton Manuscript
     itself). Malory did, however, make changes in his source when
     writing Book 5. The Winchester Manuscript also offers proof
     that the Thornton Manuscript of the Alliterative MORTE ARTHURE
     has lost original lines, which Malory's copy of the MORTE

ARTHURE did contain. His copy and the Thornton Manuscript show
"extensive textual change in one tradition or the other" (p. 88),
but the Thornton Manuscript is close enough to Malory's copy to
help interpret the MORTE DARTHUR. Each version is helpful in
editing the other, and any new edition of the Alliterative
MORTE ARTHURE should make use of the Winchester Manuscript.

502. Vorontzoff, Tania. "Malory's Story of Arthur's Roman Campaign."
     MEDIUM AEVUM, 6 (1937), 99-121.

     Vorontzoff states that Malory shortened Book 5 not, as in other
     books, by cutting characters and events but by reducing dialogue,
     shortening speeches, and cutting description of scenery. His
     narrative technique in Book 5 is similar to that used through-
     out the work.
          a. Ivor D. C. Arnold, MEDIUM AEVUM, 7 (1938), 74-75.

503. Coulton, George Gordon. MEDIEVAL PANORAMA: THE ENGLISH SCENE
     FROM CONQUEST TO REFORMATION. Cambridge: Cambridge University
     Press, 1938; rpt. New York: W. W. Norton, 1974.

     See Chapter 21. Coulton asserts that the late fifteenth century
     was an age of conflicting ideals and that this is illustrated
     both in the personality of Malory and in the MORTE DARTHUR.

504. Loomis, Roger Sherman, and Laura Hibbard Loomis. ARTHURIAN LEG-
     ENDS IN MEDIEVAL ART. London: Oxford University Press; New
     York: MLA, 1938.

     Commentary on the woodcuts in the 1498 Wynkyn de Worde edition,
     pp. 143-44. Some of the woodcuts are reproduced in figures
     415-20.
          a. J. E., MEDIUM AEVUM, 8 (1939), 168-69.
          b. G. H. Gerould, SPECULUM, 14 (1939), 252-54.
          c. William A. Nitze and Archer Taylor, MP, 36 (1939), 307-12.
          d. John J. Parry, JEGP, 38 (1939), 156-57.
          e. Howard R. Patch, RR, 30 (1939), 192-94.
          f. Friedrich Ranke, GERMANIC REVIEW, 14 (1939), 219-21.
          g. Hannah Cross, BURLINGTON MAGAZINE, 77 (1940), 33.

505. Reid, Margaret J. C. THE ARTHURIAN LEGEND: COMPARISON OF TREAT-
     MENT IN MODERN AND MEDIAEVAL LITERATURE. Edinburgh and London:
     Oliver and Boyd, 1938; rpt. New York: Barnes and Noble; London:
     Methuen, 1970.

     See pp. 120-22, 191-203. Reid discusses the relationship be-
     tween Welsh myth and the MORTE DARTHUR. She is indebted to
     Vinaver [nos. 420 and 441] for her discussion of the TRISTRAM
     section.

506. Baldwin, Charles Sears. RENAISSANCE LITERARY THEORY AND PRACTICE.
     Ed. Donald Lemen Clark. New York: Columbia University Press,
     1939.

See Chapter 5 ("Romance"). Malory "escapes from the bitter
War of the Roses to Camelot" (p. 11). Though Malory is chiefly a translator, he shows ability as a story-teller and his
style has a "grave simplicity that ranges from homeliness to
eloquence" (p. 99).

507. Bühler, Curt F. "Two Caxton Problems." THE LIBRARY, Ser. 4,
vol. 20 (1939-40), 266-71.

Bühler replies to Vinaver's argument concerning leaves 308,
311, 380, and 383 (r. and v.) in the Pierpont Morgan and John
Rylands copies of the Caxton edition [see no. 510]. Bühler
claims that the leaves were in folio, not in quarto, and that
their corresponding pages (pp. 5, 6, 11, and 12 of gatherings
N and Y) "merely comprise the printed matter of the third sheet
of the two gatherings." Pressmen probably made too many copies
of one sheet and too few of another and therefore had to reset
type for the lacking pages. [See also no. 872.]

508. Loomis, Roger Sherman. "Malory's Beaumains." PMLA, 54 (1939),
656-68. Rpt. in STUDIES IN MEDIEVAL LITERATURE: A MEMORIAL
COLLECTION OF ESSAYS. New York: Burt Franklin, 1970.

Loomis asserts that the name "Beaumains" is a corruption of
the French Gauvains and denies Vinaver's hypothesis [no. 441]
that it is based on the name of Richard Beauchamp, Earl of
Warwick.
    a. Lewis Thorpe, RBPH, 52 (1974), 198-201.

509. Renwick, W. L., and Harold Orton. THE BEGINNINGS OF ENGLISH LIT-
ERATURE TO SKELTON, 1509. London: Cresset Press, 1939; 2nd ed.
rev., 1952; 3rd ed. rev. by Martyn F. Wakelin, 1966.

A general discussion of the MORTE DARTHUR--the "first monument
of artistic prose since the days of Aelfric" (p. 95)--with
special emphasis on Malory's style. A brief bibliography is
on pp. 318-20.

510. Vinaver, Eugène. "A Note on the Earliest Printed Texts of Malory's MORTE DARTHUR." BJRL, 23 (1939), 102-06.

While collating the two copies of the Caxton edition, Vinaver
found "four long passages in which conflicting readings occur
in practically every line" (folios 308, 311, 380, and 383, r.
and v., which equal pages 5, 6, 11, and 12 of gatherings N and
Y when the pages in each gathering are numbered). He maintains
that each gathering equals two quarto sheets, one inserted
within the other ("quarto in eights") and that the Rylands copy
is the earlier since it preserves forms also found in the Winchester Manuscript. [See replies to this argument in nos. 507
and 872.]

511. Wilson, Robert H. "Malory, the Stanzaic MORTE ARTHUR, and the
      MORT ARTU." MP, 37 (1939), 125-38.

      Wilson disagrees with the theories of Bruce [nos. 358, 365,
      and 374] and Sommer [nos. 123 and 372] about the relationship
      between the MORTE DARTHUR and the Stanzaic MORTE ARTHUR. He
      believes that Malory must have employed the Stanzaic MORTE
      ARTHUR, whose poet had in turn adapted in an original manner
      the MORT ARTU. Malory therefore used two sources. Wilson
      notes that "Malory's general faithfulness to his sources, and
      tendency to compress, need have been no bar to changes serving
      a specific purpose, particularly in the highly significant pas-
      sages at the end of the story" (p. 138).

512. Workman, Samuel K. FIFTEENTH CENTURY TRANSLATION AS AN INFLUENCE
      ON ENGLISH PROSE. [Princeton Studies in English, No. 18.]
      Princeton, N. J.: Princeton University Press; London: Oxford
      University Press, 1940.

      Workman says that the "elementary simplicity of structure" in
      the MORTE DARTHUR is characteristic of English prose before
      1470. The work should be considered a recension and not a
      translation.

*513. Atabay, Ercüment. "Büyuk Ingiliz Destanlari (The Great English
      Epics), Morte D'Arthur." YENITÜRK, 9 (1941), 706-09.

514. Brugger, E. "Der schoene Feigling in der arthurischen Literatur."
      ZRP, 61 (1941), 1-44; 63 (1943), 123-73, 275-328; 65 (1949),
      121-92, 289-433; 67 (1951), 289-97.

      Brugger studies the sources and relationships of versions of
      the "fair unknown" romances, including Malory's Book 7, the
      Gareth story. Though unknown, its source is probably French.
      Brugger summarizes and assesses critical opinion on the proba-
      ble source of the GARETH. He is critical of Vinaver's views
      [no. 441]. In Brugger's study, see esp. vol. 63, pp. 275 ff.
      and vol. 65, pp. 121 ff.

515. Bennett, Josephine W. THE EVOLUTION OF THE FAERIE QUEENE. Chi-
      cago, 1942.

      Bennett discusses Spenser's use of the MORTE DARTHUR and con-
      cludes that it was not Spenser's source for the earlier books
      of the FAERIE QUEENE since no borrowing is discernible until
      Book 6.

516. McNeir, W. F. "A Possible Source for the Irish Knight." MLN,
      58 (1943), 383-85.

      The story of Launceor and Colombe in the MORTE DARTHUR may be

the source of a lost play entitled THE IRISSHE KNYGHT performed
at Elizabeth's court in 1576/7.

517. Nitze, William A. "The ESPLUMOIR MERLIN." SPECULUM, 18 (1943),
     69-79.

     Nitze compares Malory's version of the story of Merlin's im-
     prisonment with versions found in other romances.

518. Wilson, Robert H. "The 'Fair Unknown' in Malory." PMLA, 58
     (1943), 1-21.

     Wilson summarizes critical opinion on the source of Malory's
     story of GARETH and seeks to determine its source. He believes
     that it derives from a source whose author used LA COTE MAL
     TAILE (as found in the Prose TRISTAN), the BEL INCONNU, a com-
     mon source for both BEL INCONNU and LIBEAUS DESCONUS, and
     probably the EREC.
        a. P. Cézard, ROMANIA, 76 (1955), 413.

519. _____. "Malory's Naming of Minor Characters." JEGP,
     42 (1943), 364-85.

     In using his sources, Malory often cut anonymous characters
     or introduced names for them. Wilson opposes Vinaver's view
     [no. 441] that this is part of Malory's attempt to unravel the
     entrelacement of his sources. He argues that it cannot be as-
     sumed that Malory used versions of his sources which supplied
     names; it is more probable that he invented them or recalled
     them from his reading of other romances. Malory's minor char-
     acters serve the artistic function of providing a "background"
     for the action and of joining the tales together. In an Ap-
     pendix (pp. 378-85) is a list of Malory's minor characters.
     [This article is supplemented by no. 604.]

520. Williams, Charles. "Malory and the Grail Legend." DUBLIN REVIEW,
     214 (April 1944), 144 f.; rpt. in THE IMAGE OF THE CITY AND
     OTHER ESSAYS. Selected by Anne Ridler. London: Oxford Uni-
     versity Press, 1958; rpt. 1970; pp. 186-94.

     Williams discusses the Grail story and the Lancelot-Galahad
     relationship as it appears in the "English imagination," and
     especially in the MORTE DARTHUR.

521. Bennett, H. S. "Fifteenth-Century Secular Prose." RES, 21 (1945)
     257-63.

     Bennett asserts that Chambers [no. 452] "rightly saw that the
     main stream could not flow through the prose of Pecock, For-
     tescue, or Malory. Important as these are in the full story
     of our prose, they do not help us to understand which way it
     was moving" (p. 257).

522. Chambers, E[dmund] K. ENGLISH LITERATURE AT THE CLOSE OF THE
      MIDDLE AGES. [Oxford History of English Literature, Vol. 2,
      Pt. 2.] Oxford: Clarendon Press, 1945; rpt. 1964.

      See Chapter 4, "Malory" (pp. 185-205). Chambers discusses the
      eight divisions of the Winchester Manuscript. He believes
      that Malory was not a "political thinker" but a "story-teller,
      intent on the development of a very dramatic theme" (p. 197),
      which is the story of Arthur and Lancelot. The latter is the
      chief protagonist of the work. Chambers also discusses Malo-
      ry's style and his identity; he accepts the Warwickshire
      candidate proposed by Kittredge [nos. 329 and 339].
        a. John Bryson, SPECTATOR, 177 (July 12, 1946), 44.
        b. H. B. C., MANCHESTER GUARDIAN, Feb. 6, 1946, p. 3.
        c. Hermann Peschmann, ENGLISH, 6 (1946), 87-88.
        d. TLS, March 16, 1946, p. 127.
        e. Beatrice White, MLR, 41 (1946), 426-28.
        f. CHICAGO SUN BOOK WEEK, Jan. 5, 1947, p. 6.
        g. CHRISTIAN SCIENCE MONITOR, Feb. 15, 1947, p. 16.
        h. S. C. Chew, N.Y. HERALD TRIBUNE WEEKLY BOOK REVIEW,
            Mar. 30, 1947, p. 6.
        i. L. H. Loomis, MLQ, 8 (1947), 497-98.

523. Loomis, Roger Sherman. "The Combat at the Ford in the DIDOT
      PERCEVAL." MP, 43 (1945), 63-71.

      The Book of GARETH contains a motif common in Arthurian ro-
      mances--the combat of the hero who encounters one or more
      antagonists at a ford. See p. 64.

524. Parsons, Coleman O. "A Scottish 'Father of Courtesy' and Malory."
      SPECULUM, 20 (1945), 51-64.

      See p. 62. Parson states that, in his version of Arthur's
      final battle, Malory may have drawn on Scottish chronicles or
      oral tradition. Arthur is reminiscent of Sir David Lindsay,
      the magnanimous and chivalrous Scottish knight who fought at
      the battle of Gasklune in the 1390's. There are "interesting,
      rather than striking, general similarities" between the two
      battles.

525. Reese, Gertrude. "Political Import of THE MISFORTUNES OF ARTHUR."
      RES, 21 (1945), 81-91.

      Reese maintains that this play, presented in 1588 before Eliza-
      beth, contains political references to Mary Queen of Scots.
      The plot, however, is not consistent with earlier legend in
      the works of Malory and Geoffrey of Monmouth.

526. Scherer, Margaret Rosemary. ABOUT THE ROUND TABLE: KING ARTHUR
      IN ART AND LITERATURE. New York: Arno, 1945; rpt. 1974.

Scherer makes references to the MORTE DARTHUR in relation to other treatments of the Arthurian stories.

527. Walker, R[ainforth] A. "Le Morte Darthur." TLS, Mar. 31, 1945, p. 156.

A bibliographical note on the 1893 Dent reprint of the Caxton edition [no. 124].

528. "The Malory Enigma." TLS, Mar. 16, 1946, p. 127.

An argument against the existence of a "moral paradox" between the morality of the MORTE DARTHUR and the immorality of its author.

529. Richards, Gertrude R. B. "An Early Edition of the 'Morte d'Arthur.'" MORE BOOKS, Jan. 1946, pp. 18-20.

Richards announces the Boston Public Library's acquisition of a copy of the Thomas East edition of the MORTE DARTHUR. She describes the book, its format, and its woodcut illustrations.

530. Ackerman, Robert W., ed. SYRE GAWENE AND THE CARLE OF CARELYLE: AN EDITION. [University of Michigan Contributions in Modern Philology, No. 8.] Ann Arbor: University of Michigan Press, 1947.

Ackerman refutes the claim that the character of Sir Ironsyde appears only in the MORTE DARTHUR (see line 64 in SYRE GAWENE).

531. Bennett, H[enry] S. CHAUCER AND THE FIFTEENTH CENTURY. [Oxford History of English Literature, Vol. 2, Pt. 1.] Oxford: Clarendon Press, 1947; rpt. 1965.

See pp. 200-03. A compressed analysis of the MORTE DARTHUR. Bennett states that Malory had "no great skill" in shaping the materials in his sources; with the exception of the last books, the work is best read for its individual scenes. He praises Malory's prose for its dialogue, its narrative techniques, and its ability to convey irony, dignity, and sorrow. Supporting the opinion of Chambers [no. 452], Bennett states that Malory is outside the "mainstream" of English prose: "Malory remains as a beautiful inland lake cut off from the outer world" (pp. 202-03).
    a. John Bryson, SPECTATOR, 180 (Feb. 20, 1948), 230.
    b. S. C. Chew, N.Y. HERALD TRIBUNE, Nov. 7, 1948, p. 26.
    c. H. S. Davies, NEW STATESMAN AND NATION, 35 (May 1948), 360.
    d. Paul Dinkins, CATHOLIC WORLD, 168 (Dec. 1948), 253.
    e. H. B. Charlton, MANCHESTER GUARDIAN, Jan. 27, 1948, p. 3.
    f. Theodore Maynard, COMMONWEAL, 48 (Oct. 8, 1948), 624.
    g. TLS, Apr. 17, 1948, p. 221.

532. Gilbert, Allan H. "Belphoebe's Misdeeming of Timias." PMLA, 62
     (1947), 622-43.

  See p. 622. Gilbert notes there is a resemblance between
  the story in the MORTE DARTHUR of Lancelot's lying with Elaine
  and being subsequently banished by the Queen, and the story of
  Timias in the FAERIE QUEENE.

533. Housman, John E. "Higden, Trevisa, Caxton, and the Beginnings
     of Arthurian Criticism." RES, 23 (1947), 209-17.

  See pp. 216-17. Housman cites Caxton's "half-hearted preface"
  as proof that Caxton had serious reservations about the moral
  value and the historical validity of the MORTE DARTHUR.

534. Kenyon, F. G. "Letter to the Editor: MORTE DARTHUR." TLS,
     June 7, 1947, p. 281.

  Kenyon claims that Oakeshott should have received more recognition from Vinaver in his edition of the Winchester Manuscript--
  acknowledgement of Oakeshott's discovery of the manuscript and
  of Oakeshott's waiver of his own right to edit it.

535. [Lewis, C. S.] "The MORTE DARTHUR." TLS, June 7, 1947, pp.
     273-74. Rpt. in C. S. Lewis, STUDIES IN MEDIEVAL AND RENAIS-
     SANCE LITERATURE, collected by Walter Hooper. Cambridge: Cam-
     bridge University Press, 1966, pp. 103-10.

  Lewis praises Vinaver's edition of the Winchester Manuscript,
  the "stellar" discovery of which, he claims, "reduced the study
  of Malory to a state of suspense for thirteen years." But
  he claims that the Caxton edition must always be regarded as
  important. "The new WORKS OF MALORY is the restoration; but
  the cathedral, our old familiar Caxton, is still there. We
  should all read the WORKS; but it would be an impoverishment
  if we did not return to the MORTE." Lewis discusses the alleged
  paradox of Malory's immorality and the moral nature of his work,
  the "unity" controversy, Malory's style, his treatment of the
  supernatural, and the Quest story. [Discussion of these topics
  is expanded in no. 657.2.]
  a. Douglas Bush, CE, 28 (1966), 254-55.
  b. Graham Hough, THE LISTENER [London], Aug. 18, 1966, p. 245.
  c. LJ, 91 (1966), 3730.
  d. Jared Lobdell, NATIONAL REVIEW, 18 (Dec. 27, 1966), 1332.
  e. TLS, July 14, 1966, p. 616.
  f. J.-P. Barricelli, ITALIAN QUARTERLY, 1967, p. 102.
  g. J. Burrow, ESSAYS IN CRITICISM, 17 (1967), 89-95.
  h. CHOICE, 3 (1967), 1011.
  i. B. D. Cheadle, ENGLISH STUDIES IN AFRICA, March 1967,
     p. 109.
  j. Lionel J. Friedman, RP, 22 (1968), 119-20.
  k. Dieter Mehl, ARCHIV, 205 (1969), 68-70.

536. Loomis, Roger Sherman. "From Segontium to Sinadon--the Legends of a 'Cité Gasté.'" SPECULUM, 22 (1947), 520-33.

See p. 530. Loomis believes that Malory's Book of GARETH derives from a lost twelfth-century romance. Since there are similarities between the GARETH and Renaud de Beaujeu's LE BEL INCONNU (c. 1200), Loomis conjectures that Malory's hypothetical source and LE BEL INCONNU have "a more or less remote common source."

537. Whiting, B. J. "Gawain: His Reputation, His Courtesy, and His Appearance in Chaucer's 'Squire's Tale.'" MEDIAEVAL STUDIES, 9 (1947), 189-234.

Whiting claims that Malory's inconsistent treatment of Gawain can be attributed to his sources.

538. Baugh, Albert C. "The Middle English Period." A LITERARY HISTORY OF ENGLAND. New York: Appleton-Century-Crofts, 1948; 2nd ed., 1967.

See pp. 305-07. A succinct discussion of the MORTE DARTHUR.

539. Newstead, Helaine. "The Besieged Ladies in Arthurian Romance." PMLA, 63 (1948), 803-30.

See pp. 803-08. Newstead discusses the Besieged Lady of Malory's Book of GARETH, Dame Lyones, whose name means the Lady of Lothian. There are resemblances between GARETH and the thirteenth-century romance FERGUS: both have structural similarities and both have the same heroine, the Lady of Lothian. Newstead concludes that the story of a besieged lady, who is rescued from a castle by a young knight to whom she offers her love, is a "traditional narrative pattern" which the romancers found useful and adaptable because it could be expanded or compressed, offered opportunities for knights to display their prowess, and combined the themes of love and war.
  a. P. Cézard, ROMANIA, 76 (1955), 416.

540. Williams, Charles. "The Figure of Arthur." ARTHURIAN TORSO. Ed. C. S. Lewis. New York and London: Oxford University Press, 1948; rpt. 1969.

See Chapter 5, "The Coming of the Grail" (pp. 60-90). Williams interprets Balin's dolorous stroke as man's wounding himself and sees the Grail story as a "tale of the Fall--individual or universal" (p. 85). Lancelot is an affirmative force and serves as a foil to the passive Arthur.
  a. J. E. Housman, RES, N.S. 1 (1950), 84-85.
  b. M. M. Mahood, MLR, 45 (1950), 238-39.

541. Loomis, Roger Sherman. ARTHURIAN TRADITION AND CHRÉTIEN DE
      TROYES. New York: Columbia University Press, 1949.

      Loomis comments on parallels between the MORTE DARTHUR, the
      works of Chrétien de Troyes, and Celtic materials.

542. Vinaver, Eugène. "La genèse de la SUITE DU MERLIN." MÉLANGES
      DE PHILOLOGIE ROMANE ET DE LITTÉRATURE MÉDIÉVALE OFFERTS À
      ERNEST HOEPFFNER. Paris: Les Belles Lettres, 1949, pp. 295-
      300.

      Vinaver describes the history of the SUITE DU MERLIN and
      assesses Malory's use of it as a source. Until 1945, the only
      copy of the thirteenth-century SUITE was British Museum MS.
      38117 (the Huth manuscript), first edited by Paris and Ulrich
      [no. 29]. In that year, Vinaver identified a Cambridge Uni-
      versity manuscript as another version of the SUITE which ac-
      counts for sections of the MORTE DARTHUR which Malory could
      not have translated from a copy related to the Huth manuscript.
      Those sections are not original additions by Malory. Vinaver
      postulates that Malory used an earlier version of the story
      now represented by the Cambridge SUITE and the Spanish DEMANDA
      versions for the material in the MORTE DARTHUR not found in
      the Huth version.

543. Altick, Richard D. "The Quest of the Knight-Prisoner." THE
      SCHOLAR ADVENTURERS. New York: Macmillan, 1950, pp. 65-85.

      Altick describes the process by which scholars, through careful
      "detective" work and some luck, arrived at the identification
      of Thomas Malory of Warwickshire as the author of the MORTE
      DARTHUR. Kittredge's hypothesis [nos. 329 and 339] was elab-
      orated by Williams, Chambers, Hicks, and Baugh. Altick believes
      that the Winchester explicit "knight prisoner" establishes the
      identification. He discusses the supposed paradox of the
      immoral Malory and the moral nature of his work by arguing that
      social and political factors of the late fifteenth century
      should extenuate the alleged charges against Malory's character.
         a. S. C. Chew, N.Y. HERALD TRIBUNE BOOK REVIEW, Dec. 31,
                1950, p. 5.
         b. Delancey Ferguson, NEW YORK TIMES, Dec. 10, 1950, p. 6.
         c. J. H. Jackson, SAN FRANCISCO CHRONICLE, Dec. 25, 1950,
                p. 22.
         d. KIRKUS, 18 (Oct. 1, 1950), 625.
         e. [No. 548.]
         f. SCHOOL AND SOCIETY, 72 (Dec. 9, 1950), 382.
         g. E. F. Walbridge, LJ, 75 (Oct. 15, 1950), 1822.
         h. Carl Bode, AMERICAN HISTORICAL REVIEW, 56 (July 1951),
                844.
         i. BOOKLIST, 47 (Jan. 15, 1951), 185.
         j. CLEVELAND OPEN SHELF, Mar. 1951, p. 5.

k. Milton Crane, CHICAGO SUNDAY TRIBUNE, Jan. 7, 1951, p. 10.
l. W. E. G., CHRISTIAN CENTURY, 68 (Jan. 24, 1951), 113.
m. Robert Halsband, NATION, 172 (Jan. 6, 1951), 16.
n. Marjorie Nicolson, SATURDAY REVIEW OF LITERATURE, 34
    (Mar. 17, 1951), 17.
o. P. O., CANADIAN FORUM, 31 (Oct. 1951), 165.
p. SPRINGFIELD REPUBLICAN, Jan. 7, 1951, p. 8B.

544. Anderson, George K. OLD AND MIDDLE ENGLISH LITERATURE FROM THE
      BEGINNINGS TO 1485. [A History of English Literature, Vol. 1.]
      Ed. Hardin Craig. London: Oxford University Press, 1950; rpt.
      New York: Collier Books, 1962.

      In this survey, Anderson states that Malory's narrative tech-
      nique is stronger than his characterizations. "Malory boiled
      down the massive French romances into something approaching a
      coherent narrative" (p. 121, Collier ed.).

545. Dichmann, Mary E. "Characterization in Malory's TALE OF ARTHUR
      AND LUCIUS." PMLA, 65 (1950), 877-95; revised in MALORY'S
      ORIGINALITY. Ed. R. M. Lumiansky [no. 673.2], pp. 67-90.

      Dichmann asserts that an examination of Book 5, which Vinaver
      believes that Malory wrote before he wrote Books 1-4, provides
      evidence to disprove Vinaver's theory that Malory wrote eight
      separate romances. She believes that when Malory wrote Book
      5, he knew more Arthurian romances than the Alliterative MORTE
      ARTHURE (the source for Book 5). Malory's intention to unify
      his work is shown in the special emphasis which he places on
      Lancelot, in his transformation of Arthur from a primitive
      warrior to a chivalric king, and the attention he gives to
      knights who will play roles in later events.

546. Donaldson, E. Talbot. "Malory and the Stanzaic LE MORTE ARTHUR."
      SP, 47 (1950), 460-72.

      Donaldson denies Vinaver's opinion that Malory did not use the
      Stanzaic MORTE ARTHUR in Book 18 of the MORTE DARTHUR and as-
      serts that Vinaver, in citing the lack of verbal parallels be-
      tween the two, bases his argument on "negative evidence."
      Donaldson sees important similarities between the MORTE DARTHUR
      and the Stanzaic MORTE ARTHUR, which indicate that Malory did
      draw on the latter; he does not support Vinaver's opinion that
      the two have a common source which derived from the MORT ARTU.

547. Livermore, Harold V. "El caballero salvaje; ensayo de identifi-
      catión de un juglar." REVISTA DE FILOLOGIA ESPAÑOLA, 34 (1950),
      166-83.

      Livermore compares the characterization of Dinadin in the MORTE
      DARTHUR and Italian/Spanish versions, and that in the Prose

TRISTAN. He concludes that in the former, Dinadin is not so
much a satiric critic of the Arthurian world; Malory took
this theme seriously and therefore cut or omitted Dinadin's
irony.

548. "Lost and Found." TIME, 56 (Dec. 18, 1950), 60.

A brief discussion of the scholarship concerning Malory's
identity. [A review of no. 543.]

549. Micha, A[lexandre]. "Sur les sources de la 'Charrette.'" RO-
MANIA, 71 (1950), 345-58.

Micha favors the view that the river and bridge incidents in
the MORTE DARTHUR derive from the CONTE DE LA CHARRETTE of
Chrétien de Troyes. He claims, however, that Malory "ration-
alizes" these marvellous elements so that only vestiges of
the original story remain.

550. Wilson, Robert H. "Malory's Early Knowledge of Arthurian Romance." TEXAS STUDIES IN ENGLISH, 29 (1950), 33-50.

Unlike some critics, Wilson thinks that Malory had "considerable" knowledge of Arthurian romances; this knowledge is particularly evident in the early tales such as the TALE OF ARTHUR
AND LUCIUS. "Malory apparently retained, when he began to
write, a greater familiarity with Arthurian personages, cir-
cumstances, and chronology than has been recognized" (p. 50).
It is probable that Malory got names and/or information about
characters from a number of Arthurian romances, though Wilson
admits that the information might be interpolated or that Malory might have used another version of the source which he is
believed to have used.

551. _____. "Malory's French Book Again." COMPARATIVE
LITERATURE, 2 (1950), 172-81.

Wilson argues that Malory used a number of sources and not one
book (the "French book"), as some critics have maintained, and
examines Malory's 70-odd references to the "French book." Of
these, 25 are found in extant sources; 22 show additions or
alterations when compared with "closely parallel source texts";
and 23 cannot be located. Though it cannot be asserted that
the last two categories are original simply because they cannot
be located in extant sources, it can be argued that some are
"original because they are in harmony with other variations in
Malory or because they have an apparent literary motive" (p.
175). Malory's references to the "French book" increase the
credibility of his material and function as a "stylistic man-
nerism." Wilson says that his conclusion that Malory used
more than one book is supported by the evidence of references

which give "details of a narrative rather than its origin" (p. 178), the occasional mention of multiple works, and the statement in Caxton's preface that the MORTE DARTHUR was taken from "certeyn bookes of Frensshe."

552. Wroten, Helen Iams. "Malory's TALE OF KING ARTHUR AND THE EM-PEROR LUCIUS Compared with its Source, the Alliterative MORTE ARTHURE." Dissertation. University of Illinois at Urbana-Champaign, 1950. MICROFILM ABSTRACTS, 11 (1951), 127.

A line-by-line comparison of the Caxton edition, the Winchester Manuscript, and the Alliterative MORTE ARTHURE for Tale 2. Wroten disagrees with Vinaver's view that the MORTE DARTHUR consists of eight tales and that Tale 2 was written before Tale 1.

553. Davies, R. T. "Quelques Aspects Sociaux de l'oeuvre de Malory, en particulier sa conception de l'amour." BBIAS, 3 (1951), 103.

This is a summary of a paper delivered at the third meeting of the International Arthurian Society in August, 1951. Davies states that Malory had no systematic philosophy about love but that he did exalt faithfulness and love-service. In some passages, however, he exalts spiritual love above human love; the latter serves as preparation for the former. [Expanded in no. 596.]

554. Kane, George. MIDDLE ENGLISH LITERATURE: A CRITICAL STUDY OF THE ROMANCES, THE RELIGIOUS LYRICS, 'PIERS PLOWMAN.' [Methuen's Old English Library.] London: Methuen, 1951; rpt. New York: Barnes and Noble, 1970.

Kane discourages comparison between the Stanzaic MORTE ARTHUR and the MORTE DARTHUR because they are "separated by a funda-mental difference of conception" (p. 67).

555. Kettle, Arnold. AN INTRODUCTION TO THE ENGLISH NOVEL. London: Hutchinson's Univ. Library, 1951.

Kettle asserts that Malory avoided the "crudities" of simplis-tic presentation of ethical problems. Malory's work is there-fore closer to a realistic depiction of life than that found in many romances. See vol. 1, pp. 34-35.

556. Kurvinen, Auvo, ed. SIR GAWAIN AND THE CARL OF CARLISLE IN TWO VERSIONS. [Annuales Academiae Scientiarum Fennicae, Ser. B, vol. 71, no. 2.] Helsinki, 1951.

See pp. 107-09 in the Introduction ("The Ironside Episode"). A comparison of Malory's Ironside (the Rede Knyght of the Rede Laundys) with the Ironside of SIR GAWAIN AND THE CARL OF

CARLISLE. Both knights represent "a type of cruel and powerful knight, used by the romancers as the adversary of their
chief hero whose valour is thus enhanced" (p. 109). Malory's
Ironside derives from French sources, but the antecedents of
the Ironside of SIR GAWAIN are British.

557. Robinson, M. G., and Leah Dennis, eds. THE CORRESPONDENCE OF
THOMAS PERCY AND THOMAS WARTON. [The Percy Letters. Ed. Da-
vid Nichol Smith and Cleanth Brooks. Vol. 3.] Louisiana
State University Press, 1951.

The editors state that in his OBSERVATIONS ON THE FAERIE
QUEENE [no. 272], Warton "discovered" Malory and approached
him "as a critic and literary historian. . . the first to do
so" (p. xv). See the letter from Percy to Warton (May 28,
1761), pp. 1-8. Percy had the theory that "the Author of
MORT ARTHUR. . . only drew up a prose narrative of, and threw
together into a regular story the Subject of a hundred Old Ballads, which had been the delight of our Ancestors for many
ages before" (p. 2). Percy and Warton discussed the ballad
"King Ryence's Challenge [see nos. 289 and 446] in a series of
letters on pp. 22-30.

558. Vinaver, Eugène. "La manuscrit de Winchester." BBIAS, 3 (1951),
75-82.

Vinaver believes that the Winchester Manuscript is important
because it allows critics to judge better Malory's aim and to
distinguish more fully between Malory the author and Caxton
the editor. He emphasizes that the MORTE DARTHUR is eight
separate tales and not a "unified" work.

559. Webster, Kenneth G. T. GUINEVERE: A STUDY OF HER ABDUCTIONS.
Milton, Mass.: Turtle Press, 1951.

Webster discusses the two-part structure of Guinevere's rape
by Maliagraunce in Book 19. He agrees generally with Gaston
Paris that the first section (to the break in the narrative
when Lancelot is named Knight of the Cart) derives from a pre-
Christian rape, though Malory's immediate source was the
Prose LANCELOT.
   a. J. Frappier, RLC, 27 (1947), 101.

560. Wilson, Robert H. "How Many Books Did Malory Write?" TEXAS
STUDIES IN ENGLISH, 30 (1951), 1-23.

An examination of the explicits of each of the tales of the
MORTE DARTHUR leads Wilson to conclude that Malory had "formed
a unifying plan for his work, at least part way through it"
(p. 2). He argues against Vinaver's theory that Malory wrote
eight separate tales. "Malory had not abandoned the general

tradition of a complex narrative in which separate and often
entirely episodic accounts are yet, in a way, parts of a larger whole; and in spite of the particular formality of some of
the tale divisions, they do not stand in the way of our believing that he put the eight tales in a single manuscript because he thought of them as connected" (p. 7). This "partial
unity" is demonstrated by Malory's choice of source materials,
which use the same characters and provide some links in the
action, and Malory's attempt to eliminate or mitigate contradictions which appear in his sources. Wilson believes that,
as Malory wrote, he became more intent on writing a "unified"
series of tales; yet Wilson does agree with Vinaver that the
tales should be studied individually so that Malory's development as a writer can be better understood.

561. _____. "Notes on Malory's Sources." MLN, 66 (1951),
      22-26.

Wilson takes issue with Vinaver's opinions concerning Malory's
use of his sources. He claims that Malory made more extensive
use of more sections of the LANCELOT in Book 6 than Vinaver
believes and that similarities between Book 18 of the MORTE
DARTHUR and the Stanzaic MORTE ARTHUR make improbable Vinaver's
opinion that in Book 18, Malory used a text of the MORT ARTU
and not the Stanzaic MORTE ARTHUR. The absence of close verbal
parallels between Book 18 and the Stanzaic MORTE ARTHUR may
indicate that Malory relied on his memory.

562. Ackerman, Robert. AN INDEX OF THE ARTHURIAN NAMES IN MIDDLE
      ENGLISH. [Stanford University Publications in Language and
      Literature, No. 10.] Stanford: Stanford University Press,
      1952.

This index consists of all personal and place-names in Middle
English versions of the Arthurian legend, including the MORTE
DARTHUR. [See also no. 846.]
      a. J. A. W. Bennett, MLR, 49 (1954), 221.
      b. A. Kurvinen, NM, 55 (1954), 223-25.
      c. R. S. Loomis, SPECULUM, 29 (1954), 244.
      d. R. H. Wilson, JEGP, 53 (1954), 101.

563. Bivar, A. D. H. "Lyonnesse: The Evolution of a Fable." MP,
      50 (1953), 162-70.

See pp. 168-69. Malory's use of the name "Lyonnesse."

564. Brewer, D. S. "Form in the MORTE DARTHUR." MEDIUM AEVUM, 21
      (1952), 14-24. Revised as "'the hoole book'" in ESSAYS ON MA-
      LORY, ed. J. A. W. Bennett [no. 657.4], pp. 41-63.

Brewer claims that inconsistencies in the MORTE DARTHUR do not
provide enough evidence to prove that the work is eight separate

tales; the characters of Arthur and his knights and the tone
do give an "impression of unity." The theory of eight separate
tales is also unsupported by the evidence of the explicits;
these do not, according to Brewer, mark the ends of the individual tales but serve as "points of departure for further
development." Brewer points out links between the tales which
seem to indicate that Malory saw them as connected; he emphasizes Malory's development of progressive themes, especially
the rise, glory, decline, and fall of the kingdom.
    a. Helaine Newstead, MEDIUM AEVUM, 33 (1964), 234.
    b. T. C. Rumble, SPECULUM, 39 (1964), 116.

565. Kunitz, Stanley Jasspon, and Howard Haycraft, eds. BRITISH AU-
THORS BEFORE 1800; A BIOGRAPHICAL DICTIONARY. New York: H. W.
Wilson, 1952.

Biography of Thomas Malory of Warwickshire, proposed by Kittredge as author [nos. 329 and 339].

566. Myers, Alec Reginald. ENGLAND IN THE LATE MIDDLE AGES, 1307-1536.
[Pelican History of England, Vol. 4.] Baltimore and Harmonds-
worth, Middlesex: Penguin, 1952; rpt. 1959.

Myers asserts that the MORTE DARTHUR is more than a compilation
since Malory adapted it to his own uses, and that the work must
be studied in its historical context. "The decay of the old
chivalric social order and the horrors of civil war made men
look back nostalgically to the idealized chivalry of a remote
and fabulous past; but they wanted its fantasies to be presented
in a coherent, credible, and sympathetic form" (p. 233).

567. Prins, A[nton] A. FRENCH INFLUENCE IN ENGLISH PHRASING. Leiden:
Leiden University Press, 1952.

See Chapter 2 (pp. 10-20). Prins states that Malory was very
strongly influenced by French but that "for all the gallicisms
in vocabulary, this kind of prose is far less gallicized in
phraseonomy or latinized in syntax" than that of either Nicholas
Love or Thomas More (p. 18). [Compare with Chambers, no. 452.]

568. Wilson, Robert H. "The Rebellion of the Kings in Malory and in
the Cambridge SUITE DU MERLIN." TEXAS STUDIES IN ENGLISH, 31
(1952), 13-26.

Wilson believes that Malory's inclusion of the "rebellion of
the kings" episode after the coronation scene in the MORTE DAR-
THUR was not an independent addition by Malory of material from
the Vulgate Cycle, since the Cambridge SUITE DU MERLIN, discovered by Vinaver in 1945, and which represents Malory's source,
depicts the same sequence of events. He thinks that the "rebellion of the kings" section was not originally part of the

SUITE DU MERLIN. Malory compressed the action of the episode
as he found it in his source. [See nos. 586 and 613.]

569. Wilson, R[ichard] M. THE LOST LITERATURE OF MEDIEVAL ENGLAND.
      London: Methuen; New York: Philosophical Library, 1952;
      2nd ed., rev., London: Methuen, 1970.

      Wilson states that Malory derived the name of the hero Wade
      ('were he as wight as ever was Wade') from the Alliterative
      MORTE ARTHURE.

570. Burchfield, R. W. "Malory." CASSELL'S ENCYCLOPAEDIA OF LITERA-
      TURE. Vol. 2. London: Cassell, 1953.

      Brief biography of Thomas Malory of Warwickshire, proposed by
      Kittredge as the author [nos. 329 and 339].

571. Falconer, Sheila, ed. and trans. LORGAIREACHT EN TSOIDHIGH
      NAOMHTHA; AN EARLY MODERN IRISH TRANSLATION OF THE 'QUEST OF
      THE HOLY GRAIL.' Dublin: Dublin Institute for Advanced Stud-
      ies, 1953.

      In the Introduction, Falconer discusses the MORTE DARTHUR and
      its relation to the Irish translation of the QUEST.

572. Hughes, Merritt Y. "The Arthurs of the FAERIE QUEENE." EA, 6
      (1953), 193-213.

      Hughes denies that the MORTE DARTHUR exerted strong influence
      on the FAERIE QUEENE. [The opinion that Malory influenced
      Spenser was first expressed by Warton, no. 272.]

573. Levy, G. R. THE SWORD FROM THE ROCK: AN INVESTIGATION INTO THE
      ORIGINS OF EPIC LITERATURE AND THE DEVELOPMENT OF THE HERO.
      London: Faber and Faber, 1953.

      Levy stresses the importance of the MORTE DARTHUR as an "epic"
      and compares it with other epics. He briefly discusses the
      roles of Arthur, Lancelot, and Galahad.
      a. H. R. E. Davidson, FOLK-LORE, 64 (1953), 504.
      b. John L. Myers, ANTIQUITY, 27 (1953), 248-49.
      c. TLS, May 15, 1953, p. 318.

574. Loomis, Roger Sherman. "Edward I, Arthurian Enthusiast." SPECU-
      LUM, 28 (1953), 114-27.

      See p. 124. Loomis states that the French QUESTE is the source
      of the knights' vow in the MORTE DARTHUR to seek the Grail for
      a year and a day. The vow derives ultimately from the Irish
      saga THE SECOND BATTLE OF MOYTURA.

575. Lumiansky, R[obert] M. "The Relationship of Lancelot and Guine-
     vere in Malory's 'Tale of Lancelot.'" MLN, 68 (1953), 86-91.

     For annotation, see the revised version, "'The Tale of Lance-
     lot': Prelude to Adultery" in MALORY'S ORIGINALITY, ed. R. M.
     Lumiansky [no. 673.3], pp. 91-98.

576. Nitze, William A. "Arthurian Problems." BBIAS, 5 (1953), 69-84.

     See pp. 80-84. Nitze accepts Vinaver's opinion that Malory
     wrote eight separate tales and that he shifted emphasis from
     the spiritual quest to a conflict of human loyalties. He also
     compares Malory's version of the Arthurian stories with the
     French prose romance cycles.

577. Šimko, Ján. "Malory a Caxton." ČASOPIS PRO MODERNÍ FILOLOGII,
     35 (1953), 213-19 [in Polish]; English summary, p. 254.

     Šimko states that Malory wished to glorify the ideals of a
     chivalry which he saw decay during the War of the Roses; Cax-
     ton shared Malory's attitude. Šimko believes that Caxton's
     version of the MORTE DARTHUR is closer to Malory's original
     than the Winchester Manuscript, though the latter is more
     complete. [See also no. 603.]

578. Smithers, G. V. "Story-Patterns in Some Breton Lays." MEDIUM
     AEVUM, 22 (1953), 61-92.

     See pp. 69-71. Smithers notes that the "episode of the dwarf
     and the castle in which the fairy mistress is lying asleep"
     in DÉSIRÉ has parallels only with episodes in Malory's GARETH,
     Chrétien de Troyes' YVAIN, and SIR DÉGARÉ.

579. Tucker, P. E. "The Place of the 'Quest of the Holy Grail' in
     the 'Morte Darthur.'" MLR, 48 (1953), 391-97.

     Tucker states that the QUEST OF THE HOLY GRAIL "can best be
     understood as part of the story of Lancelot" (p. 391). The
     QUEST serves the important function of developing the character
     of Lancelot and of emphasizing his conflict of loyalties. Ma-
     lory does not agree with his sources that love-service is a
     part of earthly chivalry, and in his view "Lancelot's life of
     chivalry is blameworthy only when it is devoted to her service"
     (p. 392). It is his love and devotion to Guinevere which makes
     Lancelot an imperfect knight. At the end of the MORTE DARTHUR,
     he comes to realize that love-service degrades earthly chivalry.

580. Wilson, Robert H. "The Prose LANCELOT in Malory." TEXAS STUDIES
     IN ENGLISH, 32 (1953), 1-13.

     Wilson denies the opinion that Malory incorporated materials

from the Prose LANCELOT and other sources in Books 6 and 19 in
a way which seems uncharacteristic of his usual practice of
following his source carefully and condensing rather than ex-
panding his materials. Wilson does not believe that a hypothetical "Suite de Lancelot" should be invented to solve the
problem, or that it must be thought that Malory had access to
a version of the Vulgate LANCELOT which is no longer extant.
It is more likely that Malory combined the materials himself.

581. Dietz, Howard. "The Anomalous Sir Thomas Malory." NEW YORK
      TIMES, Jan. 10, 1954, Sec. 2, p. 5.

      A commentary on the alleged paradox between the immoral Malory
      and the idealism of his work.

582. Ferrier, Janet M. FORERUNNERS OF THE FRENCH NOVEL. Manchester:
      Manchester University Press, 1954.

      See pp. 14-16. In her analysis of the French story of Pelleas
      and Arcade, Ferrier comments on Whitehead's view concerning
      Malory's version of the story [no. 471]. Whitehead states that
      the French version shows a docile Pelleas, compelled by senti-
      ments of courtly love, a version which Malory was unable to
      accept. Ferrier agrees with Whitehead that Malory "evidently
      found Pelleas a sorry figure and in his own version saw to it
      that he behaved more gallantly" (p. 16).

583. Phillipps, K. C. "Contamination in Later Middle English." ENG-
      LISH STUDIES, 35 (1954), 17-20.

      Phillipps gives examples from the Caxton edition and the Win-
      chester Manuscript to show how the accusative-infinitive con-
      struction and noun-clause construction were used and sometimes
      mixed by Malory.

584. Speirs, John. "A Survey of Medieval Verse." THE AGE OF CHAUCER.
      Ed. Boris Ford. [Penguin Guide to English Literature.] Balti-
      more and Harmondsworth, Middlesex: Penguin, 1954; rpt. 1965,
      pp. 17-67.

      See pp. 41-43. Speirs is primarily interested in Malory's
      style. Characteristic of the MORTE DARTHUR are "those lovely
      elegaic cadences of prose, that diffused tone of wistful regret
      for a past age of chivalry, that vague sense of the vanity of
      earthly things. Yet the charm of the prose is a remote charm;
      the imagery is without immediacy; there is a lifelessness,
      listlessness, and fadedness about this prose for all its. . .
      loveliness" (p. 42).

585. Tillyard, E. M. W. THE ENGLISH EPIC AND ITS BACKGROUND. London:
      Chatto and Windus, 1954; published as a Galaxy Book, 1966.

See pp. 176-78. Tillyard compares Malory and Thucydides. He
calls the MORTE DARTHUR "tragic" and nostalgic rather than
"epic" and believes that Malory's forte--depiction of "time-
less passions and the logic of destiny" (p. 177)--is shown in
the final books.

586. Bogdanow, Fanni. "The Rebellion of the Kings in the Cambridge
     SUITE DU MERLIN." TEXAS STUDIES IN ENGLISH, 34 (1955), 6-17.

     The article opens with a summary of critical opinion about the
     origin of the SUITE DU MERLIN in the MORTE DARTHUR and the
     Cambridge manuscript: Vinaver thinks a "remodeled version of
     the Vulgate rebellion section" preceded the SUITE DU MERLIN;
     Wilson thinks the SUITE DU MERLIN is an independent work and
     the "rebellion of the kings" story a later interpolation. Bog-
     danow then expresses the opinion that the SUITE originally con-
     tained the rebellion episode but that some later redactors
     omitted it, a fact which would explain the differences between
     the MORTE DARTHUR and the Cambridge manuscript, which retain
     it, and other versions such as the Huth manuscript and the
     DEMANDA DEL SANCTO GRIAL, which omit it. [See nos. 568 and
     613.]

587. Davies, R. T. "Malory's Launcelot and the Noble Way of the World."
     RES, N.S. 6 (1955), 356-64.

     [This article is incorporated in no. 688.] Davies asserts that
     Launcelot represents the ideal of secular chivalry, the "middle
     way" between the extremes of the evil King Mark and the saintly
     Galahad. Launcelot is unable to reject the "middle way" and
     to achieve absolute perfection. Malory, however, is sympathe-
     tic to Launcelot and the "middle way" and vindicates him in the
     final books. "Launcelot loved as nobly as can a man who frank-
     ly accepts and does not renounce his disposition to sin" (p.
     356).

588. Graves, Robert. "Kynge Arthur is Nat Dede." THE CROWNING PRIVI-
     LEGE: THE CLARK LECTURES 1954-55. London: Cassell, 1955,
     pp. 206-11; rpt. in COLLECTED ESSAYS ON POETRY. Garden City,
     N.Y.: Doubleday, 1956, pp. 210-15.

     Graves calls King Arthur a "national obsession" (p. 208) and
     the MORTE DARTHUR the "Briton's counter-Bible" (p. 210).

589. Lumiansky, R. M. "The Question of Unity in Malory's MORTE DAR-
     THUR." TULANE STUDIES IN ENGLISH, 5 (1955), 29-39.

     Lumiansky surveys the critical reception of Vinaver's theory,
     announced in the 1947 edition of the Winchester Manuscript,
     that Malory wrote eight separate romances. He examines articles
     by Wilson [no. 560] and Brewer [no. 564], who want to accept

both the theory that the books have unity and the theory that
they can be read separately. In Lumiansky's opinion, critics
should recognize two types of unity: historical unity (i.e.
did Malory intend to write a single book?) and critical unity
(i.e. does the MORTE DARTHUR exist as a single work, regardless of Malory's authorial intentions?). Opposing Wilson and
Brewer, who claim that the MORTE DARTHUR contains critical but
not historical unity, Lumiansky claims that it has both types.
As evidence for historical unity, he points to explicit one,
which seems to indicate that Malory intended to continue his
work, and to the fact that explicits two and three have a
connecting link. As evidence for critical unity, he points
to the internal chronology of the MORTE DARTHUR, the inconsistencies of which can be explained by Malory's occasional use
of "retrospective narrative."
    a.   D. S. Brewer [no. 606].
    b.   R. H. Wilson [no. 762].

590.   _____. "Tristram's First Interviews with Mark in Malory's MORTE DARTHUR." MLN, 70 (1955), 476-78.

A denial of Vinaver's statement that Tristram's visit to Mark
in Tale 5 is repetitious because Tristram announces his identity at both interviews. Lumiansky claims that, the first
time, Tristram does not say he is Mark's nephew, only that
"I come from kynge Melydas that wedded your systir" and "my
name is Trystrams." In the second interview he identifies himself as Mark's nephew when Mark says that Marhalt will only
fight royal blood.

591. Miller, Betty. "Tennyson and the Sinful Queen." TWENTIETH CEN-
TURY, 158 (1955), 355-63.

Miller states that the tragic downfall of Arthur's kingdom is
caused by Arthur's incestuous siring of Mordred.

592. Rumble, Thomas C. "The Tristram Legend and Its Place in the MORTE
DARTHUR." Dissertation. Tulane University, 1955.

[Revised in no. 673.5.] Rumble opposes the view that the TRIS-
TRAM section weakens the structure of the MORTE DARTHUR and
that Malory, as his use of TRISTAN materials shows, is not a
literary artist. "Malory does succeed in integrating the Tristan and Arthurian stories, and . . . the interruption of the
principal story by the Tristan material serves a specific
structural purpose in the overall plan of Malory's work."
Rumble also seeks to prove that Malory's choice of the French
Prose TRISTAN as his source was appropriate.

593. Tucker, P. E. "A Source of 'The Healing of Sir Urry' in the
'Morte Darthur.'" MLR, 50 (1955), 490-92.

Tucker states that the source for this incident in Tale 7 is the "wounded knight" of the Agravain section of the Prose LANCELOT, though Malory must have worked from a lost redaction.

594. Arthos, John. ON THE POETRY OF SPENSER AND THE FORM OF ROMANCE. London: George Allen and Unwin, 1956.

See "The Questing" (pp. 65-91). Arthos discusses the importance of the image and setting of the "omnipresent forest," which serves both as a frame for the action and as a symbol of the search for self in the MORTE DARTHUR. He says that duty is an important theme. "This is what the quest has become for Malory, not so much the seeking of adventure, for the assertion of courage or strength, or for the righting of wrongs, or for the salvation of souls—although all these motives are to be recognized in various actions—but the quest is for Malory above all else, more than a service voluntarily assumed for God, the way a knight fulfills the demands of destiny" (p. 88). Lancelot represents the ideal knight, self-reliant and true to himself, an ideal which Arthos believes Malory thought necessary.

595. Blaess, Madeleine. "Arthur's Sisters." BBIAS, 8 (1956), 69-77.

Blaess finds that Malory presents approximately the same relationships among Arthur's family which are found in French romances.

596. Davies, R. T. "Malory's 'Vertuous Love.'" SP, 53 (1956), 459-69.

[A revision of no. 553; incorporated in no. 688.] Davies claims that although Malory's treatment of love is inconsistent, he generally presents love as "romantic adultery." Malory most approves of "vertuous love," the subordination of love for lady to love for God. This type of love is characterized by staby- lite (loyalty and faithfulness) and mesure (moderation).

597. Donner, Morton. "The Backgrounds of Malory's 'Book of Gareth.'" Dissertation. Columbia University, 1956. DA, 16 (1956), 1249.

Donner states that Malory's Book of GARETH derives from a twelfth-century romance based on a story preserved in THE SICK- BED OF CUCHULAINN and that Gareth is a hero whose attributes can be traced to Cuchulainn. The GARETH section draws on many stories and elements from Celtic tradition.

598. Kennedy, Elspeth. "The Two Versions of the False Guinevere Epi- sode in the Old French Prose LANCELOT," ROMANIA, 77 (1956), 98-104.

Kennedy refers briefly to Malory as one writer who made a "serious attempt to unravel or to cut the threads of the

entrelacement and to break up the long cyclic romance into a
series of tales" (p. 104).

599. Moorman, Charles. "Malory's Treatment of the Sankgreall." PMLA,
      71 (1956), 496-509.

      For annotation, see the revision, "'The Tale of the Sankgreall':
      Human Frailty" in MALORY'S ORIGINALITY, ed. R. M. Lumiansky
      [no. 673.6], pp. 184-204. [This article was later incorporated
      into THE BOOK OF KING ARTHUR, no. 680.]

600. Muir, Lynette R. "A Detail in Milton's Description of Sin."
      N & Q, N.S. 3 (1956), 100-01.

      Muir suggests that a detail in Milton's description of Sin--
      the barking hounds that kennel in the womb of Sin--in PARADISE
      LOST, Book 2, may be derived from Malory's description of the
      Questing Beast in Book 9 of the MORTE DARTHUR.

601. Rumble, Thomas C. "The First Explicit in Malory's MORTE DARTHUR."
      MLN, 71 (1956), 564-66.

      Rumble denies Vinaver's assertion that the first explicit is
      proof that the first tale is a separate work. Rumble believes
      that Malory refers not to his own work but to his source, some
      French version of the MERLIN. Malory therefore only disclaims
      henceforth to follow that particular source.

602. Schlauch, Margaret. ENGLISH MEDIEVAL LITERATURE AND ITS SOCIAL
      FOUNDATIONS. Warszawa: Państwowe Wydawnictwo Naukowe, 1956.

      See pp. 297-99. Schlauch states that Malory managed to give
      unity to diverse material in the MORTE DARTHUR, which is the
      "most impressive monument of late chivalrous literature" and
      the "summa and the swan-song of English Arthurian fiction"
      (p. 297). She interprets the fictional world of the work from
      a Marxist perspective. "The partial society shown in the
      MORTE D'ARTHUR lacks a foundation: its wandering knights and
      fair ladies and cruel villains move endlessly from castle to
      castle, through enchanted forests remote from towns, rarely
      if ever encountering the traders, the peasants, the craftsmen
      who created the material culture on which they lived" (p. 299).

603. Šimko, Ján. "A Linguistic Analysis of the Winchester Manuscript
      and William Caxton's Edition of Sir Thomas Malory's MORTE DAR-
      THUR." PHILOLOGICA, 8 (1956), 1-2.

      A summary of a more comprehensive study [no. 577]. Šimko com-
      pares Caxton's Book 5 with the corresponding section in the
      Winchester Manuscript, where the two versions differ radically,
      and finds that Caxton tended to reshape word order into a

subject-finite verb-extension pattern (i.e. strong declarative
sentences) which shows his desire for "regularity and clarity."

604. Wilson, Robert H. "Addenda on Malory's Minor Characters." JEGP,
      55 (1956), 563-87.

      This article supplements no. 519. Wilson revises the list of
      minor characters and his former conclusions in the light of re-
      cent critical studies and discoveries--the 1947 edition of the
      Winchester Manuscript, which provides name variants and a long-
      er version of Caxton's Book 5; and two new manuscripts, the
      Cambridge SUITE DU MERLIN and MS. 41 of the Prose TRISTAN.

605. _____. "Some Minor Characters in the MORTE ARTHURE."
      MLN, 71 (1956), 475-80.

      Wilson claims that Malory's text provides some evidence for de-
      termining the identification of minor characters in the MORTE
      ARTHURE.

606. Brewer, D. S. Review of THE TALE OF THE DEATH OF KING ARTHUR,
      ed. Eugène Vinaver [no. 154]; and of R. M. Lumiansky, "The
      Question of Unity in Malory's MORTE DARTHUR" [no. 589].
      MEDIUM AEVUM, 25 (1957), 22-26.

      Brewer states that the MORTE DARTHUR is a "series" of tales
      and emphasizes that there are links between them. He also
      points out that the tales were passed down as a group in their
      textual tradition and that none of the tales is found in a
      separate manuscript. Brewer summarizes and gives a favorable
      review of Lumiansky's argument for the unity of the MORTE DAR-
      THUR.

607. Davies, R. T. "Was Pellynor Unworthy?" N & Q, N.S. 4 (1957),
      370.

      Davies discusses the scene in which Pellynor, who refuses to
      help a lady who holds the body of her wounded knight and later
      finds that she has slain herself and that the two have been
      eaten by lions, rebukes himself that he might have saved her
      He is accused by Gwenyver of being responsible for the lady's
      death. According to Vinaver, Pellynor's first duty is to save
      his own life; Davies claims that the lady's death is not Pel-
      lynor's responsibility because she had no right to kill herself.

608. Loomis, Roger Sherman. "Onomastic Riddles in Malory's BOOK OF
      ARTHUR AND HIS KNIGHTS." MEDIUM AEVUM, 25 (1957), 181-90.

      Loomis discusses the origins of curious names in the MORTE DAR-
      THUR, such as Sir Ozanna le Cure Hardy and Colgrevaunce of
      Goore.

609. Lumiansky, R. M. "Gawain's Miraculous Strength: Malory's Use
      of 'Le Morte Arthur' and 'Mort Artu.'" EA, 10 (1957), 97-108.

      Lumiansky traces the references to Gawain's increase in strength
      at noon from the MORT ARTU to LE MORTE ARTHUR and the MORTE DAR-
      THUR to prove that Malory was not simply borrowing from his
      sources but chose details from them to suit his own literary
      purposes. The argument is presented as evidence for the unity
      of the MORTE DARTHUR.

610. _____. "Malory's 'Tale of Lancelot and Guinevere' as
      Suspense." MEDIAEVAL STUDIES, 19 (1957), 108-22.

      For annotation, see the revision, "'The Tale of Lancelot and
      Guinevere': Suspense." MALORY'S ORIGINALITY, ed. R. M. Lumi-
      ansky [no. 673.7], pp. 205-32.

611. _____. "Two Notes on Malory's 'Morte Darthur.' I. Sir
      Urry in England. II: Lancelot's Burial Vow." NM, 58 (1957),
      148-53.

      I. Lumiansky asserts that the narration makes it clear that
      Urry's mother says she has brought him to England to be healed,
      yet Arthur then asks why she has brought him to England. In
      reply to Vinaver [no. 129, p. 1597], who claims that this is
      an inconsistency, Lumiansky interprets Arthur's words not as
      an unnecessary question but as a question about why she brought
      Urry to England ("to that londe"). II. Lumiansky contests
      Vinaver's opinion that Malory's characterization of Lancelot
      is inconsistent.

612. Šimko, Ján. WORD-ORDER IN THE WINCHESTER MANUSCRIPT AND IN WIL-
      LIAM CAXTON'S EDITION OF THOMAS MALORY'S 'MORTE DARTHUR' (1485)
      --A COMPARISON. Halle, 1957.

      Simko compares the linguistic differences between Caxton's
      Book 5 and Tale 2 of the Winchester Manuscript, which are based
      on the Alliterative MORTE ARTHURE, and concludes that Caxton
      revised the relatively free word-order of the Winchester Manu-
      script into a stricter, more regular and formal subject-verb
      (declarative) pattern. Whereas Malory had used the MORTE
      ARTHURE with some freedom, Caxton revised by regularizing Ma-
      lory's language. This tendency toward a fixed word-order is
      an important characteristic of the later fifteenth century.
      Šimko also states that the archaic style of Book 5, when com-
      pared to the simpler and more natural style of Book 4, gives
      credence to Vinaver's theory that Malory wrote Book 5 before
      Books 1-4.
          a. Rolf Berndt, ZAA, 7 (1959), 77-82.
          b. Archibald A. Hill, LANGUAGE, 35 (1959), 561-64.
          c. Herbert Pilch, ANGLIA, 77 (1959), 496-98.

d. Priscilla Preston, MLR, 54 (1959), 252-53.
e. Tauno F. Mustanoja, NM, 61 (1960), 391-92.
f. Gerd Mann, ARCHIV, 197 (1960-61), 213-14.

613. Wilson, Robert H. "The Cambridge SUITE DU MERLIN Re-examined."
TEXAS STUDIES IN ENGLISH, 36 (1957), 41-51.

Wilson summarizes the debate between Bogdanow and himself
about the rebellion of the kings episode in the SUITE DU MER-
LIN [see nos. 568 and 586]. He claims that the episode originally came between the coronation scene at the end of the
MERLIN and the begetting of Mordred at the beginning of the
SUITE DU MERLIN. The rebellion episode derives from the ES-
TOIRE, a continuation of the MERLIN, and is therefore an interpolation in the Cambridge Manuscript. Bogdanow believes
that it may be part of the original SUITE, excised in the Huth
manuscript and the Spanish DEMANDA versions. Wilson repeats
his former conclusion that the episode is an interpolation.

614. Bogdanow, Fanni. "The Character of Gauvain in the Thirteenth-
Century Prose Romances." MEDIUM AEVUM, 27 (1958), 154-61.

Bogdanow states that Malory used the two Gauvain traditions
which he inherited from his French sources: the hero (twelfth-
century tradition) and the villain (thirteenth-century tradition). She examines how the changes in Gauvain's character
developed in the French romances.

615. Bradbrook, Muriel C. SIR THOMAS MALORY. [British Writers and
Their Work, No. 1.] London: Published for the British Coun-
cil and the National Book League by Longmans, 1958; Lincoln:
University of Nebraska Press, 1963.

Bradbrook discusses topics such as Malory the man, the MORTE
DARTHUR in epic and romance tradition, Malory's concept of the
Round Table, and tragic themes in the work. Of all loyalties,
that of knight to lord (the "masculine bond of fidelity") over-
shadows that of knight to lady; by loving Guinevere, Lancelot
divides his loyalties. In depicting the adventures of the
Round Table knights, Malory concentrates on action rather than
description, and their actions indirectly parallel the civil
strife of Malory's own society. The theme of religion is subordinated to themes of love and war. When the social loyalties
of the Round Table disintegrate, the characters revert to the
more primitive loyalties of kinship and the destruction of the
kingdom is imminent. Bradbrook believes that "it is in depicting heroic tragic action that Malory attains his full stature"
for he confronts the "unshirkable mysteries of anger and
fidelity, courage and grief, love and death" (p. 37).
    a. Rolf Berndt, ZAA, 7 (1959), 76-77.
    b. Agostino Lombardo, BELFAGOR, 14 (1959), 123.

616. Guerin, Wilfred Louis. "The Function of 'The Death of Arthur'
      in Malory's Tragedy of the Round Table." Dissertation. Tulane
      University, 1958. DA, 19 (1959), 2089. Revised as "'The Tale
      of the Death of Arthur': Catastrophe and Resolution." MALORY'S
      ORIGINALITY, ed. R. M. Lumiansky [no. 673.8], pp. 233-74.

      Guerin believes that Tale 8 is an artistic and successful con-
      clusion of the MORTE DARTHUR. He concludes that the Stanzaic
      MORTE ARTHUR is a more important source for Tale 8 than the
      MORT ARTU, that the first seven tales foreshadow the events
      of the eighth, and that the tragedy has cathartic value because
      the characters realize that they wrought their own destruction.

*617. Kuriyagawa, Fumio. "The Language of Malory's TALE OF ARTHUR AND
      LUCIUS." SEL, 24 (1958), 253-69. [In Japanese.]

618. Magill, Frank Northen, ed. CYCLOPEDIA OF WORLD AUTHORS. New
      York: Harper, 1958.

      Brief biography of Thomas Malory of Warwickshire, proposed by
      Kittredge as author [nos. 329 and 339].

619. Vinaver, Eugène. "King Arthur's Sword, or the Making of a Medie-
      val Romance." BJRL, 40 (1958), 513-26.

      Vinaver states that the Arthurian romances should be assessed
      not as predecessors of the modern novel or vestiges of folklore
      and legend, but as artistic creations. He discusses the story
      of Arthur's sword Excalibur in the romances to show what atti-
      tudes, themes, and emphases were important to each writer.

620. Adams, Robert P. "'Bold Bawdry and Open Manslaughter': The Eng-
      lish New Humanist Attack on Medieval Romance." HUNTINGTON LI-
      BRARY JOURNAL, 23 (1959-60), 33-48.

      Adams aims to provide an understanding of and rationale for
      humanists' attacks on the romances. Ideas the humanists op-
      posed--tyranny, war, and destruction of society, false concepts
      of "honor" and "glory," women as objects of passion--are glori-
      fied in the romances.

621. Jones, David. "The Myth of Arthur." EPOCH AND ARTIST. Ed. Har-
      man Grisewood. New York: Chilmark; London: Faber and Faber,
      1959, pp. 212-59.

      See pp. 243-53. Jones believes that Malory described knight-
      hood with realism and force. The driving intensity of the
      MORTE DARTHUR provides it with a kind of unity, but Jones finds
      most critical discussions of "unity" artifical and unsatisfac-
      tory. He praises Malory's originality and his style, through
      which Malory "frequently conveys [the] feeling of men doing

things, good or bad, 'to the uttermost'" (p. 247).

622. Lumiansky, R. M. "Malory's Steadfast Bors." TULANE STUDIES IN
      ENGLISH, 8 (1959), 5-20.

      Lumiansky argues that Malory added to and altered his sources
      to make Bors a consistent supporting character whose main func-
      tion is to serve as a foil to Lancelot. Bors provides a con-
      trast to Lancelot's instability and serves as the "patient
      bearer of protective responsibility for Lancelot" (p. 5). Ma-
      lory's characterization of Bors suggests that the MORTE DARTHUR
      is a "unified" work and not eight separate tales.
        a. Hume Dowe, AUMLA, 12 (1959), 80-81.
        b. Edward Standop, ANGLIA, 77 (1959), 252.

623. Olstead, Myra Mahlow. "The Role and Evolution of the Arthurian
      Enchantress." Dissertation. University of Florida, 1959.
      DA, 24 (1963), 731.

      Olstead states that the Arthurian enchantresses originated in
      Celtic myth and evolved distinct traditions. Morgan le Fay
      is an especially important figure. The Arthurian enchantresses
      play a very important role in the MORTE DARTHUR.

624. Rioux, Robert N. "Sir Thomas Malory, Créateur Verbal." EA, 12
      (1959), 193-97.

      Rioux assesses the influence of French on Malory's vocabulary.
      He believes that Malory adapted nineteen words from the French,
      only six of which are attributed to him in the NEW ENGLISH DIC-
      TIONARY. [See criticism in no. 783.]

625. Sandved, Arthur Olav. "A Note on the Language of Caxton's Malory
      and That of the Winchester MS." ENGLISH STUDIES, 40 (1959),
      113-14.

      Sandved states that although the Winchester and Caxton versions
      generally have no endings on the present plural, Caxton some-
      times uses -en when the Winchester Manuscript contains -yth.
      He believes that the latter probably retains the usage of their
      common source.

626. Schirmer, Walter F. GESCHICHTE DER ENGLISCHEN UND AMERIKANISCHEN
      LITERATUR. Tübingen, 1959. Vol. 1, pp. 184-86.

      A general discussion of the MORTE DARTHUR. Schirmer stresses
      Malory's importance as a prose writer and the antithesis be-
      tween Malory's world and the idealized Arthurian world which
      he creates.

627. Vinaver, Eugène. "Sir Thomas Malory." ALMA. Ed. Roger Sherman
      Loomis. Oxford: Clarendon Press, 1959, pp. 541-52.

A survey of the Malory biography controversy, the MORTE DARTHUR, and its sources. Vinaver says that the work and its sources should be studied together, not separately, so that Malory's artistic development can be understood.
a. Thomas A. Kirby, YALE REVIEW, N.S. 49 (1960), 627-29.
b. Jean Marx, ÉTUDES CELTIQUES, 9 (1960), 253-59.
c. Philippa Moody, MEANJIN, 19 (1960), 328-29.
d. P. Richard, FRENCH STUDIES, 14 (1960), 242-44.
e. Mario Roques, ROMANIA, 81 (1960), 124-26.
f. John Speirs, SPECTATOR, 204 (Jan. 8, 1960), 46.
g. VQR, 36 (Summer 1960), lxxxii.
h. Ronald N. Walpole, RR, 51 (1960), 288-92.
i. M. O'C. Walshe, MLR, 55 (1960), 609-10.
j. Mary Williams, FOLK-LORE, 71 (1960), 134-35.
k. R. T. Davies, RES, N.S. 2 (1961), 66-68.
l. Mary E. Giffin, CL, 13 (1961), 179-83.
m. Urban T. Holmes, SPECULUM, 36 (1961), 144-49.
n. Howard R. Patch, RP, 14 (1961), 295-302.
o. H. L. Rogers, SOUTHERLY, 21 (1961), 60.
p. T. C. Rumble, CRITICISM, 3 (1961), 67-70.
q. M. T., PERSONALIST, 42 (1961), 250.
r. Dorothy Bethurum, JEGP, 61 (1962), 160-64.
s. F. Whitehead, MEDIUM AEVUM, 31 (1962), 202-05.
t. John Leyerle, UTQ, 32 (1963), 205.
u. Alan Renoir, ENGLISH STUDIES, 47 (1966), 57-63.

628. Wilson, R[ichard] M. "On the Continuity of English Prose." MÉLANGES DE LINGUISTIQUE ET DE PHILOLOGIE, FERNAND MOSSÉ IN MEMORIAM. Paris: Didier, 1959, pp. 486-94.

Wilson states that Chambers [no. 452] underestimated the importance of Caxton and Malory in the development of modern English prose.

629. Daiches, David. A CRITICAL HISTORY OF ENGLISH LITERATURE. New York: Ronald Press; London: Secker and Warburg, 1960. Vol. 1, pp. 139-42.

Daiches characterizes Malory's style as epic and elegaic and agrees with Chambers [no. 452] that Malory is outside the mainstream of English prose tradition. He agrees with Vinaver that "it is not the clash between courtly love and heavenly love so much as the clash between courtly love and feudal loyalty that interests Malory" (pp. 140-41).

630. Ferguson, Arthur B. THE INDIAN SUMMER OF ENGLISH CHIVALRY: STUDIES IN THE DECLINE AND TRANSFORMATION OF CHIVALRIC IDEALISM. Durham, N.C.: Duke University Press; London: Cambridge University Press, 1960.

See pp. 42-58. Ferguson discusses Malory in relation to his

cultural and historical backgrounds. He says that Malory is
concerned with the "ethical value of chivalry in his own day"
(p. 58) and that he reworked his Arthurian materials with the
didactic purpose of making the MORTE DARTHUR an exemplum for
his own time. Although the fall of the Round Table society
does parallel the fratricidal War of the Roses, Malory does
not present a "systematic political allegory" (p. 44). His
chivalric code--a "practical code of conduct" (p. 46)--differs
from the courtly love ideal of his sources. Ferguson states
that Malory is concerned with the religious aspects of the work
and the problem of salvation, but though Malory recognizes the
importance of heavenly chivalry, he is more concerned with both
spiritual and worldly chivalry, and virtuous living is necessary to both.

    a. B. A. Robie, LJ, 85 (Mar. 15, 1960), 1111.
    b. D. S. Brewer, N & Q, N.S. 8 (1961), 195-96.
    c. William H. Dunham, Jr., JOURNAL OF MODERN HISTORY, Sept.
       1961, p. 313.
    d. J. R. L. Highfield, RES, Aug. 1961, pp. 287-88.
    e. Richard A. Newhall, AMERICAN HISTORICAL REVIEW, 66 (1961),
       504.
    f. M. R. Powicke, SPECULUM, 36 (1961), 482-84.
    g. D. M. S., ENGLISH, 13 (1961), 159.
    h. A. R. Wagner, HISTORY, N.S. 46 (June 1961), 136.
    i. Denys Hay, ENGLISH HISTORICAL REVIEW, 77 (Jan. 1962),
       145-46.
    j. Helaine Newstead, JEGP, 61 (1962), 373.

631. Hassall, W. O. WHO'S WHO IN HISTORY. Oxford: Blackwell, 1960.
     Vol. 1, pp. 242-43.

    A discussion of the Malory biography controversy. Hassall says
    that the author is practically unknown, for no "claim" as to
    his identity is undeniably valid. The Warwickshire Malory pro-
    posed by Kittredge [nos. 329 and 339] has the "least shadowy
    claim."

632. Lascelles, Mary. "Sir Dagonet in Arthur's Show." SHAKESPEARE
     JAHRBUCH, 96 (1960), 145-54.

    Lascelles suggests that Shakespeare read the MORTE DARTHUR and
    discusses Warton's commentary on the work [no. 272].

633. Matthews, William. THE TRAGEDY OF ARTHUR; A STUDY OF THE ALLIT-
     ERATIVE 'MORTE ARTHURE.' Berkeley and Los Angeles: University
     of California Press, 1960.

    See pp. 172-77. Matthews says that Malory adapted the MORTE
    ARTHURE by shortening it considerably; most importantly, he
    omitted the last quarter of his source so that he could make
    Arthur triumphant in the battle. In adapting the first three
    quarters of the MORTE ARTHURE, Malory reveals a special attitude

to Arthur and to his war: he makes Arthur more self-controlled and charitable, and makes the war more justified and less brutal.

a. Larry D. Benson, SPECULUM, 36 (1961), 673-75.
b. D. M. S., ENGLISH, 13 (1961), 242.
c. R. T. Davies, MLR, 57 (1962), 407.
d. H. Newstead, RP, 16 (1962), 188-92.
e. T. C. Rumble, CRITICISM, 4 (1962), 381-84.
f. R. W. Ackerman, JEGP, 62 (1963), 362.
g. J. Finlayson, MEDIUM AEVUM, 32 (1963), 74-77.
h. J. L. N. O'Loughlin, RES, N.S. 14 (May 1963), 179-82.
i. TLS, Nov. 21, 1963, p. 952.
j. David C. Fowler, RR, 55 (April 1964), 112.

634. Moorman, Charles. ARTHURIAN TRIPTYCH: MYTHIC MATERIALS IN CHARLES WILLIAMS, C. S. LEWIS, AND T. S. ELIOT. [Perspectives in Criticism, No. 5.] Berkeley: University of California Press, 1960.

Moorman states that two themes unify the MORTE DARTHUR: courtly love (in the Lancelot-Guinevere and Tristram-Isolde relationships) and the Holy Grail.

635. _____. "Courtly Love in Malory." ELH, 27 (1960), 163-76.

Moorman's purpose is to "define the part played by the system of courtly love in the history of Arthur's kingdom as Malory conceived it" (p. 164). Of the three narrative threads—the Lot-Pellinore feud, the Grail quest, and the love affair of Lancelot and Guinevere—the latter is most important. Malory exploits the paradoxical nature of courtly love so that it serves as a catalyst for the tragic theme of the fall of Arthurian civilization. [Incorporated in no. 680.]

636. _____. "The Relation of Books I and III of Malory's 'Morte Darthur.'" MEDIAEVAL STUDIES, 22 (1960), 361-66.

Moorman argues that Books [Tales] I and III of the MORTE DARTHUR have thematic significance because they contrast the old and new ideals of knighthood. Book [Tale] I shows a primitive society (exemplified by Gawain) and Book [Tale] III a courtly society (exemplified by Lancelot). These books [tales] also have narrative links with the important themes of the MORTE DARTHUR: the Lancelot-Guinevere relationship, the Lot-Pellinore feud, and the Grail quest.

637. Morton, A. L. "The Matter of Britain: The Arthurian Cycle and the Development of Feudal Society." ZAA, 8 (1960), 5-28. Rpt. as a monograph, 24 pp.

Morton discusses the MORTE DARTHUR as the culmination of the

English Arthurian tradition and says that Malory wrote the
"funeral oration" of English feudalism. Morton interprets
the work from a biographical perspective: "Defeated, a prisoner, sick perhaps, Malory endowed his epic with the sense of
failure and decay which he felt for his own life and his own
cause" (p. 24).

638. Pickford, Cedric E. L'ÉVOLUTION DU ROMAN ARTHURIEN EN PROSE VERS
LA FIN DU MOYEN AGE. Paris: Nizet, 1960.

Pickford compares Malory's work with that of Gunnot, a copier
(and probably compiler), whose techniques are closer to those
of Caxton than of Malory. Pickford states that in the later
Middle Ages, France had no "Malory" of its own to rejuvenate
and adapt its Arthurian materials.
a. H. H. Christmann, ZFSL, 71 (1961), 110-15.
b. S. Cigada, STUDI FRANCESI, 15 (1961), 526-27.
c. A. D. Crow, MLR, 56 (1961), 608-10.
d. R. S. Loomis, SPECULUM, 36 (1961), 683-84.
e. Alice Guillemin, BIBLIOTHÈQUE DE L'ÉCOLE DES CHARTES,
120 (1963), 226-28.

639. Rumble, Thomas C. "Malory's WORKS and Vinaver's Comments: Some
Inconsistencies Resolved." JEGP, 59 (1960), 59-69.

Rumble examines what Vinaver, in his Commentary to the 1947
edition of the Winchester Manuscript [no. 129], calls inconsistencies in the MORTE DARTHUR.

640. Stevenson, Lionel. THE ENGLISH NOVEL: A PANORAMA. Boston:
Houghton-Mifflin, 1960.

Stevenson refers to the importance of Malory and the early
printed book in the development of prose fiction. "Though Malory may have been merely a conscientious historian, compiling
material from the huge mass of Arthurian romances, he seems to
have worked rather in the manner of a modern historical novel-
ist, following his sources as far as they were available and
effective, but feeling free to invent details and to elaborate
character in order to give artistic as well as factual validity"
(p. 11).

641. Wright, Thomas Lundy. "Originality and Purpose in Malory's
'Tale of King Arthur.'" Dissertation. Tulane University, 1960.
DA, 21 (1960-61), 2280-82.

Wright examines thematic problems in Tale 1 of the MORTE DAR-
THUR, studies Malory's source (the SUITE DU MERLIN), and offers
a new interpretation of the subdivisions in Tale 1. He argues
that Malory's changes in his source demonstrate that he attempts to unify and develop his own interpretation of the material. [See no. 673.1.]

642. Angelescu, Victor. "The Relationship of Gareth and Gawain in Malory's 'Morte D'Arthur.'" N & Q, N.S. 8 (1961), 8-9.

Angelescu states that the mention of Gawain's vengeful nature in the Book of GARETH foreshadows and prepares for its eruption in the later books. He presents this as evidence that Malory wrote one unified work and not eight separate tales.

643. Barber, R. W. ARTHUR OF ALBION: AN INTRODUCTION TO THE ARTHURIAN LITERATURE AND LEGENDS OF ENGLAND. New York: Barnes and Noble, 1961.

See the revised version, KING ARTHUR IN LEGEND AND HISTORY [no. 816].

644. Davis, Norman. "Styles in English Prose of the Late Middle and Early Modern Period." ACTES DU VIIIe CONGRÈS DE LA FÉDÉRATION INTERNATIONALE DES LANGUES ET LITTÉRATURES MODERNES. Liège: Université de Liège, 1961, pp. 165-81.

Davis disagrees with Chambers [no. 452] that Malory is outside the "mainstream" of the English prose tradition. He concludes that although English religious prose is important in the development of modern English prose, French prose has had more influence than is generally credited.

645. Hillyer, Robert. "Speaking of Books." NEW YORK TIMES BOOK REVIEW SECTION, Sept. 10, 1961, p. 2.

A general appreciation of the MORTE DARTHUR.

646. Jacob, Ernest Fraser. THE FIFTEENTH CENTURY, 1399-1485. [Oxford History of England.] Oxford: Clarendon Press, 1961.

Jacob agrees with Chambers' assessment [no. 452] of Malory's place in the English prose tradition. "It could not be claimed that either in his language or in his thought Malory is typical of the prose of the fifteenth century" (p. 658).

647. Lumiansky, R. M. "Arthur's Final Companions in Malory's MORTE DARTHUR." TULANE STUDIES IN ENGLISH, 11 (1961), 5-19.

Lumiansky examines Malory's version of the "passing of Arthur." Malory adds the inscription from the Alliterative MORTE ARTHURE (hic jacet Arthurus, rex quondam rexque futurus) to leave open two possibilities: that Arthur's body lies in the tomb of the chapel, and that Arthur is taken to Avalon to be healed and may return. Lumiansky believes that the names given to the ladies in the boat have special significance: Morgan le Fay and the Queen of North Wales represent the evil use of supernatural powers, and Nineve and the Queen of the Wastelands represent

their good use. He discusses the character of Morgan le Fay
and argues that her evil is not fortuitous but shows that evil
is inherent in Arthurian society.

648. Moorman, Charles. "Internal Chronology in Malory's MORTE DAR-
THUR." JEGP, 60 (1961), 240-49.

Moorman argues that the chronological inconsistencies which
Vinaver finds in the MORTE DARTHUR are not evidence that Malory
wrote eight separate tales but are actually proof that the
MORTE DARTHUR has unity. He claims that the inconsistencies
point to a "planned chronology which makes use of cross reference and retrospective narrative in order to establish its
sequence of events" (p. 243). The internal chronology is
therefore proof of "planned unity." It allowed Malory to emphasize themes rather than time structure and to develop his
version of the Arthurian stories in an artistic and climactic
way. [See nos. 757 and 762.]

*649. Noguchi, Shunichi. "Malory's English: An Aspect of Its Syntax."
HIROSHIMA STUDIES IN ENGLISH LANGUAGE AND LITERATURE, 7 (1961).

650. Ryding, William Wellington. "Structural Patterns in Medieval
Narrative." Dissertation. Columbia University, 1961. DA, 26
(1965), 3308-09.

Ryding claims that Malory changed the interlace structure of
his source into a more unified narrative structure. [This dissertation is revised in no. 799.]

651. Seaton, Ethel. SIR RICHARD ROOS, c. 1410-1482: LANCASTRIAN
POET. London: Rupert Hart-Davis, 1961.

Seaton thinks that the name "Beaumains" may have been suggested
by the name of Richard Beauchamp, Earl of Warwick, Malory's
commander in France.

652. Dubois, Marguerite-Marie. LA LITTÉRATURE ANGLAISE DU MOYEN AGE
(500-1500). Paris: Presses Universitaires de France, 1962.

See pp. 142-43. Dubois calls Malory an "adapteur de génie."
The strengths of the MORTE DARTHUR are its dialogue and Malory's
prose style; its weaknesses are inadequate depiction of emotion
and poor portrayal of the symbolic aspects of its sources.

653. Dundes, Alan. "The Father, the Son, and the Holy Grail." LIT-
ERATURE AND PSYCHOLOGY, 12 (1962), 101-12.

A psychoanalytic analysis of the MORTE DARTHUR. Dundes iden-
tifies a father-son motif: the rise of the son to power. Both
Arthur and Lancelot have father-son roles. In his role as son,
Arthur rises to power by pulling the sword from the stone (a

phallic symbol). He also serves as a father figure for Lancelot, who in turn assumes the father role for Galahad.

654. Goodman, John Stuart. "The Syntax of the Verb 'To Be' in Malory's
      Prose." Dissertation. University of Michigan, 1962. DA, 23
      (1963), 3363.

      Goodman concludes that Malory's verbal constructions are the
      same as those generally used in 1470.

655. Guerin, Wilfred L. "Malory's MORTE DARTHUR, Book VII." EXPLI-
      CATOR, 20 (1962), no. 64.

      Guerin argues that Malory invented the name "beaumains." Kay's
      application of the name to Gareth is ironic since it implies
      that a kitchen knave has the hands of a knight.

656. Bartholomew, Barbara Gray. "The Thematic Function of Malory's
      Gawain." CE, 24 (1963), 262-67.

      Bartholomew argues that the characterization of Gawain is in-
      consistent because "Malory accepts the inconsistency as the
      paradox inherent in the human condition" (p. 266). Gawain, a
      typical Round Table knight, shows the "failure of the ideal."
      The article contains a brief review of criticism about Malory's
      characterization of Gawain.

657. Bennett, J. A. W., ed. ESSAYS ON MALORY. Oxford: Clarendon
      Press, 1963.

      The articles in this collection are listed below in the order
      in which they appear. Bennett says that the essays do not
      represent a concensus of opinion but are replies to Vinaver's
      1947 edition of the Winchester Manuscript and to his chapter
      "Sir Thomas Malory" in ALMA [nos. 129 and 627].

657.1 Oakeshott, W[alter] F. "The Finding of the Manuscript." ES-
      SAYS ON MALORY, pp. 1-6.

      Oakeshott, librarian of the Moberly Library at Winchester
      College, describes the series of events leading to his dis-
      covery of the Winchester Manuscript of the MORTE DARTHUR in
      the Fellows Library of the College in 1934.

657.2 Lewis, C. S. "The English Prose MORTE." ESSAYS ON MALORY,
      pp. 7-28.

      [A revision of no. 535.] Lewis disagrees with five of Vina-
      ver's critical statements about the MORTE DARTHUR: 1. Malory
      and his work present a "moral paradox"; 2. Malory reduces the
      marvellous elements of his sources; 3. he unweaves the

entrelacement of his sources; 4. he misunderstood or ignored
the religious significance of the Grail quest; and 5. he
wrote eight separate tales. 1. Lewis maintains that the
paradox of the moral themes of the work and the alleged
criminal activities of its author is not important; furthermore, Malory cannot be called a "criminal" according to
modern standards. 2. While marvellous elements are less
prominent in the MORTE DARTHUR than in its sources, Malory's
omissions actually intensify the supernatural effect. 3. In
spite of Malory's effort to unweave the interlace structure
of his source, the "polyphonic" and interwoven narrative
still remains. 4. In the "Sankgreal," Malory does place emphasis on the ethical rather than the mystical, but the two
are not at odds. 5. The question whether the MORTE DARTHUR
is a unified work or eight separate tales would not concern
Malory. [See reply by Vinaver in no. 657.3.]

657.3   Vinaver, Eugène. "On Art and Nature." ESSAYS ON MALORY,
        pp. 29-40.

        A reply to Lewis [no. 657.2]. 1. Vinaver argues that a
        "cleavage" between the character of Malory and the tone of
        his book is possible. To stress the argument that the man
        and his work present a "moral paradox" is to use biography
        for the wrong critical purposes. 2 and 4. Vinaver agrees
        with Lewis that Malory seems to succeed in increasing the
        "Marvellous" and instilling religious significance in the
        Quest while he appears to have intended the opposite effect,
        but he credits this achievement to Malory's art, the "dis-
        crepancy between the intention and the result" (p. 33).
        5. Lewis's statement that the question of "one book or eight"
        would be foreign to Malory is pertinent, but Vinaver maintains
        that the critic must examine the author's result, not his in-
        tention. The tales do have unity but can exist as separate
        units. 3. In disentangling the structure of his sources,
        Malory showed creativity. His work is not a "grand paradox
        of nature" but a "lasting work of art" (p. 40).

657.4   Brewer D. S. "'the hoole book.'" ESSAYS ON MALORY, pp. 41-63.

        [A revision of no. 564.] Brewer's thesis is that the tales
        are "structurally connected, and fit into a particular order"
        and that the best critical term to describe the structure of
        the MORTE DARTHUR is "cohesion" (a term suggested to him by
        Vinaver). Cohesion is apparent in the "unity of tone and
        atmosphere" in the work, in the continuity of the main char-
        acters and events, in the references ahead. and backwards to
        the major characters and events, and in the joining of the
        tales by specific links. Brewer stresses that "Malory's
        conscious intentions are undiscoverable and unimportant, ex-
        cept in so far as they reveal themselves in the book" (p. 48).

657.5   Tucker, P. E.   "Chivalry in the MORTE."   ESSAYS ON MALORY,
         pp. 64-103.

         Tucker states that chivalry is the chief theme of the MORTE
         DARTHUR but that Malory's concept of chivalry differs from
         that of his sources.   In Books [Tales] 1 and 2, he depicts
         a martial chivalry which emphasizes knightly prowess and
         "worship."   In Book [Tale] 3, he depicts a courtly chivalry,
         though he does not see love as its proper goal. Malory seems
         to view the courtly love in his sources as artificial and
         immoral, and he depicts a love which is natural, spontaneous,
         and faithful--a form of loyalty. Although religious ideals
         can influence earthly chivalry, the latter remains an impor-
         tant goal for Malory. He does not therefore misunderstand
         his French sources. Malory's originality is evident in his
         use of Lancelot to unify the materials in the QUEST and the
         MORT ARTU and in his development of the concept of choice
         and free will so that Fate is no longer a predominant force
         in the fall of Arthur's kingdom. Tucker concludes that Ma-
         lory's concept of chivalry is practical, governed by Chris-
         tian values, and unified by the theme of loyalty. [See
         criticism of this article in no. 688.]

657.6   Whitehead, F[rederic].   "Lancelot's Penance."   ESSAYS ON MA-
         LORY, pp. 104-13.

         Whitehead compares the treatment of "Lancelot's penance" in
         the MORTE DARTHUR and in its sources, the MORT ARTU and the
         Stanzaic MORTE ARTHUR.   In the MORT ARTU, Lancelot behaves
         as a "chivalrous gentleman" but kills his friend Gareth by
         mischance. Lancelot wishes to make amends to Gawain and to
         avoid war, but he does not wish to tarnish his honor (his
         reputation among peers).   The last scene shows Lancelot's
         deep piety and faith but not his penance. In the Stanzaic
         MORTE ARTHUR, he does penance for Guinevere's sake. In the
         MORTE DARTHUR, he does not seek a religious life and would
         prefer earthly love if he could have it; he is not truly
         penitent but laments lost love and friendship.

657.7   Shaw, Sally.   "Caxton and Malory."   ESSAYS ON MALORY, pp. 114-
         45.

         After examining Caxton's editorial procedures in the MORTE
         DARTHUR, especially Book 5, Shaw concludes that Caxton did
         much to emphasize the unity of the rather "unsophisticated"
         text that he worked with.

         Note: The following are reviews of the whole of ESSAYS ON
         MALORY.
            a. B. K. Martin, AUMLA, 24 (Nov. 1963), 357.
            b. Marjory Rigby, N & Q, N.S. 10 (1963), 433-34.

c. J. Lawlor, MLR, 59 (1964), 99-100.
d. R. M. Lumiansky, MP, 62 (1964), 158-59.
e. Helaine Newstead, MEDIUM AEVUM, 33 (1964), 233-40.
f. Edmund Reiss, JEGP, 63 (1964), 147-49.
g. T. C. Rumble, SPECULUM, 39 (1964), 116-21.
h. R. H. Wilson, CRITICISM, 6 (1964), 92-95.
i. S. S. Hussey, ARCHIV, 201 (1965), 206-07.
j. Marie-Claude Blanchet, CCM, 9 (1966), 73-74.
k. Peter H. Salus, ENGLISH STUDIES, 48 (1967), 439-47.

658. Güller, Karl Heinz. KÖNIG ARTHUR IN DER ENGLISCHEN LITERATUR DES
      SPÄTEN MITTELALTERS. [Palaestra, Bd. 238.] Göttingen: Vander-
      hoeck and Ruprecht, 1963.

      See Chapter 5 (pp. 144-65). Güller argues that the development
      of Arthur's character in the MORTE DARTHUR from a heroic char-
      acter in the early tales to a fallen king whose decline mirrors
      the fate of man tends to give the work unity. Güller examines
      each tale of the work but emphasizes Malory's use of the Allit-
      erative MORTE ARTHURE in the early tales, and his treatment of
      theTristram and Grail stories.
      a. Dieter Mehl, GERMANISCH-ROMANISCHE MONATSSCHRIFT, 46
          (1965), 106-07.
      b. R. M. Wilson, MLR, 60 (1965), 240.
      c. Ulrich Broich, ARCHIV, 202 (1966), 64-65.
      d. A. J. Bliss, N & Q, N.S. 14 (1967), 32-33.

659. Hungerford, Harold Roe. "Comparative Constructions in the Work
      of Sir Thomas Malory: A Synchronic Study." Dissertation. Uni-
      versity of California at Berkeley, 1963. DA, 24 (1964), 5399.

      Transformational grammar of comparative constructions in the
      MORTE DARTHUR.

660. Loomis, Roger Sherman. "Sir Thomas Malory." THE DEVELOPMENT OF
      ARTHURIAN ROMANCE. London: Hutchinson Univ. Library, 1963;
      New York: Harper and Row, 1964, pp. 166-85.

      A general introduction to Malory and his work consisting of
      topics such as Malory's identity, his sources, his prose style,
      and the "unity" of the MORTE DARTHUR. Loomis states that if
      the work is not "unified" in a modern sense, it does show evi-
      dence of a general design.
      a. Christopher Hollis, TABLET, July 20, 1963, p. 791.
      b. TLS, Nov. 21, 1963, p. 952.
      c. R. M. Lumiansky, JEGP, 63 (1964), 762.
      d. W. Matthews, SPECULUM, 39 (1964), 717.
      e. Lewis Thorpe, FRENCH STUDIES, 18 (1964), 362-63.
      f. R. T. Davies, RES, N.S. 16 (1965), 58.
      g. A. Macdonald, MLR, 60 (1965), 588.
      h. C. E. Pickford, MEDIUM AEVUM, 34 (1965), 84.

661. Matthews, William. LATER MEDIEVAL ENGLISH PROSE. New York:
      Appleton-Century-Crofts, 1963.

      See p. 20. Matthews stresses that Malory's style is indebted
      to its French sources.

662. Moorman, Charles. "Lot and Pellinore: The Failure of Loyalty
      in Malory's 'Morte Darthur.'" MEDIAEVAL STUDIES, 25 (1963),
      83-92.

      [Incorporated in no. 680.] Moorman argues that the failure
      of loyalty, symbolized by the Lot-Pellinore feud, is a major
      theme in the MORTE DARTHUR which contributes to the fall of
      the Round Table. The article is an argument for the unity of
      the MORTE DARTHUR.

663. Morgan, Henry Grady. "The Role of Morgan le Fay in Malory's
      MORTE DARTHUR." SOUTHERN QUARTERLY, 2 (1963-64), 150-68.

      Morgan argues that Malory de-emphasizes the positive character-
      istics of Morgan le Fay (her powers of healing and prophecy)
      to make her strengthen the theme of disloyalty. She is a
      "symbol of the weakness in loyalty which is the ultimate down-
      fall of the society" (p. 166).

*664. Noguchi, Shunichi. "Notes on the Linguistic Differences Between
      Caxton's Edition and the Winchester Manuscript of Sir Thomas
      Malory's Works." FUKUI UNIVERSITY STUDIES IN THE HUMANITIES,
      No. 12 (1963). [In Japanese.]

665. Schlauch, Margaret. ANTECEDENTS OF THE ENGLISH NOVEL, 1400-1600
      (FROM CHAUCER TO DELONEY). London: Oxford University Press;
      Warszawa: Polish Scientific Publishers, 1963.

      See pp. 75-78. Schlauch claims that Malory's emphasis on human
      relationships and his reduction of supernatural elements mark
      his work as a forerunner of modern fiction. Old folk motifs,
      such as the Perilous Bed motif in the GARETH section, are some-
      times present. The MORTE DARTHUR is the "culmination and con-
      clusion of an old style in tale-telling rather than the
      announcement of a new" (p. 78).
      a. Dorothy Jones, AUMLA, 22 (1964), 300-01.
      b. R. M. Wilson, ENGLISH, 15 (Summer 1964), 63.
      c. Mark Eccles, RENAISSANCE NEWS, 18 (Winter 1965), 329-30.
      d. G. R. Hibbard, MLR, 60 (1965), 242-43.
      e. A. C. Kettle, RES, N.S. 16 (1965), 305-07.
      f. Merritt Lawlis, JEGP, 64 (1965), 297.
      g. Juliet Snow, MEDIUM AEVUM, 34 (1965), 73.
      h. M. Stam, NEOPHILOLOGUS, 49 (1965), 192-93.
      i. Ludwig Borinski, ERASMUS, 17 (1966), 339.
      j. Douglas Gray, N & Q, N.S. 13 (1966), 74-75.

666. Schmidz, Cornelia C. D. SIR GARETH OF ORKENEY: STUDIEN ZUM
      SIEBENTEN BUCH VON MALORY'S 'MORTE DARTHUR.' Groningen: J. B.
      Wolters, 1963.

          See Chapter 1 (pp. 1-33). This chapter summarizes the argu-
          ment that Malory's GARETH is related to the "fair unknown" ro-
          mances and discusses the controversy about the origin of the
          name "Beaumains."

667. Van Duzee, Mabel. A MEDIEVAL ROMANCE OF FRIENDSHIP: EGER AND
      GRIME. Preface by Roger Sherman Loomis. New York: Burt Frank-
      lin, 1963.

          Van Duzee discusses resemblances between EGER AND GRIME and the
          Book of GARETH. She compares Gareth's battle with the Red
          Knight of the Red Laundes with an episode in EGER AND GRIME.

668. Ackerman, Robert W. "Malory's Ironsyde." RESEARCH STUDIES [Wash-
      ington State University--Pullman], 32 (1964), 125-33.

          Ackerman discusses how the character of Ironsyde can help to
          identify Malory's source for the Tale of GARETH. Comparing
          GARETH with other romances that contain a character called
          Ironsyde, such as SIR LAMBEWELL and SYRE GAWENE AND THE CARLE
          OF CARELYLYE, Ackerman concludes that in Malory's source this
          knight was also called Ironsyde and that the source was written
          in English, though it may have been adapted from a French
          version.

669. Brengle, Richard L., ed. ARTHUR, KING OF BRITAIN. New York:
      Appleton-Century-Crofts, 1964.

          Brengle reprints excerpts from the Everyman edition of the
          MORTE DARTHUR, Bradbrook's SIR THOMAS MALORY [no. 615], and
          Vinaver's 1947 edition [no. 129].

670. Davis, Gilbert R. "Malory's 'Tale of Sir Lancelot' and the Ques-
      tion of Unity in the MORTE DARTHUR." PAPERS OF THE MICHIGAN
      ACADEMY OF SCIENCE, ARTS, AND LETTERS, 49 (1964), 523-30.

          An argument for the unity of the MORTE DARTHUR. Davis examines
          the structure of the Tale of LANCELOT. He states that Malory's
          intensification of the importance of Lancelot in the Tale of
          ARTHUR AND LUCIUS (to a degree not found in its source, the
          Alliterative MORTE ARTHURE) shows his preparation for Lancelot's
          emergence as the central character in the next tale. In it,
          references to Lancelot's chivalrous deeds for Guinevere provide
          a link with later tales, and the references to the growing love
          of Lancelot and Guinevere, many of which are Malory's additions,
          serve the same purpose. In the Tale of LANCELOT, the chief
          protagonist achieves full knightly stature and Malory presents
          Arthurian society in its glory.

671. Effland, Evelyn Leigh. "Plot, Character, Theme: A Critical
      Study of Malory's 'Works.'" Dissertation. University of Den-
      ver, 1964. DA, 26 (1965), 354.

      Effland states that Malory developed more skill with plot
      and structure as he wrote the tales and that the last two
      tales best demonstrate his writing skill. Malory de-empha-
      sized the marvellous and supernatural, the courtly love tra-
      dition, and the mystic spiritualism of the Grail. He presents
      a vision of a society almost without flaw which failed because
      it contained the weaknesses inherent in human nature.

672. Greaves, Margaret. "The Dream of Sir Thomas Malory." THE BLAZON
      OF HONOUR: A STUDY IN RENAISSANCE MAGNANIMITY. London: Me-
      thuen; New York: Barnes and Noble, 1964, pp. 46-61.

      Greaves asserts that a combination of chivalric and spiritual
      ideals constitutes Malory's concept of "magnanimity." Arthur
      is the chief embodiment of this ideal because he is "true both
      to the world of chivalry and the world of the spirit" (p. 60).

673. Lumiansky, R[obert] M., ed. MALORY'S ORIGINALITY: A CRITICAL
      STUDY OF 'LE MORTE DARTHUR.' Baltimore: Johns Hopkins Press,
      1964.

      Lumiansky claims that Malory wrote a "single unified book" and
      not, as Vinaver says, eight separate tales. He is concerned
      with Malory's "final intention." Each essay examines how an
      individual tale operates in the work as a whole and how it re-
      lates to its source(s). The essays are based on two critical
      assumptions: that source study is useful in assessing Malory's
      work, and that Malory was in control of his source materials.

673.1 Wright, Thomas L. "'The Tale of King Arthur': Beginnings and
      Foreshadowings." MALORY'S ORIGINALITY, pp. 9-66.

      Source: The SUITE DU MERLIN. Malory "aims at a more secular
      idealism and--with Lancelot as chief protagonist--at a more
      comprehensive Arthurian history than that foreseen in the
      SUITE" (p. 12). Malory does not abandon entrelacement but
      uses it and "retrospective narrative" to tie together stories
      within the tale and to link all the tales. He includes allu-
      sions which are important for establishing themes and linking
      episodes. The great theme of the failure inherent in Round
      Table society underlies Tale 1. [See no. 641.]

673.2 Dichmann, Mary E. "'The Tale of King Arthur and the Emperor
      Lucius': The Rise of Lancelot." MALORY'S ORIGINALITY, pp.
      67-90.

      [A revised version of no. 545.] Source: The Alliterative

MORTE ARTHURE. Dichmann suggests that Malory knew and used
sources other than the MORTE ARTHURE because he made structural changes at the end of the tale and altered the characterization of Arthur and his knights. These changes show
that Malory intended to link this tale with those that followed. The chief function of this tale is to establish
Lancelot as Arthur's chief knight and therefore prepare for
future events.

673.3   Lumiansky, R. M.   "'The Tale of Lancelot': Prelude to Adul-
        tery." MALORY'S ORIGINALITY, pp. 91-98.

        [This article appeared first as no. 575.] Source: The Agra-
        vain section of the Prose LANCELOT. Lumiansky states that
        Malory unified widely separated story lines in his sources.
        Four of the five references in the tale to Lancelot and
        Guinevere are original and "should be viewed as Malory's
        intentional effort to fit the 'Tale of Lancelot' into the
        progressive development of the Lancelot-Guinevere relation-
        ship which runs through LE MORTE DARTHUR" (p. 97). Malory
        established Lancelot as the chief hero but was more concerned
        with foreshadowing the Lancelot-Guinevere relationship.

673.4   Guerin, Wilfred L.   "'The Tale of Gareth': The Chivalric Flow-
        ering." MALORY'S ORIGINALITY, pp. 99-117.

        Source: Unknown. Though many critics believe that the
        source is a lost French romance, Guerin thinks that it is
        original. This tale represents a flowering of the chivalric
        ideal, a period of happiness and prosperity of the Round Ta-
        ble. The love ideal--married affection and loyalty--is seen
        in the relationship of Gareth and Lyonesse. Gareth serves
        as foil to show the merits and frailties of his brothers,
        especially Gawain. The tale serves as a backdrop for the
        coming catastrophe; Gareth's love for Lancelot prepares for
        the irony of Lancelot's inadvertent killing of Gareth later.
        [See no. 764 for criticism.]

673.5   Rumble, Thomas C.   "'The Tale of Tristram': Development by
        Analogy." MALORY'S ORIGINALITY, pp. 118-83.

        Source: A lost version of the French Prose TRISTAN. Rumble
        states that it is difficult to assess Malory's intention
        since the exact version of his source is unknown. His prob-
        able changes are the gradual, sinister evolution of Mark's
        character; the fact that the love of Tristram and Isolt is
        not caused by a potion; and the lack of treachery in Isolt's
        character. Malory subordinates Tristram to Lancelot, and
        the Arthur-Lancelot-Guinevere relationship parallels and is
        complemented by that of Mark-Tristram-Isolt to demonstrate
        that the former is not an isolated phenomenon in Arthurian

society. The TRISTRAM section provides time for the development of the "discrepancy" between the ideals of the Round
Table and the human limitations that will destroy it. [See
no. 592.]

673.6   Moorman, Charles. "'The Tale of the Sankgreal': Human Frailty." MALORY'S ORIGINALITY, pp. 184-204.

[This article first appeared as no. 599; it is incorporated
in no. 680.] Source: The Vulgate QUESTE DEL SAINT GRAAL.
Moorman opposes Vinaver's view that Malory secularized the
Grail story and that the TALE OF THE SANKGREAL is a translation and is not unified with the rest of the MORTE DARTHUR.
Moorman examines changes in "religious material," in characterization, and changes which show Malory's attempt to weld
the Grail story into the larger work. He claims that the
failure of Lancelot, who is unable to abandon his secular
ideals, is the failure of the society which he represents.
It is Galahad, the heavenly knight, who exposes the frailty
of Round Table society. References in other tales foreshadow
the Grail quest and the downfall of the Round Table society.

673.7   Lumiansky, R. M. "'The Tale of Lancelot and Guenevere': Suspense." MALORY'S ORIGINALITY, pp. 205-32.

[This article first appeared as no. 610.] Source: The MORT
ARTU, the Stanzaic MORTE ARTHUR, the Prose LANCELOT, and an
unknown source. Lumiansky states that Malory utilized his
materials in Tale 7 to heighten suspense. At the end of the
Grail section, Arthur is aware of the adulterous love of his
queen and his best knight, but he is willing to grant for-
giveness and trust Lancelot in order to save his kingdom.
The important question is whether Lancelot will keep his word
Tale 7 sets up two suspenseful situations: Will further dif-
ficulties between Lancelot and Guinevere produce a rift between them? And when will Arthur become aware of the renewed
adultery?

673.8   Guerin, Wilfred L. "'The Tale of the Death of Arthur': Catastrophe and Resolution." MALORY'S ORIGINALITY, pp. 233-74.

Source: The MORT ARTU and the Stanzaic MORTE ARTHUR. Opposing the general view that the MORT ARTU was Malory's primary
source, Guerin claims that "Malory turned to the English poem
as narrative guide, but desired greater elaboration of the
thoughts of his characters and deeper analysis of their emotional reactions than the poem provided. For this material
he turned either to the French or to his own invention"
(p. 244). The tale has three tragic figures: Lancelot, Arthur, and Gawain. Malory wrote a "tragedy of the Round Table
a human device intended to weld king and vassals into an

ordered society, but one which fails through human error" (p. 270). [See no. 616.]

Note: The following reviews refer to the whole of MALORY'S ORIGINALITY.
a. L. W. Griffith, LJ, 89 (1964), 3009.
b. Alison White, HUMANITIES ASSOCIATION BULLETIN, 15 (1964), 68-69.
c. CHOICE, 1 (1965), 479.
d. Christopher Dean, QUEEN'S QUARTERLY, 72 (1965), 418.
e. George Doskow, CE, 26 (1965), 490-91.
f. M. Dubois, EA, 18 (1965), 408-09.
g. Michael H. Means, THOUGHT, 40 (1965), 449-50.
h. Nathan Comfort Starr, MLQ, 26 (1965), 333-34.
i. Rosemary Woolf, CRITICAL QUARTERLY, 7 (1965), 386-87.
j. W. Matthews, SPECULUM, 41 (1966), 155-59.
k. P. E. Tucker, N & Q, N.S. 13 (1966), 39-40.
l. J. A. W. Bennett, RES, N.S. 18 (1967), 190-91.
m. Richard L. Greene, JEGP, 66 (1967), 120-24.
n. Peter H. Salus, ENGLISH STUDIES, 48 (1967), 439-47.
o. Derek Pearsall, MLR, 63 (1968), 934-35.

674. Watkins, John Pierce. "The Hero in Sir Thomas Malory." Dissertation. University of Pittsburgh, 1964. DA, 26 (1965), 1637.

Watkins states that the human and knightly qualities of seven characters (Arthur, Gawayne, Palomydes, Launcelot, Bors, Percyvale, and Galahad) are a mixture of greatness and frailty, success and weakness.

675. Matthews, William. "Alliterative Song of an Elizabethan Minstrel." RESEARCH STUDIES [Washington State University--Pullman], 32 (1964), 135-46.

According to Matthews, the minstrel who sang a song for the Queen's entertainment at Kenilworth that was "'warraunted for story out of King Arthurz acts, the first booke and 26. chapter'" shows a general awareness of the entire MORTE DARTHUR. [See no. 289.]

676. Nakashima, Kunio. "Impersonal Verbs in Malory." BULLETIN OF THE ENGLISH LITERARY SOCIETY OF NIHON UNIVERSITY, 15 (1964), 1-45. See Appendix in the BULLETIN, 18 (1968), 23.

This study concerns "quasi-impersonal verbs" which were changing to personal verbs in the Middle English period. Malory's usage represents a transitional stage in which both forms appear.

677. Doskow, George. "Contrasting Narrative Forms in the Works of Thomas Malory: A Critical Study of 'The Tale of King Arthur' and 'The Death of King Arthur.'" Dissertation. University of Connecticut, 1965. DA, 26 (1966), 6694.

Doskow states that a major shift in narrative form can be seen
in the first and last tales of the MORTE DARTHUR. The first
seems to rely on random causes, multiplicity of incident, little progress; the last shows a modern modern, ordered structure

678. Frappier, Jean. "Les romans de la Table Ronde et les lettres en
France aux XVIe siècle." RP, 19 (1965), 178-93.

See p. 193. Frappier says that France had no "Malory" to syn-
thesize the national Arthurian materials at the end of the Middle Ages.

679. Kane, George. THE AUTOBIOGRAPHICAL FALLACY IN CHAUCER AND LANG-
LAND STUDIES. [The Chambers Memorial Lecture delivered 2 March
1965 at University College London.] Published for the College
by H. K. Lewis, London.

Kane uses Malory as one example of the situation in which "biographical data exist which appear incongruent to the image of
the poet set up by his works" (p. 5). He stresses that the
personality of an author projected in his work is a construct
and does not constitute biographical evidence unless verified
by external data.

680. Moorman, Charles. THE BOOK OF KYNG ARTHUR: THE UNITY OF MALORY'
'MORTE DARTHUR.' Lexington: University of Kentucky Press, 196

[This incorporates material from nos. 599, 673.6, 635, 636, 662
and also nos. 681 and 717.] In the Prologue, Moorman discusses
the term "unity" in reference to the MORTE DARTHUR. He believe
that the work contains both "critical" and "historical" unity,
i.e. that Malory wrote a unified work and that he intended to
write such a work [see no. 589]. Chapter 1 examines the chrono
logy of the MORTE DARTHUR. Moorman claims that the chronological inconsistencies in Tales 2, 3, 4, and part of 5 show that
Malory used a "planned chronology which makes use of cross
references and retrospective narrative in order to establish it
sequence of events" (p. 5). Chapters 3, 4, and 5 discuss the
failures in love, religion, and chivalry which contribute to the
downfall of Round Table society. The plot is unified by three
"narrative threads": Lancelot and Guinevere (failure in love),
the Grail quest (failure in religion), and the Lot-Pellinore
feud (failure in chivalry). The last chapter discusses the
whole of the MORTE DARTHUR and its theme, which is the "rise,
flowering, and downfall of a well-nigh perfect civilization."
Moorman calls the work "tragic," not didactic.
  a. R. W. Ackerman, SPECULUM, 41 (1966), 758-61.
  b. CHOICE, 2 (1966), 861.
  c. R. T. Davies, RES, N.S. 17 (1966), 428-30.
  d. U. T. Holmes, SOUTH ATLANTIC QUARTERLY, 65 (1966), 294-95.
  e. D. S. Brewer, MLR, 62 (1967), 109.

f. George Doskow, CE, 27 (1967), 579.
g. K. H. Güller, ANGLIA, 85 (1967), 92-95.
h. Peter H. Salus, ENGLISH STUDIES, 48 (1967), 439-47.
i. Edward Vasta, JEGP, 66 (1967), 571-74.
j. Helaine Newstead, MEDIUM AEVUM, 37 (1968), 219.
k. Ellyn Olefsky [no. 757].
1. R. H. Wilson [no. 762].

681. Moorman, Charles. "Malory's Tragic Knights." MEDIAEVAL STUDIES, 27 (1965), 117-27.

For annotation, see no. 717.

682. Quinn, Esther Casier. "The Quest of Seth, Solomon's Ship, and the Grail." TRADITIO, 21 (1965), 185-222.

See pp. 185-87. Quinn says that the "Solomon's ship episode" in Book 17 is never adequately explained in the MORTE DARTHUR. She accepts Vinaver's opinion that Malory misunderstood his source, the French QUESTE, and says that his changes "obscure both its religious significance and poetic integrity" (p. 186).

683. Rexroth, Kenneth. "Le Morte d'Arthur." SATURDAY REVIEW OF LIT-ERATURE, 48 (July 10, 1965), 19. Reprinted as "Malory: Le Morte d'Arthur." CLASSICS REVISITED by Kenneth Rexroth. New York: Avon, 1968, pp. 164-68.

A general assessment of Malory's appeal for his readers.

684. Scott-Giles, C. W. "Some Arthurian Coats of Arms." THE COAT OF ARMS [Heraldry Society], 8 (Oct. 1965), 332-39; 9 (Jan. 1966), 30-35.

The names and arms of 150 knights of the Round Table appear in the appendix of a treatise entitled "La forme quon tenoit des tournoys et assemblees au temps du roy uterpendragon et du roy artus" by (it is thought) Jacques d'Armagnac, Duc de Nemours. Scott-Giles discusses only those knights who appear in the MORTE DARTHUR. He lists each character, identifies him, describes his arms, and furnishes a drawing of each coat of arms.

685. Steinbeck, John. "Great Find in English Castle: 3d 'Morte d'Arthur' Version." PHILADELPHIA BULLETIN, Dec. 1965/Jan. 1966. [Page numbers unknown.]

Steinbeck reports the supposed discovery, later proven false, of a third version of the MORTE DARTHUR in the library of Alnwick Castle in Northumberland. [See nos. 704 and 865.3.]

686. Bogdanow, Fanni. THE ROMANCE OF THE GRAIL: A STUDY OF THE STRUC-TURE AND GENESIS OF A THIRTEENTH-CENTURY ARTHURIAN PROSE ROMANCE. Manchester: Manchester University Press; New York: Barnes and Noble, 1966.

[Also listed as no. 35.] This book contains references to the
relationship between the MORTE DARTHUR and the SUITE DU MERLIN.
   a. G. S., BROTERIA, 83 (1966), 580.
   b. Jean Fourquet, EA, 20 (1967), 180.
   c. E. von Richthofen, SPECULUM, 42 (1967), 357-58.
   d. W. P. Gerritsen, NEOPHILOLOGUS, 52 (1968), 196-97.
   e. D. G. Hoggan, MLR, 63 (1968), 245-47.
   f. R. S. Loomis, ARCHIV, 204 (1968), 215-18.
   g. B. K. Martin, AUMLA, 29 (1968), 104-05.
   h. Bernhard König, ZRP, 85 (1969), 281-86.
   i. F. Lecoy, ROMANIA, 90 (1969), 429-32.
   j. A. Micha, CCM, 12 (1969), 299-301.

687. Cosman, Madeleine P. THE EDUCATION OF THE HERO IN ARTHURIAN RO-
MANCE. Chapel Hill: University of North Carolina Press, 1966.

Cosman believes that Malory's account of the _enfance_ of Tristram, which differs from that presented in the French Prose
TRISTAN, may be derived from a version other than the extant
manuscript, or may be, as Vinaver thinks, Malory's own invention. Though the elements of the story resemble those in earlier versions of the TRISTAN, in the MORTE DARTHUR the
"education of the hero merely spans the time between infancy
and knighthood" and does not contain special interest. A bibliographical note on TRISTAN studies is on p. 46.
   a. CHOICE, 4 (1967), 528.
   b. E. R. Harvey, N & Q, N.S. 15 (1968), 147-48.
   c. E. Eisner, ARIZONA QUARTERLY, 25 (1969), 283.
   d. J. L. Grigsby, RR, 60 (1969), 188-89.
   e. E[lspeth] Kennedy, MEDIUM AEVUM, 38 (1969), 322.
   f. R. E. Roberts, RP, 22 (1969), 355.

688. Davies, R. T. "The Worshipful Way in Malory." PATTERNS OF LOVE
AND COURTESY: ESSAYS IN MEMORY OF C. S. LEWIS. Ed. John Lawlor. London: Edward Arnold, 1966, pp. 157-77.

[This incorporates material from nos. 587 and 596.] Davies
discusses love and chivalry in the MORTE DARTHUR and replies
to Tucker [no. 657.5]. Davies says that virtuous love in the
MORTE DARTHUR is characterized by _stabylite_ and _mesure_. Loyal
service is emphasized in the Lancelot-Guinevere and Lancelot-
Arthur relationships (loyalty of man to lady and of man to man).
Honor (worldly "worship") and truth are separate concepts.
Davies claims that it is difficult to arrive at a single interpretation of the MORTE DARTHUR but sees this ambiguity as evi-
dence of Malory's sensitivity and not, as Tucker thinks, of
Malory's carelessness.

689. Fiester, Ben Francis. "The Function of the Supernatural in Malory's 'Morte Darthur.'" Dissertation. Pennsylvania State
University, 1966. DA, 28 (1968), 4124A-25A.

Fiester analyzes five supernatural figures (Merlin, Morgan le Fay, Nyneve, Balin, and Galahad) to determine whether Malory reduced the supernatural elements in his sources because he was averse to them or because he wished to use them for his own artistic purposes. He concludes that the supernatural is used to "support and interpret the realistic events of his narrative."

690. Hood, Edna Sue. "Sir Perceval of Galles: Medieval Fiction." Dissertation. University of Wisconsin, 1966. DA, 27 (1966), 1030A-31A.

Hood argues that of the four romances--SIR PERCEVAL, Malory's GARETH, LIBEAUS DESCONUS, and Malory's LA COTE MALE TAYLE-- the first two are more successful in developing the "fair un- known" theme.

691. Hyman, Stanley Edgar. "The English Iliad." STANDARDS: A CHRON- ICLE OF BOOKS FOR OUR TIMES by S. E. Hyman. New York: Horizon Press, 1966, pp. 143-47.

Hyman claims that the MORTE DARTHUR is not an "English ILIAD" because Malory did not fuse his materials into an epic form. He discusses the modernization of the work by Keith Baines [no. 203].

692. Lagorio, Valerie Marie. "The Legend of Joseph of Arimathea in Middle English Literature." Dissertation. Stanford University, 1966. DA, 27 (1967), 3431A.

Lagorio argues that the MORTE DARTHUR represents a last phase in the development of the Joseph of Arimathea legend in England in which the latter becomes an ecclesiastical figure and is patriotically associated with Glastonbury as an English saint.

693. Loomis, Roger Sherman. "The Structure of Malory's GARETH." STUDIES IN LANGUAGE AND LITERATURE IN HONOR OF MARGARET SCHLAUCH. Warsaw: Polish Scientific Publishers, 1966, pp. 219-25.

In this structural analysis of the GARETH section, Loomis traces parts of it to probable source s. The main structure is supplied by THE SICKBED OF CUCHULAINN, and most of the story derives from Welsh and Irish saga tradition. Malory's immediate source, however, was an Anglo-Norman romance.

694. Lundie, R. S. "Divided Allegiance in the Last Two Books of Ma- lory." THEORIA, 26 (1966), 93-111.

Lundie believes that in Malory's "telling and profound recogni- tion of the impermanence of human relationships lies one of the main elements of tragedy, and that in the theme of divided allegiance which rings through his last books he creates a

power that far surpasses gloom—a power that is essentially
tragic" (p. 94). He examines the characters of Lancelot,
Guinevere, and Arthur as "prime movers" of the events that
lead to catastrophe. Lancelot remains a great hero because
he maintains his loyalty both to Arthur and to Guinevere.

695. Martin, Lynn Simpson. "Sir Thomas Malory's Vocabulary in 'The
     Tale of Arthur and Lucius,' 'The Tale of Sir Gareth,' and
     'The Tale of the Sankgreal': A Comparative Study." Disser-
     tation. University of Pennsylvania, 1966. DA, 27 (1966),
     1376A.

     Martin seeks to determine whether Malory was a "translator" or
     an original writer. Martin compares the vocabularies of these
     three tales with the vocabularies of their respective sources
     (the Alliterative MORTE ARTHURE, the QUESTE DEL SAINT GRAAL,
     and an unknown source) and concludes that, although Malory was
     influenced by his sources, he does show some originality.

696. Marx, Jean. "Le thème du coup félon et le roman de Balain."
     MOYEN AGE, 72 (1966), 43-57.

     See pp. 43-44. Marx mentions that the Huth MERLIN lacks two
     folio pages which contain the "dolorous stroke" episode. Until
     the discovery of the Cambridge SUITE DU MERLIN by Vinaver in
     1945, the MORTE DARTHUR was the only source for this incident.

697. Matthews, William. THE ILL-FRAMED KNIGHT: A SKEPTICAL INQUIRY
     INTO THE IDENTITY OF SIR THOMAS MALORY. Berkeley: University
     of California Press, 1966.

     Matthews assesses the arguments for candidates proposed as au-
     thor of the MORTE DARTHUR [see nos. 339 and 349] and advances
     the candidacy of Thomas Malory of Yorkshire. Matthews admits
     that Kittredge's Warwickshire knight is the strongest claimant
     among the opposition, but he raises objections to him on the
     grounds of "moral paradox" (the discrepancy between Malory's
     character and the nature of his work) and "bibliographical par-
     adox" (the improbability that Malory could have written the
     work in Newgate prison, or that Grayfriars library nearby held
     a collection of manuscripts similar to Malory's sources). In
     support for the Yorkshire Malory, Matthews points to the number
     of northernisms in the text, Malory's use of northern romances
     and geographical locations, and his "fondness for alliterative
     phrases." He also attempts to prove that a flaw in his argu-
     ment—that it cannot be proven that the Yorkshire Malory was
     either a knight or a prisoner—is not so serious as it seems.
     The term "knight-prisoner" may mean "prisoner of war" and would
     therefore explain how Malory had access to materials and the
     leisure to write, and why no account of his imprisonment has
     been found, since no such records were kept for prisoners of war.
     The book contains a number of appendices, including pedigrees

and linguistic comparisons and analyses, and bibliographical
notes.
  a. Sigmund Eisner, ARIZONA QUARTERLY, 23 (1967), 93-95.
  b. CHOICE, 4 (1967), 158.
  c. Martin Seymour-Smith, "Doubting Sir Thomas," SPECTATOR,
      218 (1967), 368-69.
  d. TLS, Nov. 30, p. 1126.
  e. Hugh Trevor-Roper, [Sunday] TIMES, Mar. 5, 1967, p. 52.
  f. VQR, 43 (1967), lxxii.
  g. R. W. Ackerman, SPECULUM, 43 (1968), 182-85.
  h. E. R. Jacob and A. McIntosh, MEDIUM AEVUM, 37 (1968),
      344-48.
  i. E. Vinaver [no. 156, introduction].
  j. Pasquale DiPasquale, CL, 21 (1969), 168-71.
  k. Edward Vasta, JEGP, 68 (1969), 285-89.

698. Miko, Stephen J. "Malory and the Chivalric Order." MEDIUM AEVUM,
      35 (1966), 211-30.

      Miko states that the chivalric code provides "order" for the
      knights; it also stresses the importance of appearance, of up-
      holding one's reputation. Malory, however, is critical of
      chivalry because it forgets that men can be base. Miko calls
      the end of the MORTE DARTHUR a "tragic emulsion" (p. 299). In
      essence, "our sense of tragedy is a complex combination of
      recognition of the tragic ironies and sympathy with the value
      of what is being destroyed" (p. 230).

699. Reiss, Edmund. SIR THOMAS MALORY. [Twayne's English Authors
      Series, No. 35.] New York: Twayne Publishers, 1966.

      Reiss notes the small number of book-length studies of the
      MORTE DARTHUR. His objective is to study how the MORTE DARTHUR
      "functions as a work of literary art" and "to suggest how the
      MORTE DARTHUR can and should be read" (preface). The intro-
      duction is a general survey of MORTE DARTHUR criticism; it dis-
      cusses the "moral paradox" of the Warwickshire knight and his
      work, Malory's presentation of chivalry as an idealized past,
      the "unity controversy," and Malory's use of entrelacement.
      Reiss cautions against the use of source study which denies
      Malory's artistry and claims that Malory's authorial intentions
      are irrelevant to study of the work. The rest of the book is
      a general introduction to the MORTE DARTHUR and consists of a
      combination of summary and commentary based on Robertsonian
      critical theories.
        a. CHOICE, 4 (1967), 158.

700. Richmond, Velma Bourgeois. LAMENTS FOR THE DEAD IN MEDIEVAL NAR-
      RATIVE. [Duquesne Studies, Philological Series, No. 8.] Pitts-
      burg, Penn.: Duquesne University Press, 1966.

      Richmond discusses Ector's lament for Lancelot, Lancelot's

lament for Guinevere, and Arthur's lament for the Duchess of Brittany.

701. Roach, William. "Transformations of the Grail Theme in the First Two Continuations of the Old French PERCEVAL." PROCEEDINGS OF THE AMERICAN PHILOSOPHICAL SOCIETY, 110 (1966), 160–64.

Roach states that Malory used two concepts of the Grail story, evidently derived from Robert de Boron: the association of the Grail with the dish used at the Last Supper, and Joseph of Arimathea's collection of Christ's blood during the Crucifixion.

702. Scholes, Robert, and Robert Kellogg. THE NATURE OF NARRATIVE. New York and London: Oxford University Press, 1966.

A brief discussion of the MORTE DARTHUR and the term "medieval romance" is on pp. 248–49.

703. Šimko, Ján. "Thomas Malory's Creed." STUDIES IN LANGUAGE AND LITERATURE IN HONOR OF MARGARET SCHLAUCH. Warsaw: Polish Scientific Publishers, 1966, pp. 437–44.

This article is based on no. 577. Šimko argues that the MORTE DARTHUR is politically oriented and reflects the turbulent fifteenth century. Malory lamented the disintegration of the feudal system and the bond of mutual loyalties on which the system was based. Although the feudal system lost its validity, Malory wished to retain it.

704. "Steinbeck Find Said to Be First 'Morte d'Arthur' Manuscript." NEW YORK TIMES, Jan. 2, 1966, p. 52, col. 4.

This article states that Steinbeck believes that a fifteenth-century manuscript discovered at Alnwick Castle in Northumberland is the original draft of the MORTE DARTHUR. [See nos. 685 and 865.3.]

705. Tuve, Rosamund. ALLEGORICAL IMAGERY: SOME MEDIEVAL BOOKS AND THEIR POSTERITY. Princeton, N.J.: Princeton University Press, 1966.

See Chapter 5 ("Romances"). Tuve opposes general critical opinion in claiming that Malory exerted considerable influence on Spenser. She says that both Malory and Spenser were "unabashedly idealistic about chivalry" (p. 342). She compares the French QUESTE and Malory's version and states that "although truncated in Malory, and not artistically so subtle and tense, the allegorical reading does not differ in character, and the mystical sense is clear and powerful" (p. 431).

706. Vinaver, Eugène. "Epic and Tragic Patterns in Malory." FRIENDSHIP'S GARLAND: ESSAYS PRESENTED TO MARIO PRAZ ON HIS

SEVENTIETH BIRTHDAY. Ed. Vittorio Gabrieli. Rome: Edizioni di Storia e Letteratura, 1966. Vol. 1, pp. 81-85.

Vinaver states that Malory heralds the "modern tragic form" through his emphasis on a single tragic theme.

707. _____. "Form and Meaning in Medieval Romance." THE PRESIDENTIAL ADDRESS OF THE MODERN HUMANITIES RESEARCH ASSOCI- ATION. Leeds, England, 1966.

Vinaver expounds and defends the theory that the aesthetic ideals which governed the writers of medieval romance cycles are not those of twentieth-century writers and that critics cannot interpret these works by the principles of Aristotelian criticism. The romances are "polycentric," incorporating many themes and actions, and yet they have "cohesion," a sense of design. The aesthetic ideal of the romance is multiplicity and diversity. Malory is important for adapting the cycle tradition of entrelacement by unweaving its threads and pro- ducing a more "straightforward" narrative that appealed to his time; yet the MORTE DARTHUR has both types of structure. Vina- ver proposes that no value judgments should be made about the interlace form or the "unified" form because each is an inde- pendent aesthetic ideal.

708. Bennett, William K. "Sir Thomas Malory's Gawain: The Noble Villain." WEST VIRGINIA UNIVERSITY PHILOLOGICAL PAPERS, 16 (1967), 17-29.

Bennett does not share the view of many critics that Gawain's character is inconsistent. He says that Gawain may be imper- fect, but such imperfect men bring about the destruction of ideal society. Were Gawain other than he was, the Round Table might not have fallen.

709. Blamires, David. "'Kynge Arthur ys nat dede.'" AGENDA, 5 (1967), 159-71.

Blamires discusses the use of the MORTE DARTHUR and Arthurian materials in the works of David Jones and Malory's "art and technique," especially his emphasis on martial chivalry and the great intensity of action in the MORTE DARTHUR.

710. Carter, John, and Percy H. Muir. PRINTING AND THE MIND OF MAN: THE IMPACT OF PRINTING ON FIVE CENTURIES OF WESTERN CIVILIZA- TION. London: Cassell, 1967.

A brief description of the MORTE DARTHUR is on p. 17.

711. Davis, Norman. "Style and Stereotype in Early English Letters." LEEDS STUDIES IN ENGLISH, 1 (1967), 7-17.

Davis sees a stylistic resemblance between Malory's description of Lancelot and John Paston III's description of a knight in 1472. He believes that fifteenth-century style was more dependent on epistolary and stylistic conventions than has been previously thought.

712. Gardner, John. MORTE DARTHUR. Cliffs Notes, 1967.

Plot summary.

713. Hampsten, Elizabeth. "A Reading of Sir Thomas Malory's MORTE DARTHUR." NORTH DAKOTA QUARTERLY, 35 (1967), 29-37.

A reading of the MORTE DARTHUR as "prose fiction."

714. Hobar, Donald. "The Oral Tradition in Malory's 'Morte Darthur.'" Dissertation. University of Pittsburgh, 1967. DA, 28 (1968), 3639A.

Hobar argues that the MORTE DARTHUR furnishes evidence that it was read to an audience; such an explanation accounts for its repetition, inconsistencies, simplicity of syntax, and divisions. The MORTE DARTHUR is an integrated work, though the eight tales can be read separately.

715. Ingham, Muriel Brierley. "Some Fifteenth-Century Images of Death and Their Background." Dissertation. University of California at Riverside, 1967. DA, 28 (1968), 4132A-33A.

Ingham states that the MORTE DARTHUR is a fifteenth-century work which shows a positive attitude toward death and toward life in its secular sphere.

716. Kennedy, Edward D. "King Arthur and King Mark: Aspects of Kingship in Malory's MORTE DARTHUR." Dissertation. University of Illinois at Urbana-Champaign, 1967. DA, 28 (1968), 3145A-46A.

Kennedy examines Malory's theory of kingship in the MORTE DARTHUR with reference to its sources and to medieval political theory. The traditional limitations on the king's power, the commons and the church, are not influential in the MORTE DARTHUR, but Malory does follow his sources in giving Arthur a few advisors. The characters of King Arthur and King Mark show the contrast between the "king's desire for bonum commune and the tyrant's concern for bonum privatum." In the TRISTRAM section, Malory's aim is to present Mark as a foil to Arthur.

717. Moorman, Charles. "The Tragic Knight: Malory's MORTE DARTHUR." A KNYGHT THERE WAS: THE EVOLUTION OF THE KNIGHT IN LITERATURE. Lexington: University of Kentucky Press, 1967, pp. 96-112.

[This article is a revision of no. 681.] Moorman argues that
the MORTE DARTHUR is a tragic work, showing the vulnerability
of the chivalric ideal to defeat. He rejects the view that
Malory's depiction of chivalry is didactic [Vinaver, no. 441;
Ferguson, no. 630; Tucker, no. 657.5]. The tragedy, however,
is not Aristotelian, for the characters die ignorant of their
failings and disillusioned. The theme of the MORTE DARTHUR,
the rise and fall of Arthurian civilization, is seen in three
story lines, each of which contains a rise-and-fall pattern
and each of which illustrates a separate principle of knighthood: the Lot-Pellinore feud (loyalty), the Grail quest (religion), and Lancelot and Guinevere (love).
  a. George Doskow, CE, 27 (1966), 579.
  b. R. W. Ackerman, SPECULUM, 41 (1966), 758-60.
  c. R. T. Davies, RES, N.S. 17 (1966), 428-30.
  d. D. S. Brewer, MLR, 62 (1967), 109.
  e. K. H. Güller, ANGLIA, 85 (1967), 92-95.
  f. LJ, 92 (1967), 1625.
  g. J. E. Barnie, MLR, 63 (1968), 932.
  h. W. Matthews, SPECULUM, 43 (1968), 525-27.
  i. H. Newstead, MEDIUM AEVUM, 37 (1968), 219-21.
  j. Georgia R. Crampton, CL, 21 (1969), 266-71.
  k. D. S. Brewer, MEDIUM AEVUM, 39 (1970), 216-18.
  l. Larry M. Sklute, RP, 24 (1971), 640-44.

718. Nakashima, Kunio. "Gerund in Malory." BULLETIN OF THE ENGLISH
      LITERARY SOCIETY OF NIHON UNIVERSITY, 17 (1967), 1-18.

      A discussion of form, function, nominal nature, gerund with ad-
      verbs, object and subject of the gerund, tense and voice, and
      gerund preceded by on, an, a.

* 719. Noguchi, Shunichi. "The Paradox of the Character of Malory's
      Language." HIROSHIMA STUDIES IN ENGLISH LANGUAGE AND LITERA-
      TURE, No. 13 (1967), 115.

720. Olstead, Myra. "Morgan le Fay in Malory's 'Morte Darthur.'"
      BBIAS, 19 (1967), 128-38.

      Olstead states that the character of Morgan le Fay is important
      in the MORTE DARTHUR because she is gradually exposed to be a
      constant threat to Arthur and the Round Table society. Inter-
      play between Morgan and her foil, the benevolent Lady of the
      Lake, is thematically important, heightens suspense, and con-
      tributes to "unity." At the end, the two characters are recon-
      ciled in the character of the healing Morgan who is present at
      Arthur's death, so that Morgan le Fay becomes the "basis of
      tragic reconciliation."
      a. C. Cordié, PAIDEIA, 23 (1968), 71.

721. V[inaver], E[ugène]. "Sir Thomas Malory." CHAMBERS'S ENCYCLOPAE-
      DIA. New rev. ed. Oxford and London: Permagon Press, 1967.

See Vol. 9, pp. 14-15. Vinaver accepts Kittredge's Warwickshire Malory as the author of the MORTE DARTHUR.

722. W[hitehead], F[rederic]. "Sir Thomas Malory." ENCYCLOPAEDIA BRITANNICA; A NEW SURVEY OF UNIVERSAL KNOWLEDGE. London and Chicago: Encyclopaedia Britannica, 1967.

See Vol. 14, pp. 706-07. A discussion of the Warwickshire and Yorkshire candidates for the authorship of the MORTE DARTHUR. In absence of proof that the Yorkshire Malory proposed by Matthews [no. 697] was a knight, Whitehead favors the Malory proposed by Kittredge [no. 339]. Whitehead lists Malory's sources and discusses his treatment of their entrelacement.

723. Benson, Larry D. "Sir Thomas Malory's LE MORTE DARTHUR." CRITICAL APPROACHES TO SIX MAJOR ENGLISH WORKS. Ed. R. M. Lumiansky and Herschel Baker. Philadelphia: University of Pennsylvania Press, 1968, pp. 81-131.

A survey of scholarship about the MORTE DARTHUR with a bibliography of important scholarship in the footnotes. Benson's discussion centers around Vinaver's 1947 edition of the Winchester Manuscript. He discusses Malory's reputation, editions of his work, and structural issues raised by Vinaver's edition. Benson stresses the importance of recognizing the thematic unity of the work and calls for studies which consider Malory's place in the English romance tradition.
    a. CHOICE, 6 (1969), 1388.
    b. TLS, Sept. 25, 1969, p. 1067.

724. Blake, N[orman] F. "Caxton and Courtly Style." ESSAYS AND STUDIES, N.S. 21 (1968), 29-45.

See pp. 40-41. Blake examines Caxton's alterations of the MORTE DARTHUR and concludes that "in general, Caxton's version is more courtly and less specific" than the Winchester version. A comparison of Caxton's Book 5 and the corresponding section in the Winchester Manuscript (Tale 2) shows that Caxton avoided alliterative phrases, employed French words, used vague adjectives, and achieved a more elevated tone.

*725. Couroux, Gerard Oliver. "Courtly Love in Malory's 'Le Morte Darthur.'" Dissertation. Loyola University of Chicago, 1968.

726. DsPasquale, Pasquale, Jr. "Malory's Guinevere: Epic Queen, Romance Heroine, and Tragic Mistress." BUCKNELL REVIEW, 16 (1968), 86-102.

DiPasquale claims that any discussion of Guinevere's character must consider Malory's genre, prose fiction. As queen of the Round Table, the wife of Arthur, and the mistress of Lancelot,

Guinevere represents a fusion of the romantic, the epic, and
the tragic. The article is indebted to the theories of North-
rup Frye. It contains a bibliography of critical attitudes
toward Guinevere.

727. Field, P. J. C. "Description and Narration in Malory." SPECULUM,
      43 (1968), 476-86.

Field argues that Malory's style effectively combines narration
(stark story) and description (emotional evocation), both of
which create "unity" in the work. Malory's narration, which
cuts the length and increases the pace of his materials, is
characterized by simple sentence structure and the stringing
together of coordinate main clauses to "convey a series of actions, facts, or perceptions" and also by "stylised formulaic
expressions," stock words and phrases which contribute to a lack
of imagery and therefore a less pictorial effect. Malory's description is characterized by the use of moral judgments rather
than individual personal characteristics to describe characters
and by the elimination of much description found in his French
sources. The combination of these narrative and descriptive
techniques creates an impression of realism because the reader
feels the presence of a narrator who relates the story in an
austere, blunt manner that "emphasises the moral implications
of the story which in the end dominate the effect" (p. 486).
[See no. 783.]

728. _____. "Four Functions of Malory's Minor Characters."
      MEDIUM AEVUM, 37 (1968), 37-45.

Field agrees with and summarizes the opinions of Wilson on the
function of Malory's minor characters [nos. 519 and 604].
Field's thesis is that the "minor characters provide continuity
of background, contrast of character, historical authenticity,
and enhance the stature of Lancelot" (p. 38). Minor characters
provide contrasts in terms of both theme and character; they
help to delineate the social structure of the Round Table society (the minor characters stand in relation to the major knights
as the knights to Arthur); and they serve to glorify Lancelot,
as in the TRISTRAM section, where Lancelot is a focus and standard for the other knights, and where the development of a fac-
tion against Lancelot first appears.

729. Gray, J. M. "Fact, Form and Fiction in Tennyson's Balin and Ba-
      lin." RENAISSANCE AND MODERN STUDIES, 12 (1968), 97-107.

Gray discusses the differences between the works of Malory and
Tennyson. Malory wrote a "primitive conflict tale." Tennyson
wrote a "modern drama of the divided self where the quest for
some ultimate value. . . is largely internal" (p. 107).

730. Miller, Russell Harrison. "The Ethos of Sir Thomas Malory."
      Dissertation. University of Maryland, 1968. DA, 29 (1969),
      4462.

      Miller argues that the world of the MORTE DARTHUR is "practi-
      cal and heroic," not "romantic" or "religious." To establish
      whether Malory's orientation was primarily religious or secu-
      lar, he analyzes the meaning in context of key words such as
      "honor," "chivalry," "knighthood," "noble," "truth," and
      "shame."

731. Moore, Arthur K. "Medieval English Literature and the Question
      of Unity." MP, 65 (1968), 285-300.

      Moore's thesis is that one must know the critical principles
      of the author's age before applying modern principles of "uni-
      ty" to his work. Consideration of the "conditions" for deter-
      mining unity is lacking in modern criticism. This is
      demonstrated in the controversy over the "unity" of the MORTE
      DARTHUR. "The exchanges provoked by Eugène Vinaver's denial
      of unity to the MORTE DARTHUR first of all demonstrate the
      sheer fatuousness of affirming or denying unity without refer-
      ence to the conditions of its achievement." They also show
      "confusion of matters of opinion and of fact, critical inten-
      tionalism, and abuse of rules of evidence" (p. 297). Moore
      assesses the work of Vinaver, Brewer, Lumiansky, and Moorman.

732. Moorman, Charles. "King Arthur and the English National Charac-
      ter." NEW YORK FOLKLORE QUARTERLY, 24 (1968), 103-12.

      A discussion of Malory's influence on later treatments of
      Arthur.

733. Morris, Celia B. "The 'Makaris' of Camelot." Dissertation.
      City University of New York, 1968. DA, 29 (1968), 1516A-17A.

      An examination of the work of Tennyson and Robinson, with some
      commentary on the MORTE DARTHUR.

734. Nakashima, Kunio. "Present Participle in Malory." BULLETIN OF
      THE ENGLISH LITERARY SOCIETY OF NIHON UNIVERSITY, 18 (1968),
      1-22.

      Nakashima claims that the form of the present participle in
      the MORTE DARTHUR (-yng[e] instead of -ing) has less verbal
      quality in Middle English than in modern English. He discusses
      adjectival use, predicate use, progressive form, participial
      construction, and use as other parts of speech such as adverb,
      preposition, and conjunction. A summary of the main points of
      the article is on pp. 21-22.

735. _____. "Reflexive Verbs in Malory." IN SPITE OF THE
     THIRTEEN SUPERSTITION, 2 (1968), 1-27.

     Nakashima states that the reflexive verbs are more common in
     Malory's usage than in modern English because of the tendency
     in the latter to drop reflexive pronouns. The simple personal
     pronoun (e.g. hym) is more commonly used than the compound per-
     sonal pronoun (self). The reflexive verbs in the MORTE DARTHUR
     are alphabetically arranged and discussed in terms of usage,
     with examples and indications of whether the form is now obso-
     lete.

736. Owen, Douglas D. R. THE EVOLUTION OF THE GRAIL LEGEND. [St. An-
     drews University Publications, No. 68.] Edinburgh and London:
     Oliver and Boyd, 1968.

     Owen states that part of the GARETH story derives from the BEL
     INCONNU. The gold jeweled cup which Lady Lyones sends to Ga-
     reth at the hermitage before the fight at Castle Perilous
     is the Grail.

737. Patterson, Lee Willing. "Heroism and the Rise of Romance: An
     Essay in Medieval Literary History." Dissertation. Yale Uni-
     versity, 1968. DA, 30 (1969), 694A.

     In the MORTE DARTHUR, Malory presents a "world in which change
     is no longer possible, and consequently in which the deadly
     capacities of the self cannot be disarmed. No real attempt is
     made to relate the self to a virtually irrelevant code, and
     the romantic hero loses the flexibility that characterizes him
     and approaches more and more closely to the fixity of an alle-
     gorical figure."

738. Richardson, Susan Strong. "Thematic Unity in Malory's 'Morte
     Darthur.'" Dissertation. University of Kansas, 1968. DA, 29
     (1968), 1878.

     Richardson regards the "attempt by Arthur and his knights to
     establish, through the Round Table and the ideals of chivalry,
     stability and certainty in the midst of constantly encroaching
     forces of evil and chaos" as an element of thematic unity, and
     she offers it as an argument against Vinaver's view that the
     MORTE DARTHUR is eight separate tales.

739. Sandved, Arthur O. STUDIES IN THE LANGUAGE OF CAXTON'S MALORY
     AND THAT OF THE WINCHESTER MANUSCRIPT. [Norwegian Studies in
     English, No. 15.] Oslo: Norwegian University Press; New York:
     Humanities Press, 1968.

     The purposes of this study are to cast light on the relation-
     ships of the Caxton and Winchester versions of the MORTE DARTHUR,

to establish their relation to Malory's original, and to determine Caxton's role in the development of "standard" English.
Sandved claims that Caxton's own language and that which he
uses in his revision of the MORTE DARTHUR do differ. Caxton
seems to have preserved the language which he found in his
manuscript. The book contains a bibliography of language studies of the Caxton and Winchester versions and a critique of them
a. CHOICE, 5 (1968), 960.
b. N. F. Blake, MEDIUM AEVUM, 38 (1969), 216–18.
c. Basil Cottle, JEGP, 68 (1969), 289–90.
d. Pamela Gradon, RES, N.S. 20 (1969), 485–87.
e. R. Hagenbüchle, ERASMUS, 20 (1969), 332.
f. K. Faiss, LINGUISTICS, 64 (Dec. 1970), 103–07.
g. Peter H. Salus, ENGLISH STUDIES, 52 (1971), 264–65.
h. Ján Šimko, YES, 1 (1971), 219–22.
i. J. R. Simon, EA, 25 (1972), 56.
j. Michael J. Wright, SN, 41 (1972), 475–76.
k. B. Carstensen, ANGLIA, 90 (1972), 228–30.
l. E. G. Williams, ARCHIVUM LINGUISTICUM, N.S. 1 (1970),
    104–06.
m. J. F. Vanderheyden, ORBIS, 18, p. 272.
n. Bertil Sundby, NORSK TIDSSKRIFT FOR SPROGVIDENSKAP, 24,
    pp. 326–29.

740. Schueler, Donald G. "The Tristram Section of Malory's MORTE DAR-
      THUR." SP, 65 (1968), 51–66.

Schueler argues that the MORTE DARTHUR is a thematically unified
work. "The story of Tristram makes sense in the overall narrative pattern only if it is considered an analogue to the main
drama of Arthur's Round Table, paralleling that story in its
action and characterization as it does in time. Only in its
subplots, such as the Lotte-Pellinore feud, is the history of
the Round Table advanced. The main story—of Tristram himself—
is a correlative of, not a sequel to, the story of Arthur's fellowship, and acts as a literary counterpart to the larger
theme" (p. 53). Schueler disagrees with Moorman and Rumble,
who believe that the Tristram-Isolt affair merely demonstrates
that the Lancelot-Guinevere relationship is not an isolated
phenomenon in Arthurian society. Malory emphasizes the similarities between Tristram and Lancelot to underscore their
essential differences: Tristram is an "aimlessly wandering
knight-errant of chivalry in its decline," and Lancelot is the
"archetype of Arthur's ideal fellowship, the heroic right arm
of a heroic king" (pp. 65–66). The article has a bibliography
of the "unity" controversy.

741. Starr, Nathan Comfort. "The Moral Problem in Malory." DALHOUSIE
      REVIEW, 47 (1968), 467–74.

Starr argues that Malory is concerned with the good and evil innate in every man and how these opposing qualities can be reconciled. The problem is especially apparent in the character of Lancelot.

742. Turner, Elizabeth Jane. "The Arthurian Legend as an Historical Ideal of Life: Political Theory in Sir Thomas Malory's 'Le Morte D'Arthur.'" Dissertation. University of Pennsylvania, 1968. DA, 29 (1969), 3590.

[This is revised as no. 798.] According to Turner, "there is a central paradox in LE MORTE DARTHUR which arises from the fact that although Malory initially seems to have designed the Arthurian ideal along the lines of medieval political theory, by doing so he inevitably uncovered much in the Arthurian story which made it unsuitable as an historical ideal of life." [The phrase "historical ideal of life" is taken from Johan Huizinga and means the "literary revival and literary recreation of a cultural model."]

743. Vonalt, Joyce Ouzts. "The Thematic Design of Malory's 'Morte Darthur.'" Dissertation. University of Florida, 1968. DA, 30 (1969), 296.

Vonalt states that the MORTE DARTHUR reveals a dual concern: man's relation to God and providence, and man's relation to man and problems of government. Arthur, who governs on earth by the rules of God, attempts to reconcile the two in one community.

744. Baron, Francis Xavier. "The Alienated Hero in Arthurian Romance." Dissertation. University of Iowa, 1969. DA, 30 (1970), 2960A.

Baron regards the alienation of the hero as one of the main themes of Arthurian legend. As Lancelot increases in importance next to Arthur, he is shown as more and more alienated from the corrupt Arthurian society. The final scenes reveal Lancelot's virtual retirement from all worldly concerns.

745. Blake, N[orman] F. CAXTON AND HIS WORLD. London: Andre Deutsch, 1969.

See pp. 108-13, 183-92. Blake claims that Caxton had only one manuscript of the MORTE DARTHUR and that the tales in the manuscript were in the order in which he printed them; that Caxton sometimes altered the language of the manuscript and added or deleted portions; and that Caxton's revisions aim to give the work order and unity. In Book 5, Caxton's cutting of battle description, geographical references, and speeches by minor characters place emphasis on the actions of the principal characters, Arthur and Gawain, and on the theme of Christian chivalry. His changes also show the desire to eliminate "common words which were obsolete and literary words which were no

longer fashionable" (p. 188). Caxton did not, however, make
excessive changes in word order.

746. Dillon, Bert. "Formal and Informal Pronouns of Address in Malo-
      ry's LE MORTE DARTHUR." ANNUALE MEDIAEVALE, 10 (1969), 94-103.

      Dillon states that throughout the MORTE DARTHUR, Malory's pro-
      noun usage varies but remains "consistent within a given con-
      text." Shifts in usage indicate changes of tone or situation.
      Malory did not always follow the usage of his sources. [See
      discussion in nos. 157 and 851.]

747. Fries, Maureen Holmberg. "Sir Lancelot and Sir Tristram: Char-
      acterization and 'Sens' in Malory's 'Morte Darthur.'" Disser-
      tation. State University of New York at Buffalo, 1969. DA,
      31 (1970), 1756A-57A.

      Fries argues that, in taking material for the stories of Lance-
      lot and Tristram from French sources, Malory changed the char-
      acterizations of the two knights: Guinevere encourages
      Lancelot as a "trew lover" and upholder of the chivalric code;
      Isolde, however, is not the chief inspiration for Tristram's
      knightly prowess.

748. Gaines, Barry. "A Forgotten Artist: John Harris and the Rylands
      Copy of Caxton's Edition of Malory." BJRL, 52 (1969), 115-28.

      Gaines notes that in Dibdin's supplement to the BIBLIOTHECA
      SPENCERIANA (1822), the eleven facsimile pages of the imperfect
      Caxton copy which Lord Spencer purchased in 1816 are credited
      to John Whittaker; but in his REMINISCENCES, Dibdin claims that
      a certain Harris did them. Gaines examines the careers and re-
      putations of Dibdin, Whittaker, and John Harris (1791-1873),
      and concludes that the latter was responsible for the facsimile
      pages in the Spencer copy, now in the Rylands Library.

749. Ginter, Beverly Kennedy. "The Hierarchy of Knighthood in Sir
      Thomas Malory's 'Morte Darthur.'" Dissertation. Duke Univer-
      sity, 1969. DA, 31 (1970), 356.

      Ginter states that Malory's concept of knighthood is represented
      by a "triple hierarchy," consisting of "those who attempt to ob-
      serve all three knightly loyalties, to God, to lady and to secu-
      lar lord; those who observe only two loyalties, to lord and
      lady; and those who observe only one loyalty, to their secular
      lord." These are the "trew" knights, judged by spiritual
      prowess; the "worshipful" knights, judged by physical prowess;
      and the "false" knights. There are three prototypes of the
      "trew" knight: Lancelot represents its "feudal" aspect, Gareth
      its "courtly" aspect, and Galahad its "religious" aspect. The
      "worshipful" and "false" knights are represented respectively

by Tristram and Gawain. This knightly hierarchy furnishes evidence for the structural unity of the MORTE DARTHUR.

750. Guendling, John E. "The 'Kinging' of Arthur: A Medieval Paradigm." TOPIC, 9 (Fall 1969), 30-39.

A reading of the MORTE DARTHUR with reference to Tudor politics and the Tudor monarchs' need to establish their right to rule. Guendling adopts the thesis of George H. Sabine (A HISTORY OF POLITICAL THEORY) that lawful kingship was based on inheritance, popular will, and divine will, and he interprets the story of Arthur as a perfect illustration of this theory.

* 751. Jensen, Elizabeth N. "Uoverensstemmelserne i Gawains karakter belyst ud fra SIR GAWAIN AND THE GREEN KNIGHT og Sir Thomas Malory's MORTE D'ARTHUR." EXTRACTA, 2 (1969), 195-201.

752. Kelly, Robert Leroy. "The Pattern of Triumph: Parallels Between Arthur and Galahad in Malory's 'Morte Darthur.'" Dissertation. University of Oregon, 1969. DA, 30 (1970), 4948A-49A.

Kelly asserts that the parallels between the lives of Galahad and Arthur give further evidence of unity in the MORTE DARTHUR and help to connect the Grail quest with the rest of the work. Galahad serves as a foil to Arthur. Arthur's failings demonstrate the failure of the Round Table, but he does achieve an ultimate spiritual triumph (felix culpa).

753. Kennedy, Edward D. "Malory's Use of Hardyng's Chronicle." N & Q, N.S. 16 (1969), 167-70.

Kennedy extends the arguments of Vinaver [no. 131] and Matthews [no. 633], who suggest that John Hardyng's Metrical CHRONICLE furnished the episode of Arthur's coronation as emperor of Rome in Book 2. He believes that the CHRONICLE provided certain geographical details in Book 1 and suggested the Round Table oath which Malory incorporated in the tale; moreover, the CHRONICLE could have influenced Malory's "narrative method" as much as the Alliterative MORTE ARTHURE and perhaps "suggested the overall framework" for the MORTE DARTHUR.

754. Knight, Stephen. THE STRUCTURE OF SIR THOMAS MALORY'S ARTHURIAD. [Australian Humanities Research Council Monograph, No. 14.] Sydney: Sydney University Press, 1969.

In Parts 1 and 2, Knight criticizes the opinions of Vinaver and Lumiansky on the structure of the MORTE DARTHUR. Vinaver's theory that Malory wrote eight separate tales is based on evidence in Caxton's preface, the explicits, and inconsistencies in the text, evidence which Knight finds unsatisfactory. He is also critical of the assumptions and arguments on which

Lumiansky, Moorman, and other "unity" spokesmen base their
thesis that the work is a unified whole, and especially of the
attempt to establish Malory's "intentions." In Parts 3 and 4,
Knight expounds his own view that the structure is "episodic,"
although it has "two distinct structural styles" (the "episodic" and the "polyphonic"). The structure of the first four
tales and a great part of the TRISTRAM is "episodic," a series
of knightly adventures. The episodes do contain some motifs
that occur throughout the work, but the episodic quality is
very strong. The "polyphonic" style of the last books is only
a more sophisticated version of the episodic narrative of the
earlier tales. Though the MORTE DARTHUR has some unifying
qualities, Knight believes that the two types of narrative
structure make it impossible to call the MORTE DARTHUR a "unified totality."
   a. Robert Ackerman, SPECULUM, 46 (1971), 158-60.
   b. R. T. Davies, MEDIUM AEVUM, 40 (1971), 303-05.
   c. Derek Pearsall, MLR, 66 (1971), 656-57.

755. Mead, Philip Lawrence. "A Consideration of Some Archetypes in
      Malory's 'Le Morte Darthur.'" Dissertation. University of
      New Mexico, 1969. DA, 31 (1970), 1765A.

      Mead examines the archetypal events and characters of the MORTE
      DARTHUR and concludes that the major themes of the work--
      "isolation, fruitlessness, and death"--correspond to the arche-
      type of rebirth, although regeneration does not follow. The
      story of Balin and Balan is especially significant as a micro-
      cosm of the whole work.

756. Mellizo, Felipe. "Arturo y LE MORTE." CUADERNOS HISPANOAMERICA-
      NOS, No. 229 (1969), 78-100.

      Mellizo views the identification of Thomas Malory as one of
      the most difficult historical problems in English literature.
      He discusses the history of the biography controversy, especial-
      ly the work of Kittredge, Williams, Chambers, Hicks, and Baugh.

757. Olefsky, Ellyn. "Chronology, Factual Consistency, and the Prob-
      lem of Unity in Malory." JEGP, 68 (1969), 57-73.

      The thesis of this article is that the cases for and against
      "unity" have been much overstated. Olefsky argues against the
      views of Moorman [no. 648] (that the MORTE DARTHUR has a planned
      chronology and an elaborate time scheme) and Vinaver (that in-
      consistencies in the work further the argument that it is eight
      separate tales). According to Olefsky, Moorman's reshuffling
      of sections of the tales leads to more inconsistencies, and
      that "without completely fragmenting the various books, it is
      impossible to devise a satisfactory chronology for Malory"
      (p. 63). The inconsistencies which Vinaver finds, however,

do not necessarily force a reading of eight separate tales.
Malory was not very interested in time, although he did provide
a general impression of the passage of time with Arthur's birth,
career, and death; likewise, Malory paid little heed to factual
consistency in names, numbers, and biographical details. There
are as many discrepancies within books as between them (19 of
the former, 28 of the latter). She concludes that "if there is
an over-all story plan, it is presented in terms of something
other than either detailed time or detailed consistency of
narrative fact in general" (p. 66). The MORTE DARTHUR does
lack strict unified coherence, but it gives an impression of
progression.

758. Ray, T. J. "The Book of Knights Erring." FORUM, 7 (1969), 17-23.

Ray compares the MORTE DARTHUR and handbooks of chivalry by such
authors as Christine de Pisan and Gilbert de la Haye. He believes that Malory was possibly aware of the chivalric code of
these conduct books.

759. Smith, Clare Ruggles. "The Character of Gawain in Malory." Dissertation. Texas Technical University, 1969. DA, 31 (1970),
370.

Smith argues that Malory's presentation of Gawain is consistent
and reflects the theme that "an ideal for stable national order
fails through the conflicting desires within the complex human
beings who strive toward the ideal." In his passionate devotion to his leader and to his family group, Gawain represents
the "old clan spirit." His character is more complex than has
been recognized.

760. Soudek, Ernst Herbert. "The Cart-Episode: Evolution of an Arthurian Incident from Chrétien's 'Le Chevalier de la Charrette,'
through the 'Old French Prose Lancelot,' 'the Middle High Ger-
man Prose Lancelot,' to Malory's 'Morte Darthur.'" Dissertation. University of Michigan, 1969. DA, 31 (1970), 1240.

Soudek compares Malory's version of the cart-episode with earlier ones and concludes that Malory eliminated its religious
significance and courtly love influence and emphasized Lancelot's martial prowess.

761. Tucker, Martin, ed. THE CRITICAL TEMPER: A SURVEY OF MODERN
CRITICISM ON ENGLISH AND AMERICAN LITERATURE FROM THE BEGIN-
NINGS TO THE TWENTIETH CENTURY. New York: Frederick Ungar,
1969. Vol. I: From Old English to Shakespeare.

A collection of excerpts of criticism of the MORTE DARTHUR.

762. Wilson, Robert H. "Chronology in Malory." STUDIES IN LANGUAGE,

LITERATURE AND CULTURE OF THE MIDDLE AGES AND LATER. Ed. E.
Bagby Atwood and Archibald A. Hill. Austin: University of
Texas Press, 1969, pp. 324-34.

Wilson examines two proposed chronologies of the MORTE DARTHUR
[nos. 589 and 648]. He concludes that Malory was "neither entirely indifferent to chronology nor yet invariably accurate"
(p. 333). He therefore does not agree with Lumiansky and Moorman that Malory had a careful time scheme; he also believes
that there are not enough inconsistencies to justify Vinaver's
view that the work is eight separate tales.

763. York, Ernest C. "The Duel of Chivalry in Malory's Book XIX."
PHILOLOGICAL QUARTERLY, 48 (1969), 186-91.

York attempts to furnish more evidence that English tradition
influenced Malory. He states that Lancelot's defense of Guinevere (after Meleagant accuses her of adultery) is a duel of
chivalry, a judicial test established in the reign of Richard
II and distinguished from the older duel of law. Two essential
points are that Guinevere technically is charged with treason
and that knights fight on horseback rather than on foot. York
explains how the scene does and does not follow the usual legal
procedures of the duel of chivalry and concludes that Malory
followed the English, not the French, tradition.

764. Ackerman, Robert W. "'The Tale of Gareth' and the Unity of LE
MORTE DARTHUR." PHILOLOGICAL ESSAYS: STUDIES IN OLD AND MID-
DLE ENGLISH LANGUAGE AND LITERATURE IN HONOUR OF HERBERT DEAN
MERITT. Ed. James L. Rosier. Hague: Mouton, 1970, pp. 196-
203.

Ackerman's article is primarily a critique of Guerin's essay
[no. 673.4]. Ackerman disagrees with Guerin's view that the
Tale of GARETH is Malory's own work, i.e. original; he concurs
with most critics in believing that it is based on a lost
source, a single romance. Though Ackerman agrees with Guerin
that there is little evidence of courtly love in the GARETH,
he finds too much evidence of lust in the Gareth-Lyones relationship to justify the conclusion that the love of Gareth
and Lyones is a criticism of the courtly love relationship of
Lancelot and Guinevere. The GARETH is representative of the
English romance tradition in cutting and abridging courtly
love elements from French romance. The article contains a
lengthy bibliographical survey of the "unity" issue, with emphasis on the Tale of GARETH and major critical issues associated with it.

765. Brewer, D. S. "The Present Study of Malory." FORUM FOR MODERN
LANGUAGE STUDIES, 6 (1970), 83-97. Rpt. in ARTHURIAN ROMANCE:
SEVEN ESSAYS. Ed. D. D. R. Owen. Edinburgh and London:

Scottish Press; New York: Barnes and Noble, 1971.

A survey of the last twenty years of Malory studies, arranged
according to topics. Brewer praises Vinaver's edition of the
Winchester Manuscript and especially Vinaver's demonstration of
how Malory simplified his French sources. Brewer's discussion
of scholarship is divided into sections on biography, language
and style, source study, and Malory's artistic achievement. He
opposes the alleged "moral paradox" of the author and his work
and assesses the arguments for the Warwickshire and Yorkshire
Malory candidates proposed by Kittredge [no. 339] and Matthews
[no. 697], respectively. He urges more studies of Malory's
cultural and historical backgrounds (e.g. Ferguson, no. 630),
Malory's language (e.g. Sandved, no. 739; and Matthews, no.
697), and studies of the structure of the MORTE DARTHUR which
dismiss twentieth-century principles of unity.
   a. CHOICE, 8 (1971), 1018.
   b. Janet M. Cowen, N & Q, N.S. 18 (1971), 267.
   c. Charles Elliott, ANGLO-WELSH REVIEW, 20 (1971), 240-43.
   d. J. Lawlor, RES, N.S. 23 (1972), 248.
   e. M.-M. Dubois, EA, 26 (1973), 224-25.
   f. Karl Reichl, ANGLIA, 91 (1973), 392-94.
   g. Roy Harris, FRENCH STUDIES, 28 (1974), 52-53.
   h. Helaine Newstead, CCM, 66 (1974), 175-77.
   i. Herman Braet, MOYEN AGE, 81 (1975), 151-52.

766. Goble, Wendy Coleman. "Repetition of Episodes in Malory's 'Morte
      Darthur.'" Dissertation. University of Wisconsin, 1970. DA,
      31 (1971), 4714.

      Goble states that repetition of episodes functions chiefly in
      the MORTE DARTHUR to provide novelty and familiar patterns for
      the reader but also contributes to structural technique and
      characterization.

767. Kennedy, Edward D. "Arthur's Rescue in Malory and the Spanish
      'Tristan.'" N & Q, N.S. 17 (1970), 6-10.

      Kennedy urges that more critical study should be given to
      Spanish TRISTAN manuscripts which have resemblances to Malory's
      Tale 5. He suggests that Malory's source for the TRISTRAM sec-
      tion was a French manuscript earlier than the six studied by
      Vinaver, one in which Arthur is not enchanted by Aunowre but
      remains true to Guinevere. This detail in the story of Arthur's
      rescue also coincides with the Spanish LIBRO DEL ESFORZADO CA-
      BALLERO DON TRISTAN DE LEONIS and EL CUENTO DE TRISTAN DE
      LEONIS, which ultimately derive from the hypothetical French
      manuscript which Malory used.

768. _____. "Malory and the Marriage of Edward IV."
      TEXAS STUDIES IN LITERATURE AND LANGUAGE, 12 (1970-71), 155-62.

Kennedy argues that Malory's view of the proper relationship
between a king and his queen was possibly influenced by Edward
IV's marriage in 1464 to Elizabeth Wydville. His work, however,
is not a "political allegory" (p. 162). In Tale 1, Arthur is
portrayed as loving to the queen; but after writing this tale,
Malory seems to have altered his attitude toward the king-queen
relationship: he plays down references to Arthur's love for
Guinevere and adds material which emphasizes Arthur's love for
his knights. This shift in attitude to the proper king-queen
relationship may have been affected by Edward IV's marriage.
"The events following Edward's marriage. . . would have clearly shown that a king who has undue concern for his wife is
neglecting his responsibilities as a ruler" (p. 162).

769. Lee, B. S. "Two Arthurian Tales: What Tennyson Did to Malory."
     UNIVERSITY OF CAPE TOWN STUDIES IN ENGLISH, 1 (1970), 1-18.

     Lee states that "Malory was working within a living tradition."

*770. McCarthy, Terence. "Style in Malory." Dissertation. University
     of Birmingham, 1970.

771. Matthews, William. "Caxton and Malory: A Defence." MEDIEVAL
     LITERATURE AND FOLKLORE STUDIES. Ed. Jerome Mandel and Bruce
     Rosenburg. New Brunswick, N.J.: Rutgers University Press,
     1970, pp. 77-95.

     Matthews asserts that Caxton did not intend to mislead his
     readers. Caxton was a "fifteenth-century English businessman
     catering to a public of merchants and their offspring as well
     as nobles," but he also worked, however modestly, in the ser-
     vice of literature. Matthews disagrees with Vinaver's opinion
     that Malory wrote eight separate tales which Caxton deliberate-
     ly tried to pass off as a whole book. It is unlikely that Cax-
     ton should try to deceive his readers and contradicts what is
     known of him and his work. His modifications reveal a "printer's
     bias toward system and economy" and not deceptive intent to
     shape the original manuscript to his own design.

772. Peters, Edward. THE SHADOW KING: 'REX INUTILIS' IN MEDIEVAL LAW
     AND LITERATURE, 751-1327. New Haven, Conn., and London: Yale
     University Press, 1970.

     See Chapter 5, "REX INUTILIS in the Arthurian Romances" (pp.
     170-209). Peters states that Malory shows the tendency of
     later romance writers to interpret the rex inutilis theme in
     political terms as it affects the welfare of the kingdom. "In
     the later prose cycles the dilemma of the rex inutilis, the
     social consequences of his failure seen in political rather
     than moral terms, is developed. The contrast between the rul-
     er's virtue (represented by the enhancing of his character and

his majesty) and his shortcomings (represented either by his
wound or by the sudden appearance of the consequences of an
old, forgotten sin) often results in a tension which governs
much of the sweep of these narratives. . . . The theme of the
rex inutilis becomes a tragic one" (p. 195).

773. Richardson, W. M. "A Tragedy Within a Tragedy: Malory's Use of
      the 'Tale of Balin' as a Thematic Analogue." ARLINGTON QUAR-
      TERLY, 3 (1970-71), 61-71.

      An argument for the unity of the MORTE DARTHUR. Richardson
      claims that the destruction in the Tale of BALIN heralds the
      forthcoming holocaust that destroys the kingdom, which is a
      failure of institutions, not of men.

* 774. Sadler, Diana. "Malory's Narrative Technique in 'The Tale of
      Lancelot.'" Thesis. University of Newcastle, 1970.

775. Senior, Michael. "Castle of the Holy Grail." COUNTRY QUEST:
      THE MAGAZINE FOR WALES, THE BORDER AND MIDLANDS, 10 (March
      1970), 18-20.

      Senior believes that the Castle "Dinas Bran" ("Bran's strong-
      hold"), above Llangollen, may be Malory's Castle of Corbin.
      The name "Bran" means "crow." Bran was a traditional king of
      Britain, a god figure, with a magic cauldron that brought the
      dead to life (a prototype of the Holy Grail). Malory's source
      for placing the Grail in the Castle of Corbin is the Old
      French LANCELOT. In Old French, "Corbin" means "crow." Dinas
      Bran is therefore likely to be the Castle of Corbin.

776. Stewart, Marilynn Zarwell. "The Protégés of Lancelot: A Study
      of Malory's Characterization of Lancelot in the 'Morte D'Ar-
      thur.'" Dissertation. University of Southern California,
      1970. DA, 31 (1970), 3522.

      Stewart argues that the "positive" and consistent characteriza-
      tion of Lancelot is a unifying element in the MORTE DARTHUR.
      Lancelot's protégés--Gareth, Galahad, Lavayne, Urry--serve as
      foils to him. Lancelot serves as a mentor for each in his
      search for knighthood, and in turn their development reflects
      favorably on the character of Lancelot.

777. Stroud, Michael James. "Malory and the 'Morte Arthure.'" Dis-
      sertation. University of Wisconsin, 1970. DA, 21 (1971), 4735.

      Stroud compares Malory's TALE OF KING ARTHUR AND THE EMPEROR
      LUCIUS and the Alliterative MORTE ARTHURE. He concludes that
      Malory was a "conscious artist" who took medieval narrative
      structure and adapted it for his own purposes.

778. Vinaver, Eugène. À LA RECHERCHE D'UNE POÉTIQUE MÉDIÉVALE. Paris: Nizet, 1970.

See Chapter 6 ("La Création Romanesque") and 8 ("Un Chevalier Errant") for brief comments on Malory.
   a. Robert Guiette, RBPH, 50 (1972), 469-71.
   b. F. Whitehead, FRENCH STUDIES, 26 (1972), 54-55.
   c. Norman B. Spector, MP, 70 (1973), 258-60.

779. Whitaker, Muriel Anna Isabel. "The Idealized World of Malory's 'Morte Darthur': A Study of the Elements of Myth, Allegory, and Symbolism in the Secular and Religious Milieux of Arthurian Romance." Dissertation. University of British Columbia, 1970. DA, 32 (1971), 406.

"Malory's MORTE DARTHUR presents dramatically the activities of a mythic aristocratic society living in a golden age." Elements of the story are unified by the motif of the quest, which reveals the ideals of the society: the quest for Rome (the ideals of kingship), the quest for fame and ladies (the idealsof chivalry), and the quest for the Grail (the ideals of religion).

780. Wilson, R. H. "More Borrowings by Malory from Hardyng's CHRONICLE." N & Q, N.S. 17 (1970), 208-10.

Wilson argues the possibility that Caxton or a scribe may have added details from Hardyng's CHRONICLE and that Malory borrowed extensively from the CHRONICLE, especially at the beginning of the MORTE DARTHUR.

781. Wolkenfeld, Suzanne. "The Christian Hero in Arthurian Romance." Dissertation. Columbia University, 1970. DA, 31 (1970), 1821A.

Wolkenfeld discusses how writers adapted traditional romance patterns to Christian themes. In the TALE OF THE SANKGREAL, Malory uses allegory in events, e.g. the appearance of a hermit to explain the significance of phenomena, and the use of temptation combat rather than martial combat.

782. Eggers, J. Philip. KING ARTHUR'S LAUREATE: A STUDY OF TENNYSON'S 'IDYLLS OF THE KINGS.' New York: New York University Press, 1971.

See pp. 36-49. In Eggers' view, "fate and conflicting desires cause the Round Table fall." In Tennyson's IDYLLS, the emphasis is on Round Table society; but in the MORTE DARTHUR, it is on the figure of Lancelot, who shows both the strengths and weaknesses of the Round Table, and on Arthur, who is a "poignant human figure," not the Christian hero of Tennyson.

783. Field, P. J. C. ROMANCE AND CHRONICLE: A STUDY OF MALORY'S
      PROSE STYLE. Bloomington: Indiana University Press, 1971.

[See no. 727.] Field discusses Malory's style as it "contributes to the meaning of the MORTE DARTHUR as a whole, not
with the way in which it expresses his personality" (p. 2).
Of primary importance is Malory's reduction of materials and
his use of the simple declarative sentence and the joining of
coordinate clauses. Such usage gives the impression of honesty
and truthfulness. Malory's narrative style, diction, and rhet-
oric resemble colloquial speech. There are few set descriptions,
connective detail is often omitted, descriptive detail within
the action is reduced, and "connective facts and reminders"
are cut. In Malory's dialogue, the emphasis is on direct
speech. Characteristics of knightly speech are the use of
stock phrases, humor, "verbal play on unknightliness" (e.g.
Dinadin), irony and understatement, and terseness and brevity.
Malory does not employ the narrative intrusions of his sources;
he does, however, include narrative intrusions which serve to
emphasize the historicity of the action and to lament loss
and death. The simple, objective narrative reveals Malory's
emphasis on action, not on his role as narrator. His "apparent
lack of control" as narrator is suitable for the world of the
MORTE DARTHUR, in which men, though free agents, lack control
over their world. As narrator, Malory lacks omniscience, lacks
the irony that would make him seem "superior" to his characters,
shows no psychological insight into his characters, and provides
little generalization. The book has appendices and a bibliography about Malory's style.
      a. CHOICE, 8 (1971), 831.
      b. E. O. Bache, JEGP, 71 (1972), 109.
      c. Brian Vickers, ELN, 10 (1972-73), 291-95.
      d. R. T. Davies, MEDIUM AEVUM, 42 (1973), 184-87.
      e. Edward D. Kennedy, CLIO, 2 (1973), 196-97.
      f. E. Reiss, STYLE, 1973, p. 236.
      g. W. Matthews, SPECULUM, 49 (1974), 114-16.

784. Gradon, Pamela. FORM AND STYLE IN EARLY ENGLISH LITERATURE. Lon-
      don: Methuen, 1971.

Gradon disagrees with Vinaver's opinion that Malory abandoned
the technique of entrelacement. She believes that he modified
it, breaking his story into larger divisions than are found in
his French sources. Malory blended reality and unreality, the
commonplace and the supernatural; a superb example of his use
of the supernatural is his version of Arthur's death, in which
his use of the supernatural raises the scene from the tragic
to the romantic. "The borderline between reality and unreality
is used by Malory in a distinctive way. The book is a recreation of the past, a past which is exemplary and ideal. The
shifting border between the natural and supernatural is a part

of this recreation of an ideal past, a past which is concrete
and immediate, yet, at the same time, remote and unreal. Malory's mode of writing is essentially romantic" (p. 237).
Gradon opposes the arguments of Tucker, Wilson, and Lumiansky,
who claim that Malory was concerned with the internal motivation and development of his characters. Characterization, she
says, is subordinated to theme. "The characters are not indi-
vidualised but draw their vitality almost entirely from their
social milieu" (p. 269).

   a. P. Rogers, HUMANITIES ASSOCIATION REVIEW, 25 (1974), 348.

785. Holbrook, Sue Ellen. "Medieval Notions of Time in Literature and
      Art with a Special Emphasis on Malory's 'Le Morte Darthur.'"
      Dissertation. University of California at Los Angeles, 1971.
      DA, 32 (1972), 6931A.

      Holbrook states that medieval concepts of time were reflected
      by chronometers, themes, and images of mutability (ubi sunt
      theme, Fortune's Wheel motif, etc.), and old age and death
      ("time as the essence of the human condition"). Malory seeks
      "characterizations of time which lie embedded in such areas as
      mutability, mortality, and the development and use of clocks"
      and is also concerned with finite and infinite time.

786. Jurovics, Raachel. "The Definition of Virtuous Love in Thomas
      Malory's LE MORTE DARTHUR." COMITATUS, 2 (1971), 27-43.

      Jurovics states that virtuous love is fulfilled in a marriage
      of mutual loyalty, affection, and passion and represents a mid-
      way point between religious denial and adulterous corruption.
      It maintains both a religious role (sanctity of marriage) and
      a social one (establishment of a stable and ordered society).
      Such an ideal love is exemplified by Gareth and Lyones.

787. Kennedy, Edward D. "The Arthur-Guenevere Relationship in Malory's
      MORTE DARTHUR." STUDIES IN THE LITERARY IMAGINATION, 4 (1971),
      29-40.
      Kennedy asserts that Arthur's attitude to Guenevere changes
      from one of affection in Tale 1 to one of less concern for her
      and more affection for his knights and the Round Table in later
      tales. The change is significant because it shows Malory's
      originality in following his own plan and not necessarily that
      of his sources; it also suggests that Malory wrote Tale 1 before
      Tale 2.

788. Kindrick, Robert Leroy. "The Unknightly Knight: Anti-Chivalric
      Satire in Fourteenth and Fifteenth-Century English Literature."
      Dissertation. University of Texas at Austin, 1971. DAI, 32
      (1972), 5742A.

      Kindrick calls Malory's TRISTRAM an "anti-romance."

789. Lagorio, Valerie M. "The Evolving Legend of St. Joseph of Glas-
      tonbury." SPECULUM, 46 (April 1971), 209-31.

      "Sir Thomas Malory manifests his awareness of Glastonbury's
      centrality to Arthurian and English history in his famous ver-
      sion of the Arthurian Grail legend. Although there is no ex-
      plicit connection of Joseph with Glastonbury, the consistent
      emphasis on Joseph's conversion activities in England and his
      dissociation from the Grail indicates that Malory incorporated
      the Glastonbury Joseph into his story. He furthermore made
      Joseph the sole ancestor of Lancelot and Galahad, thereby
      strengthening the link between the two elect knights of Arthur's
      era and the prime Christian of early Britain. This was conso-
      nant with his central purpose of writing a noble history of
      Arthur and England" (pp. 227-28).

790. Lambert, Mark Henry. "Malory : A Stylistic Approach." Disser-
      tation. Yale University, 1971. DA, 32 (1972), 6935.

      Lambert aims to "describe the Malorian presentation of reality
      and to indicate the nature of Malory's permanent artistic value
      through an examination of his narrative style." He suggests
      that "Malory's important originality as a stylist lies not in
      any innovations he makes, but in his tendency to emphasize
      certain devices he inherits from his sources and to de-empha-
      size others. [See revision in no. 869.]

*791. Lawson, Sarah. "Characterisation, Identity and Narrative Style
      in Malory's MORTE DARTHUR." Dissertation. University of Glas-
      glow, 1971.

792. McCarthy, Terence. "Malory's King of Wales: Some Facts on the
      Text of Book II." N & Q, N.S. 18 (1971), 327-29.

      A criticism of three emendations which Vinaver made in his edi-
      tion of the Winchester Manuscript. [See criticism in no. 807.]

793. _____. "Order of Composition in the 'Morte Darthur.'"
      YES, 1 (1971), 18-29.

      McCarthy assumes that "there is no reason why the final order
      should reflect the order of composition in any way" and proposes
      to establish the order of composition by analyzing Malory's
      style. He proposes the following order of composition: Tales
      6, 2, 5, 1, 3, 4, 7, and 8. Tales 6 and 2 are early because
      they are translations; Tales 5 and 1 are also early because
      they are partial translations which are close to their
      sources; Tale 3 is more an adaptation than a translation;
      Tale 4 may be original; Tales 7 and 8 are late compositions
      because they show "maturity of style and independence from his
      sources" (p. 21). McCarthy opposes Vinaver's theory that Tale 2

was written first; he believes that Tale 6 is first because Malory translated and abridged <u>all</u> of his source for Tale 6, whereas he omitted the end of his source in writing Tale 2.

794. Moorman, Charles. "The Arthur Legend." KINGS AND CAPTAINS: VARIATIONS ON A HEROIC THEME. Lexington: University of Kentucky Press, 1971, pp. 148-72.

A discussion of the MORTE DARTHUR with reference to the romance and chronicle traditions.

795. Muir, Margaret A., and P. J. C. Field. "French Words and Phrases in Sir Thomas Malory's LE MORTE DARTHUR." NM, 72 (1971), 483-500.

Muir and Field claim that Caxton mistakenly thought "le morte darthur" in Malory's colophon referred to the entire book rather than only the last section. Malory seems to have intended that the title for the whole should be "The Hoole Book of Kyng Arthur and of His Noble Knyghtes of the Rounde Table." Why Caxton failed to amend "le" to "la" in the title is not known. The authors believe there is too little French in the MORTE DARTHUR to determine the dialect of Malory's sources or Malory's own command of the language, but his command of French seems to have been greater as a passive reader than as an active writer.
    a. Felix Lecoy, ROMANIA, 95 (1974), 421.

796. Newstead, Helaine. "Malory and Romance." FOUR ESSAYS ON ROMANCE. Ed. Herschel Baker. Cambridge: Harvard University Press, 1971, pp. 3-14.

Newstead emphasizes the importance of the heroic in the MORTE DARTHUR. The winning of "worship" is of primary importance to Malory's knights, and the winning of love secondary. The work is therefore not typical in some ways of the formal romance as defined by Auerbach (MIMESIS).

797. Noguchi, Shunichi. "Malory and the Consolation of Style." SEL, English No., 1971, pp. 35-53.

Noguchi attempts to analyze Malory's style by analyzing the the ethical concepts which underlie his work.

798. Pochoda, Elizabeth T. ARTHURIAN PROPAGANDA: 'LE MORTE DARTHUR' AS AN HISTORICAL IDEAL OF LIFE. Chapel Hill: University of North Carolina Press; London: Oxford University Press, 1971.

[Originally a dissertation, no. 742.] Pochoda discusses the MORTE DARTHUR in accordance with her thesis that although Arthurian chivalry is presented in the fifteenth century as an "historical ideal of life" which seems to satisfy the need for

a viable political model, Malory is aware of its ultimate inadequacy for providing such a model. Tales 1 and 5 (Tale 5 is
a transitional tale) demonstrate the supposed appropriate ideal
that chivalry represents; Tales 6, 7, and 8 show the decline
and failure which derives from "self-deception," "self-ideali-
zation," and the lack of a clearly defined theory of kingship.
As depicted by Malory, the failure of the Round Table is not
a "gradual decay" but the result of weaknesses "built into the
structure" of the society. Malory's message to his age--that
Arthurian society is not a viable cultural or political model--
is a didactic one. This book also contains a "Review of Earlier Malory Scholarship," which is divided into discussion of
source study, structure, and theme; and an "Annotated Bibliography of All Significant Malory Scholarship," pp. 141-77.
  a. CHOICE, 8 (1971), 1020.
  b. LJ, 96 (1971), 1714.
  c. VQR, 1971, p. clxxii.
  d. P. J. C. Field, RES, N.S. 23 (1972), 466-68.
  e. Clifford C. Huffman, CLIO, 1 (1972), 70-72.
  f. Edward D. Kennedy, SPECULUM, 48 (1973), 397-402.
  g. William Matthews, MP, 71 (1973), 73-76.
  h. Lucy Mitchell, MEDIUM AEVUM, 42 (1973), 286-89.

799. Ryding, William W. STRUCTURE IN MEDIEVAL NARRATIVE. [De Pro-
     prietatibus Litterarum, Series Maior, Vol. 12.] Hague and
     Paris: Mouton, 1971.

     [Originally a dissertation, no. 650.] This study concentrates
     on twelfth and thirteenth-century French narrative, but it also
     discusses BEOWULF and the works of Boccaccio and Malory. Ryding
     defines three phases of medieval narrative structure: simple
     stories in "compound" form, narrative interlace, and a more
     simplified structure (represented by the works of Boccaccio
     and Malory). Ryding accepts Vinaver's theory that Malory re-
     presents the last phase of interlace structure, unweaving his
     sources and shaping a more modern narrative form in which mul-
     tiplicity yields to unity.
       a. Masanori Toyota, SEL, 1973, p. 274.
       b. Morton W. Bloomfield, SPECULUM, 48 (1973), 584-87.
       c. Helaine Newstead, RP, 29 (Aug. 1975), 108.
       d. R. T. Pickens, RR, 66 (1975), 140.

800. Senior, Michael. "The Phaedra Complex: Amour Courtois in Malo-
     ry's 'Morte D'Arthur.'" FOLKLORE, 82 (1971), 36-59.

     In this psychoanalytic interpretation of the MORTE DARTHUR,
     Senior relates the stories of Tristram and Isolt, Lancelot and
     Guinevere, and Mordred's treachery to a Freudian sado-masochis-
     tic reading of amour courtois.

801. Toyota, Masanori. "Forms and Functions of the Nominal Construction with Special Reference to Malory's English." SEL, English No. 1971, pp. 176-78. [An abstract of a longer article in the Japanese number.]

Toyota claims that there is significant use in Middle English of the nominal construction, which was greatly influenced by French phrasing.

802. Vinaver, Eugène. THE RISE OF ROMANCE. Oxford: Clarendon Press, 1971.

In this book, Vinaver revises nos. 31, 154, 619, 707, and 778. See Chapter 7, "A New Horizon" (pp. 123-39). Vinaver asserts that much criticism of Malory better describes Malory than the nature of his work, and he claims that discovery of Malory's apparent "intentions" in using his sources may not be an adequate method of assessing Malory's artistic achievement. Malory "modernized" the cyclic romance not by cutting its length but by unravelling its narrative themes. He unravels the interlace stories of the romance cycles in two ways: he makes a single episode in a continuous theme into an independent story (e.g. the story of Balin) and he takes separate parts of a story and creates an independent one (e.g. the story of the Maid of Astolat). Thematically, Malory is interested in specific ideas found in the older versions, such as the "conflict of loyalties inherent in the traditional doctrine and practice of chivalry" which arose from the incompatibility of courtly love and feudal allegiance. "The change from the cyclic romance to a narrative intelligible without reference to anything that lies beyond it and unrelated to any wider scheme of things brings with it a new sense of the tragic; the very restriction of the field of vision heralds the advent of tragedy as an essentially modern form" (p. 136).
   a. CHRISTIAN CENTURY, 88 (1971), 1397.
   b. J. H. Caulkins, L'ESPRIT CRÉATUR, 12 (1972), 64.
   c. CHOICE, 9 (1972), 652.
   d. R. T. Davies, RES, N.S. 23 (1972), 463-66.
   e. Robert Guiette, RBPH, 50 (1972), 469-71.
   f. Dieter Mehl, ARCHIV, 124 (1972), 136-38.
   g. C. E. Pickford, FRENCH STUDIES, 26 (1972), 439-40.
   h. VQR, 48 (1972), liii.
   i. R. M. Wilson, ENGLISH, 21 (1972), 23-24.
   j. R. W. Ackerman, MLQ, 34 (1973), 98-100.
   k. Morton W. Bloomfield, SPECULUM, 48 (1973), 584-87.
   l. D. S. Brewer, MLR, 68 (1973), 885-87.
   m. G. C. Britton, N & Q, N.S. 20 (1973), 28-29.
   n. André Crépin, EA, 26 (1973), 351-52.
   o. Klaus Heitmann, ARCHIV FÜR KULTURGESCHICHTE, 55 (1973), 234-36.
   p. Tadahiro Ikegami, SEL, English No., 1973, pp. 152-57.

q. Elizabeth Porter, MEDIUM AEVUM, 42 (1973), 168-71.
r. Paul Zumthor, ZRP, 89 (1973), 331-32.
s. B. N. Sargent, MP, 71 (1974), 405-07.
t. Eugene Vance, RR, 65 (1974), 52-54.
u. Helaine Newstead, RP, 28 (1975), 683-86.
v. Claude Thiry, MOYEN AGE, 81 (1975), 356-57.

* 803. Wheeler, Alvina Pheeny. "Causality and Morality in Malory's MORTE D'ARTHUR--the Establishment of the Kingdom, Tales I-IV." Dissertation. Brown University, 1971.

804. Barber, Richard W. THE FIGURE OF ARTHUR. Totowa, N.J.: Rowman and Littlefield, 1972.

See pp. 133-34. Barber discusses Malory's treatment of some popular beliefs, such as his "cautious" reference to Arthur's return. The identification of Camelot with Winchester shows that Malory was "in pursuit of his own private revision of the geography of the romances, which he always tried to reconcile with reality."
a. ANTIQUARIES JOURNAL, 53 (1973), 321.
b. R. H. C. Davis, EHR, 88 (1973), 871.
c. Kenneth Jackson, MEDIUM AEVUM, 42 (1973), 188-89.
d. P. A. Wilson, ARCHAEOLOGIA CAMBRENSIS, 112 (1973), 193-94.
e. Brynley F. Roberts, STUDIA CELTICA, 8-9 (1973-74), 336-39.
f. CHOICE, 11 (1974), 314.
g. R. J. Cormier, CCM, 66 (1974), 156-59.
h. A. G. Dyson, JOURNAL OF THE SOCIETY OF ARCHIVISTS, April 1974, p. 49.
i. AMERICAN HISTORICAL REVIEW, 80 (1975), 380.
j. Valerie M. Lagorio, SPECULUM, 51 (1976), 310-12.

805. Bornstein, Diane D. "Military Strategy in Malory and Vegetius' DE RE MILITARI." CLS, 9 (1972), 123-29.

Bornstein claims that Malory's attitude to his knights and to the Round Table may have been influenced by Vegetius' DE RE MILITARI. "Malory observed the knights of the Round Table not only with the admiring eye of the chivalric idealist, but also with the critical eye of the professional soldier" (p. 128).

806. Everett, Barbara. "The Waste Land." TLS, Mar. 3, 1972, p. 249.

Everett suggests that Malory's story of BALIN served as the source for T. S. Eliot's fisher king and that it is more likely that Eliot was exposed to Malory's story of "conscience and guilt" than to the works of Jessie L. Weston. [See no. 812.]

807. Field, P. J. C. "Malory's 'Morte Arthure' and the King of Wales." N & Q, N.S. 19 (1972), 285-86.

Field disagrees with McCarthy's view [no. 792] that Malory got the title "King of Wales" from the Alliterative MORTE ARTHURE and mistakenly attributed it to Arthur. Field claims that the error of identifying Arthur with the King of Wales first occurred in the E.E.T.S. edition of the MORTE ARTHURE. The King of Wales is not Arthur but one of his vassals.

808. Kellogg, Alfred L. "Malory and Color Symbolism: Two Notes on His Translation of the 'Queste del St. Graal.'" CHAUCER, LANG-LAND, ARTHUR: ESSAYS IN MIDDLE ENGLISH LITERATURE. New Brunswick, N.J.: Rutgers University Press, 1972, pp. 11-29.

Kellogg compares passages containing the visions of Gawain and Bors in both the French QUESTE and Malory's version. He concludes that Malory de-emphasized spiritual elements in his source and failed to understand their significance.
a. Barbara Raw, N & Q, N.S. 20 (1973), 437-39.
b. R. M. Wilson, YES, 4 (1974), 245.

809. Kelly, Robert L. "Arthur, Galahad, and the Spiritual Pattern in Malory." AMERICAN BENEDICTINE REVIEW, 23 (1972), 9-23.

Kelly argues that the MORTE DARTHUR has "cohesion" rather than "organic unity," and that this cohesion, which makes chronological inconsistencies unimportant, is furnished by an "all-embracing view of the age of Arthur as providential history" (pp. 9-10). He rejects Vinaver's view that Malory secularized the Grail story and claims that the role of Galahad is more central to the work than has generally been believed because there are important parallels between Galahad and Arthur.

810. Kennedy, Edward D. "Two Notes on Malory: 1. Malory and the Spanish 'Tristan': Further Parallels. 2. Tristram's Death in Malory's 'Morte Darthur.'" N & Q, N.S. 19 (1972), 7-10.

1. Kennedy states that two episodes in Tale 5 of the MORTE DARTHUR more closely resemble Spanish TRISTAN manuscripts than the six French Prose TRISTAN manuscripts which are closest to Malory's source. 2. Kennedy notes that Malory's report of Tristram's death in Tales 7 and 8 may have been suggested by a speech by Bors in the MORT ARTU which lists Tristram among men who suffered for women.

*811. Oshima, Shotaro. LA LITTÉRATURE ANGLAISE ET L'IMAGINATION POÉTIQUE--TEMPÉRAMENT CELTIQUE ET SON DÉVELOPPEMENT. Tokio: Hakusuiska, 1972.

This contains a section about Tristram and Arthur in the MORTE DARTHUR. [BBIAS, 27 (1975), no. 389.]

812. Padmanabha, Jayanta. "'The Waste Land.'" TLS, Mar. 17, 1972,
      p. 308.

      [A reply to no. 806.] Padmanabha points to a reference about
      Malory in Eliot's AFTER STRANGE GODS (1934) as proof that Eliot
      read Malory as an adult. He also suggests that Eliot's fisher
      king may have been influenced more by a passage concerning
      Galahad (Book 17, Chapter 3) than by the book of BALIN.

813. Reese, Theodore I. "The Character and Role of Guenevere in the
      Nineteenth Century." Dissertation. Brandeis University, 1972.
      DA, 33 (1973), 5138A.

      In the MORTE DARTHUR, Guenevere's role is to serve as a cata-
      lyst to the destruction of the kingdom.

814. Soudek, Ernst. "Chivalry and Thomas Malory." STUDIES IN THE
      LANCELOT LEGEND. [Monograph in Comparative Literature, Rice
      University Studies, Vol. 58, No. 1.] Houston: Rice Univer-
      sity Press, 1972, pp. 25-50.

      A discussion of the scene of Guinevere's abduction and rescue
      [see Vinaver's edition, no. 131, pp. 1119-40]. Soudek states
      that Malory artistically "telescopes" the incident from the
      Prose LANCELOT and that his reduction reflects a different
      attitude toward chivalry: Malory reprimands the present age
      and holds up for emulation the moral ideals of the old chival-
      ry. Malory cuts courtly love elements from the episode so
      that his version is an abduction and tryst story that empha-
      sizes the knightly prowess of Lancelot.

815. Walsh, John Michael. "Characterization and Structure in Malory's
      Last Two Tales." Dissertation. Yale University, 1972. DA,
      34 (1973), 290A-91A.

      Walsh states that in using his two sources for the final two
      tales of the MORTE DARTHUR, the MORT ARTU and the Stanzaic
      MORTE ARTHUR, Malory alters characterization. In Malory's ver-
      sion, the Lancelot-Guinevere relationship is very tense; the
      cart episode shows the power which Guinevere still exercises
      over him (her insecurity prompts her to test her power). Ar-
      thur is a "politic and cautious leader" in the last tale.
      Malory does not separate earthly and spiritual values, accord-
      ing to Walsh, but regards the latter as merely an extension of
      the former.

816. Barber, Richard W. KING ARTHUR IN LEGEND AND HISTORY. Totowa,
      N.J.: Rowman and Littlefield; Ipswich: Boydell Press, 1973,
      rpt. 1974.

      [A revised version of no. 643.] See Chapter 8, "The Flower of

Chivalry" (pp. 121-33). Barber favors the authorship of the Yorkshire Malory proposed by Matthews [no. 697], rejects both the idea that the MORTE DARTHUR is eight separate tales and the view that it has strict "unity," and discusses the sources of each tale. Critical discussion is indebted to Vinaver and Lumiansky.

   a. R. M. Wilson, ENGLISH, 23 (1974), 71.
   b. CHOICE, 12 (1975), 203.
   c. REVIEWS OF NEW BOOKS, 3 (1975), 176.
   d. Yvonne R. Lockwood, JOURNAL OF AMERICAN FOLKLORE, 89 (1976), 361-63.

817. Bass, Robert Gene. "The Dream as a Narrative Device in Thomas Malory's 'Le Morte D'Arthur.'" Dissertation. Miami University, 1973. DAI, 34 (1974), 4186A.

"Malory uses the dream to strengthen plot, character development, or theme." Bass argues that a comparison of Malory and authors who use dream devices shows that Malory is not so skilled in integrating dreams with the narrative and that Malory condenses material—either the dream itself or the interpretation of the dream—so that its significance is diminished.

818. Beston, John, and Rose Marie Beston. "The Parting of Lancelot and Guinevere in the Stanzaic 'Le Morte Arthur.'" AUMLA, 40 (1973), 249-59.

The authors state that the parting scene of Lancelot and Guinevere occurs in the MORTE DARTHUR and in its source, the Stanzaic MORTE ARTHUR. Since the scene does not appear in their common source, the MORT ARTU, they believe that the scene is the original work of the author of the Stanzaic MORTE ARTHUR.

819. Craft, Carolyn Martin. "Free Will in Malory's 'Le Morte Darthur' and in Some Earlier Arthurian Writings." Dissertation. University of Pennsylvania, 1973. DA, 34 (1973), 1853A.

Craft argues that as the Arthurian tradition developed, authors showed greater awareness of the problem of free will. In the MORTE DARTHUR, human interaction is very important because individual actions and decisions influence those of other individuals and of society in general. Man is left to choose good or evil and has the possibility of reforming if he chooses.

820. Ferrante, Joan M. THE CONFLICT OF LOVE AND HONOUR: THE MEDIEVAL TRISTAN LEGEND IN FRANCE, GERMANY, AND ITALY. [De Proprietatibus Litterarum, Series Practica, No. 78.] Hague and Paris: Mouton, 1973.

Ferrante discusses the MORTE DARTHUR briefly in the Introduction (p. 7). Though Malory is undeniably more interested in

Lancelot than in Tristram, his interruption of Lancelot's story
in the center of the narrative to tell that of Tristram is important. In Malory's view, the "lust and lack of control Tristan exhibits in his love is at the core of the decay in the
Arthurian world."
   a. H. Braet, STUDI FRANCESI, 56 (1975), 325.
   b. Dafydd Evans, N & Q, N.S. 22 (1975), 318.
   c. D. H. Green, MLR, 71 (1976), 119-20.
   d. Winthrop Wetherbee, SPECULUM, 51 (1976), 738-40.
   e. Reginald Hyatte, RR, 68 (1977), 63-65.

821. Gehle, Quentin Lee. "A Study of Character Motivation in Chré-
      tien's 'Cligès,' Chaucer's 'Troilus and Criseyde,' and Malory's
      'Morte D'Arthur.'" Dissertation. University of Kentucky,
      1973. DAI, 35 (1974), 1622A.

      Gehle claims that the desire for "social harmony" is more evi-
      dent in the MORTE DARTHUR than in either CLIGÈS or TROILUS AND
      CRISEYDE. Malory has sympathy with private and social motives,
      but he tends to favor the latter. In Arthur, both motives are
      strong; Tristram and Lancelot, however, are motivated by private
      interests, selfish and unselfish respectively.

822. Hartung, Albert E. "Narrative Technique, Characterization, and
      the Sources in Malory's 'Tale of Sir Lancelot.'" SP, 70 (1973),
      252-68.

      According to Hartung, Malory's use of the Agravain section of
      the Prose LANCELOT and the PERLESVAUS shows that he not only
      unravels threads of the narrative but that he also shows inter-
      est in event and characterization, particularly in the character
      of Lancelot. "It is as if Malory, looking into the future of
      the Arthurian story as represented by the QUESTE DEL SAINT GRAAL
      and the MORT ARTU, set for himself the problem of creating the
      kind of character whose lapses would be most painful, whose
      moral dilemmas would be most crucial, and whose final redemp-
      tion would be most affecting in the light of that future" (p.
      268).

823. Kermode, John Frank, and John Hollander, eds. THE OXFORD ANTHOLOGY
      OF ENGLISH LITERATURE. New York: Oxford University Press,
      1973. Vol. 1, pp. 444-58.

      The authors compare the MORTE DARTHUR and its sources and dis-
      cuss Malory's suppression of marvellous elements.

824. McCarthy, Terence. "Caxton and the Text of Malory's Book 2." MP,
      71 (1973), 144-52.

      McCarthy's premise, which is based on the editorial principles
      of Vinaver, is that whenever readings in the Caxton edition and

the Winchester Manuscript differ, one supported by Malory's
sources must be chosen; if no source is known, the Winchester
reading must be chosen because it is more likely that Caxton
altered his version than that a scribe altered the Winchester
Manuscript. Agreement between Caxton's edition and Malory's
sources may be coincidental. McCarthy questions Vinaver's
editorial emendations in Book 2, where Caxton's edition and
the Winchester Manuscript differ greatly, and states that
Vinaver fails to consider the principle by which Caxton re-
cast the work, a principle which "reveals a desire to make the
work more positively courtly" (p. 146). Material contained in
Caxton's Book 2 which is not found in the corresponding section of the Winchester Manuscript must not necessarily be
attributed to Malory since Caxton may be responsible for the
change; such material can, however, be attributed to Malory
if it is also found in Malory's source, the Alliterative MORTE
ARTHURE.

825. Merriman, James Douglas. THE FLOWER OF KINGS: A STUDY OF THE
ARTHURIAN LEGEND IN ENGLAND BETWEEN 1485 and 1835. Lawrence:
University of Kansas Press, 1973.

See pp. 16-29. Merriman states that although Vinaver has received little support for his view that the MORTE DARTHUR is
eight separate tales, the "unity" proponents are overzealous
and "overly ingenious" in their attempts to prove that the
work is a unified whole. Merriman favors the views of Lewis
and Brewer and provides a bibliography of the controversy on
pp. 186-88. Malory's style is adapted to the action and his
characters are presented through dramatic action, not psychological analysis; on the other hand, the MORTE DARTHUR has inconsistencies and structural weaknesses (e.g. the TRISTRAM and
Grail sections). "Translator, abridger, adapter, rearranger,
condenser--Malory was all of these, but it is unlikely that he
added a single important narrative element to the Arthurian
story. Quite the contrary; his real triumph--a partial one,
to be sure--lay in the fact that beneath the tangled accretions,
he discerns, consciously or unconsciously, the indispensable
elements in the legend" (p. 21).
   a. CHOICE, 10 (1973), 1385.
   b. LJ, 98 (1973), 1168.
   c. B. H. Bronson, PQ, 53 (1974), 616.
   d. Derek Pearsall, MLR, 69 (1974), 839-41.
   e. Rachel Bromwich, RES, N.S. 26 (1975), 327-29.

826. Nakashima, Kunio. "The Noun in Malory." IN SPITE OF THE THIR-
TEEN SUPERSTITION, 6 (1973), 105-42.

Nakashima discusses NUMBER (some plurals without plural endings;
a few -n plurals; collective nouns in singular and plural constructions; nouns with and without -s; a(n), this, that + plural

singular verbs and plurals); CASE (invariable genitive with
instances where there is no change in the plural; non-personal
verbs in genitive; "his" takes place of the genitive; frequent
use of post-genitive; split and group genitive; objective
genitive (rare) and adverbial genitive; and GENDER (usage similar to modern English).

827. Paxson, Diana. "The Holy Grail." MYTHLORE, 3 (1973), 10-11, 31.

A general history of the Grail legend. Paxon discusses Malory's role as adapter and editor. She states that in the MORTE
DARTHUR, Galahad is a saintly figure, but the chief interest
is concentrated on secular characters such as Lancelot and
Gawain.

828. Pickford, Cedric E. "Camelot." MÉLANGES DE LANGUE ET DE LITTÉ-
RATURE MÉDIÉVALE OFFERTS À PIERRE LE GENTIL. Ed. Jean Dufournet
and Daniel Poirion. Paris: S.E.D.E.D. et C.D.U. Réunis, 1973,
pp. 633-40.

A study of how Arthurian writers, including Malory, localize
Camelot and how Camelot is for them a symbol, whether or not
it has geographical reality in their works.

* 829. Staines, David McKenzie. "Tennyson's Camelot: A Study of Tennyson's Arthurian Poetry and Its Medieval Sources." Dissertation.
Harvard University, 1973.

830. Stevens, John Edgar. MEDIEVAL ROMANCE: THEMES AND APPROACHES.
London: Hutchinson Univ. Library, 1973.

According to Stevens, Lancelot's love for Guinevere is a love
akin to duty and loyalty. Malory saw "romantic love at its
best as a stable, abstemious, loyal friendship between two
people who happened to be of the opposite sex" (p. 48). What
Malory praises in love is stability, a quality desirable in
other relationships as well. In the MORTE DARTHUR, the Quest
is a secular adventure, more ceremonial and ritualistic than
religious. Stevens stresses Malory's role in the romance tradition.
a. TLS, Aug. 31, 1973, p. 1008.
b. R. M. Wilson, ENGLISH, 22 (1973), 112-13.
c. C. Blyth, ESSAYS IN CRITICISM, 24 (1974), 391-98.
d. D. Pearsall, RES, N.S. 25 (1974), 457.
e. G. C. Gritton, N & Q, 220 (1975), 452-54.
f. M. Mills, MEDIUM AEVUM, 44 (1975), 320.
g. Helaine Newstead, SPECULUM, 51 (1976), 359-61.

831. Whitaker, M[uriel] A. "Allegorical Imagery in Malory's 'Tale of
the Noble King Arthur and the Emperor Lucius.'" NM, 74 (1973),
496-509.

"Malory's King Arthur is an idealized character performing symbolic acts in a setting that is only intermittently realistic" (p. 508). Whitaker emphasizes the importance of the "quest" pattern. Arthur is similar to a mythic hero and he achieves his greatest glory in the Roman campaign.

832. Whitteridge, Gweneth. "The Identity of Sir Thomas Malory, Knight-Prisoner." RES, N.S. 24 (1973), 257-65.

Whitteridge opposes the views of Hicks and Baugh that Sir Thomas Malory of Newbold Revell (Warwickshire) is also Thomas Malory of Fenny Newbold. He offers evidence that they are not the same man but separate individuals: the Fenny Newbold Malory was a Yorkist rebel, and the Newbold Revell Malory was a Lancastrian sympathizer who wrote the MORTE DARTHUR. [See reply in no. 837.

833. York, Ernest C. "Legal Punishment in Malory's 'Le Morte Darthur." ELN, 11 (1973), 14-21.

York examines five instances where women are condemned to be burned at the stake. In some instances, a woman accused of adultery is charged with "treason," a charge which indicates that Malory drew on pre-twelfth-century French law rather than on Anglo-Saxon law (in which adultery was seldom a capital offense and was not punished by fire). Malory also follows French law in calling murder "treason"; in English law, only murder of royalty was called "treason." In one instance, however, "treason" refers only to the intent to kill. York concludes that Malory "depicts historically sound legal practice," draws on several periods of tradition from the eleventh through the fourteenth centuries, and generally follows French legal customs. He shows originality in using the stake as legal punishment for crime.

*834. "Arthurian Romance: The Holy Grail. . . Fire Imagery." ENGLISH LANGUAGE AND LITERATURE [English Literary Society of Korea.] No. 51-52 (Autumn-Winter 1974), 54-67. [In Korean.]

835. Bessinger, J. B. "THE GEST OF ROBIN Revisited." THE LEARNED AND THE LEWED: STUDIES IN CHAUCER AND MEDIEVAL LITERATURE (FOR BARTLETT JERE WHITING). Ed. Larry D. Benson. [Harvard English Studies, No. 5.] Cambridge: Harvard University Press, 1974, pp. 355-69.

A structural comparison of THE GEST OF ROBIN and the MORTE DARTHUR.

836. Davis, Norman. "A Ghostly Middle English Form of 'Leopard.'" N & Q, N.S. 21 (1974), 210.

Davis seeks to correct an error in the MIDDLE ENGLISH DICTIONARY

which gives "libud" (in Vinaver's edition of the Winchester
Manuscript) as an erroneous form of "libard" (leopard). The
error is not scribal (the Winchester scribe wrote "libard")
but is a misreading by Vinaver which was not corrected in the
corrigenda in the second edition of 1967.

837. Field, P. J. C. "Sir Thomas Malory, M.P." BULLETIN OF THE IN-
      STITUTE OF HISTORICAL RESEARCH, 47 (1974), 24-35.

      Field dismisses the proposal of Matthews [no. 697] that a
      Yorkshire Malory wrote the MORTE DARTHUR and accepts the War-
      wickshire candidate for authorship proposed by Kittredge [no.
      339]. Field disproves the theory of Whitteridge [no. 832] that
      there were two Thomas Malorys of Warwickshire, one of Newbold
      Revell and one of Fenny Newbold, by furnishing evidence that
      Newbold Revell and Fenny Newbold were the same place. Further-
      more, he adds information to what is known of Malory's parlia-
      mentary career and suggests the possibility that Malory shifted
      loyalties from lord to lord, including Richard Beauchamp, Earl
      of Warwick, and Humphrey Duke of Buckingham.

838. Finlayson, John. "The Alliterative MORTE ARTHURE and SIR FERUM-
      BRAS." ANGLIA, 92 (1974), 380-86.

      Finlayson replies to Griffith's argument [no. 381] that Malory's
      Book 5 derives from the Alliterative MORTE ARTHURE, which in
      turn derives from the French FIERABRAS. He suggests that the
      ultimate source is the English SIR FERUMBRAS (ca. 1380). While
      he does not state that the English version is positively the
      source of the MORTE ARTHURE, Finlayson seeks to show that it
      could as easily have been the source as the French romance.

839. Gaines, Barry. "The Editions of Malory in the Early Nineteenth
      Century." PUBLICATIONS OF THE BIBLIOGRAPHICAL SOCIETY OF AMERI-
      CA, 68 (1974), 1-17.

      Gaines discusses the histories and importance of the two popu-
      lar editions of the MORTE DARTHUR published in 1816, the Southey
      edition of 1817, and the two extant copies of the Caxton edition.
      The three editions of 1816 and 1817 were very influential during
      the nineteenth century.

840. Griffith, Richard R. "The Political Bias of Malory's MORTE DAR-
      THUR." VIATOR, 5 (1974), 365-86.

      Griffith examines the view that Sir Thomas Malory was a Lancas-
      trian sympathizer and then argues that Malory's sympathies were
      Yorkist. Griffith claims that the textual evidence advanced
      to support Malory's Lancastrian sympathies is "tenuous and
      equivocal" (p. 366) and is also "ambiguous, susceptible to dif-
      ferent explanation, or inconsistent with other portions of his

work" (p. 375). He argues that it is likely that Malory was a Yorkist sympathizer because he was writing for the aristocracy of the 1460's, who were at least nominally Yorkists. Griffith, however, admits that he cannot explain why Malory should have been in prison in the 1470's if he were a Yorkist sympathizer.

841. Hellenga, Robert R. "The Tournaments in Malory's MORTE DARTHUR." FORUM FOR MODERN LANGUAGE STUDIES, 10 (1974), 67-78.

Hellenga discusses the "tournaments of the MORTE DARTHUR and their relationship to tournament history." The battles which Malory presents are not those of his own day but those of a period between the war encounters of the twelfth century and the pageants of the fifteenth. In using the thirteenth-century prose romances, Malory inherits the more civilized tournament tradition which contrasts to the warlike games, without spectators, of earlier times. Malory does, however, sometimes make alterations and adds material of his own which follows the customs of a later period.

842. Holichek, Lindsay Eller. "Malory's French Sources and English Books: Books VI, VII and VIII and the Adaptations of Meaning." Dissertation. University of Wisconsin at Madison, 1974. DA, 35 (1975), 5348.

Holichek discusses Malory's handling of his French sources for Books [Tales] 6 through 8 in terms of form (his reaction to the structure of his sources) and content (his changes, additions, and deletions). In Book [Tale] 6, Malory retains structure but alters content (e.g. he eliminates condemnation of earthly chivalry). In Book [Tale] 7, he alters structure by placing the story of Lancelot and Guinevere between the stories of the Quest and the fall of the kingdom. In Book [Tale] 8, he makes some alterations in structure, more than in Book 6 but less than in Book 7. Malory's method for handling the structure which he inherited from the French sources is not consistent, but his thematic purpose, as revealed in the content of the work, is consistent and shows that he creatively redefined his Arthurian materials.

843. Hynes-Berry, Mary E. "Relation and Meaning in the 'Queste del Saint Graal' and Malory's 'Tale of the Sankgreal.'" Dissertation. University of Wisconsin at Madison, 1974. DA, 35 (1974), 2941A-42A.

Hynes-Berry compares the QUESTE and the SANKGREAL and concludes that allegory is structurally and thematically important to the French work and that Malory's mode of writing is "exemplary." He removes allegorical explication unrelated to the action and emphasizes dramatic action (the story of Lancelot's quest for perfection) rather than the significance of the Grail itself.

He also simplifies the language of the QUESTE so that the story becomes more and more immediate for the reader.

844. Jones, Kirkland C. "The Relationship Between the Versions of Arthur's Last Battle as They Appear in Malory and the LIBRO DE LAS GENERACIONES." BBIAS, 26 (1974), 197-205.

Jones compares one scene in the MORTE DARTHUR (romantic tradition) and the LIBRO DE LAS GENERACIONES (chronicle tradition) to show how the two works exemplify the different aims of the romance and the chronicle.

845. Kato, Tomomi, ed. A CONCORDANCE TO THE WORKS OF SIR THOMAS MALORY. Tokyo: University of Tokyo Press, 1974.

A concordance to the Vinaver edition of the Winchester Manuscript, containing all words in context (narrative dialogue, or proper name) except those in Caxton's preface and rubrics. Words are attributed either to the Winchester Manuscript (one or the other of the two scribes) or to the Caxton edition. Emendations are noted and there is a word frequency list at the end.
   a. LJ, 99 (1974), 2954.
   b. Robert Ackerman, COMPUTERS AND THE HUMANITIES, 9 (1975), 44-45.
   c. Yuji Nakao, SEL, English No., 1975, pp. 121-31.

846. Lerond, Dennis. AN ARTHURIAN CONCORDANCE. Baltimore: T-K Graphics, 1974.

A list of characters in the Arthurian romances, including the MORTE DARTHUR. [See no. 562.]

847. Luttrell, Claude. THE CREATION OF THE FIRST ARTHURIAN ROMANCE. Evanston, Ill.: Northwestern University Press, 1974.

Luttrell gives a bibliography of criticism about the source of Malory's GARETH and summarizes the views of Wilson, Brugger, Schmidz, and Loomis. He traces the GARETH, which is close to the "fair unknown" stories, to a source close to what he calls the "Ipomedon II." He also argues that the EREC ET ENIDE is a source.
   a. William Calin, FRENCH REVIEW, 49 (1975), 119.
   b. Derek Pearsall, MLR, 70 (1975), 843-45.

848. Matthews, William. "Where Was Siesia-Sessoyne?" SPECULUM, 49 (1974), 680-86.

This article discusses the geographical location of the site of Arthur's great military victory over Lucius, which is called "Sessoyne" in the MORTE DARTHUR. After reviewing critical

opinions, most of which are based on political interpretations
of the work, Matthews suggests that the site is Val-Suzon in
Burgundy.
a. Fr. Viellard, ROMANIA, 97 (1976), 573.

849. Mercer, Mary Ellen. "A Violent Order: Moral Vision in Later
Arthurian Romance, 1250-1500." Dissertation. Syracuse University, 1974. DA, 36 (1976), 6708A.

In Chapter 2, Mercer discusses Books [Tales] 1 and 2 of the
MORTE DARTHUR as "heroic chivalry," and in Chapter 6, she discusses Malory's attitude toward chivalry. Her thesis is that
the presentation of social and political problems in late Arthurian romances reveals the insecurity of the aristocratic
class in the later Middle Ages. "The Death-of-Arthur material
. . . responds to the threat of dissolution, attempting to
glorify the chivalric age and to explain somehow the downfall
of the ideal society."

850. Morris, Celia. "From Malory to Tennyson: Spiritual Triumph to
Spiritual Defeat." MOSAIC, 7 (1974), 87-98.

A discussion of Malory's and Tennyson's versions of the story
of the Holy Grail.

851. Nakashima, Kunio. "Thou and Ye in Malory." IN SPITE OF THE
THIRTEEN   SUPERSTITION, 7 (1974), 157-77.

"In Malory ye is the prevailing pronoun of address to a single
person (about 70%). It is used with far greater frequency between ladies, between kings, between husband and wife, brothers
and sisters, by knights to ladies, to hermits, etc., and to
kings, and by inferiors to kings and knights. It is also the
ordinary singular pronoun of address between knights, by kings
to knights, parents to children, and ladies to knights. Thou
marks, on the other hand, intimacy, contempt and difference of
rank. It is regularly used in address to a deady body, to a
dying knight, to a love in soliloquy, to God, and by a voice
to the knight in the quest of the Holy Grail. Two knights in
a fight usually thou each other, a lady often insultingly
thous a knight, and inferiors are commonly addressed with the
singular form." Each category is then discussed. [See also
nos. 156, 746.]

*852. Shimuzu, Aya. "Dinadin et sa satire." BULLETIN DE L'UNIVERSITÉ
GAKUGEI SCIENCES HUMANIES, Tokio, 25 (1974), 55-64.

Shimuzu claims that Dinadin's verbal attacks on arms and love
and his criticism of the age herald the modern spirit. [BBIAS,
28 (1976), no. 463.]

853. Snyder, Robert Lance. "Malory and 'Historial' Adaptation."
     ESSAYS IN LITERATURE--WESTERN ILLINOIS UNIVERSITY, 1 (1974),
     135-48.

> Snyder borrows C. S. Lewis's term "historial" to describe Ma-
> lory's technique of adaptation, which is a mixture of factual
> history and fable. His concern is "unravelling the pattern of
> human causation behind a political tragedy within Time" (p.
> 138). As an adapter, Malory tries to recreate the thematic
> significance of his Arthurian materials. He is primarily in-
> terested in the "vexing problem of the meaning of man's
> responsibility in creating social structures greater than
> himself" (p. 146).

854. Staines, David. "Tennyson's 'The Holy Grail': The Tragedy of
     Percivale." MLR, 69 (1974), 745-56.

> This article contains general remarks on the MORTE DARTHUR and
> compares the work with that of Tennyson.

855. Stroud, Michael. "Malory and the Chivalric Ethos: The Hero of
     ARTHUR AND THE EMPEROR LUCIUS." MEDIAEVAL STUDIES, 36 (1974),
     331-53.

> Stroud believes that there is no "moral paradox" between Ma-
> lory and his work and that the MORTE DARTHUR is not so "moral"
> as some have claimed. He says that Malory's attempt to re-
> establish an older order of chivalry and feudalism which is
> violent and brutal is not at odds with his character. Malory's
> concept of chivalry is based on prowess. The Tale of ARTHUR
> AND THE EMPEROR LUCIUS shows that the society of the MORTE
> DARTHUR is a "violent and unforgiving" one, "intolerant of
> weakness and disdainful of compassion" (p. 338). Instead of
> trying to escape from an intolerable present, Malory tries to
> "reassert values he still felt appropriate to feudalism as he
> knew it" (pp. 351-52). Stroud says that Malory should not be
> judged according to the ethical standards of today.

856. Takamiya, Toshiyuki. "'Wade,' 'dryvande,' and 'Gotelake'--
     Three Notes on the Order of Composition in the MORTE DARTHUR."
     SEL, English No., 1974, pp. 131-48.

> Takamiya reviews scholarship on the order of composition of the
> eight tales of the MORTE DARTHUR. This controversy was initi-
> ated by Vinaver's statement that Tale 2 precedes Tale 1. Taka-
> miya states that Tales 1 through 4, as they appear in both the
> Winchester Manuscript and the Caxton edition, are in the correct
> order of composition. He believes that Tales 3 and 4 were writ-
> ten at approximately the same time.

857. Ziegler, Georgianna. "The Characterization of Guinevere in

English and French Medieval Romance." Dissertation. University of Pennsylvania, 1974. DAI, 35 (1975), 5371A.

Ziegler uses modern theories of character analysis based on the novel genre to discuss the dual nature of the character of Guinevere in the romances. Guinevere is depicted both as a woman of low repute and as a queen of great virtue. This duality is inherited from Celtic sources and alters as the Arthurian materials are later developed. In Chapters 6 and 7, Ziegler discusses Malory's treatment of Guinevere. She regards the MORTE DARTHUR as an example of an Arthurian romance in which Guinevere does not have a "subsidiary role."

858. Barnett, D. J. "Whatever Happened to Gawain?" ENGLISH STUDIES IN AFRICA, 18 (1975), 1-16.

Barnett opposes Vinaver's view that Malory uncritically uses two conceptions of Gawain's character: the noble Gawain of the Vulgate Cycle, and the villainous Gawain of the French Prose TRISTAN. Barnett believes that Gawain is villainous in the early sections of the MORTE DARTHUR, which are based on the SUITE DU MERLIN. Malory's depiction of Gawain is therefore consistent.

859. Batten-Phelps, Carole. "An Examination of the Social Structure and Its Effects on Chivalry and Honour in Malory's MORTE DARTHUR." Dissertation. University of London, Bedford College, 1975.

Chapters are "The Structure of Malory's Arthurian Society" (an examination of social relationships), "Honour in the MORTE DARTHUR" (the conflicts between public and private honour), "Chivalry in the MORTE DARTHUR" (how Malory's heroic chivalry differs from that in his sources), and "Fighting in the MORTE DARTHUR" (fighting is seen as the most important activity of Malory's chivalry).

860. Blake, N[orman] F. CAXTON: ENGLAND'S FIRST PUBLISHER. New York: Barnes and Noble, 1975.

See pp. 141-42. Blake discusses Caxton's editorial procedures and stylistic alterations in the MORTE DARTHUR. Neither the Caxton edition nor the Winchester Manuscript was illustrated, though both were "very suitable" for illustration, so Blake assumes that Caxton's manuscript of the work was also not illustrated. "Caxton was prompted to use woodcuts only if this was suggested to him by his source."
    a. Michael Pollak, LIBRARY QUARTERLY, 48, no. 2 (April 1978), 193-96.

*861. Eto, Jun. "Soseki et la légende arthurienne." ÉTUDE COMPARATIVE

SUR 'KAÏROKO.' Tokio: University of Tokio Press, 1975.

In writing KAÏROKO, the only native Japanese treatment of the
Arthurian legend, Soseki (1867-1916) drew on the MORTE DARTHUR,
Books 18 - 20. [BBIAS, 28 (1976), no. 458.]

862. Ferrante, Joan M. "The Conflict of Lyric Conventions and Romance
     Form." IN PURSUIT OF PERFECTION: COURTLY LOVE IN MEDIEVAL
     LITERATURE. Ed. Joan M. Ferrante and George D. Economou. Port
     Washington, N.Y.: Kennikat Press, 1975, pp. 135-78.

     See pp. 171-73. Ferrante states that Malory did not reject
     courtly love, but he did see it as a potentially destructive
     force in society because it "fosters disloyalty and thus dis-
     order."
     a. R. T. Davies, MLR, 72 (1977), 385-87.
     b. Caroline Locher, CL, 29 (1977), 374-77.

863. Fries, Maureen. "Malory's Tristram as Counter-Hero to the MORTE
     DARTHUR." NM, 76 (1975), 605-13.

     Fries argues that the TRISTRAM section and its hero provide a
     contrast and a "counter-hero" to the NOBLE TALE OF SIR LANCE-
     LOT and to Lancelot, respectively. Malory relates Lancelot's
     adventures to the "growth of Arthur's rule of justice and mer-
     cy; Tristram's to the gradual discplacement [sic] of that rule
     by a system of brute force" (p. 606). The two knights are con-
     trasted in terms of their knightly prowess (Tristram is not
     just and merciful, not morally upright) and their love for
     lady (Tristram betrays Isolde) and liege. Tristram is therefore
     more important as a symbol of the decay of the Arthurian world
     and its ideals than as a knight. The article contains a sum-
     mary of important criticism of the TRISTRAM section.

*864. Harp, Richard L. "The Christian Poetic of the Search for the
     Holy Grail." CHRISTIAN SCHOLAR'S REVIEW, 4 (1975), 300-10.

     "The Grail romances, represented by Malory's LE MORTE DARTHUR
     and von Eschenbach's PARZIVAL, cannot be interpreted as a skil-
     ful patching together of Celtic folk tales. The Grail, a reve-
     of God's grace, is a serious subject for Christians, and a
     large part of its study should be devoted to its intrinsic
     significance. To explain the medieval Christians' attachment
     to the vessel (which represented for them the mystical body of
     Christ) as a product of semantic confusion is to render com-
     pletely incomprehensible the means by which the great poetic
     power of the Grail stories was achieved." [Z. J. B., ABSTRACTS
     OF ENGLISH STUDIES, 20, no. 9 (May 1977), no. 2703.]

865. Hayashi, Tetsumaro, ed. STEINBECK AND THE ARTHURIAN THEME.
     [Steinbeck Monograph Series, No. 5.] Muncie, Indiana: Ball
     State University, 1975.

865.1   Kinney, Arthur F. "TORTILLA FLAT Re-Visited." STEINBECK AND
          THE ARTHURIAN THEME, pp. 12-24.

          A discussion of tone, theme, and structure in the MORTE DAR-
          THUR. Kinney states that the "fundamental unity" of the
          work is of the "broadest sort: in an imposed atmosphere
          jointly romantic and moralizing; in the celebration of the
          past through unremitting and untarnished praise of the ideals
          of knighthood; in a focus on a half-dozen characters who de-
          velop biographically from the idealism of youth to the jaded
          disillusionment of old age. Thus the rise, flowering, and
          fall of the Round Table serves Malory as an overarching meta-
          phor for the biographies of men, of dreams, and of society
          generally" (pp. 16-17).

865.2   Simmonds, Roy S. "A Note on Steinbeck's Unpublished Arthurian
          Stories." STEINBECK AND THE ARTHURIAN THEME, pp. 25-29.

          A comparison of Steinbeck's version of the MORTE DARTHUR and
          the work itself. Simmonds estimates that Steinbeck completed
          slightly more than a quarter of his project.

865.3   _____. "The Unrealized Dream: Steinbeck's Modern
          Version of Malory." STEINBECK AND THE ARTHURIAN THEME,
          pp. 30-43.

          Steinbeck's "Letter to Alicia" (Dec. 31, 1965) discusses
          Steinbeck's first meeting with Vinaver, their trip to Alnwick
          Castle in Northumberland, and the discovery of a fifteenth-
          century copy of the BRUT, paleographically similar to the
          Winchester Manuscript. Simmonds states that the London DAI-
          LY MAIL printed on Jan. 1, 1966, a version of this letter
          and interpreted it as the discovery of another Malory manu-
          script. [See nos. 685 and 704.]

866.   Jenkins, Elizabeth. MYSTERY OF ARTHUR. New York: Coward,
          McCann and Geoghegan, 1975.

          Chapters 12 and 13 are a popular account of the MORTE DARTHUR,
          containing a summary of the story and the political history of
          the War of the Roses as it pertains to the work.
          a. Philip Rahtz, ANTIQUITY, 50 (1976), 161-63.

867.   Kennedy, Edward D. "Malory's King Mark and King Arthur." MEDI-
          AEVAL STUDIES, 37 (1975), 190-234.

          Kennedy states that Arthur is portrayed as a more worthy king
          in the MORTE DARTHUR than in its sources, the MORT ARTU and
          the Stanzaic MORTE ARTHUR. Malory's depiction of King Mark as
          vengeful and tyrannical is basically the same as that in his
          sources and is not, as some critics have said, a "blackening"

of Mark's character. Mark serves as a foil to Arthur, and in
contrasting the two, Malory illustrates the medieval political
theorists' definition of the good and bad king: the good king
is motivated by bonum commune, the bad king by bonum privatum.
The portrait of King Mark in Tale 5 influences and is juxta-
posed with the figure of Arthur in Tales 7 and 8. Malory depicts Arthur as a good king, loving to his people, generous,
just, wise, courageous, placing public good over personal af-
fection. In the last two tales, Malory emphasizes Arthur's
love for the Round Table, not for his queen.

868. Kimball, Arthur Samuel. "Merlin's Miscreation and the Repetition
      Compulsion in Malory's MORTE DARTHUR." LITERATURE AND PSYCHO-
      LOGY, 25 (1975), 27-33.

      Kimball applies Freud's theory of the repetition compulsion
      (confrontation rather than flight from reality) to the MORTE
      DARTHUR. He views Merlin as a figure simultaneously creative
      and destructive. In the MORTE DARTHUR, life struggles against
      chaos, but the latter ultimately triumphs.

869. Lambert, Mark. MALORY: STYLE AND VISION IN 'LE MORTE DARTHUR.'
      [Yale Studies in English, No. 186.] New Haven, Conn.: Yale
      University Press, 1975.

      [A revision of no. 790.] In this stylistic study of the MORTE
      DARTHUR, Lambert tries to determine Malory's "vision" and to
      assess why Malory "matters." In the opening chapter, Lambert
      discusses those characteristics of prose style which Malory
      held in common with his sources and his contemporaries. These
      characteristics—in dialogue, mixed forms of discourse, "con-
      firmation" (little distinction between the voices of the nar-
      rator and the characters in a given passage), collective
      discourse, and formality of speech; in narration, the use of
      superlatives, qualitative description (modifiers which "eval-
      uate" rather than "describe"), catalogues, and conventional and
      "blueprint" details—point toward the "objective existence of
      moral qualities and values" and give credence to the idea that
      Malory's attitude is that of an historian, not a moralist. The
      second chapter discusses the individual stylistic traits which
      distinguish Malory from his sources. He stylizes set descrip-
      tions of landscapes and cuts descriptive detail; he modifies
      action by reducing details; he stylizes characters, who are
      distinguished by their possession or lack of knightly qualities
      and by their speech. Lambert does not seek patterns of consis-
      tency in Malory's ideas on love or religion and insists that
      Malory's attitude toward them is one of "indifference." Malory
      does, however, possess a "singleness of vision" which prepares
      for the intensity of the last tales, a "vision" which allows all
      attention to be focused on events leading to the final tragedy.
      The cause of the tragedy is complex, but Lambert stresses the

importance of the code of honor which places emphasis on avoid-
ing shame and exposure and maintaining the public appearance of
virtue.
a. CHOICE, 12 (1976), 1572.
b. Peter Dronke, TLS, July 23, 1976, p. 930.
c. R. M. Lumiansky, ELN, 14 (Sept. 1976), 56–57.
d. E. M. Bradstock, AUMLA, 47 (May 1977), 73–75.
e. Edward D. Kennedy, JEGP, 76 (1977), 125–28.
f. Derek Brewer, MLR, 73 (1978), 874–75.
g. Dieter Mehl, ANGLIA, 96 (1978), 228–31.
h. Shinuchi Noguchi, SEL, English No., 1978, pp. 120–24.

870. Lappert, Stephen F. "Malory's Treatment of the Legend of Arthur's
Survival." MLQ, 36 (1975), 354–68.

Lappert discusses Malory's treatment of the story of Arthur's
survival. In the MORTE DARTHUR, the theme of destruction is of
primary importance, but at the moment of Arthur's death, Malory
projects a sense of hope. Arthur's death therefore has a "dual
focus" and shows intentional ambiguity.

871. Marino, James Gerard Americus. "Game and Romance. [A discussion
of the game-like structure of certain Middle English metrical
romances]." Dissertation. University of Pittsburgh, 1975.
DA, 37 (1976), 1538A.

In Part III, Marino examines Malory's figure of Galahad, partic-
in the Tale of the SANKGREAL, and sees Galahad as an individual
who breaks the "play spirit of Camelot."

872. Matthews, William. "Variant Printing in LE MORTE DARTHUR." THE
LIBRARY, Series 5, 30 (1975), 45–47.

Matthews examines the controversy between Vinaver and Bühler
over the two folio pages which differ conspicuously in the
Pierpont Morgan and John Rylands copies of the Caxton edition
[see nos. 507 and 510]. After comparing spelling characteristics
of the Winchester Manuscript, the two copies of the Caxton edition, and other works printed by Caxton, Matthews concludes that
the Pierpont Morgan copy is the reset text on the grounds that
it contains spellings unusual to the rest of the MORTE DARTHUR
and that the two folio pages in this copy show an attempt to correct errors in the text. He therefore concurs with Bühler that
copies of the sheets in question were too few and had to be
reset.

873. Nakashima, Kunio. "Personal Pronouns in Malory." BULLETIN OF
THE ENGLISH LITERARY SOCIETY OF NIHON UNIVERSITY, 23 (1975),
353–76.

The nominative "you" is frequent in the MORTE DARTHUR, especially

after a verb; "them" is more frequent than "hem"; editorial
"we" found with a verb in the present subjunctive indicates
command. Nakashima also discusses the third person pronoun
followed by relative clause or prepositional phrase; nominative pronoun as complement of "to be"; repetitive use of the
pronoun to avoid ambiguity or to emphasize a noun; compound
personal pronoun used as reflexive, emphatic, or both; "hit"
as subject of "to be" in reference to a proper name.

874. _____. "Possessive Pronouns in Malory." EIBUNGAKU-
RONSHU. Tokio, Université Nihon, 8 (Dec. 1975), 111-24.

Discussion of forms (e.g. "the," "of hit," "thereof" used
instead of modern English "its"; "their" used five times more
often than "hir"); objective use; use as possessive pronoun;
"both their" = "of them both"; demonstrative pronoun + possessive; possessive pronoun with determinative use as antecedent
of relative pronoun; possessive used anaphorically in reference
to a word previously mentioned; possessive after a noun preceded
by the indefinite article (or by "no," "any," "some," "many,"
or by a numeral).

875. Nash, Walter. "Tennyson: 'The Epic' and 'the Old "Morte."'"
CAMBRIDGE QUARTERLY, 6 (1975), 326-49.

Nash comments chiefly on Tennyson's MORTE D'ARTHUR (1833/34)
but does contrast the works of Tennyson and Malory.

*876. Shimuzu, Aya. "Histoire de l'Homme et de la Femme au Moyen Age."
HÉROÏNES DANS LA LITTÉRATURE ANGLAISE. [Histoire des Femmes
du Monde, Angleterre, II.] Tokio: Hyoronsha, 1975, pp. 53-87.

A study of Guinevere and the Maid of Astolat. [BBIAS, 28
(1976), no. 465.]

*877. _____. "Qui est Sir Thomas Malory?" EIBUNGAKU-RONSO.
Tokio: Université Daitobunka, 7 (1975), 40-54.

Shimuzu characterizes Malory: "conservateur et réaliste, il
envisage la vie telle qu'elle est et respect le bon sens que
l'on retrouve chez les Anglais." [BBIAS, 28 (1968), no. 464.]

878. Stugrin, Michael. Monarch Literature Notes on Sir Thomas Malory's
MORTE D'ARTHUR. Monarch, 1975.

Plot summary.

*879. Takamiya, Toshiyuki. "The Structure, Meaning, and Characteriza-
tion in Malory's 'Tale of Gareth.'" GEIBUN KENKYN, 34 (1975),
113-26. [In Japanese.]

880. Whitaker, Muriel A. I. "Flat Blasphemies--Beardsley's Illustrations for Malory's MORTE DARTHUR." MOSAIC, 8 (1975), 67-75.

Whitaker claims that the works of Malory and Beardsley show an "antithesis of purpose"--the idealism of Malory and the satire of Beardsley. Both were "black-and-white artists, depending on form rather than colour to create character and setting" (p. 69). The action of the MORTE DARTHUR contrasts sharply with the anemic quality of Beardsley's drawings. "What chiefly differentiates the two artists is their attitude to evil" (p. 71). Beardsley emphasizes the moral qualities of the MORTE DARTHUR, associating evil in the secular world with instability and loss of faith; for him, sin is "fascinating, provocative, and irresistible" (p. 72).

881. Whitworth, Charles W. "The Sacred and the Secular in Malory's TALE OF THE SANKGREAL." YES, 5 (1975), 19-29.

Whitworth argues that the Grail story should not be read in terms of the character of Lancelot and that Malory did not misunderstand his source, the French QUESTE. The Grail section of the MORTE DARTHUR, while altered from its original, does retain its religious significance. Whitworth examines the question of Malory's "secularization" of the story by discussing the roles of major characters, particularly Percival and Bors, who have thus far received little critical scrutiny. The religious impact of the Grail quest on the Round Table is seen at the end of the MORTE DARTHUR.

882. Wilson, Robert H. "Malory and the Ballad 'King Arthur's Death.'" MEDIEVALIA ET HUMANISTICA: STUDIES IN MEDIEVAL AND RENAISSANCE CULTURE, N.S. 6 (1975), 139-49.

Wilson argues that the MORTE DARTHUR is one of the sources of the ballad "King Arthur's Death" in the Percy Folio manuscript.

883. Barnden, Mrs. D. A. "Who Was the Real Sir Thomas Malory?" [Sunday] TIMES, Mar. 28, 1976, p. 14, col. b.

A reply to Hughes's statement [no. 897] that Malory was from Warwickshire. Mrs. Barnden discusses other candidates, especially the Yorkshire Malory proposed by Matthews [no. 697].

884. Benson, Larry D. MALORY'S 'MORTE DARTHUR.' Cambridge: Harvard University Press, 1976.

Benson studies Malory in the literary and historical milieu of the late fifteenth century. The book contains four sections: I. "Malory and the Arthurian Romance" (an attempt to define Malory's genre in relation to early and contemporary romance cycles). The MORTE DARTHUR, which draws on both the old Arthurian

romance tradition and the fifteenth-century prose romance tradition, is a "one-volume prose history." II. "Malory and
English Romance" (Malory's work in relation to English methods
of adaptation, i.e. narrative structure). Malory chose the
French prose narrative over the English verse narrative pattern,
yet his brevity and "modified" interlace technique distinguish
the MORTE DARTHUR from its sources. Benson emphasizes Malory's
"inventive" qualities and the thematic unity of his work. III.
"Malory and Chivalry" (the historical context in which Malory
wrote). For Malory, chivalry was a "realistic" subject, neither
nostalgic nor escapist; fifteenth-century romances dealt with
practical matters and concerns of Malory's aristocratic class.
IV. "Malory and the Fall of Camelot" (a new interpretation of
the MORTE DARTHUR with emphasis on the last three tales). Benson argues that critics have overemphasized tragic elements in
the last tales, obscuring the affirmative side of the tragedy.
Though the last tale is a tragedy, the tone is "one of forgive-
ness, of final joy."
 a. M. C. Bradbrook, TLS, July 23, 1976, p. 931.
 b. CHOICE, 13 (1976), 658.
 c. Ernest C. York, ELN, 41 (June 1977), 211-13.
 d. Robert W. Ackerman, SPECULUM, 53 (1978), 124-26.

885. Blake, N[orman] F. "Caxton Prepares His Edition of the MORTE
      DARTHUR." JOURNAL OF LIBRARIANSHIP, 8 (1976), 272-85.

      Blake discusses "why Caxton chose to publish Malory's MORTE
      DARTHUR, how this copy was prepared for printing and what steps
      the publisher took to promote it. The manuscript itself was
      prepared fairly mechanically for printing with only book 5
      being rewritten. Most of what Caxton tells us in his prologue,
      which was added after the rest of the book was in print, is
      fictitious and was designed to sell the book. The realization
      that this is so gives an important insight into Caxton's atti-
      tude towards Malory and to fifteenth-century literary taste"
      (p. 272).

886. Blakiston, J. M. G. "Malory Manuscript." [London] TIMES, Mar.
      31, 1976, p. 15, col. g.

      Blakiston claims that there was opposition from Winchester Col-
      lege and from outside sources to the selling of the Winchester
      Manuscript to the British Library.

887. Bornstein, Diane. "William Caxton's Chivalric Romances and the
      Burgundian Renaissance in England." ENGLISH STUDIES, 57 (1976),
      1-10.

      See pp. 8-9. Bornstein states that in "using his romances for
      a didactic purpose and calling attention to his aim in Prologues
      and Epilogues, Caxton was following the practice of writers at

the Court of Burgundy." She notes that Caxton emphasizes the
didactic elements of the MORTE DARTHUR in his Prologue, in his
division of the work into twenty-one books and his use of
chapter headings, and in his revisions of Book 5.

888.   Clark, Roy Peter. "Alfin: Invective in the Alliterative MORTE
       ARTHURE." ELN, 13 (1976), 165-68.

       In the Alliterative MORTE ARTHURE, Gawain, with a contemptuous
       tone, calls Lucius an "alfyne." This is the first recorded
       use of the word, which the OLD ENGLISH DICTIONARY and the
       MIDDLE ENGLISH DICTIONARY gloss as a chess piece more limited
       in movement than a bishop. In the MORTE DARTHUR, the word ap-
       pears as "elffe." Clark thinks that by Malory's time, "alfin"
       had lost its pejorative connotation.

889.   Crenshaw, William Bryan. "'Alas, that Ever I Shold See This
       Day': Patterns of Destruction in Malory's LE MORTE DARTHUR."
       Dissertation. University of South Carolina, 1976. DA, 37
       (1977), 6470A-71A.

       According to Crenshaw, the Tale of BALIN is a "microcosm" of
       the MORTE DARTHUR; it contains patterns of destruction which
       recur throughout the work and which lead finally to the destruc-
       tion of the Round Table. The presence of such patterns in the
       tale and in the work as a whole demonstrates the thematic unity
       of the MORTE DARTHUR.

890.   Custance, Michael. "Malory Manuscript." [London] TIMES, Mar. 22,
       1976, p. 15, col. f.

       Custance questions whether secrecy in the sale of the Winches-
       ter Manuscript to the British Library was desirable and whether
       public funds were used to purchase it.

891.   Deacon, Richard. A BIOGRAPHY OF WILLIAM CAXTON: THE FIRST ENG-
       LISH EDITOR--PRINTER, MERCHANT, AND TRANSLATOR. London:
       Frederick Muller Ltd., 1976.

       Deacon states that Caxton's preface shows that he was convinced
       of Arthur's authenticity. "Malory obviously convinced Caxton
       that he had some substantial reasons for accepting the Arthurian
       legend, yet curiously Caxton was sufficiently critical of Malo-
       ry's use of the English language that he treated it and re-wrote
       it with considerably less respect than more recent translators
       . . . . Caxton was a remarkably strict sub-editor of Malory,
       pruning, condensing and colouring as he saw fit" (p. 66). Dea-
       con proposes two possible reasons why Caxton printed the MORTE
       DARTHUR: great interest among his clients concerning the sub-
       ject matter, and the possibility that Caxton himself had
       considered writing such a work but had abandoned the project.

a. C. Bühler, TLS, July 29, 1977, p. 944.
b. Michael Pollak, LIBRARY QUARTERLY, 48, no. 2 (April 1978), 193-96.

892. Ford, Patrick K. "The Death of Merlin in the Chronicle of Elis Gryffydd." VIATOR, 7 (1976), 379-90.

Ford compares the story of Merlin's death in a recently discovered manuscript of Gruffydd, in the Vulgate Cycle, and in the MORTE DARTHUR. He examines how the story developed and the changes which Malory made in his version. Ford concludes that "in Malory there is internal confusion over the denizen of the lake, at least with regard to her relationship with Merlin. We may assume that in the development of the traditions about her, the Lady of the Lake was provided with a court and attendant ladies, some of whom then had their own adventures; Malory apparently knew a version of the story wherein it was one of these that Merlin loved and that brought about his downfall" (pp. 382-83).

893. Gray, Patsy Rozell. "Making Earnest of Game: A Study of the Play-Elements in Malory's LE MORTE DARTHUR." Dissertation. Southern Illinois University, 1976. DA, 37 (1977), 5850A.

Gray analyzes the game structure of the MORTE DARTHUR. After Arthurian society is established, the action consists of "recreational contests"--martial chivalry, love chivalry, and finally celestial chivalry. When the Grail quest fails, the game spirit of Arthurian society collapses. "The civilization predicated on recreational contests is destroyed by the deadly paradox inherent in its aristocratic games."

894. Hodges, Margaret. KNIGHT PRISONER: THE TALE OF SIR THOMAS MALORY AND HIS KING ARTHUR. New York: Farrar, Straus, and Giroux, 1976.

A fictional biography of Malory, based on facts about the life of Sir Thomas Malory of Warwickshire and on events and characters depicted in the MORTE DARTHUR.

895. Howard, Philip. "Archivist Resigns over Malory Manuscript." [London] TIMES, Mar. 23, 1976, p. 4, col. f.

Announcement of the resignation of Peter Gwyn, archivist of Winchester College.

896. _____. "Winchester May Sell Its Malory Manuscript." [London] TIMES, Mar. 11, 1976, p. 1, col. h.

Announcement of the plan to sell the Winchester Manuscript to the British Library, the motive of Winchester College being to "provide a financial cushion for parents, should the Government

enact a law depriving public schools of their charitable sta-
tus."

897. Hughes, Wendy. "Arise Sir Thomas--You'd Love This." [Sunday]
      TIMES, Mar. 14, 1976, p. 3, col. a.

      Hughes comments on the proposed sale of the Winchester Manu-
      script for five hundred thousand pounds. She also conjectures
      that the manuscript was first taken from Winchester Castle to
      the school during the Cromwellian period.

898. Hynes-Berry, Mary. "Language and Meaning: Malory's Translation
      of the Grail Story." NEOPHILOLOGUS, 60 (1976), 309-19.

      In writing the SANKGREAL, Malory uses the plot and vocabulary
      of his source, the French QUESTE, but his original style "trans-
      forms our perception of events" (p. 310). Malory's method of
      abridgement is both "selective" (he excises details not essen-
      tial to the action and long passages of theological doctrine)
      and "synthetic" (he compresses ideas). He abandons the hypo-
      tactic style of the QUESTE for a paratactic and therefore more
      colloquial style which encourages an empathetic response from
      the reader. [See no. 914.]

899. Jordan, Constance. "Enchanted Ground: Vision and Perspective in
      Renaissance Romance." Dissertation. Yale University, 1976.
      DA, 37 (1977), 4337A-38A.

      Jordan argues that in romance, the knight must distinguish
      between the "apparent" (what changes) and the "true" (what en-
      dures through change). "To pursue the truth, a knight needs
      to tolerate the uncertainty of questing for an end he sees only
      imperfectly, as veiled in the distance or future time." In
      LE MORTE DARTHUR, this is represented in visions of the Grail
      and Arthur's kingdom and in the romance forest.

900. Jurovics, Raachel. "Virtuous Love, Unvirtuous Queen: The Con-
      tribution of Theme and Characterization to the Unity and Orig-
      inality of Sir Thomas Malory's LE MORTE DARTHUR." Dissertation.
      University of California at Los Angeles, 1976. DA, 37 (1976),
      2198A.

      Jurovics states that "thematic consistency" is a more suitable
      criterion for discussing the "unity" of the MORTE DARTHUR than
      "narrative" or "chronological" consistency, and that "thematic
      consistency" provides evidence for the originality of Malory's
      work. To support this thesis, Jurovics examines the character
      of Malory's Gwenevere, which differs from that in his sources,
      and finds that it is consistent.

901. Kennedy, Edward D. "Malory's Version of Mador's Challenge."
      N & Q, N.S. 23 (1976), 100-03.

      Kennedy states that Mador's challenge to Arthur in Tale 7 in
      order to secure justice for his kinsman, who he thinks was
      killed by Guinevere, is a speech which departs radically from
      Malory's sources, the Stanzaic MORTE ARTHUR and the MORT ARTU.
      He thinks that Malory recalled a passage from his source for
      Tale 1, the SUITE DU MERLIN.

902. "Malory Manuscript Bought by British Library." [London] TIMES,
      Mar. 25, 1976, p. 1, col. h.

      Announcement that the Winchester Manuscript was purchased by
      the British Library for one hundred and fifty thousand pounds,
      half furnished by acquisition monies and half from "outside"
      sources. Some had valued the manuscript at five hundred thou-
      sand pounds. Also announces a forthcoming facsimile edition
      of the manuscript by the Early English Text Society [no. 109].

903. Nakashima, Kunio. "Demonstrative Pronouns in Malory." IN SPITE
      OF THE THIRTEEN   SUPERSTITION, 9 (1976), 169-80.

      A discussion of forms; weak "this," "that" used in a sense ap-
      proximating that of the definite article; use of "that one. . .
      that other," "the tone. . . the toether"; "this," "that" in
      reference to persons; adverbial use; "this same," "that same";
      "yon/yondir"; determinative uses.

904. _____. "Relative Pronouns in Malory." BULLETIN OF
      THE ENGLISH LITERARY SOCIETY OF NIHON UNIVERSITY, 24 (1976),
      1-34.

      A discussion of forms and frequency; "that"; "which"; "who";
      non-expression of relative; "what"; "whether"; compound rela-
      tive; preposition (post-position, redundant preposition,
      omission of preposition); prepositional adverbs with "where";
      relative pronoun followed by personal or possessive pronoun
      (in reference to the same subject); reference to noun in the
      genitive or to possessive pronoun made by relatives; miscella-
      neous uses.

905. Painter, George D. WILLIAM CAXTON: A QUINCENTENARY BIOGRAPHY OF
      ENGLAND'S FIRST PRINTER. London: Chatto and Windus, 1976; New
      York: Putnam, 1977.

      See pp. 146-49. Painter opposes Vinaver's opinion that the
      MORTE DARTHUR is eight separate tales. "Professor Vinaver over-
      reacted, as though he had detected two fifteenth-century English-
      men in a conspiracy to mislead a twentieth-century French textual
      editor, Malory by writing 'a series of separate romances', and

Caxton by producing it as a single book under a 'spurious and
totally unrepresentative title'" (p. 148). He finds fault with
Vinaver's opinion that the reprinting of sheets N3/6 and Y3/6
shows conscious revision [no. 510]. Painter believes the reprinting is best explained by an "accidental shortage in the
first printing" (p. 148).
   a. C. Bühler, TLS, July 29, 1977, p. 944.
   b. D. Grumbach, NEW YORK TIMES, Apr. 24, 1977, p. 16.
   c. T. Lask, NEW YORK TIMES, Mar. 24, 1977, p. 49.
   d. Michael Pollak, LIBRARY QUARTERLY, 48, no. 2 (April 1978),
      193-96.

906. Riddy, Felicity. "Structure and Meaning in Malory's 'The Fair
     Maid of Astolat.'" FORUM FOR MODERN LANGUAGE STUDIES, 12
     (1976), 354-66.

     Riddy studies Malory's technique of conjointure in "The Fair
     Maid of Astolat" and how he adapts and alters three narrative
     threads of the plot--the Lancelot-Guinevere love affair, the
     Maid's love for Lancelot, and Lancelot's wounding and healing--
     to stress a meaning other than that of his sources. Further-
     more, Malory uses the "different worlds of the court and Asto-
     lat, the tournament and the hermitage to express different,
     and largely incompatible, sets of values; the settings of the
     story. . . carry the burden of meaning" (pp. 356-57). The
     contrast between public values (i.e. Lancelot and Winchester)
     and private values (i.e. the Maid and Astolat) reveals the
     weaknesses in the Arthurian world and prepares for its imminent
     collapse.

907. Roby, Patricia Carol. "The Tripartite Structure of the WORKS OF
     SIR THOMAS MALORY." Dissertation. Marquette University, 1976.
     DA, 38 (1977), 811A-12A.

     Roby states that the MORTE DARTHUR is a unified "trilogy with
     tripartite structure." Tales 1-4 show the rise of Arthur and
     the establishment of the kingdom; Tale 5 contrasts Arthur and
     Mark; Tales 6-8 reveal the fall of the kingdom.

908. Skinner, Veronica Mary Lowe. "Guenevere: A Study in the Arthur-
     ian Legend." Dissertation. University of Massachusetts, 1976.
     DA, 37 (1976), 289A.

     Skinner asserts that Malory's version of Arthurian legends
     presents and balances two distinct views of Guenevere inherited
     from his sources: first, the political role, in which her
     adultery disrupts the Round Table; and second, the role of
     noble queen who encourages knightly prowess. In the MORTE DAR-
     THUR, she combines both roles; as a true lover to Lancelot,
     she deserves praise, but her indecision and adultery help to
     precipitate the fall of Arthur's kingdom.

909. Tristram, Philippa. FIGURES OF LIFE AND DEATH IN MEDIEVAL ENG-
      LISH LITERATURE. London: Paul Elek, 1976.

      See pp. 123-26. Tristram examines the ubi sunt theme in the
      MORTE DARTHUR, stressing the "elegaic" tone of the work and its
      emphasis on "natural transience."
      a. J. A. Burrow, TLS, Feb. 25, 1977, p. 224.
      b. Pamela Gradon, MEDIUM AEVUM, 47 (1978), 166-70.
      c. Douglas Hamer, RES, N.S. 29 (1978), 74-76.
      d. S. Wenzel, SPECULUM, 53 (1978), 638-40.

910. Whitaker, Muriel. "Sir Thomas Malory's Castles of Delight."
      MOSAIC, 9 (1976), 73-84.

      Whitaker claims that in the romances, the castle functions sym-
      bolically in reference to the supreme authority exercised by
      the aristocracy from their castles. It is also associated with
      entertainment and with healing powers.

911. Fein, Susanna Greer. "Thomas Malory and the Pictorial Interlace
      of 'La Queste del Saint Graal.'" UTQ, 46 (1977), 215-40.

      This article is chiefly a study of the French QUESTE and its
      "pictorial interlace," a term used to describe the entangled
      forest paths in which the Grail knights wander and which sig-
      nify allegorically the human search for salvation. Fein com-
      pares the "pictorial interlace" of the narrative structure
      with the art of manuscript illumination. In the MORTE DARTHUR,
      Malory cuts out many physical details from his source and in-
      creases the amount of action and dialogue, alterations which
      reduce the imaginative effect of "pictorial interlace" in the
      reader's mind. Moreover, Malory emphasizes the theme of human
      loyalty rather than the individual's search for God. Fein
      supports Vinaver's thesis that Malory's concern is with Came-
      lot and earthly society, not with Corbenic and the spiritual
      realm. She suggests "refinements" of meaning for the term
      "interlace," which was coined by Lot and popularized by Vinaver.

912. Hellenga, Lotte, and Hilton Kelliher. "The Malory Manuscript."
      THE BRITISH LIBRARY JOURNAL, 3,no. 2 (Autumn 1977), 91-113.

      The opening paragraph announces the purchase of the Winchester
      Manuscript (now called Additional Manuscript 59678) by the
      British Library in March, 1976, and its display in the Caxton
      quincentenary exhibition with the Pierpont Morgan copy of Cax-
      ton's edition (on loan). The two articles present evidence
      that the manuscript was in Caxton's Westminster workshop early
      in the 1480's and discuss the early history of the manuscript.

912.1 Hellenga, Lotte. "The Malory Manuscript and Caxton," pp. 91-
       101.

Hellenga states that an examination of the manuscript under
an infra-red viewer reveals traces of printer's ink and offsets of capital and lower-case letters belonging to Caxton's
types 2 and 4. These discoveries, according to Hellenga,
are a "strong indication of its prolonged and intensive use
in or near a printer's shop; not as   printer's copy, but
most likely in preparing a copy which was then used by the
compositors. The combination of two types of Caxton identified in the offsets, one of which was used only by Caxton,
seems to make the conclusion inescapable that this phase of
intensive use of the manuscript took place in Caxton's office.
The combination of the two types indicates that this must
have taken place after the introduction of type 4 in 1480,
and not later than 1483, when type 2 disappeared for good,
probably in the melting pot" (p. 98). Part of an indulgence
printed by Caxton in 1489 was used to mend a tear in leaf 243.
Hellenga believes that this "agrees with the evidence for the
presence of the manuscript in or near the workshop in Westminster, and shows that it must have remained there at least
as late as 1489" (p. 99). It is possible that there is a
direct link between the manuscript and Caxton's edition.

912.2   Kelliher, Hilton. "The Early History of the Manuscript," pp.
        101-11.

        Kelliher notes that the name "Richard Followell," written in
        a late sixteenth-century hand, appears on fol. 348 of the
        manuscript. His researches reveal that a family by the name
        of Followell was associated with the Malorys of Litchborough
        in Northamptonshire. He suggests the possibility that the
        manuscript was copied for a member of this family and loaned
        to Caxton, probably before 1483. The copy remained with Cax-
        ton at least until 1489, and was returned to the Malory
        family no later than the beginning of the second quarter of
        the sixteenth century. In the second part of his article,
        Kelliher discusses the transcription of the manuscript by two
        scribes "A" and "B." "Assuming that they were working simul-
        taneously we must conclude that their copy-text consisted . .
        of a number of separate manuscripts, whether bound or in
        loose gatherings comprising sometimes one tale and sometimes
        perhaps two" (pp. 110-11).

913.   Howard, Philip. "Winchester Controversy over Meads Development."
        [London] TIMES, June 24, 1977, p. 1, col. h.

        Mention of the sale of the Winchester Manuscript by Winchester
        College to the British Library.

914.   Hynes-Berry, Mary. "Malory's Translation of Meaning: THE TALE
        OF THE SANKGREAL." SP, 74 (1977), 243-57.

Hynes-Berry argues that in abridging the Grail QUESTE to a
third of its length, Malory "alters the reader's perception of
the action and of the way the story elements relate to each
other. He focuses the reader's attention on a totally different kind of meaning" (p. 255). Malory therefore shifts emphasis from allegory to exemplum, from analogy to comparison.
Hynes-Berry qualifies Vinaver's view that Malory secularizes
the Grail story: she believes that Arthurian chivalry incorporates Christian values and that knighthood is a "Christian
vocation," so the Round Table knights are the most worthy men
to undertake the Grail quest. On both narrative and thematic
levels, Lancelot and his inner conflict are of central importance. Malory presents Lancelot more sympathetically than he
is presented by the author of the French QUESTE; but though
Lancelot is the best knight in the MORTE DARTHUR, he is still
sinful. His failure shows the human struggle and failure to
attain spiritual perfection. [See no. 898.]

915. McCaffrey, Phillip. "The Adder at Malory's Battle of Salisbury:
Sources, Symbols, and Themes." TENNESSEE STUDIES IN LITERATURE,
22 (1977), 17-27.

McCaffrey discusses the scene in the MORTE DARTHUR in which an
adder bites a knight and thereby initiates the final battle
between Arthur and Mordred. Malory's version of the incident
differs from that in his source, the Stanzaic MORTE ARTHUR,
and shows that the snake is a symbol which functions thematically in the MORTE DARTHUR. McCaffrey supports his argument by
pointing to popular literary motifs associated with the snake
and to Malory's use of a snake in Arthur's dream, which foreshadows the final battle. "From the adder's role in precipi-
tating the battle and from its traditional literary associations,
the reader may conclude that Arthur's kingdom is destroyed by
a combination of lust, deceit and both domestic and political
betrayal" (p. 24).

916. Nakashima, Kunio. "Passive Voice in Malory." BULLETIN OF THE
ENGLISH LITERARY SOCIETY OF NIHON UNIVERSITY, 25 (1977), 163-
84.

Discussion of "hyght(e)"; indefinite "men" construction; "be"
+ past participle; compound tenses of perfect and pluperfect;
indirect object as subject of the passive verb, with direct object retained; "he was sent for" construction; examples of close
similarities of meaning among the passive, reflexive, and in-
transitive constructions; passive form of double object construction; and prepositions of agency.

917. Oakeshott, Walter. "The Matter of Malory." TLS, Feb. 18, 1977,
p. 193.

A review of the two facsimile publications, the E.E.T.S. facsimile edition of the Winchester Manuscript [no. 109] and the
Scolar Press facsimile of the Pierpont Morgan Library edition
of Caxton [no. 111]. Oakeshott speculates on the history of
the Winchester Manuscript and connects it with a book trans-
ferred from Winchester Cathedral in 1652 and returned in 1660.
He dismisses the argument [see no. 912.1] that Caxton might
have used the manuscript.

918. "Caxton Used Malory Manuscript." [London] TIMES, Apr. 21, 1978,
       p. 20, col. f.

       Article reports the research of Dr. Lotte Hellenga in associa-
       tion with the British Library and the London Metropolitan Po-
       lice forensic science lab which shows that Caxton used the
       Winchester Manuscript at his Westminster printing office be-
       tween 1480 and 1483. [See no. 921.]

919. Dillon, Bert. A MALORY HANDBOOK. Boston: G. K. Hall, 1978.

       In the Introduction, Dillon discusses topics such as general
       aids for study, biography, Malory and Caxton, the fifteenth-
       century background, unity, theme, characterization, and prose
       style. The book contains bibliographical references. The bulk
       of the book is an analysis (extensive summary) of each of the
       eight tales, keyed to Caxton's edition and the Winchester Manu-
       script (the manuscript itself, Vinaver's second edition of the
       WORKS OF SIR THOMAS MALORY, and Vinaver's one-volume edition).
       Before summarizing each tale, Dillon furnishes an introduction
       in which he discusses sources and bibliographical information.

920. Field, P. J. C. "The Winchester Round Table." N & Q, N.S. 25
       (1978), 204.

       Field says that of the twenty-four knights whose names appear
       on the Winchester Round Table, only one (le Biaus Desconus) is
       not found in the MORTE DARTHUR, and eleven of them are known
       only in that work. He believes that the MORTE DARTHUR is the
       "main source" for the names on the table and therefore should
       be dated no earlier than 1469/70.

921. Santinelli, Patricia. "Caxton's Malory Connexion Proved." [Lon-
       don] TIMES HIGHER EDUCATIONAL SUPPLEMENT, May 5, 1978, p. 2,
       col. d.

       Santinelli gives the same information as in no. 918, but adds
       that Kelliher's research [no. 912.2] provides further proof
       that Caxton used the Winchester Manuscript at Westminster be-
       tween 1480 and 1483. Kelliher suggests that Anthony Woodville,
       Earl Rivers, presented the manuscript to Caxton ten years after
       Malory's death.

922. Scanlon, Paul A. "A Checklist of Prose Romances in English, 1474–
      1603." THE LIBRARY, Series 5, 33, No. 2 (June 1978), 143-52.

      The checklist is divided into translations and original works.
      Scanlon says that "Malory's LE MORTE DARTHUR is perhaps the
      only one which, in this regard, there might be some dispute"
      (p. 143).

INDEX OF NAMES

Authors, Editors, Translators, and Illustrators

Morris, Charles: 138.

Morris, Mary: 396.

Morris, William: 396.

Morton, A. L.: 637.

Mott, A. S.: 113.

Muir, Lynette R.: 600.

Muir, Margaret A.: 795.

Muir, Percy H.: 710.

Murray, James A. H.: 325.

Murrel, E. S.: 42.

Myers, Alec Reginald: 566.

Nakashima, Kunio: 676, 718, 734, 735, 826, 851, 873, 874, 903, 904, 916.

Nash, Walter: 875.

Naudé, Adèle: 218.

Needham, Paul: 111.

Neill, John R.: 180.

Newcomen, George: 355.

Newstead, Helaine: 493, 539, 796.

Nicolson, William: 271.

Nitze, William A.: 78, 79, 442, 517, 576.

Noguchi, Shunichi: 649, 664, 719, 797.

Northup, Clark S.: 245.

Northup, George Tyler: 86.

Norton, Samuel Wilber: 321.

Nutt, Alfred: 302, 305.

Oakeshott, Walter F.: 478, 479, 480, 484, 485, 494, 657.1, 917.

O'Dell, Sterg: 27.

Odgers, W. Blake: 290.

Ogle, R. B.: 185.

Olefsky, Ellyn: 757.

O'Loughlin, J. L. N.: 486.

Olstead, Myra Mahlow: 623, 720.

Omer, Devorah: 225.

Orton, Harold: 509.

Oshima, Shotaro: 811.

Ososki, Gerald: 193.

Owen, Douglas D. R.: 736, 765.

Padmanabha, Jayanta: 812.

Painter, George D.: 905.

Pantzer, Katharine F.: 21.

Panzer, Georg Wolfgang Franz: 3.

Paris, Gaston: 29, 299, 344.

Paris, Paulin: 51.

Parry, John J.: 240, 242, 244, 245, 250.

Parsons, Coleman O.: 524.

Paton, Lucy Allen: 57, 96, 104, 368.

Patterson, Lee Willing: 737.

Wilson, R[ichard] M.: 569, 628.

Wilson, R[obert] H.: 260, 460,
    461, 511, 518, 519, 550, 551,
    560, 561, 568, 580, 604, 605,
    613, 762, 780, 882.

Winder, Blanche: 182.

Winkler, Gera: 472.

Woledge, Brian: 252.

Wolkenfeld, Suzanne: 781.

Worde, Wynkyn de: 112, 113, 114,
    262.

Workman, Samuel K.: 512.

Wragg, H.: 145, 430.

Wright, Thomas: 121.

Wright, Thomas L.: 641, 673.1.

Wroten, Helen Iams: 552.

Wülker, Richard Paul: 336.

Wyeth, N. C.: 136.

York, Ernest C.: 763, 833.

Zenker, Rudolf: 405, 424.

Ziegler, Georgianna: 857.

INDEX OF TITLES

"Sir Thomas Malory's Castles of Delight": 910.

"Sir Thomas Malory's Gawain: The Noble Villain": 708.

SIR THOMAS MALORY'S LE MORTE D'ARTHUR (Baines): 203.

"Sir Thomas Malory's LE MORTE DARTHUR" (Benson): 723.

SIR THOMAS MALORYS 'LE MORTE D'ARTHUR' (Schüler): 360.

"Sir Thomas Malory's Vocabulary": 695.

SIR THOMAS WYATT AND SOME COLLECTED STUDIES: 476.

SIR TRISTREM (McNeill): 301.

SIR TRISTREM; A METRICAL ROMANCE (Scott): 275.

SMERT' ARTURA: 227.

"Society of Antiquaries--June 16, 1898": 351.

"Some Arthurian Coats of Arms": 684.

SOME FACTS CONCERNING THE SYNTAX OF MALORY'S 'MORTE DARTHUR': 453.

"Some Fifteenth-Century Images of Death": 715.

"Some Minor Characters in the MORTE ARTHURE": 605.

"Some Observations in Connection with B. Trnka": 482.

"Soseki et la légende arthurienne": 861.

"A Source of 'The Healing of Sir Urry'": 593.

"The Sources of Malory's 'Le Morte Darthur'": 315.

"Sources of the Arthur Story in Chester's LOVES MARTYR": 398.

"Speaking of Books": 645.

SPECIMENS OF EARLY ENGLISH METRICAL ROMANCES: 276.

SPECIMENS OF ENGLISH PROSE-WRITERS: 277.

STANDARDS: 691.

STEINBECK AND THE ARTHURIAN THEME: 865.

"Steinbeck Find said to be First 'Morte d'Arthur' Manuscript": 704.

SUBJECT INDEX

Alliterative MORTE ARTHURE (see MORTE ARTHUR, Alliterative).

Arthur: 419, 522, 653, 658, 672, 716, 752, 768, 787, 811, 831, 867.

Arthur, death of: 410, 412, 647, 870.

"Arthur and the Emperor Lucius" (see "Tale of Arthur and the Emperor Lucius").

Ascham, Roger: 265, 389, 620.

Avalon: 412.

EL BALADRO DEL SABIO MERLIN: 80-82, 84-85, 87-89, 416.

Bale, John: 264.

Balin: 31.

Balin, Book of: 403, 428, 500, 755, 773, 806, 812, 889.

Beardsley, Aubrey: 24, 124, 527, 880.

Beauchamp, Richard, Earl of Warwick: 270, 342, 378.

Beaumains (see Gareth).

LE BEL INCONNU (see also "fair unknown romances"): 380, 466, 536, 736.

Bors: 622, 881.

British Library Additional MS. 59678 (see Winchester Manuscript).

British Library Harleian MS. 2252 (see MORTE ARTHUR, Stanzaic).

Cambridge University Additional MS. 7071 (see SUITE DU MERLIN).

Camelot: 327, 828.

Castle of Corbin: 775.

"Castle Terabil": 316, 318.

Caxton, William (see also Editions, Caxton): 771, 795, 891.

Characterization in the MORTE DARTHUR (see also under names of individual characters): 157, 376, 406, 413, 433, 460, 519, 573, 604, 673, 674, 728, 784, 791, 815, 821.

CHARRETTE, LE CONTE DE LA (see Chrétien de Troyes).

Chivalry, Malory's attitude toward: 324, 387, 389, 393, 402, 441, 462, 481, 506, 566, 577, 587, 615, 621, 626, 630, 637, 657.5, 672, 681, 688, 698, 699, 703, 709, 717, 730, 742, 749, 758, 784, 796, 798, 814, 849, 855, 859, 884.

Chrétien de Troyes: 541.
CHARRETTE: 299, 354, 442, 549, 760.
EREC: 847.
IVAIN: 364, 385, 405, 467, 578.

Chronicle tradition (see also Hardyng, John, and MORTE ARTHURE): 498, 783, 794.

Chronology in the MORTE DARTHUR: 589, 648, 680, 757, 762.